UBIQUITOUS COMPUTING

Edited by **Eduard Babkin**

Ubiquitous Computing
Edited by Eduard Babkin

Published by InTech
Janeza Trdine 9, 51000 Rijeka, Croatia

Publishing Process Manager Katarina Lovrecic

Technical Editor Teodora Smiljanic

Cover Designer InTech Design Team

Additional hard copies can be obtained from orders@intechopen.com

Ubiquitous Computing, Edited by Eduard Babkin
p. cm.
ISBN 978-953-307-409-2

For EU product safety concerns:
IN TECH d.o.o., Prolaz Marije Krucifikse Kozulić 3, 51000 Rijeka, Croatia,
info@intechopen.com or visit our website at intechopen.com.

Meet the editor

Eduard Babkin is a professor at the National Research University - Higher School of Economics in Nizhny Novgorod, in Russia. Currently, he is the head of the department of information systems and technologies at that university, and both an associate member of LITIS laboratory at National Institute of Applied Sciences (Rouen, France). Eduard Babkin has ten years of practical experience in R&D, architecting and project management of complex distributed systems for large international telecommunication companies. In 2007, Eduard Babkin obtained his PhD degree in Computer Science at the National Institute of Applied Sciences. His scientific interests include enterprise engineering, multi-agent systems, knowledge representation and processing.

Contents

Preface

The aim of this book is to give a treatment of the actively developed domain of Ubiquitous computing (also known as ubicomp). In that domain, due to miniaturization, reduced costs of electronic components and advanced information technologies, developers are now offered a wide range of practical opportunities to design, develop and deploy thousands of the coin-sized sensors and mechanical devices at multiple locations.

Originally proposed by Mark D. Weiser in 1988, the concept of Ubiquitous computing may be considered as an evolutionary development of traditional computational methods and platforms. However, ubicomp enables real-time global sensing, context-aware informational retrieval, multi-modal interaction with the user and enhanced visualization capabilities. In effect, ubiquitous computing environments give extremely new and futuristic abilities to look at and interact with in our habitat at any time and from anywhere.

Unforeseen ability to fuse rich diversity of information retrieval, processing and access methods available in ubiquitous computing environments, practically invisible devices and tight connectivity of distributed components raise many foundational, technological and engineering issues which were not even known prior to the third, ubicomp, wave of computing. Detailed cross-disciplinary coverage of those issues is really needed today for further progress and widening of application domains.

This book collects twelve original works of researchers from eleven countries, which represent different aspects of cutting-edge research and application of Ubiquitous computing. The submissions are clustered into four sections:

- Foundations
- Security and Privacy
- Integration and Middleware
- Practical Applications

Section Foundations is opened by the work of Mauro Marcelo Mattos where the concept of Knowledge-based Operating System (KBOS) is discussed. KBOS has ability of knowing how to perform tasks and how to self-adapt to the fluctuations of resource availability when interacting with the surrounding environment. Studies of ubicomp foundations are continued by Ren-Song Ko who presents an original concept of mutual assistant networks (MANs) which combines social networks with wireless sensor networks, and provides an infrastructure for new location-aware social network applications, in which people may share the local and timely information that cannot be obtained on time from the Internet. Uncertainty and error handling in the case of the invisibility of the devices and lacking of user's awareness is studied by Marie-Luce Bourguet. For resolving that problem the author offers exploiting users' correct mental models of the devices and data properties. Foundational technologies for content adaptation in Ubiquitous computing are considered by Wanderley Lopes de Souza1, Antonio Francisco do Prado, Marcos Forte and Carlos Eduardo Cirilo. In their work the authors describe the Internet Content Adaptation Framework (ICAF), and suggest to apply ontologies for content adaptation. Mianxiong Dong, Long Zheng, Kaoru Ota, Song Guo, and Minyi Guo shed light on and study shadows of caching mechanisms for improving communication in Ubiquitous computing environment. They discuss the concept of Ubiquitous Multi-Processor (UMP) and offer an optimized algorithm for resource allocation to a processing node, which can improve the overall performance of the UMP system.

Extremely important and challenging issues of security and privacy in Ubiquitous computing environments are considered in three consecutive works of the second Section. Hyun-Seok Kim, Jin-Young Choi, and Sin-Jae Lee propose comprehensive Security Analysis of the RFID Authentication Protocol using model checking formalism of Failure Divergence Refinement (FDR). Based on the results of model checking authors reconfirm the existence of known security flaws and propose new schemes for secure RFID communication. Vivian C. Kalempa, Rodrigo Campiolo, Lucas Guardalben, Urian K. Bardemaker, and João Bosco M. Sobral explore the challenges to ensuring privacy in ubiquitous computing environments and propose to extend a metamodel of such environments to the aspects provacy.

Section Integration and Middleware is focused on the problems of interoperability in the joint context of ubiquitous computing environment, existing IT-infrastructure and people society. In their work, Nicolas Ferry, Vincent Hourdin, St′ephane Lavirotte, Ga¨etan Rey, Michel Riveill and Jean-Yves Tigli propose WComp, which is a middleware for ubiquitous computing capable of managing the dynamicity and heterogeneity of entities in the software infrastructure. The proposed middleware solution is built in accordance with the principles of Web Service Oriented Architecture for Device (WSOAD). Habib Abdulrab, Eduard Babkin and Oleg Kozyrev describe semantically enriched integration framework for ubiquitous computing environment, which is called Ontology Mediator.

The last section of the application of ubicomp in practical settings starts with the work of R. Francese, I. Passero & Genoveffa Tortora. The authors discuss current challenges for mobile location-based pervasive content sharing applications. Interesting factual information and observations are presented by Dewi Agushinta R. , Tb. Maulana

Kusuma, Bismar Junatas and Deni Trihasta in the case study research which is about ubiquitous computing applications in Indonesia. Orlewilson B. Maia, Nairon S. Viana and Vicente F. de Lucena Jr observe benefits and opportunities of using the interactive Digital Television (iDTV) systems as the Center of and Ubiquitous Environment in particular circumstances of Brasilia.

Upon acquaintance with the presented scientific works, the readers will obtain consistent comprehension of major foundations of Ubiquitous computing environments, their exciting opportunities and challenges, relevant scientific methods and practice-oriented technologies. The editor of the book strongly believes that as a result, the research community will be expanded with new pioneers and enthusiasts who have a goal to advance the ubicomp as "that which informs but doesn't demand our focus or attention."

Eduard Babkin
National Research University,
Higher School of Economics
Nizhny Novgorod,
Russia

Part 1

Foundations

1

Machine Biological Clock: Exploring the Time Dimension in an Organic-Based Operating System

Mauro Marcelo Mattos
FURB – University of Blumenau
Brazil

1. Introduction

Ubiquitous Computing (UbiCom), Autonomic Computing (AC) and Organic Computing (OC) research has produced a substantial body of work dealing with smart devices, smart environments and smart interaction technologies.

Ubiquitous computing was introduced by (Weiser, 1991) and is related to a vision of people and environments augmented with computational resources providing information and services when and where they could be desired, going beyond than just infrastructure aspects, and suggesting new paradigms of interaction inspired by widespread access to information and computational capabilities (Abowd & Mynatt, 2000) (Poslad, 2009). This vision involves social, technological, engineering and foundational questions (Milner, 2006).

UbiCom environments are increasingly challenging domains when compared with those traditional – also not so easy to deal with traditional computing applications domains. According to (Brachman, 2002) in such scenario there exists the need for a software infrastructure that supports all sorts of heterogeneities (hardware, operating systems, networks, protocols and applications).

Autonomic Computing is related to someone or something acting or occurring involuntarily. It is related to the ability to manage the computing enterprise through hardware and software that automatically and dynamically responds to the requirements of the business. This means self-healing, self-configuring, self-optimizing, and self-protecting hardware and software that behaves in accordance to defined service levels and policies (Murch, 2004)(Balasubramaniam, et al., 2005).

Organic Computing is a research field emerging around the conviction that problems of organization in complex systems in computer science, telecommunications, neurobiology, molecular biology, ethology, and possibly even sociology can be tackled scientifically in a unified way, by means of which progress in understanding aspects of organization in either field can be fruitful in the others (Würtz, 2008). OC systems are based on a general architecture, which would permit users to create specific applications by defining goal hierarchies (Malsburg, 2008) taking advantages of one of the key attributes of biological systems making it possible to adapt and change on multiple time scales as they evolve, develop, and grow, and they should do so without external direction or control (Bellman, Landauer, & Nelson, 2008).

The pervasiveness characteristic of these demands also implies the growing dependency on the expectance to obtaining the proper services when the system is fault-free and especially when it encounters perturbations. So, it is important to qualitatively and quantitatively associate some measures of trust in the system's ability to actually deliver the desired services in the presence of faults.

Since the first steps in the computing history we have seen the field of Software Engineering expand in several ways including the application of software architecture principles to the development of systems. Software architecture involves both the structure and organization by which modern system components and subsystems interact to form systems, and the properties of systems that can best be designed and analyzed at the system level. The importance of software architecture for software development is widely recognized, yet transfer of innovative techniques and methods from research to practice is slow (Krutchen, 2004) (Osterweil, 2007)(Kruchten, Capilla, & Dueñas, 2009)(Buschmann, 2010) and costly (Lagerström, von Würtemberg, Holm, & Luczak, 2010) due to rapid and continuous technology changes.

One important aspect to be pointed is that the current computing platform is made upon a vast collection of code - operating systems[1], programming languages, compilers, libraries, run-time systems, middleware - and hardware that make possible a program to execute. This platform has not evolved beyond computer architectures, operating systems (OS), and programming languages of the 1960's and 1970's (Hunt G., et al., 2005)(Hunt & Larus, 2007). In consequence, application and operating system errors are a continuing source of problems in computing. Existing approaches to software development have proven inadequate in offering a good tradeoff between the assurance, reliability, availability, and performance in such a way that software remains notoriously buggy and crash-prone (Naur & Randell, 1969) (Anderson, 1972) (Randell, 1979) (Linde, 1975)(Kupsch & Miller, 2009),(Ackermann, 2010). In this context, the OS is probably the most crucial piece of software that runs on any computer (Iyoengar, Sachdev, & Raja, 2007).

The preceding paragraphs bring us a scenario that is contrasting: from one side the landscapes of software engineering domains are constantly evolving and for the other side, the computing environments (hardware, OS, telecommunication infrastructure and tools) have historically proved not be robust enough. In this ever-changing scenario, the mainstream research in software engineering goes in a direction trying to propose innovative solutions in the realm of building, running, and managing software systems.

In order to find an appropriate solution to development and design of the new class of systems an appropriate paradigm seems necessary. We choose to take the opposite direction towards the past to try to figure out what could be changed in the beginning of the process in order to minimize the recurrent problems that we are faced in developing and using software. As a consequence we proposed a new software architecture where:

- the only alive (runnable) entity is the operating system, and
- the operating system has the ability of learning based on past experiences on what to do, how to do it and when start learning about solving tasks.

[1] In this work, we refer to the concept of *operating system* in a broader sense, involving the categories of general purpose, embedded, stand-alone or networked, because we need to get an overview first, before examining each class in depth. Moreover, the aspects under review do not require differentiation between these classes.

In the present work, we aim at attracting the reader's attention towards the conception of a system with the ability of knowing how to perform tasks and how to self-adapt to the fluctuations of resource availability when interacting with the surrounding environment. We call this system as a Knowledge-based Operating System (KBOS).

The work is organized as follows: a problem's contextualization related to the current paradigm of computing systems development is presented in section 2; some fundamental concepts are reviewed in section 3; a knowledge-based operating system concept in section 4; section 5 presents some related works and in the conclusion section the final comments are presented.

2. Current paradigm

Sequential programs can be described by a single flow of execution and by the use of simple programming structures such as loops and nested function calls. The execution context of these programs in some point of the run time is defined by the value of the program counter, the value of the cpu registers and the content of the program's stack.

The figure 1 presents an overview of the current paradigm in computing. From a software development perspective, to develop software is to follow some method (software development life cycle) in order to go from requisites analysis to implementation. Also, let us to consider that a program can be represented by a development team (figure 1b) and that a particular software development team, in general, does know nothing about other team's work. This could lead us to situations like:

- similar code continues to be developed by different teams;
- programming errors continues to be introduced in different points of the development steps;
- information about the final run-time environment remains unavailable for the OS;
- race conditions between non synchronized programs remains leading to instabilities;

In other words: the development team does not have ENOUGH information about ALL POSSIBLE ENVIRONMENTS where the software will be used[2].

From the users perspective, to use a software is a matter of clicking over some icon and expecting the corresponding program to start running. The user knows about the purpose of a program and has some expectation about its behavior.

From the operating system's perspective, all knowledge that is previously known is about slicing (and possibly trying to protect) binary (executable) code over the time (figure 1a).

Regardless of which method was chosen to develop a particular application, at some point we will move to the phase of code generation. In this moment, all the documents (and source code) will be stored in files (figure 1b) and the compiler will generate a string of bits that we used to call: a program.

At this moment, the OS comes to scene - remembering that the main purpose of an operating system is to share computational resources among competing users. To do this efficiently a designer must respect the technological limitations of these resources (Peng, Li, & Mili, 2007).

One of the difficulties of OS design is the highly unpredictable nature of the demands made upon them mainly because the relationship between different applications are not considered as a functional/non-functional requisite at the design time. This happens

[2] We should to consider that each user's machine probably will have different hardware and software configurations that in some moment could be running a particular buggy combination of factors.

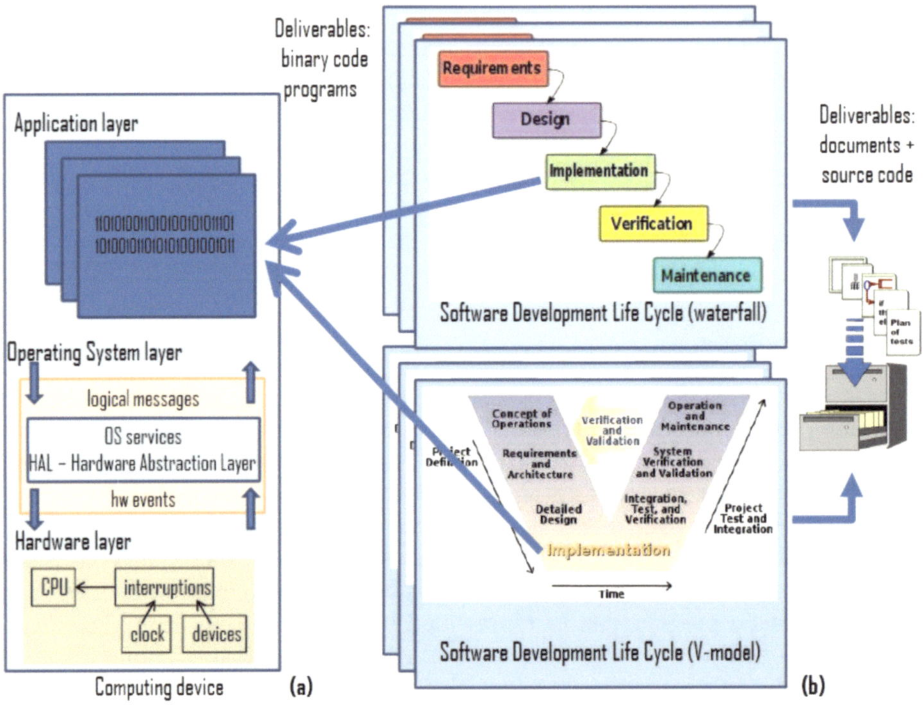

Fig. 1. Current paradigm: software from an inside-out perspective (a), and from an outside-in perspective (b).

because the structure of an OS requires a series of fine-grained event-handler functions for handling events. These event-handler functions must execute quickly and always return to the main event-loop.

Behind the "software layer that manages the hardware" concept (Tanenbaum, 2008), an OS could be better described as a software architecture (Perry & Wolf, 1992) which embeds a large number of design decisions related to hardware interface, programming languages and tools that have a direct impact in almost every software that will be deployed. So, an OS architecture involves a set of functional components related to management of processes, memories, files, devices (input/output operations), security and user interface. In general they are organized in layers.

The first level is the hardware that requires the OS attention by emitting signals to the CPU thru some kind of interrupt model. These hardware events are converted to some kind of logical messages to be dispatched to the application running on that computing device (figure 1a). This conversion exports an abstract view on hardware so that programmers do not have to deal with low level details.

The analysis on the set of clues presented leads us to speculate on the influence that some of the key concepts related to current paradigm: multiprogramming[3], operator, and program - can contribute to the recurrence of the historical problems[4].

[3] There is a class of embedded applications that, for the very specific nature, are not affected by the principle of interruption (have deterministic behavior). Even these, however, could be to some extent, included in this reflection.

2.1 Multiprogramming

The computing device, in general, can run several applications at a time leading us to some kind of multiprogramming environment. The main difficulty of multiprogramming is that the concurrent activities can interact in a time-dependent manner which makes it practically impossible to locate programming errors by systematic testing.

Perhaps, more than anything else, this explains the difficulty of making operating systems reliable (Hansen, 1973), (Hansen, 1977) (Post & Kagan, 2003).

One of the most fundamental design decisions in conceiving a new OS architecture is related to the definition of the type of kernel: non-preemptive or preemptive. This decision imposes a tradeoff between the coupling in the time domain and resource sharing. A non-preemptive kernel makes the OS able to share resources among tasks but couples the tasks in the time domain while a preemptive kernel decouples the tasks in the time domain but enforces the resource sharing (Samek, 2009).

2.2 Operator

Another interesting aspect to be considered is about the figure of a computer operator[5].

In 1961 Klausman wrote: "… I define a *computer operator* as a job responsibility of a person who is in charge of the computing equipment while it is in normal operating condition. The equipment includes the processor, its console or supervisory control panel, and the peripheral equipments on-line or off-line. The operator may have assistants to change tapes, paper forms or the like. Normal operating condition is that in which the system is able to operate in continuous or automatic mode without intervention for relatively long periods of time. These periods may be interrupted by occasional transient errors which do not cause maintenance service. The operator's responsibilities include the running of production programs, programs being *debugged*, and service routines, such as compilers, tape correction routines, etc. The operator's responsibility also includes the diagnosis and action taken as a consequence of transient errors. In addition is the general area of communications into which the operator fits. To intelligently operate the system his knowledge should transcend mere ability to push buttons, an activity which may steadily decrease with the growth in sophistication of the programming art and engineering developments during the sixties… It is conceivable that a data processing system will be completely automatic. A real time clock built into the system will turn it on in the morning or the middle of the night. Automatic tape changes will mount and dismount tapes - feed cards, forms and the like. And the operator - where is he? He isn't - the function ceases to exist. This may not happen tomorrow or next year but it is coming. In an industry which is literally begging for competent personnel it seems to me that operators have nothing to fear from this progress, for more challenging jobs have appeared and will continue to be created for decades to come…" (Klausman, 1961).

Currently, the figure of the computer operator was replaced by the figure of the end user and, in this context, one of the programmer's role is to arrange virtual buttons in a graphical user interface for user to press them and thus make the program work.

---

[4] It is important to emphasize that we are analyzing some characteristics in order to understand what could be the cause of recurring issues, and we are not arguing for or against the current paradigm.

[5] Even considering the class of embedded operating systems for the specific purpose, the concept of operator remains valid (albeit virtually) once the set of interactions between the external world and the controlled device is performed through a set of well established interfaces – replacing buttons for function calls. Under the functional perspective, there is no difference between pressing a button or calling a function.

2.3 Program

One last aspect to be discussed refers to the concept of program (Haigh, 2002): basically a program is a binary expression of some algorithm written in a programming language.

The classical computing model is based on detailed algorithmic control, rests entirely on the insight of the programmer into the specific application of the program and has a strong dependency of abstraction layers. The machine is deterministic and blindingly fast, but is considered as totally clueless. The programmer is in possession of all creative infrastructures, in the form of goals, methods, interpretation, world knowledge and diagnostic ability (Malsburg, 2008).

This approach can work for any well-defined and sufficiently narrow tasks. But, if the system fails, the programmers would diagnose and debug the errors. They would determine what knowledge to add or modify, how to program it, and how to modify and rebalance the pre-existing programs to accommodate the new performance without harming the parts that already worked well (Hayes-Roth, 2006).

Automation in adaptation, learning, and knowledge acquisition is very limited - a tiny fraction of the overall knowledge required, which the engineers mostly prepared manually. The strategy to cope with the increasing complexity of software systems is to adopt some kind of infrastructure based on several levels of abstractions (Kramer & Magee, 2007), (da Costa, Yamin, & Geyer, 2008).

3. Fundamental concepts

"…Computers, unfortunately, are not as adept at forming internal representations of the world. ... Instead of gathering knowledge for themselves, computers must rely on human beings to place knowledge directly into their memories…" (Arnold & Bowie, 1985).

Before proceeding, we must establish a conceptual basis related to the context of this work.

3.1 Data, information, knowledge, knowledge-acquisition

To (Frost, 1986): *Knowledge* is the symbolic representation of aspects of some named universe of discourse, and *Data* is a special case of knowledge and means the symbolic representation of simple aspects of some named universe of discourse.

(Meadow & Yuan, 1997) in they work on measuring the impact of information on development affirm that "we can consider that the terms *data, information* and *knowledge* represent regions in an epistemological continuum. They are not specific points, because each one has many definitions and variations. *Data* generally means a set of symbols with little or no meaning to a recipient, *information* is a set of symbols that have meaning or significance to its recipient, and *knowledge* means the accumulation and integration of information received and processed by a recipient".

Although there is no unanimity (Lenat & Feigenbaum, 1988) (Davis, Shrobe, & Szolovits, 1993) (Duch, 2007), the researchers agree that *knowledge representation* is the study of how knowledge about the world can be represented and what kinds of reasoning can be done with that knowledge.

Knowledge in the context of this work is conceived as being a set of logical-algebraic operational structures that makes possible to organize the system's functioning according to interconnection and behavior laws.

It is well known that a significant obstacle to the construction of knowledge-based systems is the process of *knowledge acquisition*(Shadbolt, O'hara, & Crow, 1999). The key to this process is how we may effectively acquire the knowledge that will be implemented in the knowledge base. In an operating system environment, this is not an easy task. It is usually done by hooking the calls to operating system application programming interface (API) and recording logs for further analysis (Skjellum, et al., 2001). This approach is a time and resources consuming process and presents, as the main drawbacks:

i. the data gathering process impacts the overall performance, influencing other applications that aren't involved in the application context being considered;
ii. this impact on performance also interferes with the application being considered;
iii. and this scenario probably will be different from that of where the application was developed.

3.2 Intelligence, machine intelligence and finite state machines

Also, there is no consensus on the definition of intelligence. (Legg & Hutter, 2007) in their work on "machine intelligence" states that, in general, most definitions share the fact that *intelligence* is a property of an entity (an *agent*) which interacts with an external problem or *situation* (usually unknown or partially known), and has the ability to succeed with respect to one or more goals (the *goals*) from a wide range of possibilities (not just some specific situations).

A particular view for machine intelligence is presented by (Costa, 1993) where he introduces a definition for the concept of machine intelligence, shows the practical possibility to this definition and provides an indication of its need, it gives you an objective content and shows the value and usefulness that such a definition may have to the computing science in general, and artificial intelligence in particular. Rocha Costa started from the intelligence definition given by J. Piaget and established how the conditions for such a definition could be interpreted in the machine domain. The definition presented assumes that it must be recognized the *operating autonomy* of the machines. This leads to abandon, or at least put on second plan, the perspective of contrived imitation for intelligent behavior from humans or animals and adopt the point of view that he calls *naturalism* - to consider machine intelligence as a natural phenomenon on the machines.

A common and straight way of modeling behavior is extending the event-action paradigm to explicitly include the dependency on the execution context through a finite state machine (FSM). An FSM is an efficient way to specify constraints of the overall behavior of a particular system. Also FSMs have an expressive graphical representation in the form of state diagrams - directed graphs in which nodes denote states, and connectors denote state transitions. The FSM has a drawback, the phenomenon known as state explosion, related to the fact that there is an implicit notion of repetition of states. To make its use more practical, state machines can be supplemented with variables. In this case, they are called extended state machines, and can apply the underlying formalism to much more complex problems than could be practical without including the variables (Samek, 2009).

3.3 Time and cognition

"...I'm trying to understand how time works. And that's a huge question that has lots of different aspects to it. A lot of them go back to Einstein and space-time and how we measure

time using clocks. But the particular aspect of time that I'm interested in is *the arrow of time*: the fact that the past is different from the future. We remember the past, but we don't remember the future. There are irreversible processes. There are things that happen, like you turn an egg into an omelette, but you can't turn an omelette into an egg. ..."(Biba, 2010)
Despite the importance, of the concept of time has been discussed in several venues (Church, 2006), (Stenger, 2001). However, it is undeniable that THE CONCEPT is implicitly linked to daily activities by establishing a sequence, seemingly logical, of real-world events.
According to (Carroll, 2008), from the perspective of physics, "the nature of time is intimately connected with the problem of quantum gravity. At the classical level, Einstein's general relativity removes time from its absolute Newtonian moorings, but it continues to play an unambiguous role; time is a coordinate on four-dimensional space-time, however, it measures the space-time interval traversed by objects moving slower than light.
Under the Quantum Mechanics perspective, there are considered some fundamental aspects like the position and momentum of a particle what imperfectly reflect the reality of the underlying quantum state. It is therefore perfectly natural to imagine that, in a full theory of quantized gravity, the space-time itself would emerge as an approximation to something deeper. And if space-time is an emergent phenomenon, surely time must be".
Once the knowledge representation is captured, inferences can be made including extending forward from the known past and present to the unknown (prediction or statistical syllogism) and/or determining the causality by extending from the known data back to hypothesis (explanation or abduction) (Josephson & Josephson, 1994).
Thus, every knowledge representation model requires a representation of time, of the temporal relationship between events and has to deal with uncertainty. In some systems, the time model is such that the actions should be considered instantaneous, and only one action can occur at some given time, while in others, where there is an association between an action and a time reference, the inference module can automatically derive other relations.
In a more philosophical perspective (Overton, 1994) states that the cycle of time is a deep metaphor entailing a relational field of both nonclosed cycles (spirals) and direction that emerges in a broader sense across a several scientific disciplines. In the context of the organic narrative, the cognition and personality are understood as emerging from a fundamental relational theory of the embodied mind. In the context of the mechanical narrative, the development is understood as being limited to variation (and only variation), and cognition and personality emerge from a theory of the computational mind.
In computing, a more practical approach on this subject has been addressed in research on intelligent agents. To illustrate, we selected two works in which the relationship between time and are intrinsic cognition although greater attention is devoted to the cognitive aspect. A promising approach called *action awareness* is based on to provide agents with reflective capabilities where agents can reflect on the effects and expected performance of their actions (Stulp & Beetz, 2006). Another approach is based on an *efficient thought* concept (Hayes-Roth, 2006) that is based on a list of eight steps that the most complex organizations, in general, perform in parallel. This approach states that the intelligent being:

- observes what's happening in the environment,
- assesses the situation for significant threats and opportunities,
- determines what changes would be desirable,

- generates possible plans to operate those changes,
- projects the likely outcomes of those plans,
- selects the best plan, and
- communicates that plan to key parties before implementing it.

Throughout the process, the intelligent being validates and improves its model.

3.4 Biological clock

According to (Schmidt, Collette, Cajochen, & Peigneux, 2007) "... There is evidence that the interaction between homeostatic and circadian factors is not linear throughout the day and can affect a wide range of neuro behavioral events. However, the impact of potential time-of-day variations on brain activity and cognitive performance remains largely ignored in cognitive psychology and neuropsychology, despite the fact that Ebbinghaus (1885/1964) already reported more than one century ago that learning of nonsense syllables is better in the morning than in the evening...".

According to (GSLC, 2010), "living organisms evolved an internal biological clock, called the circadian rhythm, to help their bodies adapt themselves to the daily cycle of day and night (light and dark) as the Earth rotates every 24 hours. The term 'circadian' comes from the Latin words for about (*circa*) a day (*diem*). Circadian rhythms are controlled by *clock genes* that carry the genetic instructions to produce proteins. The levels of these proteins rise and fall in rhythmic patterns. These oscillating biochemical signals control various functions, including when we sleep and rest, and when we are awake and active. Circadian rhythms also control body temperature, heart activity, hormone secretion, blood pressure, oxygen consumption, metabolism and many other functions. A biological clock has three parts: a way to receive light, temperature or other input from the environment to set the clock; the clock itself, which is a chemical timekeeping mechanism; and genes that help the clock control the activity of other genes".

People (and other animals) are able to perceive the duration of intervals between events however the organism's internal clocks are not exactly 24 hours long. Associative learning is dependent upon time perception, and the mechanisms of time perception are related to an internal clock. In situations in which there are many different time intervals, these can be combined for the assessment of the typical interval (Schmidt, Collette, Cajochen, & Peigneux, 2007).

3.5. Situated agents

"...unfortunately, programming situated agents is quite difficult. Interacting with a dynamic and largely unpredictable environment introduces a number of significant problems. Most of these problems are related to the way the agents use the plans that determine their behavior. Traditionally, plans were used literally; the agent did exactly what the plan said. This placed a heavy burden on the plan maker, because it had to foresee all the possible ways in which the agent's interaction with the environment might unfold. Today, it becomes clear that an agent should have the ability to interpret plans in a more sensible and context-dependent way; it should be able to improvise, to interrupt, resume and sequence activities, to actively forage for information and to use the current situations to disambiguate references in its plans" (Schaad, 1998).

We find that statement important to resume the actual paradigm. In our point of view, the actual paradigm can be introduced as follows: "unfortunately, programming is quite difficult. Interacting with a dynamic and largely unpredictable environment introduces a number of significant problems. Most of these problems are related to the way the programmers develop programs that determine their behavior. Traditionally, programs are used literally; the program does exactly what was programmed to do. This place a heavy burden on the programmer, because he has to foresee all the possible ways in which the program's interaction with the environment might unfold.
Unfortunately, our programs, in general, continues to be forged as static pieces of instructions.

3.6 World model

One aspect of fundamental importance in the robotics research area, and one that it is neglected by the operating systems designers refers to the fact that in robotics projects there is always a mapping function between reality and an internal representation denominated "world model". In other words, there is some form of explicit environment representation where the robot will operate. And it is this world model that determines what decisions are made.
It is important to make a distinction between two types of world models:
i. those that only describe the current state of the agent's surroundings, and
ii. those that include more general knowledge about other possible states and ways of achieving these states. The first models are commonly referred as environment models and typically include some kind of spatial 3-D description of the physical objects in the environment. It contains dynamic and situation-dependent knowledge and can be used, for instance, in navigation tasks. The models of the second kind are referred as world models, and typically include more stable and general knowledge about: objects, properties of objects, relationships between objects, events, processes, and so on (Davidsson, 1994).
Accordingly Grimm et. al (2001), the main requirements to be reached in this class of projects are: robustness; reliability; modularity; flexibility; adaptability; integration of multiple sensors; resolution of multiple objectives; global reasoning, and intelligent behavior.
This aspect is also considered in autonomous agents research area. As stated in (Franklin & Graesser, 1996) "... Autonomous agent means a system situated in, and part of, an environment, which senses that environment and acts on it, over time, in pursuit of its own agenda. It acts in such a way as to possibly influence what it senses at a later time...".
That is, the agent is structurally coupled to its environment. If an operating system does not have an internal representation of its own relationship with surroundings, how can we suppose that it can make intelligent decisions? That is one of the main problems to be solved by the designers of new generation operating systems. It must be clear that by affirming that the operating system doesn't have an internal representation of its internal state we mean that it's not enough to collect statistical data about all the processes and other countable things that occur when the system is running. Instead, it has to collect them in order to be able to infer something about what is happening at some particular moment. This is a much more complex process that cannot be achieved by writing multitudes of scripts and building lots of administration tools.

3.7 Comments

In this section, we presented a set of concepts for which there is no unanimity among researchers. It was not our intention to present a complete review of the disciplines, but point out a few aspects that we consider important in the context of this work.
We followed a path starting from the more abstract concepts (knowledge, intelligence, time) towards the more concrete ones (biological clock).
We are considering the biological clock as the starting point to establish a time unit compatible with that found in humans and over which we do our daily tasks (including learning, planning and dealing with uncertainties - requisites from Ubicom, AC, and OC) and that does have no relationship with the real time clock used in machines.
After these considerations we can conclude that the complex and dynamic nature of the environment were software solutions are developed (and where they will be executed) has the effect that the operating system:

- does not have complete control over the environment;
- does not have the capacity to devise complete models of its environment (not only its counters and pointers);
- does not possess complete information about the environment, and
- cannot completely trust the information it does have, because it is usually uncertain, imprecise, noisy, or outdated due to the nature of its perceptual processes.

At this point we have collected evidences pointing to the expectation that we need to build systems capable to export some kind of intelligent behavior. To achieve these goal artificial systems must have direct access to their environments beyond the information stored in logs It is not enough to have elaborated reasoning, learning and planning capabilities because such an intelligent entity has to be able to autonomously acquire its required information through perception and carry out contemplated actions. In other words, it is necessary to make those "intelligent entities" more sensitive to context, enabling them to sense their environment, decide which aspects of a situation are really important, and infer the user's intention from concrete actions. Those actions may be dependent on time, place end/or even the past interactions with user.
These limitations have been a central driving force behind the creation of a new operating system based on knowledge abstraction. The main goal is to bring together knowledge about artificial intelligence, robotics and physics in order to produce a new class of operating systems able to cope with the presented challenges.

4. A Knowledge-based operating system model

The novel concept introduced in Mattos (2003) says that a knowledge-based operating system (KBOS) is: "an embodied, situated, adaptive and autonomic system based on knowledge abstraction which has identity and intelligent behavior when executed". The whole system is built inside a shell which gives the endogenous characteristic. A hyper dimensional world model enables the entire system to perceive evolving and/or fluctuating execution conditions.
The endogeneity characteristic of the system insofar as the world model is surrounded by the hardware, i.e. the world model *is* the system. The world model can be characterized as the surrounding membrane of a biological cell. The nucleus is the hardware. Therefore, the membrane acts as an interface between the external environment and internal environment. Using the analogy of the cell, we cannot break through the membrane to access the inner

parts of it. So any form of influence in the cell must occur in a process similar to osmosis, i.e. provide stimulus to the interface which will translate the stimulus to the internal representation of the cell.

4.1 A KBOS World Model

We have identified 3 dimensions over which such a new operating system paradigm has to be based:

- physical dimension,
- behavioral dimension, and
- temporal dimension

The physical dimension describes the physical hardware components and their structural relationship. The behavioral dimension is described by extended state machines. Each device has a state machine for describing is physical primary behavior we called this as: *physical context of a device* (PCD). A state machine describes the dynamic aspects of the component's behavior. The current state of some device is represented by a string of bits (figure 2).

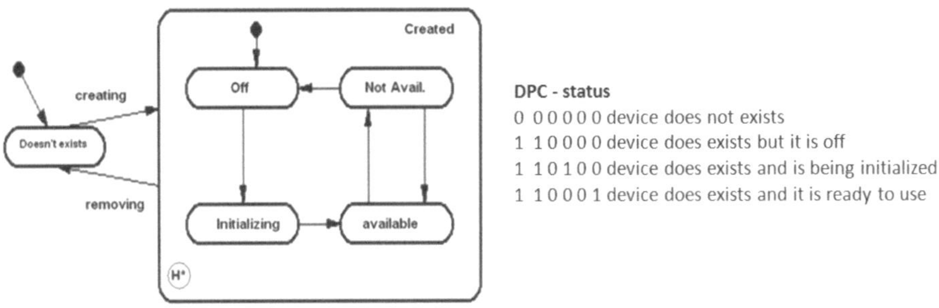

Fig. 2. Physical context of a device

Each device has a state machine that describes, in a more high level of abstraction, the functional aspects of it - we call it a *logical context of a device* (LCD) (figure 3).

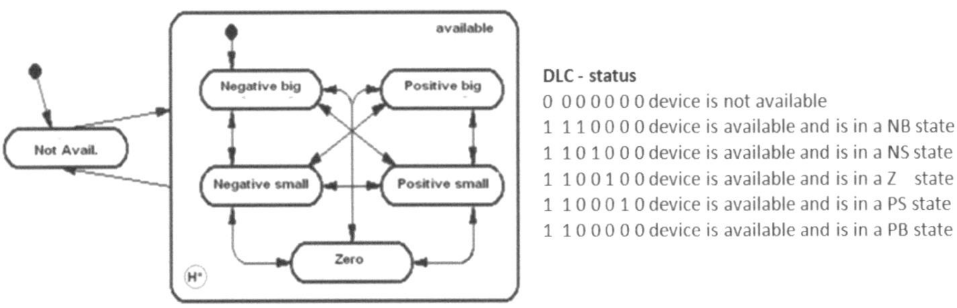

Fig. 3. Logical context of a device

One aspect that we would like to point is that the LCD use a fuzzy notation to express functional aspects of a particular device like available space (i.e. a disk unit could express space availability ranging from completely full to completely empty), communication link availability and so on.

Merging all the PCD and LCD results in a bit mask that represents the current state of the world (figure 4). This *world status word* (WSW) is used to trigger the execution of plans that were conceived as context-sensitive. It can be observed that the status word may also to represent some world's configurations for which yet there are no plans available.

For example, we could have an action plan describing what TO do in a situation where the network connection is good and the disk space is at least 50% available - let's call it the ideal solution. In a situation where the network connection is bad and disk space is less than 20% could lead to bad behavior in the plan. Perceiving this, a KBOS can start the learning stage, where it will test whether the optimal solution will work well or it will fail at some point of the present situation. If the solution works well, the system learns and registers at its knowledge base that the ideal solution also works for this situation. If not, the system will take to choose alternative plans in order to cope with the situation.

One could to observe that the bit mask is highly sensitive to fluctuations of the possible states of the world what can lead to a combinatorial explosion of states. Thus, a requirement for development of applications for a KBOS is explicitly to conceive exception conditions for each individual application. This characteristic leads to the development of more context-sensitive applications.

The description above characterizes one difference in designing software when compared with the traditional way of doing (figure 1). In our approach, the software development process should be guided by the dynamics of the application. Furthermore, we believe it should be abolished the phase of binary code generation - at the end of the compiling process as we always have done until now.

In this new perspective, the process of building a program should to finish by delivering a set of technical information to be provided to the assimilation interface of a KBOS which is the module effectively responsible for to transform that information into execution plans.

The act of transforming a program in an execution plan for a KBOS is a three-step process.

The first step involves the traditional process of software development (conception, design, implementation, testing) - including the constraints demanded by the context of a KBOS environment.

The second step involves generating, instead of an executable code, a meta-model containing:

- an extended state machine describing the dynamic behavior of the entire application and,
- the source code associated with the effective implementation of the application logic for each state/sub-state.

The third step involves submitting the meta-model to the KBOS assimilation interface for effective generation of a set of execution plans.

Our contribution stems from the fact that we are recognizing the importance of providing for the KBOS more than binary code (executable) to manage. Figure 5 reinforces the fact that we are not arguing about how we use to obtain information about the domain of a particular application, or how we should map this information in terms of software architecture or even trying to change the current paradigm of programming.

An execution plan is built in a parallel functional decision tree (Schaad, 1998) format and represents the lowest level of code that KBOS recognizes and executes. So, in a broader sense, of knowledge of a KBOS emerges from a library of execution plans and from the system's experience in to execute them according to environment fluctuations.

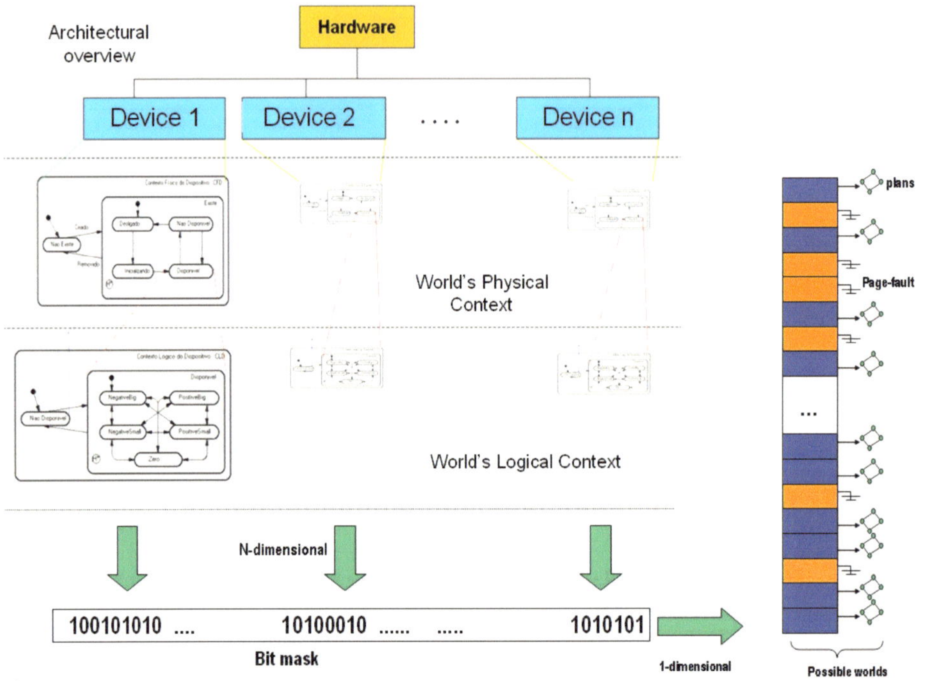

Fig. 4. A KBOS world model in an overall perspective

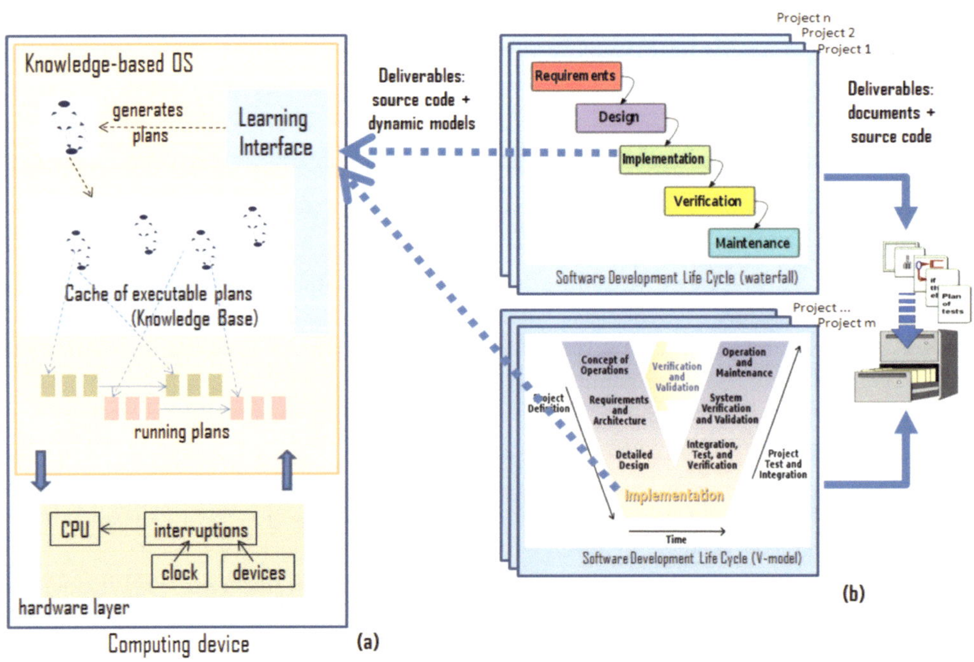

Fig. 5. Overview of the proposed software development process.

We should point some important characteristics:

- Knowledge = source code + dynamic models: traditionally, the last phase of compiling process is the binary code generation. An executable code doesn't carries additional information about the intentions of a particular program. In function of that, operating systems has to be prepared for both - well behavior and non-conforming programs;
- Learning interface: in a KBOS environment the assimilation interface grabs the input pack (source code + dynamic models) and analyses its own knowledge base in order to identify similar procedures. If it finds two different solutions for the same problem it could produce plans to be evaluated by itself in order to identify which one is the best to be adopted. The outcome is a new set of plans to be inserted in its knowledge base.
- Executable plans (Schaad, 1998) instead programs: in our point of view, at same time that the program represents the programmer's knowledge about some domain, it also carries no additional information when executed by some computing device. In a KBOS, we bring to the environment that knowledge and make it available to the OS.

Traditionally, a plan is regarded as an ordered collection of executable primitives, or macros, that are decomposable into primitives. We have chosen decision trees as a plan representation structure in KBOS in function of a number of distinct advantages over other representations for reactive plans (Schaad, 1998):

- simplicity: decision trees are easy to implement in any programming language and the associated run-time system can also be simple;
- efficiency: decision trees execute very efficiently.
- stepped execution model: decision trees are a natural fit with the stepped, ex-ante arbitrated execution model and with the design principle of improvisation underlying it
- transparency: decision trees are easy to understand and debug
- layering: layering is important for expressing temporal coherence, such as persistence and sequences, and for code reuse.

In this context, a plan is a data structure that maps a state machine and the program source code to a set of parallel functional decision trees (PFDT) using the notation described in (Schaad, 1998). A plan consists of a set of instructions expressed in the notation of PFDT - the *steppables* (figure 6a). Each plan is encapsulated by an envelope, which, among other things allows the recording of information about the context of the world (physical, behavioral and temporal) at any given time.

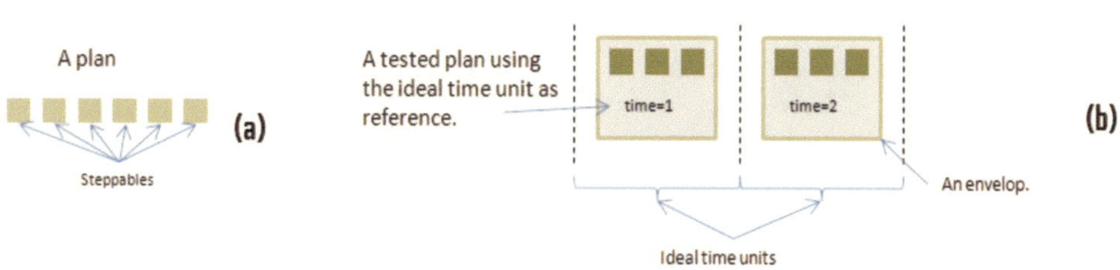

Fig. 6. An execution plan (a), and the plan tested in an ideal development environment (b)

The development of applications for KBOS introduces a requirement that the developer use an ideal development environment - an environment where it is possible to implement plans without interference from other applications/tasks (equivalent to running a program in a single-TASK operating system). This ideal environment has an abstract clock unit which

is used only for purposes of temporal ordering of the plans. The recording the execution time of a plan is a matter of increment the time counter (figure 6b).
If a plan is completely executed during an abstract interval, we register the value 1 as the time that plan needs to complete its task. Otherwise, if a plan requires more than one time unit, for each subsequent block of commands, that fits inside a time unit, we will increment this value until we get the end of the plan - observing that this procedure happens only at testing/debugging time.
In the situation where some sub-plans (any path within a program) have not been validated by the testing phase, the time of this path is recorded as invalid (-1). This information will allow the KBOS to become aware that the path was not previously tested and makes the KBOS to switch to a stage of learning.
At this stage, the plan being executed is monitored to assess effects on other plans being executed. As time passes and newer executions of this plan does not cause side effects, the plan starts being promoted to a condition in which he is regarded as reliable. Thus, one of the ways the KBOS acquires knowledge about the effects of some plan's behavior is by reinforcement learning.
If some error condition is detected, the system can provide to programmer the set of envelops with information about the environmental conditions at the error time. This adds important information about the timing in which the error occurred. Naturally it is not our expectation that a KBOS will develop the ability to correct programming logic errors.

4.2 The time dimension

Different definitions of time granularity have been proposed in the literature. All these definitions use partitions of a fixed temporal domain to represent temporal structures (Clifford & Rao, 1987), (Puppis, 2006).
In the current paradigm of computing systems, the time is a variable that has to be explicitly read (*get-time()/get-date() functions*) in order to enable software entities to perceive the time flow. The structure that we propose for the temporal domain is suitable for the needs of a KBOS and it is represented by a quadtree-like bit structure which enables to represent since the smallest observable or interesting time unit as well as a very coarse granularity (fig. 7).

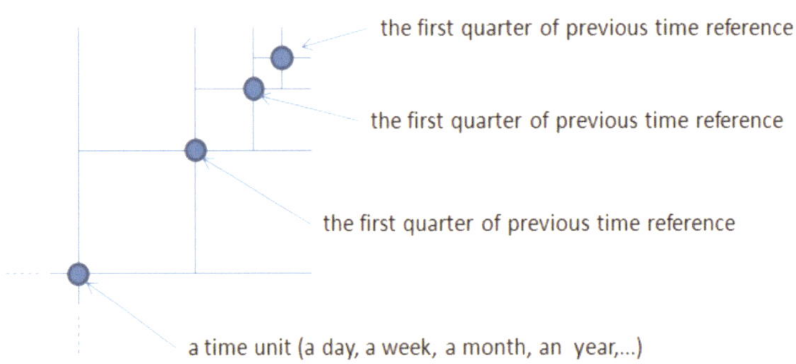

Fig. 7. The quadtree-like structure for representing time units (sub-units) in KBOS.

The term quadtree is used to describe a class of hierarchical data structures whose common property is that they are based on the principle of recursive decomposition of space.

Hierarchical data structures are useful because of their ability to focus on the interesting subsets of the data, resulting in an efficient representation and improved execution times, and it is thus particularly useful for performing set operations. Hierarchical data structures are attractive because of their conceptual clarity and ease of implementation (Samet, 1984).
This model allows to record and check the occurrence of an event on various time scales (figure 8) using the same universal structure, and with a very small computational cost. In this context, the manipulation of events is just a matter of bitwise operations (AND, OR, XOR, NOT) against the structure.

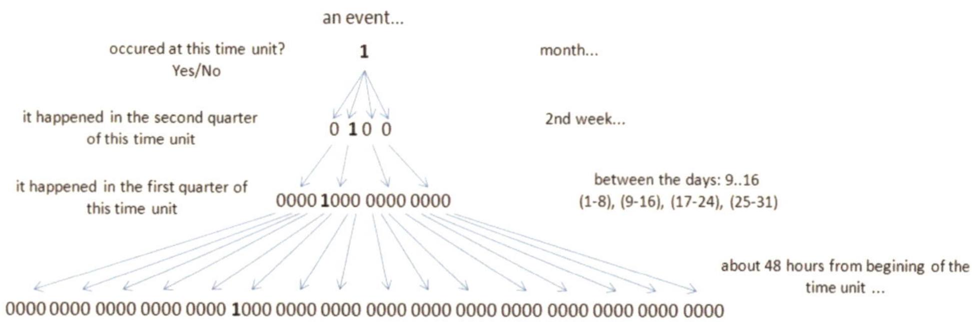

Fig. 8. Recording the occurrence of an event

There is a single global structure to represent the time for all instances of execution plans. Each execution plan can use sub-structures of the overall structure to represent time units in the application's domain. Thus, a reference to a specific unit of time is characterized as an index in this structure.
Once we have identified an universal structure to represent time units, the next step was to define the machine biological clock (MBC) and its computational representation.

4.3 Machine biological clock

As seen before, living organisms have some sort of internal biological clock that helps to define what is called: the circadian rhythm - the rhythm used to synchronize the internal actions within the body.

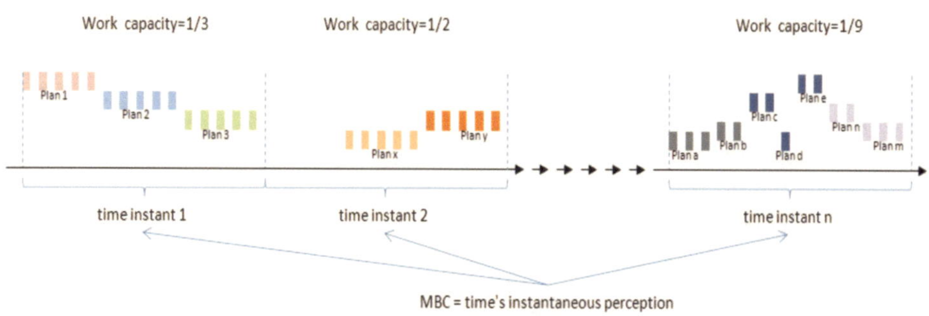

Fig. 9. Machine biological clock and work capacity

The MBC follows the same principle - a unit of time observable in the time's system structure (figure 9). However, we should to highlight that the events and actions taken during this time interval are considered as *instantaneous* in such a way that a KBOS can only to consider this timescale for inference purposes. For analogy, in general, people do not perceive time units smaller than 1 second but we know that the internal functioning of the body works in smaller fractions of a second. In the same way, a KBOS is still capable of performing operations in fractions of seconds according to the characteristics of hardware but it will only perceive the time flow from the MBC units.

The MBC is a unit of time derived from the real time clock of the computing device. Thus, the size of the MBC (in units of fractions of seconds) is a matter of individual adjustment - each class of devices that share the same hardware characteristics should also share the same MBC. In the same way, different classes should have different MBC.

From the MBC concept it is possible to derive the concept of *work capacity* (WC) - a unit that measures the device's ability to perform tasks, which is measured in units of MBC (fig.8).

As more tasks needs to be executed by unit of MBC, less WC the device will present, and vice-versa.

This characteristic allows the system perceive that it is in an overcharged situation and this "feeling" will be propagated for all active plans instantly- i.e. in the time interval between two MBC time units. In this moment, all plans automatically will start to adapt themselves to that fluctuation condition. In the current paradigm, this situation could be evidenced, for example, because the queue of processes is long, or because the rate of context switching is high. However, if all processes are not context-aware, the system cannot adapt easily.

In a fairly high level of abstraction, this unit of *work capacity* enables a KBOS to make decisions when interacting with other devices in a community(Goumopoulos & Kameas, 2009) and to discover "*how good it is*" when comparing with the neighborhood devices - again, this characteristic could lead to some kind of measure of "*social behavior*" of the machine.

4.4 Time perception

Perceiving a time flow is a matter of to be situated. In order to achieve this goal, we had to conceive a complementary data structure to PFDT, refered before as envelop. We will depict a sample of how we made possible for plans to perceive the time flow without the need of explicitly asking it to the operating system.

The figure 10a shows a plan previously tested at the development environment by the programmer. This plan when comes to the user's machine and is assimilated will have the time units adjusted to the real MBC of the target device.

The figure 10b shows the plan being executed in a real situation sharing the cpu time with other plans but running according the time units previously defined.

The figure 10c shows a tipical situation where the availability of cpu is reduced by the fact the system needs to execute more plans. In this case, some part of the first envelop is sliced and scheduled to be executed in a time further. When the unfinished part of the first envelop starts running, its time recorded will be different from the actual MBC making with all further function calls be made with an indication of a delayed situation.

To a better understanding, the figure 11 shows an example of a java program that is time dependent as a sample of how we deal with time in the current paradigm.

In general, the program needs to call the *System.currentTimeMillis()* function in order to discover the current time and make some calculation to discover if it is delayed, on time or ahead of time (when comparing with previous execution of the same plan). Also, in general,

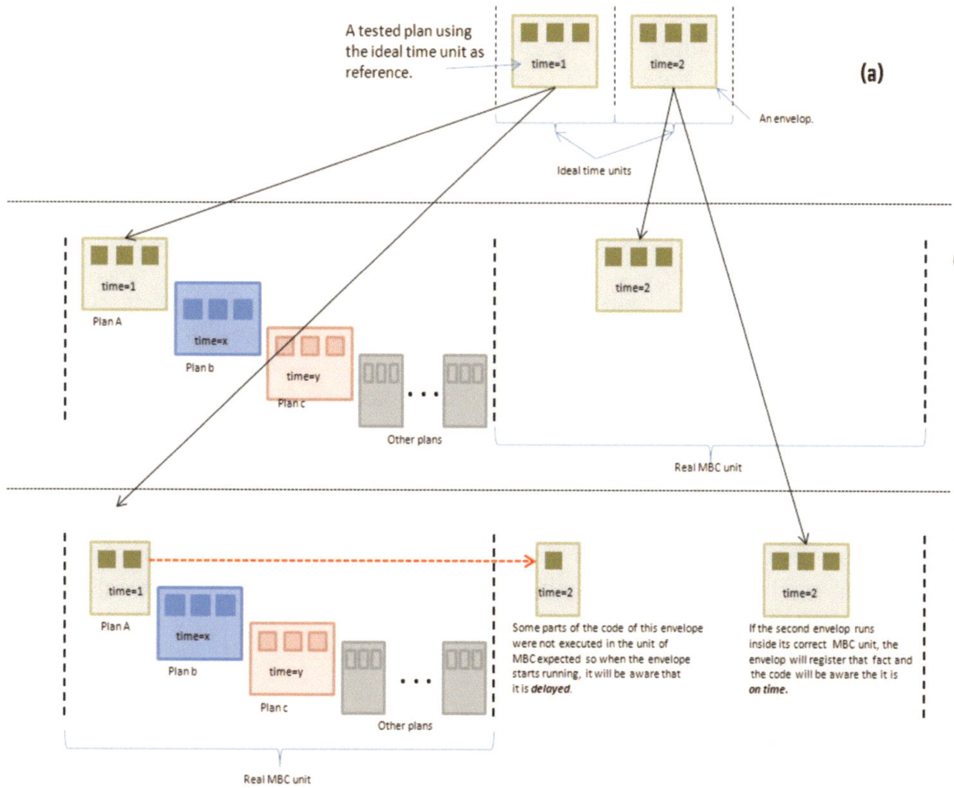

Fig. 10. A tested plan (a), the plan running in a real environment (b), and a plan perceiving it is delayed (c).

```
public class AdaptationWithExplicitTimeManagement {
   private long deadline1, deadline2;
   private boolean hasSomethingToDo = true;
   public void doSomethingLate() { }
   public void doSomethingExactlyOnTime() { }
   public void doSomethingWithTimeLeft() { }
   public void processChanges1() {
      while (hasSomethingToDo) {
         if (System.currentTimeMillis() > deadline1)      doSomethingLate();
         else if (System.currentTimeMillis() < deadline1) doSomethingWithTimeLeft();
         else                                             doSomethingExactlyOnTime();
      }//while
   }
   public void processChanges2() {
      while (hasSomethingToDo) {
         if (System.currentTimeMillis() > deadline2)      doSomethingLate();
         else if (System.currentTimeMillis() < deadline2) doSomethingWithTimeLeft();
         else                                             doSomethingExactlyOnTime();
      }//while
   }
```

Fig. 11. Explicit time example

only some portions of the code running in a system have to deal with such constraints, so we have a mix of code dealing with time and code that was not conceived to deal with time running together in the same environment. For example, the method *doSomethingExactlyOnTime()* could be started exactly on time, but become late because the multitasking environment could be scheduled other code to run changing the time when *doSomethingExactlyOnTime()* will effectively receive the CPU. If the code structure of that method is not build as the sample code (lines 14-16), the late execution could cause the entire system to present some strange behavior. And we are not talking about real-time applications, but desktop ones.

The figure 12 shows how a plan (in KBOS context) deal with time perception: each procedure/function has to explicitly declare sections where the time dimension has to be considered as a functional requisite.

In this example we can observe that there are three methods implementing the logic for *processChanges()* each one ending with one of the reserved words: *_Late*, *_OnTime* and *_AheadOfTime*.

During the execution of a plan, the system activates the appropriated section (*late*, *onTime* or *aheadOfTime*) according to the situation of the world model as previously described. If the developer does not know what to do in some situation, he can explicitly use an *IDoNotKnowWhatToDo* clause and the KBOS run-time will start trying to learn how to deal with that situation. This leads to some possibilities:

- the knowledge-base already have some other plan that already was tested before - this plan is activated;
- the knowledge-base does not have other plan - then the KBOS starts to follow the execution of the plan verifying what happens, for example, if the plan is delayed or cancelled.

In the example (figure 10), the method *processChanges1...()* was developed dealing with the three situations but in the situation where method *processChanges2...()* is dispatched late, the programmer explicitly declared that *iDontKnowWhatToDoInThisSituation()* (on line 20).

To support this model of function dispatch, the KBOS adopts a mapping function that makes possible to convert a n-dimensional world status to an one-dimensional status word The way we have implemented this functionality is changing the standard procedure call protocol:

call [memory address].

Instead, we have adopted the protocol:

call [memory address [World Status Word, CurrentMBC]].

When the destination address points to an *iDontKnowWhatToDoInThisSituation*, the system switches to a learning state. Under this condition, the KBOS can decide to let the procedure/function called run in one of the other possibilities programmed, or to cancel the call once the "programmer" doesn't know how his program could behave under that condition.

If the system let the procedure/function call to continue, the system will learn what happens and will register the behavior of that part of the code under inadequate conditions in the PLAN'S state machine. So that the system will develop the capacity of observing the way a module works in order to decide, in the future, if it will allow or not that code to run again. Notice that this cannot grant that the code will do it right in the future.

```
public class AdaptationWithImplicitTimeManagement {
   private boolean hasSomethingToDo = true;
   public void doSomethingLate() { }
   public void doSomethingExactlyOnTime() { }
   public void doSomethingWithTimeLeft() { }

   public void processChanges1_Late() {
      while (hasSomethingToDo) { doSomethingLate(); } }
   public void processChanges1_OnTime() {
      while (hasSomethingToDo) { doSomethingExactlyOnTime(); }}
   public void processChanges1_AheadOfTime() {
      while (hasSomethingToDo) { doSomethingWithTimeLeft(); }}

   public void processChanges2_Late() {
      iDontKnowWhatToDoInThisSitutation(); }
   public void processChanges2_OnTime() {
      while (hasSomethingToDo) { doSomethingExactlyOnTime(); }}
   public void processChanges2_AheadOfTime() {
      while (hasSomethingToDo) { doSomethingWithTimeLeft();} }
```

Fig. 12. Implicit time example.

The possibility to deal with time perception information is made explicit to the programmer in development time so, it allows him to make decisions for building/conceiving self-adaptive plans. On the other hand this introduces an additional level of difficulty because the programmers are not traditionally accustomed to thinking of time dimension in the conception of their programs.

The time dimension also makes it possible to introduce the vague notion of space concept if two different plans perceive that both are delayed it is equivalent to say to each one that there is someone else sharing resources within the same MBC unit. This could leads, for example, that the logical path of some plan could be changed to another path that implements the same functionality but demands less resources. The self-adaptive and self-reconfigurable characteristics of the system are based on this facility.

5. Related work

In general, the operating system designers are concerned primarily with problems of a purely quantitative nature (e.g. performance) (Hansen, 2000) (Peng, Li, & Mili, 2007) while qualitative aspects should receive more attention. Before continuing, it is important to look at the efforts already made towards changing the situation presented. We emphasize that we are excluding from this analysis those works aimed at improving the current model like (Hunt & Larus, 2007) (Lee, et al., 2010) mainly because we are interested in going deeper in the area of knowledge-based systems at operating system level.

By reviewing the literature, it is possible to find some references to a knowledge-based operating system. ((Sansonnet, Castan, Percebois, Botella, & Perez, 1982),(Vilensky, Arens, & Chin, 1984),(Blair, Mariani, Nicol, & Shepherd, 1987),(Chikayama, Sato, & Miyazaki, 1988),(Moon, 1985),(Larner, 1990),(Ali & Karlsson, 1990), (Xie, Du, Chen, Zheng, & Sun, 1995),(Patki, Raghunathan, & Khurshid, 1997), (Jankowski & Skowron, 2007)). Other approaches involve the application of artificial intelligence techniques through kernel

implants[6] to achieve better interfaces in traditional operating systems ((Pasquale, 1987), (Chu, Delp, Jamieson, Siegel, & Whinston, 1989), (Zomaya, Clements, & Olariu, 1998);(Kandel, Zhng, & Henne, 1998); (Holyer & Pehlivan, 2000),(Lim & Cho, 2007)).
However, all failed to achieve its objectives because the conceptual basis for the meaning of "knowledge" or "intelligence" was not properly established. In general, due to project's time constraints, prototypes are constructed using existing and proven technologies wherever possible, rather than implementing core technologies from scratch.
In (Stulp & Beetz, 2006) was proposed a novel computational model for the acquisition and application of action awareness, showing that it can be obtained by learning predictive action models from observed experience and also demonstrating how action awareness can be used to optimize, transform and coordinate underspecified plans with highly parametrizable actions in the context of robotic soccer. The system works in two moments:
i. idle time, when the agent learns prediction models from the actions in the action library; and
ii. operation time, when action chains are generated.
In (Tannenbaum, 2009) we found that self-awareness means learned behaviors that emerge in organisms whose brains have a sufficiently integrated, complex ability for associative learning and memory. Continual sensory input of information related to the organism causes its brain to learn its (the organism's) physical characteristics, and produce neural pathways, which come to be reinforced, so that the organism starts recognizing, several features associated to each reinforced pathway. The self-image characteristic provides a mechanistic basis for the rise of the concept of emergency of behavior that, on its turn, is connected to the concepts of self-awareness and self-recognition. On the basis of all that process there is the notion of time perception.

6. Conclusion

We have given an overview of an endogenous self-adaptive and self-reconfigurable approach to operating system design that we call: knowledge-based operating system.
In order to get there, we presented some evidences that lead us to go back in the origins of the modern computing and figure out what could be the reasons why we still are dealing with problems identified a long time ago.
In our point of view, the concepts of program, multitasking and operator are strong candidates to be considered.
A *program* is a rigid expression of the programmer's knowledge acquired during the software development life cycle that is transformed into a string of bits and expected to be managed by the OS. As the hardware was expensive, the OS designers found in the *multitasking* a way to better share the computational resources between different users. The *operator* was needed in order to make the installation ready for all users demanding computational resources.
We do not eliminate the concepts of program multitasking and operator, but instead, repositioned these concepts in the perspective of:

- a program shall be replaced by a plan of execution, whose code is generated internally by the system and externally to the user's environment by the traditional process of generating executable code; this changes the perspective of software setup towards a software learning;

[6] See (Seltzer, Small, & Smith, 1995) for a kernel implant explanation.

- The concept of multitasking becomes a tool to support the concept of MBC in that it now plans are explicitly able to: (a) perceive when they were sliced, and (b) perceives the fluctuation of resources availability of the computing device.

This characteristic allows the conception and development of really context-aware applications.
Insofar as the characteristics of adaptability become part of the system, the characteristics of the user-machine relationship become enriched.
We demonstrate that the concept of knowledge in this phase of the project is a matter of self-knowledge, or the computing device knowledge about its ability to perform tasks and to self-adapt to the fluctuations of resource availability in the environment.
To the extent that context-aware applications begin to take into account these characteristics, a new concept of intelligence and perception of intelligent behavior becomes evident.
In the context of this work, the role of the programmer now has a double function:

- on the one hand, it continues to map the knowledge of some application's domain for an encoding tool;
- on the other hand, it assumes the role of teaching the system how to perform the application's role.

This relationship expands the possibilities of what we call today the reuse of code for the reuse of knowledge.
Based on what was presented we could start thinking in terms of the machine's identity concept, which is resultant from the embodiment, situatedness, adaptiveness and autonomic characteristics of a KBOS. This leads to the emergence concept - a property of a total system which cannot be derived from the simple summation of properties of its constituent subsystems.
In this sense, the set of characteristics enables the system to perceive, in an individualized manner, a set of events occurring in some instant of time. Thus, the intelligent behavior emerges from the previous characteristics plus the relationship between the system and the surrounding environment (Müller-Schloer, 2004).
We believe that the major contribution of this work has been to present a new way of designing systems that can evolve in a natural way for the machines (Costa, 1993) opening an avenue for research in conceiving really embodied software artifacts on the context of ubiquitous computing environment.

7. References

Abowd, G. D., & Mynatt, E. D. (2000, March). Charting Past, Present, and Future Research in Ubiquitous Computing. Transactions on Computer-Human Interaction, 7, pp. 29-58.

Ackermann, T. (2010). Quantifying Risks in Service Networks:Using Probability Distributions for the Evaluation of Optimal Security Levels. AMCIS 2010 Proceedings.

Ali, K. A., & Karlsson, R. (1990). The Muse Or-parallel Prolog model and its performance. In S. Debray, & M. Hermenegildo (Ed.), Proceedings of the 1990 North American Conference on Logic Programming (Austin, Texas, USA) (pp. 757-776). Cambridge, MA: MIT Press.

Anderson, J. P. (1972). Computer Security Technology Planning Study Vol. 1. HQ Eletctronic Systems Division (AFSC), Deputy for Command and Management Systems, Bedford,Massachusetts.

Arnold, W. R., & Bowie, J. S. (1985). Artificial intelligence: a personal, commonsense journey. Upper Saddle River, NJ, USA: Prentice-Hall.

Balasubramaniam, D., Morrison, R., Kirby, G., Mickan, K., Warboys, B., Robertson, I., et al. (2005). A software architecture approach for structuring autonomic systems. ACM SIGSOFT Software Engineering Notes, 30 (4), 1-7.

Barham, P., Isaacs, R., Mortier, R., & Harris, T. (2006). Learning Communitacion Patterns in Sigularity. First Workshop on Tackling Computing Systems Problems with Machine Learning Techniques (SysML) - Co-located with SIGMETRICS 2006. Saint-Malo, France.

Bellman, K. L., Landauer, C., & Nelson, P. R. (2008). Systems Engineering for Organic Computing. In R. P. Würtz (Ed.), Understanding Complex Systems (p. 355). Bochum, Germany: Springer-Werlag.

Biba, E. (2010, March 01). Physicist Sean Carroll on "What is time"? Retrieved July 15, 2010, from Wired Science: http://www.wired.co.uk/news/archive/2010-03/01/physicist-sean-carroll-on-what-is-time

Blair, G. S., Mariani, J. A., Nicol, J. R., & Shepherd, D. (1987). A Knowledge-base Operating System. The Computer Journal, 30 (3), 193-200.

Brachman, R. J. (2002, Nov/Dec). Systems that know what they're doing. IEEE Intelligent Systems, 67-71.

Buschmann, F. (2010, September-October). On architecture styles and paradigms. IEEE Software, 92-94.

Carroll, S. M. (2008). What if Time Really Exists? arXiv:0811.3772v1 .

Chikayama, T., Sato, H., & Miyazaki, T. (1988). Overview of the parallel inference machine operating system (PIMOS). Proceedings of the International Conference of Fifth Generation Computer Systems., pp. 230-251.

Chu, C. H., Delp, E. J., Jamieson, L. H., Siegel, H. J., & Whinston, A. B. (1989, June). A model for an intelligent operating system for executing image understanding tasks on a reconfigurable parallel architecture. Journal of Parallel and Distributed Computing, pp. 598-622.

Church, R. M. (2006). Behavioristic, cognitive, biological, and quantitative explanations of timing. In E. A. Wasserman, & T. R. Zentall (Eds.), Comparative cognition: Experimental explorations of animal intelligence. (pp. 24-269). New York, NY, EUA: Oxford University Press.

Costa, A. C. (1993). Inteligência de máquina: esboço de uma abordagem construtivista. Federal University of Rio Grande do Sul, Institute of Informatics, Porto Alegre, Brazil.

da Costa, C. A., Yamin, A. C., & Geyer, C. F. (2008). Toward a general software infrastructure for ubiquitous computing. IEEE Pervasive Computing, 7 (1), 64-73.

Davidsson, P. (1994). Autonomous Agents and the Concept of Concepts (Thesis). Lund University.

Davis, R., Shrobe, H., & Szolovits, P. (1993). What Is a Knowledge Representation? AI Magazine, 14 (1), 17-33.

Duch, W. (2007). What is computational intelligence and where is it going? Challenges for Computational Intelligence, 63, 1-13.

Fleisch, B. D. (1983). Operating systems: a perspective on future trends. SIGOPS Operating Systems Review, 17 (2), pp. 14-17.

Franklin, S., & Graesser, A. (1996). Is it an Agent, or Just a Program?: A Taxonomy for Autonomous Agents. In J. P. Muller, M. Wooldridge, & N. R. Jennings (Eds.), Lecture Notes in Computer Science (Vol. 1193, pp. 21-35). London, UK: Springer-Verlag.

Frost, R. A. (1986). Introduction to Knowledge Base Systems. Collins.

Grimm, R., Davis, J., Lemar, E., Macbeth, A., Swanson, S., Tom, S. G., et al. (2001). System-level Programming Abstractions for Ubiquitous Computing. Proceedings of the 8th Workshop on Hot Topics in Operating Systems (HotOS-VIII).

GSLC. (2010, May 28). The time of our lives. Retrieved September 29, 2010, from Learn.Genetics - Genetic Science Learning Center: http://learn.genetics.utah.edu/content/begin/dna/clockgenes/

Haigh, T. (2002, January-March). Software in the 1960s as concept, service, and product. IEEE Annals of the History of Computing, 24 (1), pp. 5-13.

Hansen, P. B. (1973). Operating systems principles. Upper Saddle River, NJ, USA: Prentice-Hall,Inc.

Hansen, P. B. (1977). The architecture of concurrent programs. Upper Saddle River, NJ, USA: Prentice-Hall,Inc.

Hansen, P. B. (2000). The evolution of operating systems. In Classic operating systems: from batch processing to distributed systems (pp. 1-36). New York, NY, USA: Springer-Verlag New York, Inc.

Hayes-Roth, R. (2006). Puppetry vs. creationism: why AI must cross the chasm. IEEE Intelligent Systems, 21 (5), 7-9.

Holyer, I., & Pehlivan, H. (2000). A Recovery Mechanism for Shells. The Computer Journal, 43 (3), 168-176.

Hunt, G. C., & Larus, J. R. (2007). Singularity: rethinking the software stack. SIGOPS Operating Systems Review, 41 (2), 37-49.

Hunt, G., Larus, J., Abadi, M., Aiken, M., Barham, P., Fähndrich, M., et al. (2005). An overview of the Singularity project. Redmond, WA: Microsoft Research.

Iyoengar, K., Sachdev, V., & Raja, M. K. (2007). A security comparison of open-source and closed-source operating systems. Proceedings of South West Decision Sciences Thirty-eighth Anual Conference. San Diego, CA, USA.

Jankowski, A., & Skowron, A. (2007). A Wistech Paradigm for Intelligent Systems. (J. Peters, A. Skowron, I. Düntsch, J. Grzymala-Busse, E. Orlowska, & L. Polkowski, Eds.) Lecture Notes in Computer Science:Transactions on Rough Sets VI, 4374, pp. 94-132.

Josephson, J. R., & Josephson, S. G. (1994). Abductive Inference:Computation, Philosophy,Technology. New York: Cambridge University Press.

Kandel, A., Zhng, Y.-Q., & Henne, M. (1998). On use of fuzzy logic technology in operating systems. Fuzzy Sets and Systems, 99 (3), 241-251.

Klausman, E. F. (1961). Training the computer operator. ACM '61:Proceedings of the 1961 16th ACM national meeting (pp. 131.401-131.404). New York, NY, USA: ACM.

Kramer, J., & Magee, J. (2007). Self-Managed Systems: an Architectural Challenge. 2007 Future of Software Engineering (May 23 - 25, 2007). International Conference on Software Engineering (pp. 259-268). Washington, DC, EUA: IEEE Computer Society.

Kruchten, P., Capilla, R., & Dueñas, J. C. (2009). The decision view's role in software architecture practice. IEEE Software, 26 (2), 36-42.

Krutchen, P. (2004). An Ontology of Architectural Design Decisions in Software Intensive Systems. 2nd Groningen Workshop Software Variability, (pp. 54-61).

Kupsch, J. A., & Miller, B. P. (2009). Manual vs. automated vulnerability assessment: a case study. First International Workshop on Managing Insider Security Threats (MIST 2009). West Lafayette, IN.

Lagerström, R., von Würtemberg, L. M., Holm, H., & Luczak, O. (2010). Identifying factors affecting software development cost. Proc. of the Fourth International Workshop of Software Quality and Maintainability (SQM).

Larner, D. L. (1990). A distributed, operating system based, blackboard architecture for real-time control. IEA/AIE '90: Proceedings of the 3rd international conference on Industrial and engineering applications of artificial intelligence and expert systems (pp. 99-108). Charleston, South Carolina, US: ACM.

Lee, S.-M., Suh, S.-B., Jeong, B., Mo, S., Jung, B. M., Yoo, J.-H., et al. (2010). Fine-grained I/O access control of the mobile devices based on the Xen architecture. of the 15th Annual international Conference on Mobile Computing and Networking (Beijing, China, September 20 - 25, 2009) (pp. 273-284). Beijing, China: ACM, NY, USA.

Legg, S., & Hutter, M. (2007, December). Universal intelligence: a definition of machine intelligence. Minds and Machines, pp. 391-444.

Lenat, D. B., & Feigenbaum, E. A. (1988). On the thresholds of knowledge. Proceedings of the International Workshop on Artificial Intelligence for Industrial Applications (IEEE AI'88), (pp. 291-300). Hitachi City, Japan.

Lim, S., & Cho, S.-B. (2007). Intelligent OS process scheduling using fuzzy inference with user models. IEA/AIE'07: Proceedings of the 20th international conference on Industrial, engineering, and other applications of applied intelligent systems (pp. 725-234). Kyoto, Japan: Springer-Verlag.

Linde, R. (1975). Operating Systems Penetration. AFIPS Conference Proceedings, 44.

Malsburg, C. v. (2008). The Organic Future of Information Technology. In R. P. Würtz (Ed.), Understanding Complex Systems (p. 355). Bochum: Springer-Verlag.

Mattos, M. M. (2003). Fundamentos conceituais para a construção de sistemas operacionais baseados em conhecimento (thesis). thesis, UFSC - Universidade Federal de Santa Catarina, PPGEP - Programa de Pós-Graduação em Engenharia de Produção, Florianópolis, Brazil.

Meadow, C. T., & Yuan, W. (1997). Measuring the impact of information: defining the concepts. Information Processing & Management, 33 (6), 697-714.

Milner, R. (2006, March). Ubiquitous computing: shall we understand it? The Computer Journal, 383-389.

Moon, D. A. (1985, June). Architecture of the Symbolics 3600. SIGARCH Computer Architecture News., 13 (3), pp. 76-83.

Müller-Schloer, C. (2004). Organic omputing: on the feasibility of controlled emergence. 2nd IEEE/ACM/IFIP International Conference on Hardware e Software Codesign and System Synthesis. Stockholm,Sweden: ACM Press.

Murch, R. (2004). Autonomic Computing. IBM Press.

Naur, P., & Randell, B. (1969). Software Engineering: Report of a Conference Sponsored by the NATO Science Committee. In P. Naur, & B. Randell (Ed.). (p. 136). Garmisch, Germany: Scinetific Affairs Division, NATO.

Osterweil, L. J. (2007). A future for software engineering? FOSE '07: 2007 Future of Software Engineering (May 23-25,2007) International Conference on Software Engineering (pp. 1-11). Washington, DC, USA: IEEE Computer Society.

Overton, W. F. (1994). The arrow of time and the cycle of time: concepts of change, cognition, and embodiment. (L. A. Pervin, Ed.) Psychological Inquiry: An International Journal of Peer Commentary and Review., 5 (3), 215-237.

Pasquale, J. C. (1987). Using expert systems to manage distributed computer systems. Berkeley, CA, USA: University of California at Berkeley.

Patki, A. B., Raghunathan, G. V., & Khurshid, A. (1997). FUZOS - Fuzzy Operating System Support for Information Technology. Proceedings of Second On-line World Conference on Soft Computing in Engineering,Design and Manufacturing. (pp. 23-27). Bedfordshire,UK: Cranfield University.

Peng, Y., Li, F., & Mili, A. (2007). Modeling the evolution of operating systems: an empirical study. Journal of Systems Software, 80 (1), 1-15.

Perry, D. E., & Wolf, A. L. (1992, October). Foundations for the study of software architecture. (ACM, Ed.) ACM SIGSOFT Software Engineering Notes, 17 (4), pp. 40-52.

Pfleeger, S. L. (2010, July/August). Anatomy of an Intrusion. IEEE IT Professional, 12 (4), pp. 20-28.

Poole, D., Mackworth, A., & Goebel, R. (1997). Computational intelligence: a logical approach. Oxford, UK: Oxford University Press.

Poslad, S. (2009). Smart Devices and Services, in Ubiquitous Computing: Smart Devices, Environments and Interactions. Chichester,UK: John Wiley & Sons, Ltd.

Post, G., & Kagan, A. (2003). Computer security and operating system updates. Information and Software Technology, 45 (8), 461-467.

Ragunath, P. K., Velmourougan, S., Davachelvan, P., Kayalvizhi, S., & Ravimohan, R. (2010, January). Evolving a new model (SDLC Model-2010) for software development life cycle (SDLC). International Journal of Computer Science and Network Security, 10 (1), pp. 112-119.

Randell, B. (1979). Software engineering in 1968. ICSE '79: Proceedings of the 4th international conference on Software engineering (pp. 1-10). Munich, Germany: IEEE Press.

Samek, M. (2009). Practical UML Statechars in C/C++, Second Edition: Event-Driven Programming for Embedded Systems (2a ed.). Newton, MA, USA: Newnes.

Sansonnet, J. P., Castan, M., Percebois, C., Botella, D., & Perez, J. (1982, March). Direct execution of lisp on a list-directed architecture. SIGARCH Computer Architecture News, 10 (2), pp. 132-139.

Schaad, R. (1998). Representation and Execution of Situated Action Sequences (Thesis). Universitat Zürich.

Schmidt, C., Collette, F., Cajochen, C., & Peigneux, P. (2007). A time to think: circadian rhythms in human cognition. Cognitive Neuropsychology, 24 (7), 755-789.

Seltzer, M., Small, C., & Smith, K. (1995). The case for extensible operating systems. Harward Computer Center for Research in Computing Technology.

Shadbolt, N., O'hara, K., & Crow, L. (1999, October). The experimental evaluation of knowledge acquisition techniques and methods: history, problems and new directions. International Journal of Human-Computer Studies, 51 (4), pp. 729-755.

Shibayama, S., Sakai, H., & Takewaki, T. (1988). Overview of knowledge base mechanism. Proceedings of the International Conference on Fifth Generation Computer Systems, pp. 197-207.

Skjellum, A., Dimitrov, R., Angaluri, S. V., Coulouris, G., Uthayopas, P., Scott, S. L., et al. (2001, May). Systems Administration. International Journal of High Performance Computing Applications, 15 (2), pp. 143-161.

Stenger, V. J. (2001). Time's arrows point both ways: the view from nowhen. Skeptic, 8 (4), 92-95.

Stulp, F., & Beetz, M. (2006). Action awareness – enabling agents to optimize, transform, and coordinate plans. Proceedings of the Fifth International Joint Conference on Autonomous Agents and Multiagent Systems (AAMAS) (pp. 8-12). Hakodate, Hokkaido, Japan: ACM.

Tanenbaum, A. S. (2008). Modern Operating Systems. Prentice Hall.

Tannenbaum, E. (2009, June). Speculations on the emergence of self-awareness in big-brained organisms. Consciousness and Cognition, 18 (2), pp. 414-427.

Vilensky, R., Arens, Y., & Chin, D. (1984, June). Talking to UNIX in English: an overview of UC. Communications of ACM, 27 (6), pp. 574-593.

Weiser, M. (1991, September). The Computer for the Twenty-First Century. Scientific American, 94-10.

Wilensky, R., Chin, D. N., Luria, M., Martin, J., Mayfield, J., & Wu, D. (2000, April). The Berkeley UNIX Consultant Project. Artificial Intelligence Review, 14 (1-2), pp. 43-88.

Würtz, R. P. (2008). Introduction: Organic Computing. In R. P. Würtz (Ed.), Understanding Complex Systems (p. 355). Bochum, Germany: Springer-Verlag.

Xie, L., & Yi, J. (1998). A model for intelligent resource management in a large distributed system. Science in China Series E: Technological Sciences, 41 (1), pp. 13-21.

Xie, L., Du, X., Chen, J., Zheng, Y., & Sun, Z. (1995). An introduction to intelligent operating system KZ2. SIGOPS Operating Systems Review, 29 (1), pp. 29-46.

Yokote, Y. (1992). The Apertos reflective Operating System: the concept and its implementation. Conference Proceedings on Object-Oriented Programming Systems, Languages, and Applications -OOPSLA '92. 27, pp. 414-434. New York, NY,EUA: ACM.

Yuhua, Z., Honglei, T., & Li, X. (1993, May). And/Or parallel execution of logic programs: exploiting dependent And-parallelism. SIGPLAN Notices, pp. 19-28.

Zomaya, A. Y., Clements, M., & Olariu, S. (1998, March). A framework for reinforcement based scheduling in parallel processor systems. IEEE Transactions on Parallel and Distributed Systems., 249-260.

2

Anywhere/Anytime Software and Information Access via Collaborative Assistance

Ren-Song Ko
National Chung Cheng University
Taiwan

1. Introduction

The development of computing has recently been dominated by three trends: the emergence of a wide range of embedded systems with diverse architectures and purpose; the rise of relatively high-speed mobile communication devices such as smart phones, personal digital assistants (PDAs), portable media players, ebook readers, etc; and the development of cloud computing, offering virtually unlimited data storage and computing resources, which may extend the capabilities of resource-constrained mobile devices. As a consequence, these devices and infrastructures have begun to pervade our daily life, creating a new paradigm in the interaction between people and computing environments along the lines of that envisioned by Weiser (Weiser, 1991), and thus opening up the potential of many novel applications.

For instance, the ubiquitous presence of computers allows people to carry with them only a minimal amount of computing hardware and software, depending on ambient computers to boost performance as needed. A smart phone may not have sufficient computation power to playback a high-definition movie but,rather than running the media playback software on a single device, one could look for available computers nearby and connect them together to constitute an *ad-hoc system* (Ko et al., 2008). The software can then utilize the resources of all participating devices to accomplish the execution collaboratively. Such a system is unplanned and organized on a temporary basis, usually to execute a specific task.

Another possible application is the timely information query. Even with sophisticated search engines available nowadays, the answers to some questions (e.g., "is the department store crowed now?" or "can someone take a snapshot of the car race now?") are time-sensitive and may become less significant if they cannot be obtained immediately; only people who are currently near the store or the race track can provide the appropriate responses. Similarly, with the ubiquity of mobile network-connected devices, it is highly possible to find such people and thus applications requiring timely information become feasible.

1.1 Problems

However, the scale of ubiquitous computing is huge, and so is the need to enable interoperability among mobile devices and infrastructures. Thus, realizing a system for ubiquitous applications as described above may face the following research challenges.

1.1.1 Software reuse

Given the number and variety of mobile and embedded devices, software development is, in most cases, a complex and time-consuming process since heterogeneous environments raise problems above and beyond source code level portability, which has a significant impact on ease of software reuse. With careful coding, the software may be compiled into native code for various platforms. Nevertheless, the software will probably be difficult to deploy and use. The source code has to be compiled for the target platform, either by vendors or users, and the computing environment needs to be correctly configured to the required hardware and shared libraries. While this problem may be alleviated by platform-independent intermediate bytecode and virtual machines (e.g., Java), a higher level of portability vis-a-vis performance also needs to be considered (Ko & Mutka, 2002). For instance, while a multimedia application may run perfectly on a desktop, it may run so slowly on a mobile device as to be unusable. One way to improve performance would be to reduce the output quality. An alternative would be to improve software to detect and exploit special the functionality of particular devices.

To achieve a higher level of portable performance, information on the resources available on the target devices is necessary but, unfortunately, not available until run time. Therefore, instead of making assumptions regarding the capabilities of target devices, developers specify performance and resource requirements during the software development stage. The software may then determine at run time whether it can run on the target platform, or, even better, adapt itself to the computing environment by adjusting performance and resource requirements.

1.1.2 Dynamic computing environment

These computing environments are open and dynamic; i.e., usage is not confined to a fixed location, and people carrying computers may join and leave the environment at will. Thus, the environment may change during the execution of an application, leading to problems such as resource variability, system errors, and changing requirements.

To improve system dependability, robustness, and availability, software execution has to be aware of environmental changes and take appropriate actions to accommodate these changes. Traditionally, such auto-adapting mechanisms may be implemented at the code level, e.g., explicit coding of environmental conditions and corresponding remedial actions. However, such approaches are specifically targeted and the adaptive capabilities are often limited in scope, brittle, costly to change, and difficult to reuse. Furthermore, they lack a global view of software systems, so they usually only detect the symptoms but not true sources of environmental changes and thus may not be able to determine the most suitable response.

1.1.3 Resources and information location

Dramatic improvements in the quality of and accessibility to networks makes it increasingly feasible to use collections of networked commodity devices as computational resources. Thus, the widespread use of dynamically-assembled collections of computers, located on local and even wide area networks, as powerful computational resources is becoming possible. For instance, a computational task might be initially mapped to available computers within a workgroup, but then extended or migrated to other resources provided by a commercial computational services provider because of changes in computational characteristics or resource availability. However, locating computational resources or information that are relevant to users' interests can be challenging for ubiquitous computing since it needs to

determine which resource is the best candidate at minimum cost given the heterogeneous, dynamic nature of the resources involved.
For example, searching for devices to constitute an ad-hoc system, a good resource discovery mechanism may need to consider many factors including user interfaces, architectures, or physical locations to minimize the costs of interoperability among participants. In addition, it is preferable that all ad-hoc system participants be in geographic proximity to promote ease of interaction. It is also highly likely that people currently close to the store would have an answer to the query, "is the department store crowed now?". Therefore, a range of physical locations must be incorporated within a resource discovery mechanism; e.g., routing mechanisms using geographic parameters such as Greedy Forwarding (GF) (Finn, 1987) may be used to locate participants and initiate communication among them.

1.2 Possible solutions

Due to the problems described above, the rapid the development of ubiquitous applications usually requires identifying appropriate middleware abstractions and organizing successful protocols, algorithms, and software modules into generic middleware platforms. An ideal platform should allow applications to handle the resource constraints of the ubiquitous devices but, at the same time, exploit their unique features such as availability of location information, embedded sensors, mobility, and spontaneous interaction.

1.2.1 Adaptive systems

To cope with dynamic computing environments, the concept of reflective systems that have the capability to reason and act autonomously was proposed (Maes, 1987). Such a system provides a representation of its own behavior which is amenable to inspection and adaptation, and so is able to observe its current state and alter its behavior at run time. Reflection has been added into various systems, including languages (*Java Platform Standard Edition API Specification*, n.d.), operating systems (Jr & Kofuji, 1996; Yokote, 1992), and middleware (Blair et al., 1998; Kon et al., 2000; Wang & Lee, 1998). These systems allow users to inspect internal states and modify several aspects of implementation, execution, and communication at run time and can adapt themselves flexibly to heterogeneous and dynamic environments.
Many projects have proposed to implement reflection from various perspectives to provide possible solutions for adaptive software development in ubiquitous computing. The paper (da Costa et al., 2008) describes the fundamental issues such as heterogeneity, dependability and security, privacy and trust, mobility, transparent user interaction, etc. A number of software architectures have provided solutions for particular classes of systems and specific domains of concerns to allow users simultaneously interact and collaborate using multiple heterogeneous devices.
For instance, the projects outlined in (Cheng et al., 2006; Garlan et al., 2004; Oreizy et al., 1999) adopt an architecture-based approach in which system architectural models are maintained at run time and used as the basis for system adaptation. External control mechanisms, considered in separable modules, allow system adaptation to become the responsibility of components outside the system which can thus can be analyzed, modified, extended, and reused across different systems. The architectural models usually provide a global view of the system, allowing one to better identify the sources of environmental changes.
BEACH (Tandler, 2001) provides a software infrastructure for synchronous collaboration with many different devices, supporting different forms of interaction and hardware configurations. The layered architecture of Aura (Garlan et al., 2002) can anticipate requests

from a higher layer by observing current demands, and adjust its performance and resource usage characteristics accordingly. HESTIA (Hill et al., 2004) provides a secure infrastructure for ubiquitous computing environments. It addresses the incompatible interoperation problem of securing critical information services in large-scale environments. Analysis of extensive surveys on software infrastructures and frameworks which support the construction of ubiquitous systems is given in (Endres et al., 2005).

Furthermore, many systems (de Lara et al., 2001; Flissi et al., 2005; Gu et al., 2004; Stevenson et al., 2003) adopt component-based software infrastructure for ubiquitous environments, which can take advantage of the exported interfaces and the structured nature of these applications to perform adaptation without modifying the applications. These applications are designed as assemblies of distributed software components and are dynamically discovered according to the end-user's physical location and device capabilities. With this approach, an application can add new behaviors after deployment. In addition, the system will dynamically partition the application and offload some components to a powerful nearby surrogate. This allows for delivery of the application in a ubiquitous computing environment without significant fidelity degradation. McKinley, et al. (Mckinley et al., 2004) provide a review of technologies related to compositional adaptation.

1.2.2 Service composition

An approach similar to that of component-based software systems is to combine multiple primitive programs for a complex task. For example, shell pipes in Unix provide useful data I/O mechanisms, employing multiple programs to work together, and complex tasks are accomplished by coordinating sequences of primitive programs. These programs are "connected" by pipes which facilitate exchange of data among them. Truong and Harwood (Truong & Harwood, 2003) extended this concept and proposed a shell that provides distributed computing over a peer-to-peer network and is characterized by good scalability.

Another related topic is the composition of web services. Programmers may use the Web Services Description Language (WSDL) to specify characteristics and access of web services, and thus web services can be composed to provide a complicated service. However, WSDL does not support semantic descriptions; thus, a composition always requires intervention by a programmer. To enable web services to perform a dynamic composition by themselves, Martin et al. (Martin et al., 2004) proposed the OWL-S approach, in which a client program and web services may have a common consensus on the semantics of the terms in WSDL by a third-party ontology, and thus a web service can automatically interact with another web service by a priori setting the rule for the semantics. Mokhtar et al. (Mokhtar et al., 2007) extended the OWL-S approach and proposed a conversation-based service composition method named COCOA that aims for the dynamic composition of services to complete a user task. With COCOA, a service as well as a user task is transformed to an automata, and an algorithm is proposed to combine the automata of different services.

QoS-aware composition is another important issue of web service composition. For example, Li et al. (Li et al., 2001) propose a hierarchical adaptive QoS architecture for multimedia applications. A multimedia service is delivered by multiple service configurations, each of which involves a different set of service components. Each service component is executed as a process. Components cooperate through protocols over network communication. Usually, the composition of web services needs to satisfy given optimization criteria, such as the overall cost or response time, and can be formulated as a NP-hard optimization problem (Canfora et al., 2005). Canfora et al. (Canfora et al., 2005) proposed a genetic algorithm for the NP-hard

QoS-aware composition problem. In addition, Wada et al. (Wada et al., 2008) proposed a multi-objective genetic algorithm to deal with optimization criteria with trade-offs, and Berbner et al. (Berbner et al., 2006) proposed a fast heuristic that was 99% close to optimal solutions in most cases. Furthermore, various middleware and frameworks (Issa et al., 2006; Yu & Lin, 2005; Zeng et al., 2004) have been proposed to realize QoS-aware web service compositions.

1.2.3 Resource discovery

As mentioned earlier, design of such a resource discovery mechanism becomes increasingly difficult under ubiquitous computing conditions in which useful information servers are not known a priori. Porter and Sen (Porter & Sen, 2007) classified two approaches for resource discovery mechanisms, namely referral (Candale & Sen, 2005; Sen & Sajja, 2002; Singh et al., 2001; Yolum & Singh, 2005) and matchmaker (Albrecht et al., 2008; Iamnitchi & Foster, 2004; Jha et al., 1998; Ogston & Vassiliadis, 2001). In the referral approach, the resource providers provide both services and referrals to other providers. Providers which provide high quality services are likely to be recommended by many providers. Providers must, however, ascertain the trustworthiness and expertise of other providers to measure the value of a recommendation. For example, in (Candale & Sen, 2005), the performance of a provider is measured by the satisfaction obtained by its clients. This mechanism requires learning both the performance levels of different service providers as well as the quality of referrals provided by other providers by exchanging information.

Another possible solution to this problem is to use a matchmaker: a dedicated resource discovery server that arranges the connections. Assuming clients are truthful in their interactions with the matchmaker, optimal matches can be found. For example, in the SWORD architecture (Albrecht et al., 2008), a resource query will be processed by a distributed query processor to find candidate nodes whose characteristics match the specified requirements. Then, the optimized subset of the candidate nodes will be determined by the optimizer component accounting for desired device characteristics, such as load and network location, and inter-device characteristics, such as latency and bandwidth.

Furthermore, several efforts (Albrecht et al., 2008; Balazinska et al., 2002; Huang & Steenkiste, 2003) have explored resource discovery mechanisms in large-scale environments. The system must scale to thousands of devices and be highly available. It also has to support high rates of measurement updates from participating devices, from static characteristics such as operating system, processor speed, and network coordinates to more dynamic characteristics such as available CPU capacity, memory, and disk storage.

1.3 Organization of this article

The remainder of this article is organized as follows. Section 2 describes the idea of ad-hoc systems in detail and how it may be realized by the adaptive software framework, FRAME, implemented as part of the adaptive software architecture project, ASAP. Under FRAME, software components can be discovered, loaded, combined, adapted, and executed on the target platforms in accordance with available resources and performance constraints. Software may have a list of specifications, specified during the development stage, to gather information about its environment. During execution, the software may check the list for environmental changes, and then respond accordingly. Therefore, an ad-hoc system can be constructed and executed without human intervention.

Section 3 introduces the Distributed Shell System, or DISHES, in which a mobile user can issue a shell script of a task, and DISHES will automatically locate the required programs and retrieve the necessary data. The required programs will be dispatched and executed on their host computers. Intermediate results will be piped between the host computer through networks, and final result will be I/O redirected to the user-specified location.
In Sec. 4, we present the basic idea of mutual assistant networks (MANs) which combine social networks and wireless sensor networks (WSNs) to query local and timely information. The proposed infrastructure uses routing protocols commonly adopted in WSNs, such as GF, to forward the query to someone who may have an answer. Conceptually, people in MANs serve the role played by sensors in WSNs; they may accept queries from others, gather information based on queries, and then respond. Such a new social network application will promote the sharing of knowledge and bring people closer together. Finally, a summary is given in Sec. 5.

2. Ad-Hoc systems

2.1 Overview

As mentioned earlier, the ubiquity of computers makes it possible to combine several resource-limited devices as an ad-hoc system to complete a complex computing task. Imagine a scenario in which a user watches a movie on his smart phone. Referring to Fig. 1, to completely execute on the smart phone, the media player software needs to decoding the multimedia stream, output video and audio, and interact with the user. Due to limited computing capability, the performance or quality of the video and audio may be unacceptably poor. In addition, the small size of the phone may lead to an unpleasant interaction experience.

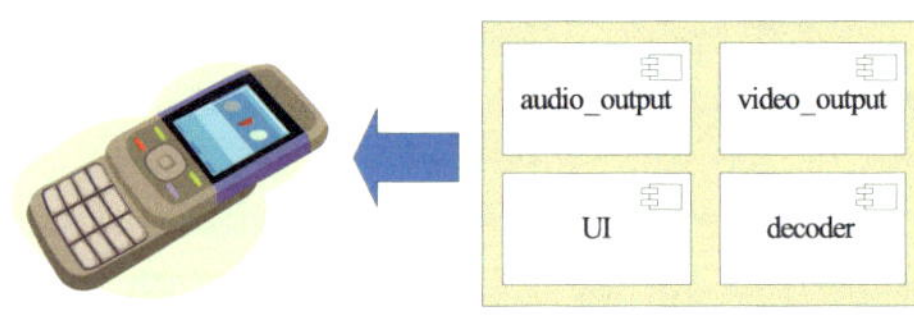

Fig. 1. The media player software needs to decode the multimedia stream, output video and audio, and interact with the user. Due to limited computing capability, the performance or quality of the video and audio may be unacceptably poor.

Alternatively, the user may search ambient devices for their hardware features. For example, he may find a TV for its big LCD display, a Hi-Fi audio system for its stereo sound quality, and a PC for its computing power. He can connect these devices together to form an ad-hoc system as shown in Fig. 2. After the media player software is launched, the appropriate part of the code will be distributed to each device, i.e., the code for audio processing to the Hi-Fi audio system, the code for video processing to the TV, and the code for decoding the multimedia stream to the PC. As a consequence, instead of watching the movie on the smart phone, the user may enjoy the smoother movie on the ad-hoc system with a larger image on the TV and better sound from the Hi-Fi audio system.
One challenge to realizing ad-hoc systems is the diversity of participating devices. It is impossible to know the performance of components on each device in advance to determine the appropriate component distribution. In Fig. 2, before distributing the video processing component to the TV, one must first know if the TV has the appropriate resource for video processing. Such performance information can only be known after the ad-hoc system is formed. Manually probing the performance of each participating device is difficult for the

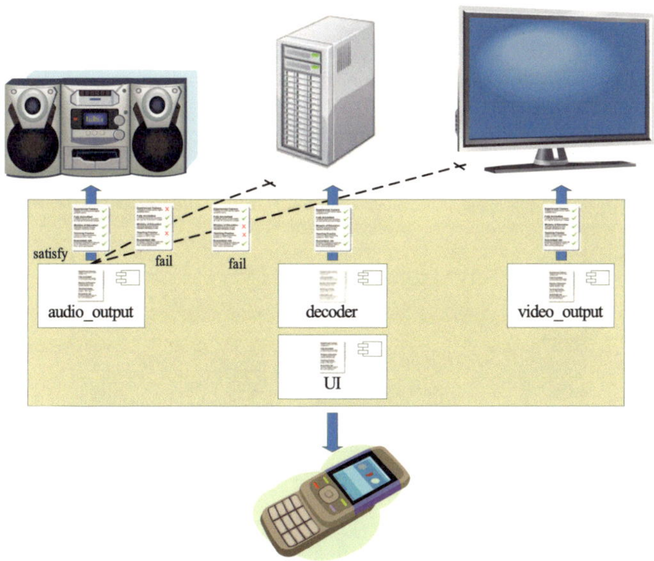

Fig. 2. The media player software executes on an ad-hoc system consisting of a smart phone, a TV, a Hi-Fi audio system, and a PC. The components are distributed to the appropriate participating devices in which all specifications are satisfied for a better movie watching experience.

average user, but the adaptive software framework, FRAME (Ko & Mutka, 2002), may provide a better solution to alleviate this configuration problem.

2.2 The adaptive software framework, FRAME

In many mass production industries, such as automobiles and electronics, final products are assembled from parts. The parts may be built by various vendors, but they are plug-in compatible if they have the required functionality. It is technically impossible for vendors to develop parts that may work perfectly in every environment. As a consequence, vendors usually specify how well the parts may perform in certain environments, and users can select appropriate parts based on these specifications. If, under certain conditions, a part fails or does not perform as required, it can be replaced with an appropriate part. For example, regular tires are designed for normal weather conditions, but may be prone to skidding on snow and thus may not meet safety requirements. Consequently, special snow tires may be used to achieve better safety.

A similar idea was adopted in FRAME. In addition to function implementation as normal components, specifications for required resources were added as shown in Fig. 3(a). The specifications allow FRAME to identify an appropriate participating device for execution.

FRAME is a middleware which provides APIs for Java applications to adapt themselves to heterogeneous environments. Figure 3 illustrates the component structure and its middleware architecture. A component provides abstract function interfaces without exposing detailed implementations. Similar to components in the automobile and electronic industries, a component may have multiple implementations developed by various vendors. Different implementations may require different resources and produce different quality of results; these are specified as specifications. The components of an application are not linked during the development stage, but are "assembled" at run time after determining the resources

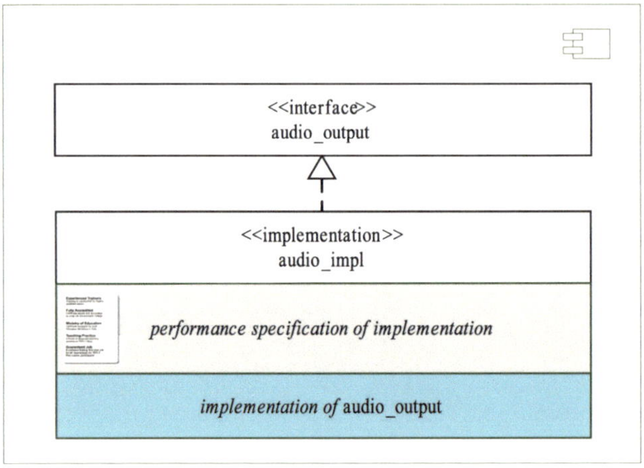

(a) Component

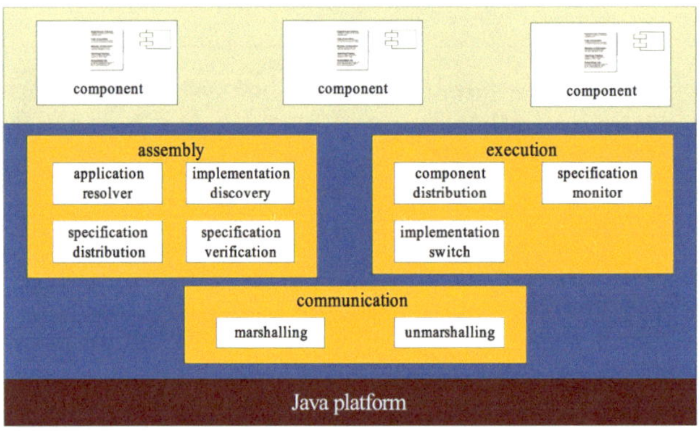

(b) Middleware architecture

Fig. 3. The adaptive software framework, FRAME consists of three modules, namely assembly, execution, and communication. In addition to function implementation, specifications for required resources are added for components in FRAME.

of the computing environment with their specifications. If the application fails to work appropriately because of dynamic environmental changes, it may also use the FRAME APIs to replace component implementations for better performance or quality of execution without down-time. In summary, FRAME provides the following features:

- Developers may specify specifications for component implementations.
- Application components may be automatically distributed to single or multiple participating devices.
- Before execution, FRAME may probe the available resources from the computing environment and then adapt themselves to the computing environment via a special process called *assembly*.
- During execution, FRAME may detect run-time environmental changes and, if necessary, invoke the assembly process without down-time.

Referring to Fig. 3(b), these features are implemented as three modules, namely assembly, execution, and communication. The assembly module resolves the components of an application and discovers all possible component implementations, then distributes and verifies the implementation specifications for participating devices to determine the appropriate execution devices. The execution module distributes each component to the selected execution device following the assembly process. It also monitors the specifications during run-time and, if necessary, invokes the assembly process for more appropriate implementations without down-time. The communication module provides necessary data marshalling/unmarshalling mechanisms for cooperation among components on different devices.

The assembly process is worthy of special attention. The traditional approach to component implementation selection is to use condition statements such as `if-else` statements as shown in Table 1. There may be nested if-else statements and each is used to decide the appropriate implementation of a component. Once an implementation is selected, execution flow may go into the inner `if-else` statements to select the appropriate implementation of other components. However, from a software engineering perspective, the condition statements approach is primitive. As the numbers of components and their implementations increase, the code tends toward so-called "spaghetti code" that has a complex and tangled control structure and the software will become more difficult to maintain or modify. The most important limitation of this approach is that condition statements are hard-coded, so the availability of all implementations needs to be known during the development stage. It is impossible to integrate newly-developed implementations without rewriting and recompiling the code, and, of course, the down-time.

```
if (constraints of component 1 with implementation 1)
{ // select component 1 with implementation 1

  if (constraints of component 2 with implementation 1)
  { // select component 2 with implementation 1

    // check each implementation of component 3, 4,...
  }
  else if (constraints of component 2 with implementation 2)
  { // select component 2 with implementation 2

    // check each implementation of component 3, 4,...
  }
  ... // more else if blocks for other implementations of component 2
}
else if (constraints of component 1 with implementation 2)
{ // select component 1 with implementation 2

  // similar as the code in the if block of
  // component 1 with implementation 1
}
... // more else if blocks for other implementations of component 1
```

Table 1. `if-else` statement structure for the component implementation selection

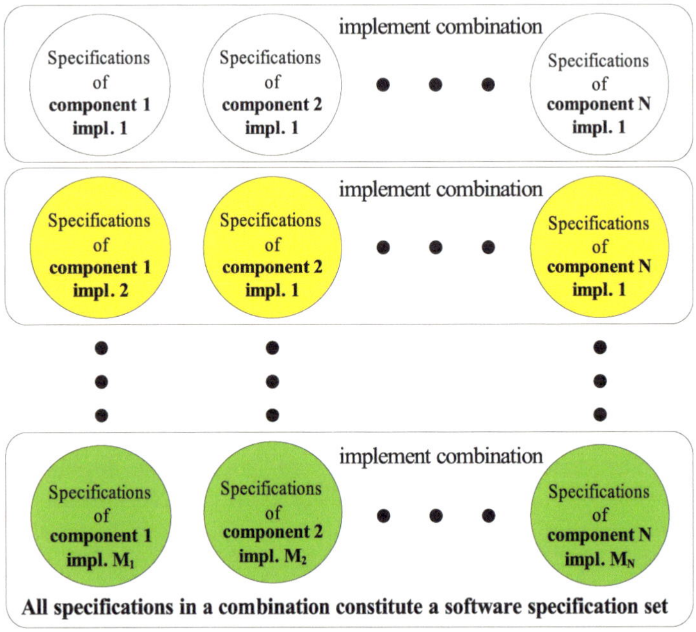

Fig. 4. All possible implementation combinations of an application: each row represents a possible implementation combination and the constraints of a combination constitute a software constraint set.

FRAME uses a different approach than condition statements to select appropriate component implementations. By identifying all component implementations of an application via service discovery, the assembly module builds all possible combinations of the application as shown in Fig. 4. Each combination has a set of specifications, called a *software specification set*, which consists of all the specifications from the involved component implementations. Since no two implementations should have same set of specifications, the mapping between combinations and software specification sets is one-to-one. By solving which specification set is *feasible*, i.e., all specifications in the software specification set are satisfied, the corresponding feasible combination will be found.

To realize ad-hoc systems, the assembly module distributes components to participating devices prior to constructing the software specification sets. There might be more than one possible distribution of components, and we call each possibility a *distribution*. For each distribution, the assembly module constructs all possible software specification sets and determine whether a feasible specification set exists. A distribution is *feasible* if it has a feasible software specification set, and then the application is assembled from the feasible distribution. In other words, the assembly process for an ad-hoc system application is to find a feasible distribution from all possible distributions. For the example of the media player software in Fig. 2, there may be an implementation for the audio component with good sound quality, and all its specifications are satisfied on the Hi-Fi audio system, but not the PC and the TV. Thus the audio component implementation will be executed on the Hi-Fi audio system. As a consequence, an ad-hoc system for the media player is constituted without human intervention.

3. Distributed Shell System

This section introduces another approach for accomplishing a resource intensive task by using ambient computing resources. The approach is based on the concept that many single machine systems provide a command line interface (e.g., shell) which allows a user to issue a command consisting of many primitive programs to accomplish a complex task. These programs are coordinated by the *pipe* mechanism and the result may be stored as a file via the *I/O redirection*. DISHES (DIstributed SHEll System) (Lai & Ko, 2010) extends this idea to ubiquitous computing environments, in which a mobile device user can issue a command specifying the data location and a sequence of programs to process the data. When a mobile device receives the command, it will seek out appropriate ambient devices which have the required programs and send tasks-to-do to these devices. Each device may retrieve the data from the specified location and execute the designated program to process the data. Once finished, it will send the result to other devices for further processing or back to the user's mobile device. Thus, a complicated task can be achieved by the sequential cooperation of multiple primitive programs.

Imagine a scenario in which a student in a school library is looking for research literature with the keywords "ubiquitous computing" in descending order of the year published. He may issue the following command with his smart phone:

```
grep ''ubiquitous computing'' http://myschool.edu.tw/reference_list |
sort -k 2,2 -r > sorting_result
```

Based on the command, the student's smart phone will find devices providing the required programs (`grep` and `sort`). Suppose computer `A` provides `grep` and computer `B` provides `sort`, as depicted in Fig. 5. Then `A` will retrieve the client information from the specified data location, `http://myschool.edu.tw/reference_list`, execute `grep "ubiquitous computing"` to pick up the literature containing the phrase `"ubiquitous computing"`, and send the intermediate result to `B` via the pipe. After receiving the intermediate result from `A`, `B` will execute `sort -k 2,2 -r` to sort the literature by publication year. The final sorted result will be sent back to the student's smart phone and stored as the file, `sorting_result`, via the I/O redirection.

In the above example, the student only specifies the data location and a sequence of programs. DISHES will automatically seek out appropriate computers with the required programs to process the data retrieved from the specified location. Moreover, a complicated task may be accomplished by gluing multiple primitive programs (`grep` and `sort`). These primitive programs do not have to be stored in or executed on the student's smart phone. They can be executed on the other computers (`A` and `B`) for better performance, and the results will be returned to the user. With this approach, the hardware and software of a mobile device may be kept as simple as possible, allowing the device volume, weight, and cost to be minimized. Thus, DISHES boosts people's mobility. Besides, gluing together multiple primitive programs to perform a complicated task can reduce software development costs. Note that though both DISHES and FRAME use ambient computing resources to execute resource intensive tasks, their fundamental purposes and approaches are different. DISHES tries to reuse the software that has been well established on single machine systems without making any modifications. There is no software migration involved in DISHES and the shared resources are software oriented; that is, users look for ambient computing resources completely from a software perspective. On the other hand, when building an ad-hoc system, users select a device based

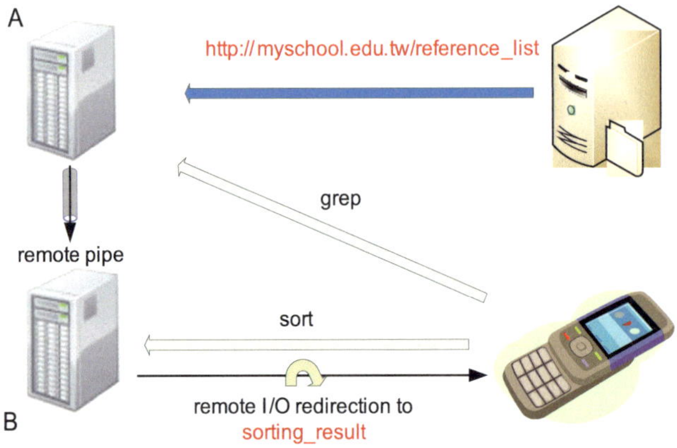

Fig. 5. The student issues the command with his smart phone to find research literature with the keyword "ubiquitous computing". DISHES finds computers providing the specified programs, and coordinates their execution via the remote pipe and I/O redirection mechanisms.

on the hardware features it provides. For example, in Fig. 2, the user may consider adding the TV into the ad-hoc system for the multimedia application because of its big LCD display.
The main feature of DISHES is the implementation of the remote version of the pipe and I/O redirection without any modification to the original programs. The remote pipe allows the standard output of one process to be fed directly as the standard input to another over networks. It may be realized by the assistance of two agent processes as depicted in Fig. 6(a). For example, to construct a remote pipe from process P_1 of device A to process P_2 of device B, two agent processes, AP_1 on A and AP_2 on B, are created with two regular UNIX pipes, from P_1 to AP_1 and AP_2 to P_2. Moreover, a socket connection between AP_1 and AP_2 is constructed. Thus, AP_1 may receive the output of P_1 from the regular UNIX pipe and relay it to AP_2 via the socket connection, and then AP_2 may feed the output to P_2 via the other regular UNIX pipe. Consequently, we have a remote pipe from P_1 to P_2. Note that the tasks of the agent processes AP_1 and AP_2 are to relay the information, regardless of the output of P_1. Therefore, the remote pipe is realized without any modification to the original programs.
Similar to the remote pipe, two agent processes, AP_3 on A and AP_4 on B, are needed for remote I/O redirection, as illustrated in Fig. 6(b). The output of P_3 is fed to AP_3 via a regular UNIX pipe, and then to AP_4 via a socket connection. Finally, the output is saved to file via a regular UNIX I/O redirection mechanism.
Traditional shells on single machine systems use an explicit specified list of directories (e.g., via the environment variable PATH under UNIX) for searching programs by name. However, due to the dynamic characteristics of ubiquitous computing environments, program locations are usually unknown in advance. Therefore, similar to the assembly module in FRAME, service discovery mechanisms may be incorporated to search programs in an unfamiliar environment. In addition, the intermediate results of one computer may be transmitted to another computer for subsequent program execution via the network, so performance optimization may need to be considered during the service discovery (e.g., to find a sequence of computers so that the total communication time for transmitting the intermediate results is minimized). The problem can be formulated as a minimum sequential workflow problem in static environments and solved by a polynomial algorithm (Lai & Ko, 2010). However, it

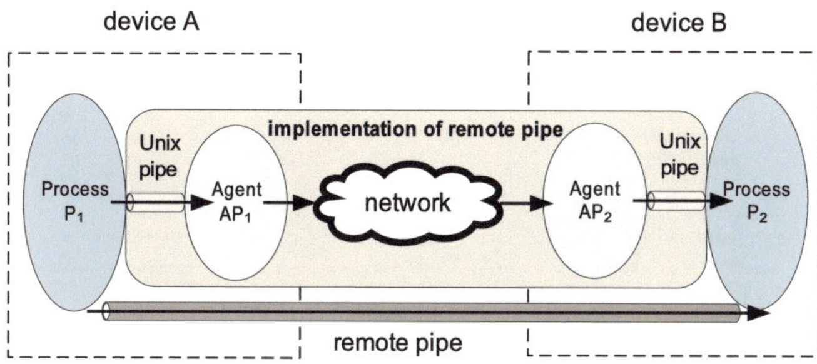

(a) remote pipe

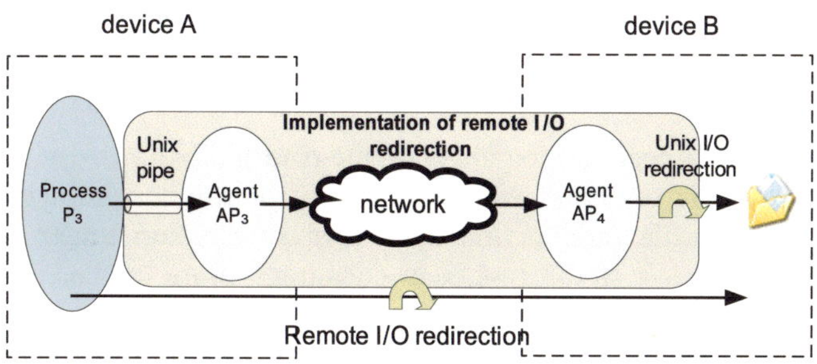

(b) remote I/O redirection

Fig. 6. Implementation of remote pipe and I/O redirection. Agents are needed to relay information between processes on different devices.

becomes an on-line problem under ubiquitous computing environments and requires further study.

4. Mutual Assistant Networks

In this section, we introduce the concept of integrating social networks which connect people and ubiquitous computing which connects computers, allowing people to use not only ambient computing resources, but also human resources. For example, a user may want to know if a festival is worth going to before setting out. Such information is timely; it becomes useless after the festival ends and thus must be answered by someone who is currently near the festival. Given the ubiquitous existence of people carrying network-connected devices, finding people close to the festival who are willing to help is quite feasible. Thus, the objective of mutual assistant networks (MANs) is to provide necessary mechanisms to bridge the user and these people. Referring to Fig. 7, a MAN will forward the user's question about the festival to people near the festival to collect their opinions. Similar to WSNs, a MAN may analyze and aggregate the data, and then return the results to the user.

The features of MAN applications and WSN applications are similar in some aspects. WSNs can collect information about physical environments from sensors while MANs collect knowledge or opinions from people. Both can use geographical parameters to specify whether data is collected from sensors or people. Therefore, many proposed WSN infrastructures may also be adopted for MANs, such as geographic routing, network configuration and coordination, data dissemination, and data aggregation, to name just a few.

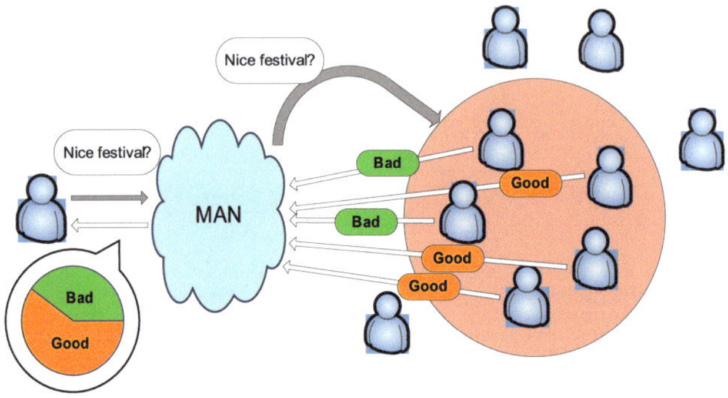

Fig. 7. A MAN can forward a user's question about the festival to the people close to the event and collect their responses. The MAN then analyzes and aggregates the data, and then returns the results to the user.

The current prototype has been implemented on the Android platform, with the architecture illustrated in Fig. 8. It provides APIs for MAN applications implemented into four modules. The user profile module manages user information under MAN, including identity. It also maintains a credit system to encourage users to share knowledge and a reputation system to track the validity of information that users have provided depending on feedback ratings provided by questioners. The networking module can deliver messages to destinations via routing techniques using geographic parameters such as GF (Finn, 1987) and GPSR (Karp & Kung, 2000). The data processing module provides various functions for manipulating information collected from people, including statistics, indexing, aggregation, and dissemination. The sensor module is basically an abstraction layer allowing applications to access the various hardware sensors present in devices.

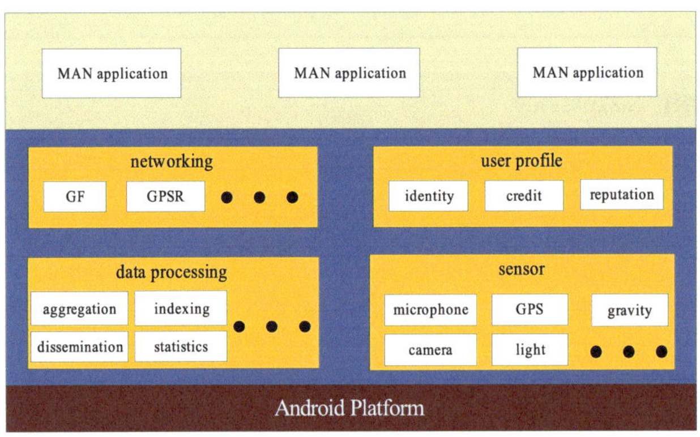

Fig. 8. The architecture of the current MAN prototype. MAN applications are developed through four modules, namely networking, user profile, data processing, and sensor.

Several social networking projects have been prosed to connect people, including WhozThat (Beach et al., 2008), SocialFusion (Beach et al., 2010), MoSoSo (Tsai et al., 2009), and Micro-Blog (Gaonkar et al., 2008). SocialFusion is a system capable of systematically integrating diverse data streams including sensors for mobile social networks that enable new context-aware applications such as context-aware video screens and mobile health applications. Note that one conceptual difference between the MAN and SocialFusion is that MAN uses people as sensors. As many of the infrastructure design considerations for

MANs originate from WSNs, the infrastructure can handle thousands or millions of nodes, i.e., people, spread over a large area. Many of constraints and challenges facing WSNs are also found in MANs. For example, a MAN is more expansive and dynamic than the current TCP/IP network and may create new types of traffic patterns that are quite different from the conventional Internet and raise demand for new approaches to minimize the amount and range of communication through local collaboration, such as aggregation or duplicate data suppression. How, where, and what information is generated and consumed by users will affect the way information is compressed, routed, and aggregated. Furthermore, MANs connect people who may not have had any prior social interaction, so it is more appropriate to address people by physical properties, such as location or proximity, than by names or IP addresses. There is also a need for advanced query interfaces and resource discovery engines to effectively support user-level functions.
MAN is still a developing project that requires further improvements. The goal of the architecture design is to provide service abstractions as a base for the development of new applications. The modular architecture design allows new protocols or algorithms, along with the integration of third party services; e.g., Google Maps for specifying geographic parameters.

5. Conclusion

This article illustrates three possible approaches for people to access the computing and information resources from ambient devices and other people anytime and anywhere. FRAME can realize the concept of ad-hoc systems in which a user may utilize hardware features from the computers nearby for better performance and interfaces. DISHES allows a user to coordinate the execution of a sequence of programs located on different devices without modifications. MANs provides an infrastructure for new location-aware social network applications, in which people may share the local and timely information that cannot be obtained in time from the Internet. With the ubiquitous existence of computers, there is no need to carry excess software and hardware, and thus people's mobility will be boosted. In addition, the ubiquitous existence of people carrying mobile devices may promote sharing of knowledge and thus extend the senses of human beings to a normally inaccessible locations via knowledge sharing.

6. References

Albrecht, J., Oppenheimer, D., Vahdat, A. & Patterson, D. A. (2008). Design and Implementation Tradeoffs for Wide-Area Resource Discovery, *ACM Transactions on Internet Technology* 8(4): 1–44.

Balazinska, M., Balakrishnan, H. & Karger, D. (2002). INS/Twine: A Scalable Peer-to-Peer Architecture for Intentional Resource Discovery, *Proceedings of the First International Conference on Pervasive Computing*, Springer-Verlag, Zurich, Switzerland, pp. 195–210.

Beach, A., Gartrell, M., Akkala, S., Elston, J., Kelley, J., Nishimoto, K., Ray, B., Razgulin, S., Sundaresan, K., Surendar, B., Terada, M. & Han, R. (2008). WhozThat? Evolving an Ecosystem for Context-Aware Mobile Social Networks, *IEEE Network* 22(4): 50–55.

Beach, A., Gartrell, M., Xing, X., Han, R., Lv, Q., Mishra, S. & Seada, K. (2010). Fusing Mobile, Sensor, and Social Data To Fully Enable Context-Aware Computing, *Proceedings of the Eleventh Workshop on Mobile Computing Systems & Applications*, ACM, Annapolis, Maryland, pp. 60–65.

Berbner, R., Spahn, M., Repp, N., Heckmann, O. & Steinmetz, R. (2006). Heuristics for QoS-aware Web Service Composition, *Proceedings of the IEEE International Conference on Web Services*, IEEE Computer Society, Washington, DC, USA, pp. 72–82.

Blair, G. S., Coulson, G., Robin, P. & Papathomas, M. (1998). An Architecture for Next Generation Middleware, *Proceedings of the IFIP International Conference on Distributed Systems Platforms and Open Distributed Processing*, Springer-Verlag, London.

Candale, T. & Sen, S. (2005). Effect of referrals on convergence to satisficing distributions, *Proceeding of the 4th International Joint Conference on Autonomous Agents and Multiagent Systems*, Utrecht, The Netherlands, pp. 347–354.

Canfora, G., Di Penta, M., Esposito, R. & Villani, M. L. (2005). An Approach for QoS-aware Service Composition based on Genetic Algorithms, *Proceedings of the 2005 conference on Genetic and Evolutionary Computation*, ACM, Washington DC, USA, pp. 1069–1075.

Cheng, S.-W., Garlan, D. & Schmerl, B. (2006). Architecture-based Self-Adaptation in the Presence of Multiple Objectives, *Proceedings of the 2006 International Workshop on Self-Adaptation and Self-Managing Systems*, ACM, New York, NY, USA, pp. 2–8.

da Costa, C. A., Yamin, A. C. & Geyer, C. F. R. (2008). Toward a General Software Infrastructure for Ubiquitous Computing, *IEEE Pervasive Computing* 7(1): 64–73.

de Lara, E., Wallach, D. S. & Zwaenepoel, W. (2001). Puppeteer: Component-based Adaptation for Mobile Computing, *Proceedings of the 3rd USENIX Symposium on Internet Technologies and Systems*, San Francisco, California.

Endres, C., Butz, A. & MacWilliams, A. (2005). A Survey of Software Infrastructures and Frameworks for Ubiquitous Computing, *Mobile Information Systems* 1(1): 41–80.

Finn, G. G. (1987). Routing and Addressing Problems in Large Metropolitan-Scale Internetworks, *Research ISI/RR-87-180*, Information Sciences Institute.

Flissi, A., Gransart, C. & Merle, P. (2005). A Component-based Software Infrastructure for Ubiquitous Computing, *Proceedings of the 4th International Symposium on Parallel and Distributed Computing*, IEEE Computer Society, Washington, DC, USA, pp. 183–190.

Gaonkar, S., Li, J., Choudhury, R. R., Cox, L. & Schmidt, A. (2008). Micro-Blog: Sharing and Querying Content Through Mobile Phones and Social Participation, *Proceeding of the 6th International Conference on Mobile Systems, Applications and Services*, ACM, Breckenridge, CO, USA, pp. 174–186.

Garlan, D., Cheng, S.-W., Huang, A.-C., Schmerl, B. & Steenkiste, P. (2004). Rainbow: Architecture-Based Self-Adaptation with Reusable Infrastructure, *Computer* 37(10): 46–54.

Garlan, D., Siewiorek, D., Smailagic, A. & Steenkiste, P. (2002). Project Aura: Toward Distraction-Free Pervasive Computing, *IEEE Pervasive Computing* 1(2): 22–31.

Gu, X., Messer, A., Greenberg, I., Milojicic, D. & Nahrstedt, K. (2004). Adaptive Offloading for Pervasive Computing, *IEEE Pervasive Computing* 3(3): 66–73.

Hill, R., Al-Muhtadi, J., Campbell, R., Kapadia, A., Naldurg, P. & Ranganathan, A. (2004). A Middleware Architecture for Securing Ubiquitous Computing Cyber Infrastructures, *IEEE Distributed Systems Online* 5(9).

Huang, A.-C. & Steenkiste, P. (2003). Network-Sensitive Service Discovery, *Proceedings of the 4th conference on USENIX Symposium on Internet Technologies and Systems*, USENIX Association, Seattle, WA.

Iamnitchi, A. & Foster, I. (2004). A Peer-to-Peer Approach to Resource Location in Grid Environments , *Grid Resource Management: State of the Art and Future Trends*, Kluwer Academic Publishers, Norwell, MA, USA, pp. 413–429.

Issa, H., Assi, C. & Debbabi, M. (2006). QoS-Aware Middleware for Web Services Composition - A Qualitative Approach, *Proceedings of the 11th IEEE Symposium on Computers and Communications*, IEEE Computer Society, Washington, DC, USA, pp. 359–364.

Java Platform Standard Edition API Specification (n.d.).
URL: *http://download.oracle.com/javase/6/docs/api/*

Jha, S., Chalasani, P., Shehory, O. & Sycara, K. (1998). A Formal Treatment of Distributed Matchmaking, *Proceedings of the second International Conference on Autonomous Agents*, ACM, Minneapolis, Minnesota, United States, pp. 457–458.

Jr, J. M. A. & Kofuji, S. T. (1996). Bootstrapping the Object Oriented Operating System Merlin: Just Add Reflection, *in* C. Zimmerman (ed.), *Advances in Object-Oriented Metalevel Architectures and Reflection*, CRC Press, chapter 5.

Karp, B. & Kung, H. T. (2000). GPSR: Greedy Perimeter Stateless Routing for Wireless Networks, *Proceedings of the 6th Annual International Conference on Mobile Computing and Networking*, ACM, Boston, MA, US, pp. 243–254.

Ko, R.-S., Lai, C.-C., Yen, C.-K. & Mutka, M. W. (2008). Component-Based Ad Hoc Systems for Ubiquitous Computing, *International Journal of Pervasive Computing and Communications Special Issue on Towards merging Grid and Pervasive Computing* 4(4): 333–353.

Ko, R.-S. & Mutka, M. W. (2002). A Component-Based Approach for Adaptive Soft Real-Time Java within Heterogeneous Environments, *A special issue of Parallel and Distributed Real-Time Systems* 5(1): 89–104.

Kon, F., Román, M., Liu, P., Mao, J., Yamane, T., MagalhÃčes, L. C. & Campbell, R. H. (2000). Monitoring, Security, and Dynamic Configuration with the dynamicTAO Reflective ORB, *Proceedings of the IFIP/ACM International Conference on Distributed Systems Platforms and Open Distributed Processing (Middleware'2000)*, number 1795 in *LNCS*, Springer-Verlag, New York, pp. 121–143.

Lai, C.-C. & Ko, R.-S. (2010). DISHES: A Distributed Shell System Designed for Ubiquitous Computing Environment, *International Journal of Computer Networks & Communications* 2(1): 66–83.

Li, B., Kalter, W. & Nahrstedt, K. (2001). A Hierarchical Quality of Service Control Architecture for Configurable Multimedia Applications, *Journal of High Speed Networks, Special Issue on Management of Multimedia Networking*, IOS Press.

Maes, P. (1987). *Computational Reflection*, PhD thesis, Laboratory for Artificial Intelligence, Vrije Universiteit Brussel, Brussels, Belgium.

Martin, D. L., Paolucci, M., McIlraith, S. A., Burstein, M. H., McDermott, D. V., McGuinness, D. L., Parsia, B., Payne, T. R., Sabou, M., Solanki, M., Srinivasan, N. & Sycara, K. P. (2004). Bringing Semantics to Web Services: The OWL-S Approach, *Proceedings of the first International Workshop on Semantic Web Services and Web Process Composition*, San Diego, CA, USA, pp. 26–42.

Mckinley, P. K., Sadjadi, S. M., Kasten, E. P. & Cheng, B. H. (2004). Composing Adaptive Software, *IEEE Computer* 37(7).

Mokhtar, S. B., Georgantas, N. & Issarny, V. (2007). COCOA: COnversation-based service COmposition in pervAsive computing environments with QoS support, *Journal of Systems and Software* 80(12): 1941–1955.

Ogston, E. & Vassiliadis, S. (2001). Matchmaking Among Minimal Agents Without a Facilitator, *Proceedings of the 5th International Conference on Autonomous Agents*, ACM, Montreal, Quebec, Canada, pp. 608–615.

Oreizy, P., Gorlick, M. M., Taylor, R. N., Heimbigner, D., Johnson, G., Medvidovic, N., Quilici, A., Rosenblum, D. S. & Wolf, A. L. (1999). An Architecture-Based Approach to Self-Adaptive Software, *IEEE Intelligent Systems* 14(3): 54–62.

Porter, J. & Sen, S. (2007). Searching for Collaborators in Agent Networks, *Proceedings of the 2007 IEEE/WIC/ACM International Conferences on Web Intelligence and Intelligent Agent Technology - Workshops*, IEEE Computer Society, Washington, DC, USA, pp. 508–511.

Sen, S. & Sajja, N. (2002). Robustness of Reputation-based Trust: Boolean Case, *Proceeding of the first International Joint Conference on Autonomous Agents and Multiagent Systems*, ACM, Bologna, Italy, pp. 288–293.

Singh, M. P., Yu, B. & Venkatraman, M. (2001). Community-based service location, *Communications of the ACM* 44(4): 49–54.

Stevenson, G., Nixon, P. & Ferguson, R. I. (2003). A General Purpose Programming Framework for Ubiquitous Computing Environments, *System Support for Ubiquitous Computing Workshop*, Seattle, USA.

Tandler, P. (2001). Software Infrastructure for Ubiquitous Computing Environments: Supporting Synchronous Collaboration with Heterogeneous Devices, *Proceedings of the 3rd international conference on Ubiquitous Computing*, Springer-Verlag, London, UK, pp. 96–115.

Truong, M. T. & Harwood, A. (2003). Distributed Shell over Peer-to-Peer Networks, *Proceedings of the International Conference on Parallel and Distributed Processing Techniques and Applications*, Las Vegas, Nevada, USA, pp. 269–278.

Tsai, F. S., Han, W., Xu, J. & Chua, H. C. (2009). Design and development of a mobile peer-to-peer social networking application, *Expert Systems with Applications* 36(8): 11077–11087.

Wada, H., Champrasert, P., Suzuki, J. & Oba, K. (2008). Multiobjective Optimization of SLA-Aware Service Composition, *Proceedings of the 2008 IEEE Congress on Services - Part I*, IEEE Computer Society, Washington, DC, USA, pp. 368–375.

Wang, Y.-M. & Lee, W.-J. (1998). COMERA: COM Extensible Remoting Architecture, *Proceedings of the 4th USENIX Conference on Object-Oriented Technologies and Systems (COOTS)*, USENIX, pp. 79–88.

Weiser, M. (1991). The Computer for the 21st Century, *Scientific American* 265(3): 66–75. Reprinted in IEEE Pervasive Computing, Jan-Mar 2002, pp. 19-25.

Yokote, Y. (1992). The Apertos Reflective Operating System: The Concept and Its Implementation, *in* A. Paepcke (ed.), *Proceedings of the Conference on Object-Oriented Programming Systems, Languages, and Applications (OOPSLA)*, Vol. 27, ACM Press, New York, NY, pp. 414–434.

Yolum, P. & Singh, M. P. (2005). Engineering Self-Organizing Referral Networks for Trustworthy Service Selection, *IEEE Transactions on Systems, Man and Cybernetics, Part A* 35(3): 396–407.

Yu, T. & Lin, K.-J. (2005). A Broker-Based Framework for QoS-Aware Web Service Composition, *Proceedings of the 2005 IEEE International Conference on e-Technology, e-Commerce and e-Service*, IEEE Computer Society, Washington, DC, USA, pp. 22–29.

Zeng, L., Benatallah, B., H.H. Ngu, A., Dumas, M., Kalagnanam, J. & Chang, H. (2004). QoS-Aware Middleware for Web Services Composition, *IEEE Transactions on Software Engineering* 30(5): 311–327.

3

Uncertainty and Error Handling in Pervasive Computing: A User's Perspective

Marie-Luce Bourguet
School of Electronic Engineering and Computer Science,
Queen Mary, University of London
U.K.

1. Introduction

From this chapter's perspective, pervasive computing is a new class of multimodal systems, which employs passive types of interaction modalities, based on perception, context, environment and ambience (Abowd & Mynatt, 2000; Feki, 2004; Oikonomopoulos et al., 2006). By contrast, early multimodal systems were mostly based on the recognition of active modes of interaction, for example speech, handwriting and direct manipulation. The emergence of novel pervasive computing applications, which combine active interaction modes with passive modality channels raises new challenges for the handling of uncertainty and errors. For example, context-aware pervasive systems can sense and incorporate data about lighting, noise level, location, time, people other than the user, as well as many other pieces of information to adjust their model of the user's environment. In affective computing, sensors that can capture data about the user's physical state or behaviour, are used to gather cues which can help the system perceive the user's emotions (Kapoor & Picard, 2005; Pantic, 2005). In the absence of recognition or perception error, more robust interaction is then obtained by fusing explicit user inputs (the active modes) and implicit contextual information (the passive modes). However, in the presence of errors, the invisibility of the devices that make up the pervasive environment and the general lack of user's awareness of the devices and collected data properties render error handling very difficult, if not impossible.

Despite recent advances in computer vision techniques and multi-sensor systems, designing and implementing successful multimodal and ubiquitous computing applications remain difficult. This is mainly because our lack of understanding of how these technologies can be best used and combined in the user interface often leads to interface designs with poor usability and low robustness. Moreover, even in more traditional multimodal interfaces (such as speech and pen interfaces) technical issues remain. Speech recognition systems, for example, are still error-prone. Their accuracy and robustness depends on the size of the application's vocabulary, the quality of the audio signal and the variability of the voice parameters. Signal and noise separation also remains a major challenge in speech recognition technology.

Recognition-based multimodal interaction is thus still error prone, but in pervasive computing applications, where the capture and the analysis of passive modes are key, the possibilities of errors and misinterpretations are even greater. Furthermore, in pervasive computing applications, the computing devices have become invisible and the users may not be aware of their behaviour that is captured by the system. They may also have a wrong understanding of what data is captured by the various devices, and how it is used. In most cases, they do not receive any feedback about the system's status and beliefs. As a result, many traditional methods of multimodal error correction become ill adapted to pervasive computing applications. When faced with errors, users encounter a number of new challenges: understanding the computer's responses or change of behaviour; analysing the cause of the system's changed behaviour; and devising ways to correct the system's wrong beliefs.

This chapter addresses these problems. It exposes the new challenges raised by novel pervasive computing applications for the handling of uncertainty and errors, and it discusses the inadequacies of known multimodal error handling strategies for this type of applications. It is organised as follows. In the next section, we explain our usage of the words multimodal and pervasive computing and we propose our own definitions, which are based on the notions of active and passive modes of interaction. We also describe a number of pervasive computing applications, which will serve in the remainder of the chapter to illustrate the new challenges raised by this type of applications. In section 3 of the chapter, we briefly review the various recognition error handling strategies that can be found in the multimodal interaction literature, then in section 4, we show that many of these multimodal error handling strategies, where active modes only are used, are ill adapted to pervasive computing applications. We also discuss the new challenges arising from the deployment of novel pervasive computing applications for error correction. In section 5, we suggest that promoting users' correct mental models of the devices and data properties that make up a pervasive computing environment can render error handling more effective. Section 6, finally, concludes the chapter.

2. Multimodal and pervasive computing

The concepts of multimodal interaction and of pervasive computing share many commonalities, one of which is the lack of an accepted definition.

2.1 Active and passive modes

The concept of multimodal interaction partly arose from the difficulties met by the speech recognition research community, in the early eighties, to implement satisfactorily robust speech-based interfaces. The idea was to complement the error prone voice inputs with more deterministic ones, such as mouse and keyboard inputs (i.e. direct manipulation and typing). In parallel with the deployment of more robust touch screen and pen input technologies, alternative recognition-based modalities of interaction (pen-based 2D gestures and hand-writing) also started to emerge. Vision-based recognition modalities, i.e. inputs captured by a camera, soon followed, complementing the list of recognition-based input modalities, while at the same time opening new possibilities for context awareness and the perception of passive modes of interaction (e.g. gaze and facial expressions). Until now, the concept of multimodal interaction has never stopped evolving, encompassing yet more input modes, which are increasingly based on perception and sensory information. The various mission statements made by the Multimodal Interaction Working Group (MIWG) of the W3C (World Wide Web Consortium) offer a good evidence of this evolution. In 2002 (W3C, 2002), the MIWG aimed to develop new technology to create "web pages you can speak to and gesture at". According to its charter, the MIWG was "tasked with the development of specifications covering the following goals: To support a combination of input modes, including speech, keyboards, pointing devices, touch pads and electronic pens; To support the combination of aural and visual output modes; To support a combination of local and remote speech recognition services; To support the use of servers for speech synthesis and for streaming pre-recorded speech and music; To support a combination of local and remote processing of ink entered using a stylus, electronic pen or imaging device; To support varying degrees of coupling between visual and aural interaction modes; To support the use of a remote voice dialog engine, e.g. a voice gateway running VoiceXML; To support the coordination of interaction across more than one device, e.g. cell phone and wall mounted display." The MIWG's charter, in 2002, was still resolutely geared towards speech and pen interaction. In 2003, however, the same Working Group (W3C, 2003), in a document dedicated to their multimodal interaction framework, was listing the following input modes: speech, handwriting, keyboarding and pointing device, but with the assumption that "other input recognition components may include vision, sign language, DTMF (Dual-tone multi-frequency signaling), biometrics, tactile input, speaker verification, handwritten identification, and other input modes yet to be invented". Beside the recognition component, The W3C also included a "System and Environment component", which "enables the interaction manager to find out about and respond to changes in device capabilities, user preferences and environmental conditions", hence incorporating in their system specifications some of the aims of a pervasive computing system.

Nowadays, in the HCI literature, the expression "pervasive computing" is mostly used to describe connected computing devices in the environment. For example, the following description of pervasive computing has been proposed by TechTarget©: in pervasive computing, "the goal of researchers is to create a system that is pervasively and unobtrusively embedded in the environment, completely connected, intuitive, effortlessly portable, and constantly available"; and also: pervasive computing is the "possible future state in which we will be surrounded by computers everywhere in the environment that respond to our needs without our conscious use." In these statements, the notions of being "unobtrusive" and "without our conscious use" add a dimension which was not present in earlier (often speech-based) multimodal systems. To be unobtrusive and to not require our conscious use, pervasive computing applications must rely on novel sources of information which are called "passive" modes of interaction. Examples of passive modes include vision-based modes captured by cameras (e.g. gaze and facial recognition for affective computing), sensory information (levels of lighting, temperature, noise, as well as biometrics information), GPS (Global positionning System, for positioning and time information) and tag technologies such as RFID (Radio Frequency Identification). In other words, the term pervasive is used to qualify the system (the devices, their type and their connectivity), whereas the term multimodal is often used to qualify the interaction. In this context, the multimodal interface becomes the mean to interact with the pervasive system.

In this chapter, we will use the term "multimodal" to qualify systems, which make use of several active modes of interaction, at least one of them being recognition-based (failing that, we will simply talk of "interactive" systems). We will use the word "pervasive" to qualify systems, which combine both active and passive modes of interaction. The next section provides some examples of pervasive computing applications.

2.2 Pervasive computing applications

Novel pervasive computing applications have started to emerge, which address one or more aims of a pervasive computing environment: being unobtrusive, being invisible and not requiring users' conscious interaction with the system. We describe briefly here five types of pervasive computing applications: context-aware multimodal interaction systems, location-aware systems, affective computing, smart home applications and wearable computers.

2.2.1 Context-aware multimodal interaction systems

Context-aware multimodal interaction systems make up one class of pervasive computing applications where the emphasis is on using passive modalities (the context) to enhance the interaction, especially its efficiency and robustness. (Dey, 2001) provides a good definition of the word context: "context is any information that can be used to characterize the situation of an entity. An entity is a person, place, or object that is considered relevant to the interaction between a user and an application, including the user and applications themselves." Still according to (Dey, 2001), a "system is context-aware if it uses context to provide relevant information and/or services to the user, where relevancy depends on the user's task". In a context-aware multimodal interaction system, perceived contextual information is often used to complement or disambiguate an active mode of interaction, such as speech (Stillman & Essa, 2001; Macho et al., 2005). For example, (Yoshimi & Pingali, 2002) describe a video conferencing application, which combines carefully placed multiple distributed microphone pairs with calibrated cameras to identify the current speaker and their location, in order to achieve a finer control of the speech recognition process. More recently, (Luo et al., 2009) show that in a classroom environment, sources of contextual information are abundant (people, activities, location, physical environment and computing entities) that can influence the result of otherwise ambiguous multimodal fusion. Some contextual information like illumination, temperature and noise level is obtained directly from sensors, while other like user activities and location is dynamically obtained from a Virtual Interactive Classroom (VIC) software platform. The VIC platform can display to the lecturer, in real-time, emotion data, through attention detection, facial expression recognition, physiological feature detection and speech emotion recognition processes for every student in the virtual classroom and for groups of students engaged in discussion. In this application, context is used to augment lecturer-student interaction with additional information and communication opportunities. (Yue et al., 2005) describe an hypermedia mobile system able to provide users with geographic information services at any time from anywhere. This system encompasses a context-sensitive multimodal module in which explicit multimodal user inputs and implicit contextual knowledge are integrated. Context sensitive information is used to evaluate users cognitive load and attention interference from the mobile environment, in order to adapt the interaction between the user and the mobile device (e.g. adaptation of the level of complexity and detail of the displayed information) as well as some aspects of the device's interface (e.g. orientation-aware adaptation of the display mode). Finally, (Crowley, 2006) proposes a framework for context aware observation of human activity, in which a situation (i.e. the current state of the environment) is described by a configuration of relations for observed entities. The stated aim of such a framework is to provide a foundation for the design of systems that act as a "silent partner" to assist humans in their activities in order to provide appropriate services without explicit commands and configuration (i.e. unobtrusive systems that do not require users conscious intervention).

2.2.2 Location-aware systems

Location-aware systems are a special type of context-aware systems where the emphasis is on adapting a service to the user's current location. Location-aware systems are typically deployed in pervasive environments with highly mobile users. Their aim is to make mobile devices know where they are and automatically do the right thing for that location, for example automatically reconfiguring themselves, adapting their security level, or being able to share information with nearby devices. (Khoury & Kamat, 2009) describe a system that can dynamically track a user's viewpoint and identify the objects and artefacts visible in the mobile user's field of view. In this system, the user's spatial context is defined both by their location (captured by GPS) and by their three-dimensional head orientation (captured by a magnetic orientation tracking device). Indoors, GPS technology is of no use, but RFID tags can help establish the location of a particular object or spot within the range of a few centimeters. An alternative to expensive RFID tags is to use the Wireless Local Area Network (WLAN) technique to sense and detect a location, as explained in (Tsai et al., 2010). (Tsai et al., 2010) describe a location-aware tour guide system for museums where a location position agent can sense the strengths of the signals from all the access points to which the mobile devices can be linked. If the visitor changes location, a context-aware agent matches the new coordinates on the museum map, which is shown on the visitor's PDA. Nowadays, advanced web browsers have also become location-aware and allow developers to find a computer's location by looking at the surrounding WiFi networks (which is not as precise as using a GPS, but more precise than relying on a user's IP address). Websites that use location-aware browsing aim at bringing more relevant information, or saving users time while searching.

2.2.3 Affective computing

Affective computing applications, another class of pervasive computing applications, can sense users' physiological state, track their activities and perceive their behaviour to infer their psychological state, mood and level of satisfaction or dissatisfaction. The virtual classroom application (Luo et al., 2009) mentioned already is an example of context-aware affective computing application. (Kapoor & Picard, 2005) describe a framework that can automatically extract non-verbal behaviours and features from face and postures, to detect affective states associated with interest and boredom in children, which occur during natural learning situations. Features are extracted from four different channels: the upper face (brow and eye shape, likelihood of nod, shake and blink), the lower face (probability of fidget and smile), the posture (current posture and level of activity), as well as information from the status of the application (in this case an educational game). In (Benoit et al., 2007) a driving assistant system is described that relies on passive modalities only (facial expression, head movement and eye tracking) to capture the driver's focus of attention and predict their fatigue state. The driver's face is monitored with a video camera and three signs of hypo-vigilance are tracked: yawning, blinking (or eyes closure) and head motion. Complex bio-inspired algorithms are then used in order to analyse the data and predict attention and fatigue.

2.2.4 Smart homes

Smart home applications are becoming increasingly popular and an area of rapid expansion for research and development. According to the Smart Homes Association, smart home technology is: "the integration of technology and services through home networking for a better quality of living". The idea is that anything in the home that uses electricity can be put on the home network and when commands are given, either by voice, remote control, computer or mobile phone, the home reacts. Most applications relate to lighting, home security, home theater and entertainment and thermostat regulation. A smart home system may also automatically decide to turn off lights and TV sets when the user leaves the house, adjust artificial lighting levels according to changes in day light, add items to an electronic shopping list when the house fridge gets empty, etc. According to (Edmonds, 2010), "Microsoft Chairman Bill Gates' home might be the most famous smart home to date. Everyone in the home is pinned with an electronic tracking chip. As you move through the rooms, lights come on ahead of you and fade behind you. Your favorite songs will follow you throughout the house, as will whatever you're watching on television. The chip keeps track of all that you do and makes adjustments as it learns your preferences. When two different chips enter the same room, the system tries to compromise on something that both people will like."

2.2.5 Wearable computers

Finally, wearable computer applications, where the computing devices are worn on the body, implies context recognition with on-body sensors. (Ferscha & Zia, 2009) present a wearable computer, which aims at providing directional guidance for crowd evacuation, by means of a belt worn by individuals in the crowd. The vibrotactile belt notifies individuals in panic about exits. It has the capability to sense the neighbourhood, to extract the relative spatial relations (distance and orientation) of all neighbours, and to interact with the person wearing it in a natural and personal way. Smart textiles, used for example in fashion (Vieroth et al., 2009) offer an extreme example of wearable computing where the pervasive computing environment is the clothing.

3. Multimodal error Handling Strategies

This section of the chapter offers a brief review of error handling strategies in multimodal interaction systems. We will then examine in section 4 how these strategies can or cannot be applied to pervasive computing applications such as the ones presented in the previous section.

Despite recent progress in recognition-based technologies for human-computer interaction (speech, gestures, handwriting, etc.), recognition errors still occur and have been shown to reduce the effectiveness of natural input modalities (Halverson et al., 1999; Karat et al., 1999; Suhm et al., 1999). The impact of recognition errors on multimodal systems' usability varies according to the application and depends upon a number of factors such as the amount of input required, the acceptability of uncorrected errors, the benefits of using recognition-based modalities (as compared with other interaction means), the availability of adequate error handling mechanisms, etc. (Bourguet, 2006) has listed thirty different error handling strategies in recognition-based multimodal interfaces and proposed a classification (see Fig. 1). According to this classification, an error handling strategy can either be the responsibility of the machine (i.e. the multimodal interface) or of the user, and can fulfil one of the three following purposes: error prevention, error discovery and error correction.

Purpose / Actor	Error Prevention	Error Discovery	Error Correction
MACHINE	*- Error reduction by design* (1) Isolated characters (2) Single-stroke alphabets (3) Tap-to-speak interfaces (4) Restricted grammars (5) Guided dialogues (6) Context-sensitive cues (7) Consistency and symmetry (8) Structured graphics (9) Adapted modalities *- Error reduction by context* (10) Feature level integration (11) Context-aware systems	*- Automatic detection* (15) Thresholding (16) Semantic, pragmatic and common sense knowledge (17) Mutual disambiguation (18) Synchronisation models	*- Automatic correction* (16) Semantic, pragmatic and common sense knowledge (17) Mutual disambiguation (18) Synchronisation models
USER	*- User prevention* (12) Modality selection (13) Complementary inputs (14) Redundant inputs	*- Machine-led discovery* (19) Implicit confirmation (20) Explicit confirmation (21) Mediation strategies (22) Visual display of results (23) List of alternative hypotheses	*- User correction* (24) Repeat (25) Spell out (26) Rephrase (27) Contradict (28) Modality switch (29) Cross-modal correction (30) Correction marks

Fig. 1. Taxonomy of multimodal error-handling strategies (adapted from (Bourguet, 2006))

3.1 Machine error handling

It appears from Fig. 1 that most strategies for error prevention can be attributed to the machine. They work in two possible ways: either the interface is designed to influence or constrain user behaviour into less error-prone interaction (i.e. "error reduction by design"), or greater recognition accuracy is achieved through the use of additional or contextual information (i.e. "error reduction by context").

Error reduction by design techniques achieve error prevention by leading users towards the production of inputs that are easier to recognise. The different techniques differ in the level of constraints they impose on user behaviour and actions, and the degree of control the user has on the interaction. For example, "Tap-to-speak interfaces" are interfaces in which users must indicate to the system by a brief signal that they are going to talk before each utterance (Oviatt et al., 1994). Another technique consists in implementing "guided dialogues" where users are prompted to say or do something from a limited set of possible responses. Another, less constraining technique, consists in controlling the system's responses and discourse level throughout the dialogue ("consistency and symmetry") in order to shape the users' speech and actions to match that of the system's (Heer et al., 2004).

Error reduction by context techniques achieve error reduction by augmenting users' inputs with redundant or contextual information. Context-aware systems, in particular, make use of passive modalities and, according to our definitions, thus belong to the domain of pervasive computing. Similarly, "Feature level integration" exploits intrinsic properties of tightly coupled modalities such as speech and lip movements and does not require users to consciously act multimodally.

Error discovery by machine works in three possible ways: by using statistical data ("thresholding"), by exploiting cross-modal information ("mutual disambiguation" and "synchronisation models"), or by applying knowledge-based rules (Baber & Hone, 1993). (Bourguet & Ando, 1998) have shown that to be effective at disambiguating interaction, cross-modal information must be complementary but not always semantically rich. They show for example that timing information from hand gestures (i.e. speech and gesture synchronisation data) can be used to locate in the speech signal the parts that are more semantically significant, such as important nominal expressions. In (Holle & Gunter, 2007) a series of experiments are presented, which explore the extent to which iconic gestures convey information not found in speech. The results suggest that listeners can use gestural information to disambiguate speech. For example, an iconic gesture can facilitate the processing of a lesser frequent word meaning.

Finally, with knowledge-based and cross-modal strategies, the automatic discovery of recognition errors can sometimes lead to automatic correction as well. This is generally true if the correct output figures in the list of alternative hypotheses produced during the recognition process.

3.2 User error handling

On the users' side, user prevention strategies rely on users' spontaneous change of behaviour to prevent errors. This is facilitated in natural multimodal interfaces by the availability of multiple modalities of interaction, which allows users to exercise their natural intelligence about when and how to deploy input modalities effectively (Oviatt, 1999).

When a recognition error occurs, users are normally in charge of notifying the machine. It is important, however, that the machine facilitates error discovery. Machine-led discovery techniques include implicit confirmation (Narayanan, 2002), explicit confirmation (e.g. when in safety critical systems users are asked to confirm that what has been recognised or understood is correct), visually displaying recognition results, and allowing the selection of the correct result from a list of alternative hypotheses.

Once errors have been found, users can effectively help the machine resolve them, usually by producing additional inputs. Studies of speech interfaces have found that the most instinctive way for users to correct mistakes is to repeat (Suhm et al., 2002). However, although repeating might be the most obvious way to correct when the system mishears, it is often the worse for the system (Frankish et al., 1992). The main reason for this is that when repeating, users tend to adjust their way of speaking (e.g. by over-articulating) to what they believe is easier for the recogniser to interpret, which often has the opposite effect. In handwriting, a similar strategy to repeating is to overwrite a misrecognised word. Linguistic adaptation is another strategy that has been observed where users choose to rephrase their speech, in the belief that it can influence error resolution: a word may be substituted for another, or a simpler syntactic structure may be chosen (Oviatt, 2000). In multimodal systems, it has been suggested that users are willing to repeat their input at least once, after which they will tend to switch to another modality (Oviatt & van Gent, 1996). For example, if speech input failed repeatedly when entering data in a form, users may switch to the keyboard in order to type their entry. Alternative strategies include locating a recognition error by touching a misrecognised word on a writing-sensitive screen where recognition output is displayed, then correcting the error by choosing from a list of alternative words, typing, handwriting, or editing using gestures drawn on the display (Suhm et al., 1999).

To summarize this section it can be said that an extensive body of work exists in multimodal error handling and that a large number of strategies have been proposed and tried. However, most of these strategies assume the use of active modalities. In the next section of the paper, we show that many of these strategies are ill adapted to pervasive computing applications, where passive modalities play an important role.

4. Error handling in pervasive computing

4.1 Machine error handling

In "traditional" multimodal user interfaces, machine error handling plays an important role in error prevention. In particular, *error reduction by design* (see Fig. 1) is a major error handling strategy, which aims at preventing interaction errors by influencing or guiding users' behaviour. In pervasive computing, where, in general, the devices must not interfere with social interaction and human behaviour, error reduction by design goes against the fundamental principle of unobtrusiveness. In many pervasive computing applications, especially context and location aware applications (e.g. the hypermedia mobile system (Yue et al., 2005), the silent partner concept (Crowley, 2006) and the dynamic user-viewpoint tracking system (Khoury & Kamat, 2009)) as well as in smart home applications, the aim is indeed of anticipating and not influencing users' needs and actions. (Matsumiya et al., 2003) specifically address the problem of unobtrusiveness and "zero disturbance" in pervasive computing. The authors present an authentication model, which aims at authenticating mobile users without interfering with their mobile behaviour. They describe a "zero-stop" authentication model that can actively authenticate users in an environment populated with various mobile and embedded devices without disturbing users' movements. In pervasive applications, where unobtrusiveness and zero disturbance is a major concern, one of the most important error handling strategy class (error reduction by design) thus becomes inapplicable.

In contrast, the second class of machine error handling strategies for error prevention: *error reduction by context* (see Fig. 1), plays an important role in pervasive computing applications. The use of context and multi-sensors information to render user-system interaction more robust and efficient is one major aim of context-aware multimodal applications (e.g. the video conferencing application (Yoshimi & Pingali, 2002) and the virtual classroom application (Luo et al., 2009)). Another example of such strategy is provided by "machine lip reading" techniques which consist in combining acoustic information from the speech signal with visual information captured from the shapes of the speaker's lips to achieve more robust speech recognition without requiring any additional user inputs (Meier et al., 2000).

As far as the automatic correction of recognition errors is concerned, it can be achieved in current multimodal interfaces, by using *semantic, pragmatic, and common sense knowledge* (see Fig. 1). (Singh, 2002) has collected common sense statements from the public for the Open Mind Common Sense Project, resulting in a database that currently contains more than 700,000 facts. The common sense statements have been used to reorder the recognition hypotheses returned by a speech recogniser and filter out possibilities that "don't make sense". In pervasive computing, the approach can be taken further by incorporating knowledge about human behavioural and social signalling. As the field matures, such knowledge will undoubtedly become invaluable to allow machines to automatically detect and correct errors. For example, the understanding of users emotions through the analysis of facial expressions (see the affective computing applications) will allow machines to disambiguate between literal and ironic statements.

4.2 User error handling

According to the definitions we proposed in section 2.1, the main difference between a multimodal system and a pervasive one, is the nature of the interaction modes: active versus passive modes. All the user strategies for error handling described in section 3, assume active modes of interaction and users complete awareness (but not necessarily control) of all aspects of the interaction. In fact, they also assume that the source and cause of the error can somehow be located and identified by the user or by the machine. For example, to be able to "exercise their natural intelligence about when and how to deploy input modalities effectively" (user error prevention strategies), users must have a good understanding of the properties and characteristics of each modality. They must also be able to anticipate the performance quality they are likely to obtain from the systems that recognise and interpret these modalities. Similarly, user error correction strategies such as *modality switch* and *cross-modal correction* require users to be able to identify the faulty recognition process in order to choose a more appropriate alternative.

Fig. 2 summarises some characteristics of the devices that are used in pervasive computing applications as well as some properties of the data that these devices capture (passive modalities), which are likely to make error handling by users difficult and render known user error handling strategies, such as the ones presented in section 3.2, impractical.

Devices Characteristics		Data Properties	
Invisibility	Where is the device / sensor located?	**What data**	What is captured ?
Multiplicity	Which device captured the data ?	**Use**	How is the data used ?
Sensitivity	How sensitive is the device ?	**Trustworthiness**	How well is the data used ?
Disparity	How disparate are the different devices ?	**Accuracy**	How accurate is the data?
		Combination	How is the data combined with other ?

Fig. 2. Device and data issues in pervasive computing applications (adapted from (Bourguet, 2008))

First of all, many of the devices and sensors have become invisible (*Invisibility*). Several devices and sensors are connected in the pervasive environment, and it may not be possible to know which of them has collected data (*Multiplicity*). Given the multiplicity of the devices, it may also be difficult to know the specific properties of each of them, in particular how sensitive a particular device is (*Sensitivity*) and how similar or different all the devices are in their characteristics (*Disparity*). From the user's perspective, when the system seems to behave abnormally (following a recognition or sensing error), the invisibility of the devices implies that the user cannot locate the faulty system (in order, for example, to avoid using it). The multiplicity of the devices means that even if they can be located, which device(s) caused the error may not be obvious. The unknown sensitivity of the devices does not allow users to adapt their behaviour in order to provide better quality inputs, and the disparity of the devices does not allow users to devise and re-use appropriate strategies for error handling.

As far as data properties are concerned, the user may not know which data is captured by the pervasive system (*What data*) and for what purpose it has been captured (*Use*). These two properties are inherent to most affective computing applications. Not knowing what is captured and for what purpose may let the user wonder about the appropriateness of the data use and give rise to problems of miss-trust (*Trustworthiness*). Questions can also arise about the performance quality of the various recognition and sensing processes, and in particular about the accuracy of the collected data (*Accuracy*). Finally, in relation with the multiplicity of the devices, how is the data combined with other to build complex representations of the environment and of the user and make inferences is another source of uncertainty (*Combination*).

Let's imagine that an affective computing application has wrongly inferred from the analysis of an image of the user's face, combined with a low level of user's activity, that the user is anxious or in difficulty. The system may then embark on trying to comfort the user by accordingly changing its behaviour and response mode (for example by lowering the level of difficulty of the user's current activity). In this situation, the user is faced with a number of challenges: (1) understanding the computer's change of behaviour (e.g. "the system is trying to comfort me"); (2) analysing possible causes of the system's changed behaviour (e.g. "the system believes I am unhappy"); and (3) devising ways of correcting the system's wrong belief (e.g. "I should smile more!"). However, in order to devise an error correction strategy, the user must know the type of data or data combination that is at the origin of the wrong inference (*What data* and *Combination*), by which device it has been captured (*Multiplicity*), where the device is located (*Invisibility*), how to provide better inputs (*Sensitivity* and *Accuracy*). In other words, when data has been wrongly interpreted in a pervasive environment, error correction is difficult because it may be impossible to know which device is responsible, and what combination of data contributed to the wrong interpretation. Even when users are aware of what data is captured, for example images of their face, it may not be clear how the data is used by the system, and how accurate is the data. Finally, when it comes to try and influence system's behaviour and beliefs, it will be necessary to understand how sensitive the devices are, and how disparate or homogeneous they are in their properties and characteristics.

Another issue in pervasive computing, is that users may not always be aware of their own actions, which have been captured and exploited by the system to enhance the interaction (see for example the "virtual classroom" application (Luo et al., 2009). The use of passive modalities, for example through the capture of spontaneous gestures and facial expressions, is an important property of pervasive environments. However, the shift from an environment where the user is always the conscious actor of every input received by the system, to an environment where the user is only one possible source of inputs among others (see context and location aware applications), or where the inputs produced by the user are produced unconsciously (see affective computing applications), is a dramatic one. For example, the "driving assistant" application (Benoit et al., 2007) explicitly relies on the fact that users have little or no control on the data captured by the system, so it can detect dangerous behaviour in driving conditions.

Furthermore, the invisibility of the devices in pervasive computing raises one of the most important challenges for error discovery by users. This is because when the devices responsible for capturing and analysing interaction data become invisible, it becomes increasingly difficult for users to identify the causes of the errors. In multimodal interfaces, the machine is primarily in charge of enabling error discovery by providing adequate feedback on its status and beliefs (*machine-led discovery*). In pervasive computing, the additional challenge is thus to devise ways of providing the necessary feedback while remaining invisible and unobtrusive. The users' ability to devise error handling strategies is generally dependent on the availability of system's feedback about its current status and beliefs. (Bourguet, 2008) describes an experimental study that aims to test users spontaneous change of behaviour in situation of error correction, when the cause and source of the error cannot easily be identified. The context of the experiment is multimodal (speech and pen interaction) and not pervasive, but it gives an insight into users' opportunistic error handling strategies in complex error situations. The study is designed to verify if users are likely to modify some aspects of their input when repeating a complex multimodal command (a command that combines speech and gestures), in the belief that it can help error resolution. In particular, the study aims at comparing users modality synchronisation patterns in normal situations of interaction, and in situations of error correction. It was found that when repeating a multimodal command, users are likely to use different modality synchronisation patterns to try and influence the performance of recognition-based modalities, but only if the source of the error can be identified. Synchronisation patterns that significantly depart from typical patterns should thus be interpreted with in view the possibility that the user is in error recovery mode, and modality integration techniques should be able to adapt to changing synchronisation patterns. However, users only seem to be able to adapt their behaviour when they can identify the source and nature of the system error. In absence of cues about the origin of the error, they either choose to repeat the command in the same way it was originally entered or they give up on the interaction. This result let us foresee new challenges for handling errors in pervasive computing applications, where the cause and nature of the errors are likely to be difficult to anticipate and identify.
Users' ability to understand the systems and devices used in human computer interaction, allow them to make prediction about future events, which in turns allow them to devise appropriate strategies for system error handling. The "invisibility", "what data", and "use" properties shown in Fig. 2 particularly affect the ability of users to predict future events and to prevent errors from occurring. In other words, error handling necessitates accurate users' mental models of the multimodal and pervasive computing systems. In the next section, we discuss the merits and difficulties of promoting through system design good users' mental models in pervasive computing applications.

5. Towards more usable pervasive computing applications

According to (Norman, 1988), a mental model is "the model people have of themselves, others, the environment, and the things with which they interact." Mental models allow us to make predictions before carrying out an action about its possible effects. When they are correct or sufficiently accurate, we can use them to solve unexpected problems, if however they are inadequate, they can lead to difficulties. When interacting with devices, users build and employ two types of mental models: structural and functional models (Preece et al., 1994).

Users can build a structural model of a system when they have grasped, understood and stored in memory the structure of how the devices work. Typically, structural models are simplified models that enable the person using them to make predictions about the behaviour of the devices they represent. In other words, a structural model is a representation of "how-it-works". The advantage of structural models is that by explaining how a device works, they allow a user to predict the effects of any possible sequence of actions, and hence to work out how to achieve most tasks possible with the device (Preece et al., 1994). They are particularly useful when a device breaks down or, by extension, when it commits errors. However, constructing a structural model is difficult and often requires a great deal of effort.

A model that represents "how to do it" is a functional model. To build a functional model, users must have acquired procedural knowledge about how to use the devices. Functional models are normally constructed using existing knowledge of similar domains and situations, but in desktop and mobile HCI, the widely used visual interface metaphors (e.g. the office desk metaphor with its file and folder icons) have become the models that users learn. Most of the time, functional models are sufficient and people seem to get by without using structural models (very few computer users know about the internals of a computer and how it works, but every regular computer user knows how to use it in order to accomplish their task). Indeed, according to (Preece et al., 1994), users tend to develop functional-based mental models of systems while remaining largely unaware of their structural aspects.

During multimodal error handling, however, both structural and functional mental models are useful. For example, users achieve error prevention by effectively allocating inputs to modalities, sometimes producing complementary or redundant inputs. The allocation of inputs to modalities necessitates a good understanding of the devices used for data capture, of the nature of the captured data, and of the use that is made of it. In other words, it necessitates a good mental representation of "how it works" in order to predict the system's responses to a planned sequence of actions. Similarly, user correction strategies require adequate knowledge about "how to do things" in order to come up with alternative ways of inputting information, which will effectively repair system's errors.

In pervasive computing, the invisibility and unobtrusiveness requirements make it impossible to develop visual interface metaphors, which have become so familiar in more traditional computing applications. Hence even functional mental models are difficult to convey and build. Generally, users get to find out about a system through its physical interface and its behaviour, i.e. what is called the system image. In pervasive computing, the system's physical interface may have completely disappeared, rendering the system image evasive, to say the least. The system image also includes the system's behaviour, i.e. the way it responds. The difficulty in pervasive computing is that the system's response may not be in relation with any user's conscious action but with environmental changes, and hence appear to be unpredictable or incomprehensible. If the system image is not able to convey to the users the designer's model in a clear and obvious way, then it is likely that the users will develop incorrect mental models. Consequently, they will experience great difficulties in understanding the system, using the system and knowing what to do when the system doesn't behave in the way they assumed it would.

One fundamental advantage of structural models is that they allow a user to predict the effects of any possible sequence of actions. As mentioned already, an additional difficulty in pervasive computing is that users are not always aware of the actions that have been captured, and the effects that can be observed (system's response) may have been triggered by environmental changes that users have not perceived or paid attention to. Here the "what data" property, once more, is the main obstacle. Structural models, in principle, also allow to work out how to achieve most tasks possible with the device. However, in pervasive computing, the notion of task is not always relevant, as the pervasive system is sometimes working on our behalf (see the smart home applications) or is trying to automatically adapt to our needs and affective state (see location-aware systems and affective computing applications).

Some work has highlighted the importance of a user-centred approach to the design of pervasive computing applications. (Ciarletta & Dima, 2000) have adapted the OSI reference model (Open Systems Interconnection model) to pervasive computing, adding a model of the user to their pervasive computing conceptual model (see Fig. 3). In particular, the abstract layer formalizes the necessity of maintaining consistency between the user's reasoning and expectations (Mental Models) and the logic and state of the pervasive computing application (Application). The intention is that, given the limited techniques that pervasive computing applications developers can use to communicate the state of the application, the proposed conceptual model will "force pervasive developers to consider the user's point-of-view much more than developers in traditional environments".

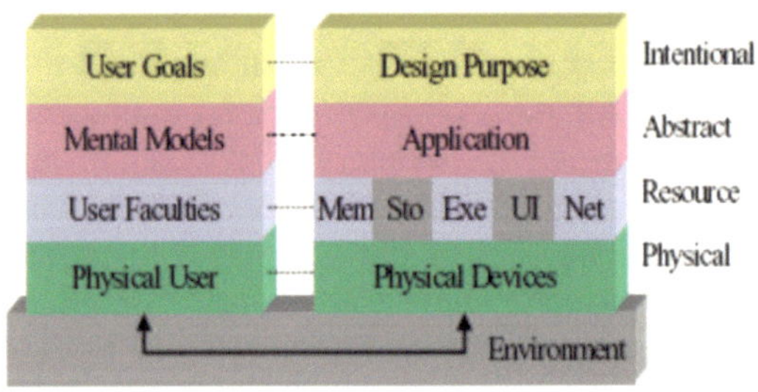

Fig. 3. Pervasive computing conceptual model (reproduced from (Ciarletta & Dima, 2000))

(Dobson & Nixon, 2004) clearly state that it is vitally important that users can predict when and how pervasive systems will adapt (i.e. respond to inputs and environmental changes), and can perceive why a particular adaptation has occurred. Arbitrary behavioural changes are incomprehensible to users and make a pervasive system completely unusable; on the other hand, single behaviour is unattractive in that it prevents a system from adapting to context. The difficulty is thus to find the optimal balance between adaptability (reactivity to contextual changes) and comprehensibility (leading to predictability). They conclude that predictability can arise in pervasive computing applications from having a close, structured and easily grasped relationship between the context and the behavioural change that context engenders. In other words, an application's behavioural variation should emerge "naturally" from the context that causes it to adapt, and any change in behaviour should be accompanied by a perceptible change in the context that "makes sense" for the application at hand. Moreover, the changes should correspond to external contextual cues that convey the need for the behavioural change to the user. This way, users should be able to build

functional mental models that allow them to use pervasive computing applications in most normal situations. Functional models might not be enough, however, to cope with abnormal situations where error handling has become necessary.
More recently, (Leichtenstern & Andre, 2008) explore the idea of using mobile phones as interfaces with pervasive computing environments, as they are devices that most users are already familiar with. The mobile interface is designed following a usage model which specifies various contexts, users and environment, as well as the user's goals and mental model. The mobile interface, while remaining familiar, is adaptable according to the current state of the usage model.

6. Conclusion

In this chapter we addressed the new challenges raised by novel pervasive computing applications for the handling of uncertainty and errors. We exposed the differences between "traditional" multimodal systems and pervasive computing applications, such as context and location aware systems, affective computing applications, smart homes and wearable computers. In particular, we discussed the inadequacies of known multimodal error handling strategies in pervasive environments, where the devices are heterogeneous and have become invisible, and where users largely remain unaware of the types and properties of the data that these devices capture and exploit. We observed that most traditional error strategies for error prevention have become impractical because they are irreconcilable with the fundamental principle of unobtrusiveness in pervasive computing. We also observed that most user strategies for handling errors were dependent on users being able to identify the source and cause of the error and on users having good structural and functional mental models of the interactive systems.
With the increasing diversity of devices, contexts of use, and users, the design of effective means of error prevention, detection, and correction will be a determinant factor of usability and users' acceptance of pervasive computing applications. This chapter has highlighted the necessity of providing users with appropriate support to allow them to devise and deploy adequate strategies for handling errors. However, error handling in pervasive computing applications is more complex than in current multimodal interfaces. In pervasive computing, it will be of paramount importance that users are supported in their forming of adequate mental models of the system. These mental models should provide users with the correct knowledge of what data is captured and recorded, and how it is used. Because of the invisibility of the devices and the necessity of being unobtrusive, supporting the development of adequate mental models is more challenging than in traditional interfaces. Provided that the pervasive computing application successfully promotes adequate mental models, it can be anticipated that users will develop whole new strategies to cope with errors in pervasive computing applications, and research to gain a better understanding of these strategies will be needed in order to devise appropriate interface designs and techniques to support them.

7. References

Abowd, G.D. & Mynatt, E.D. (2000). Charting past, present, and future research in ubiquitous computing. *ACM Transactions on Computer Human Interaction*, Vol. 7, No. 1, (2000) 29-58

Baber, C. & Hone, K.S. (1993). Modelling error recovery and repair in automatic speech recognition. *International Journal of Man–Machine Studies*, Vol. 39, No. 3, (1993) 495–515

Benoit, A.; Bonnaud, L.; Caplier, A.; Damousis, I.; Tzovaras, D.; Jourde, F.; Nigay, L.; Serrano, M. & Lawson, J.L. (2007). Multimodal signal processing and interaction for a driving simulator: component-based architecture. *Journal on Multimodal User Interfaces*, Vol. 1, No. 1, (2007)

Bourguet, M.L. & Ando, A. (1998). Synchronisation of speech and hand gestures during multimodal human–computer interaction, *Extented Abstracts CHI 1998*, pp. 241-242, Los Angeles, USA, April 1998, ACM Press

Bourguet, M.L. (2006). Towards a taxonomy of error handling strategies in recognition based multimodal human–computer interfaces. *Signal Processing journal*, Vol. 86, No.12, (December 2006) 3625–3643

Bourguet, M.L. (2008). Handling uncertainty in pervasive computing applications. Computer Communications journal, Vol. 31, No. 18, (December 2008) 4234-4241

Ciarletta, L. & Dima, A. (2000). A Conceptual Model for Pervasive Computing, *Proceedings of the 2000 International Workshop on Parallel Processing*, Washington, DC, USA, August 2000

Crowley, J.L. (2006). Things that See: Context-Aware Multi-modal Interaction. *Lecture Notes in Computer Science*, Vol. 3948, (2006) 183-198

Dey, A.K. (2001). Understanding and Using Context. *Journal of Personal and Ubiquitous Computing*, vol 25, (2001) 4-7

Dobson, S. & Nixon, P. (2004). More principled design of pervasive computing systems, *Proceedings of the Engineering for Human–Computer Interaction and Design, Specification and Verification of Interactive Systems*, pp. 292–305, Hamburg, Germany, July 2004

Edmonds, M. (2010). How Smart Homes Work, *Copyright © 2010 Discovery Communications Inc.* http://tlc.howstuffworks.com/home/smart-home1.htm

Feki, M.A.; Renouard, S.; Abdulrazak, B.; Chollet, G. & Mokhtari, M. (2004). Coupling context awareness and multimodality in smart homes concept. *Lecture Notes in Computer Science*, Vol. 3118 (2004) 906–913

Ferscha, A. & Zia, K. (2009). LifeBelt: Silent Directional Guidance for Crowd Evacuation, *Proceedings of 13th International Symposium on Wearable Computers (ISWC 09)*, pp. 19–26, Linz, Austria, September 2009

Frankish, C.; Jones, D. & Hapeshi, K. (1992). Decline in accuracy of automatic speech recognition as a function of time on task: fatigue or voice drift? I*nternational Journal of Man–Machine Studies*, Vol. 36, (1992) 797–816

Halverson, C.; Horn, D.; Karat, C. & Karat, J. (1999). The beauty of errors: patterns of error correction in desktop speech systems, *Proceedings of the INTERACT 99*, pp. 133–140, Edinburgh, UK, September 1999, IOS Press

Heer, J.; Good, N.; Ramirez, A.; Davis, M. & Mankoff, J. (2004). Presiding over accidents: system direction of human action, *Proceedings of the ACM CHI'04*, pp. 463–470, Vienna, Austria, April 2004

Holle, H. & Gunter, T.C. (2007). The role of iconic gestures in speech disambiguation: ERP evidence. *Journal of Cognitive Neuroscience*, Vol. 19, No. 7, (2007) 1175–1192

Kapoor, A. & Picard, R.W. (2005). Multimodal affect recognition in learning environments, *Proceedings of the ACM MM'05*, Singapore, November 2005

Karat, C.; Halverson, C.; Horn, D. & Karat, J. (1999). Patterns of entry and correction in large vocabulary contentious speech recognition systems, *Proceedings of the ACM CHI'99*, pp. 568–575, Pittsburgh, Pennsylvania, May 1999

Khoury, H.M. & Kamat, V.R. (2009). High-precision identification of contextual information in location-aware engineering applications . *Advanced Engineering Informatics journal*, Vol. 23, No. 4 (October 2009) 483-496

Leichtenstern, K. & Andre, E. (2008). User-centred development of mobile interfaces to a pervasive computing environment, *Proceedings of the First International Conference on Advances in Computer–Human Interaction*, pp. 114–119, Sainte Luce, Martinique, February 2008

Luo, A.; Zhou, J.; Wang F. & Shen, L. (2009). Context Aware Multimodal Interaction Model in Standard Natural Classroom. *Lecture Notes in Computer Science*, Vol. 5685, (2009) 13-23

Macho, D.; Padrell, J.; Abad, A.; Nadeu, C.; Hernando, J.; McDonough, J.; Wolfel, M.; Klee, U.; Omologo, M.; Brutti, A.; Svaizer, P.; Potamianos G. & Chu, S.M. (2005). Automatic speech activity detection, source localization, and speech recognition on the chil seminar corpus, *Proceedings of the IEEE International Conference on Multimedia and Expo*, pp. 876–879, Amsterdam, July 2005

Matsumiya, K.; Aoki, S.; Murase, M. & Tokuda, H. (2003). Active authentication for pervasive computing environments. *Lecture Notes in Computer Science*, Vol. 2609, (2003) 267–273

Meier, U.; Stiefelhagen, R.; Yang, J. & Waibel, A. (2000). Towards unrestricted lipreading. *International Journal of Pattern Recognition and Artificial Intelligence*, Vol. 14 (2000) 571–585

Narayanan, S. (2002). Towards modeling user behavior in human-machine interactions: effect of errors and emotions, *Proceedings of the ISLE Workshop on Dialogue Tagging for Multi-modal Human Computer Interaction*, Edinburgh, UK, December 2002

Norman, D.A. (1988). *The Psychology of Everday Things*, Basic Books, New York

Oikonomopoulos, A.; Patras, I. & Pantic, M. (2006). Human action recognition with spatiotemporal salient points. *IEEE Transactions on Systems, Man and Cybernetics Part B*, Vol. 36, No.3, (2006) 710–719

Oviatt, S.; Cohen, P. & Wang, M. (1994). Toward interface design for human language technology: modality and structure as determinants of linguistic complexity. *Speech Communication*, Vol. 15, (1994) 283–300

Oviatt, S. & van Gent, R. (1996). Error resolution during multimodal human–computer interaction, *Proceedings of the Fourth International Conference on Spoken Language Processing*, pp. 204–207, Philadelphia, Pennsylvania, October 1996

Oviatt, S. (1999). Ten myths of multimodal interaction. *Communication of the ACM*, Vol. 42, No. 11, (1999) 74–81

Oviatt, S. (2000). Taming recognition errors with a multimodal interface. *Communications of the ACM*, Vol. 43, No. 9, (2000) 45–51

Pantic, M. (2005). Affective Computing, In: *Encyclopedia of Multimedia Technology and Networking*, vol. 1, pp. 8–14, Hershy, PA, USA, Idea Group Reference

Preece, J.; Rogers, Y.; Sharp, H.; Benyon, D.; Holland, S. & Carey, T. (1994). Knowledge and Mental Models, In: *Human-Computer Interaction*, pp. 123-139, Addison-Wesley

Singh, P. (2002). The public acquisition of commonsense knowledge, *Proceedings of the AAAI Spring Symposium: Acquiring (and Using) Linguistic (and World) Knowledge for Information Access*, Palo Alto, California, 2002

Stillman, S. & Essa, I. (2001). Towards reliable multimodal sensing in aware environments, *Proceedings of the PUI 2001*, Orlando, Forida, November 2001

Suhm, B.; Myers, B. & Waibel, A. (1999). Model-based and empirical evaluation of multimodal interactive error correction, *Proceedings of the ACM CHI'99*, pp. 584–591, Pittsburgh, Pennsylvania, May 1999

Suhm, B.; Myers, B. & Waibel, A. (2001). Multimodal error correction for speech user interfaces. *ACM Transactions on Computer–Human Interaction*, Vol. 8, No. 1, (2001) 60–98

Tsai, C.W.; Chou, S.Y. & Lin, S.W. (2010). Location-aware tour guide systems in museums. *Scientific Research and Essays journal*, Vol. 5, No. 8, (April 2010) 714-720

Vieroth, R.; Löher, T.; Seckel, M.; Dils, C.; Kallmayer, C.; Ostmann, A. & Reichl, H. (2009). Stretchable Circuit Board Technology and Application, *Proceedings of 13th International Symposium on Wearable Computers (ISWC 09)*, pp. 33–36, Linz, Austria, September 2009

W3C. (2003) http://www.w3.org/TR/mmi-framework/

W3C. (2002) http://www.w3.org/2002/01/multimodal-charter.html

Yoshimi, B.H. & Pingali, G.S. (2002). A multi-modal speaker detection and tracking system for teleconferencing, *Proceedings of the ACM Conference on Multimedia*, pp. 427-428, Juan-les-Pin, France, December 2002

Yue, W.; Mu, S.; Wang, H. & Wang, G. (2005). TGH: A case study of designing natural interaction for mobile guide systems, *Proceedings of Mobile HCI'05*, pp. 199-206, Salzburg, Austria, September 2005

4

Content Adaptation in Ubiquitous Computing[1]

Wanderley Lopes de Souza[1], Antonio Francisco do Prado[1],
Marcos Forte[2] and Carlos Eduardo Cirilo[1]
[1]*Federal University of São Carlos*
[2]*Federal University of São Paulo*
Brazil

1. Introduction

According to the predominant computing environments, the history of Computing can be classified into the initial period of mainframes, the current one of personal computers, and the future one of Ubiquitous Computing whose goal is to provide the user with easy access to and processing of information at any time and from anywhere (Hansmann et al., 2003).

Mobile communication has contributed to drive the leap of Computing into this new era, since it has given users unprecedented choice and freedom, enabling them to search for new and rewarding ways to conduct their personal and professional affairs. In just one decade, mobile networks have allowed for a growth rate that took fixed networks almost a century to achieve, and the advances in mobile technologies have led to the transition from voice-exclusive services to web-based content services.

This globalized mobility requires new architectures and protocols that allow mobile networks to connect easily to several types of services and content providers spread over the Internet. The futuristic view of the mobile Internet presupposes users with different profiles using different access networks and mobile devices, requiring personalized services that meet their needs, availability and locations. In this context, it is necessary to describe information about people, places, devices and other objects that are considered relevant for the interaction between users and services, including the users and services themselves.

The fields of Ubiquitous Computing include content adaptation, which involves converting an original content into a large number of formats compatible with the user preferences, the access device capabilities, the access network characteristics, and the delivery context. Due to the infinity of possible adaptations, the greater the quantity of available adaptation services, the higher the chances of meeting the user's needs.

The content adaptation can occurs at several points along the data path, including the origin server, the user device, and the edge device. An essential requirement for carrying out this process is the establishment of an adaptation policy, which defines what adaptation is to be done on a given content, when, and who should do it. To be effective, this policy must take into account information on users, devices, access network, content, and service agreement.

The purpose of this Ubiquitous Computing book chapter is to do a survey on our main contributions in the field of content adaptation. The sequence of this chapter is organized as

---

[1] Supported by INCT-MACC/CNPq

follows: section 2 deals with content adaptation, the Internet Content Adaptation Protocol (ICAP), and an adaptation service that uses this protocol; section 3 deals with frameworks for content adaptation, in particular the Internet Content Adaptation Framework (ICAF); section 4 deals with ontologies and Web services for content adaptation, and an ICAF extension for the use of these technologies; and section 5 presents some concluding remarks.

2. Content adaptation

Content adaptation involves modifying the representation of Internet content in order to come up with versions that meet diverse user requirements and the distinct characteristics of devices and access networks (Buchholz & Schill, 2003). Among the Internet content adaptation services the following stand out (Beck et al., 2000):

a. *Virus scan*, searches for viruses before delivering the content to the user;
b. *Ad Insertion*, inserts advertisements into a content based on user interests and/or location;
c. *Markup Language Translation*, allows devices that do not support Hypertext Markup Language (HTML) pages but support other markup languages (e.g., Wireless Markup Language) to receive the content of such pages;
d. *Data compression*, allows the origin server to send its content in compressed form so that the edge device can extract it, thereby reducing the bandwidth used in this communication;
e. *Content Filtering*, redirects an unauthorized content request or blocks a response containing unsuitable content;
f. *Image Transcodification*, processes image files in order, for example, to transform its format, reduce its size and/or resolution, or modify its color range; and
g. *Language Translate*, translates a Web page from one language to another.

These adaptation services require from an adaptation server special processing functions, such as video and voice trans-coding, intelligent text processing and filtering, and many others. Performing the adaptation services at the origin server has the advantage that the content author has a full control on what and how to present the content to the user. On the other hand, since these functions are quite different from the basic functions needed for building Web servers, the authoring process becomes more complex and time consuming. Another major drawback is the cost and the performance scalability issue of the origin server. Performing the adaptation services at the end user device limits the adaptation to the available functionality and capability of the device. It is therefore recommended to locate these functions in a separate computer that could be shared by many different applications.

2.1 Internet Content Adaptation Protocol (ICAP)

ICAP (Elson & Cerpa, 2003) was first introduced in 1999 by Peter Danzig and John Schuster from Network Appliance and further developed by the ICAP Forum, a coalition of Internet businesses. ICAP is a client/server application protocol running on the top of TCP/IP, similar in semantics and usage to HTTP/1.1, and designed to off-load specific Internet-based content adaptation to dedicated servers. Each server may focus on a specific value added service, thereby freeing up resources in the Web servers and standardizing the way in which these services are implemented. At the core of this process there is an ICAP client that intercepts HTTP messages and transmits them to the ICAP server for processing. The ICAP server executes its adaptation service on these messages and sends them back to the ICAP client. ICAP can be used in two modes as shown in Figure 1: request modification mode (*reqmode*) and response modification mode (*respmode*).

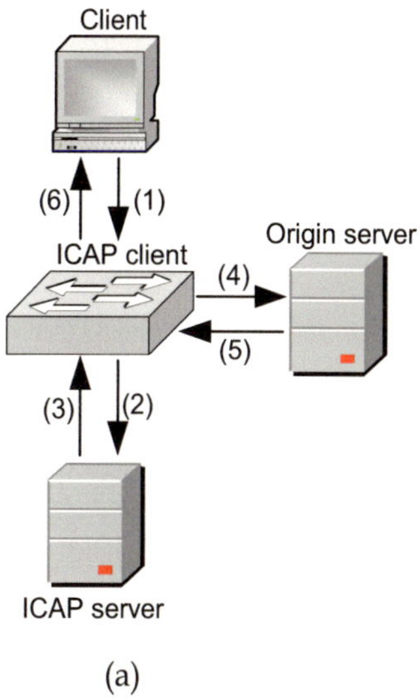

Fig. 1. (a) ICAP *reqmode* (b) ICAP *respmode*

In the *reqmode*, a user Client sends a request to an Origin server. This request is intercepted by an ICAP client, which redirects it to an ICAP server. The ICAP server may then: (a) send back a modified version of the request containing the original URI, and the ICAP client may then send the modified request to the Origin server, or may first pipeline it to another ICAP server for further modification; (b) modify the request so that it points to a page containing an error message instead of the original URI; (c) return an encapsulated HTTP response indicating an HTTP error. Figure 1(a) shows a data flow, where the message sequences in cases (a) and (b) are 1, 2, 3, 4, 5, and 6, while the message sequence in case (c) is 1, 2, 3, and 6.
The response modification mode (*respmode*) is intended for post-processing performed on a HTTP response before it is delivered to the user client. The ICAP client forwards the request directly to the Origin server. The Origin server's response is intercepted by the ICAP client, which redirects it to an ICAP server. The ICAP server may then: (a) send back a modified version of the response; or (b) return an error. Figure 1(b) shows a data flow for this case.
Although it is an essential part, the transaction semantics defined by ICAP is of limited use without a control algorithm, that determines what adaptation or processing function should be requested for what HTTP request or response passing through the ICAP client.

2.2 Adaptation policy

One fundamental aspect in content adaptation is the definition of an adaptation policy, i.e., what adaptation services are to be offered, which local or remote adaptors will execute these adaptations, and when the latter should be requested. The following information is necessary regarding the adaptation environment: characteristics and capacities of the access device; personal user information and preferences; conditions of the communication network; characteristics of the requested content; and the terms of the service agreement between the service provider and the end user. As proposed in (Forte et al., 2006) and illustrated in Figure 2, this information can be described and stored in *device*, *user*, *network*, *content* and *Service Level Agreement (SLA)* profiles.

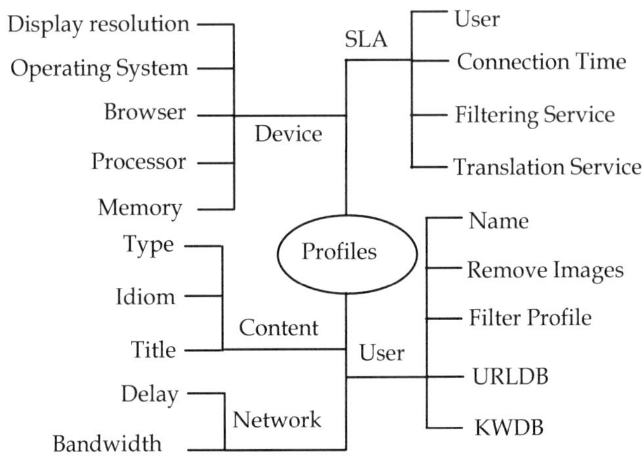

Fig. 2. Profiles and attributes

The user profile contains the user's personal information and his content adaptation preferences. Different users may wish to have different adaptations applied to a requested content (e.g., one user prefers having images removed while another prefers the sound). Adaptations not based on user preferences may be inconvenient or even undesirable.

The network profile can be dynamically obtained through agents that monitor parameters of the communication network between provider and user. Parameters such as latency and bandwidth guide some adaptation processes (e.g., images, video and audio on demand) so that the adapted content is optimized for the conditions of the network of a given context.

The content profile, also generated dynamically, is based on characteristics of the requested content. The applicable content modifications are determined based on information extracted from the HTTP header and, if it is available, the set of content metadata.

The SLA profile contains the terms of the service agreement between the user and the access provider, which can offer different plans, including bandwidth, connection time and added value services, allowing users to choose the plan that best fits their needs.

The adaptation policy must also consider adaptation rules, which comprise a set of related conditions and actions. These conditions refer to the profiles, reflecting the characteristics and needs of the entities involved in the adaptation process, and determine the action to be taken and the adaptation servers to be used. Figure 3 shows execution points for adaptation rules: points 1 and 2 during the request stage, the former before the content search in the cache and the latter after this search; points 3 and 4 during the response stage, the former before the content storage in the cache and the latter after this storage. The execution point definition for each rule depends on the adaptation service (e.g., an antivirus service should be executed at point 3 to prevent a contaminated content from being stored in the cache).

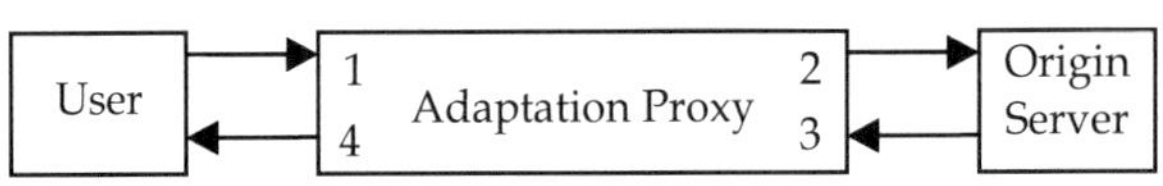

Fig. 3. Execution points for processing adaptation rules

2.3 Content Classification and Filtering Service (CCFS)

CCFS allows for controlling the access to undesirable content. Three interrelated terms are defined for this kind of service: (a) *labeling* is the process that describes a content associated to a label without requiring the user to open the file to examine its content; (b) *rating* is the process that confers values on a content based on certain suppositions/criteria, and if the content has a label, it already possesses a prequalification which may or may not be accepted by the filter; (c) *filtering* is the process aimed at blocking access to a content by comparing its classification against the system's definition of undesirable content. It should be noted that CCFS is not restricted solely to illegal (e.g., racism) or inappropriate contents (e.g., pornography), but also to undesirable contents in a corporation (e.g., shopping, chats).

The oldest and most commonly employed classification method is based on proprietary *Uniform Resource Locator (URL)* collections, in which each URL is associated to a specific content category. When a page is requested, the classifier checks its address in the database to find its category. With the category definition the filter can block or release the access to the site, according to the configured Internet policy. Keeping these collections updated is a challenge for CCFS suppliers, since the rate at which new Internet pages are created far exceeds their capacity to classify them (ICOGNITO, 2002).

A second generation of classifiers executes the analysis and classification of all Web traffic requested by the user on demand (e.g. keywords, textual analysis, labels, image analysis).When a page is received, it is classified according to its content, and the system blocks or releases that page in line with the pre-established filtering policy. The classification process is subject to the following problems: (a) *under-blocking*, when the filter fails to block undesired content, usually due to an outdated *URL* database or, in the dynamic approaches, an incorrect content classification; (b) *over-blocking*, when the filter blocks a content unduly, usually due to the use of keywords without context analysis. Pages on sexual education and medicine are the most commonly affected by this last problem (Rideout et al., 2002).

The CCFS we developed (Forte et al., 2006), illustrated in Figure 4, is part of a general architecture encompassing a set of dedicated adaptation servers and a content adaptation proxy. The purpose is to allow access to the available Internet content, independently of the device the user is employing, and to adapt the content according to the user's preferences.

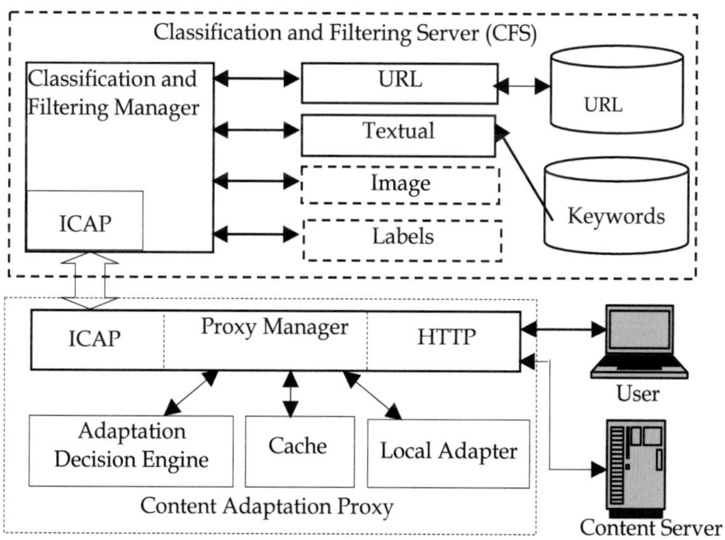

Fig. 4. CCFS general architecture

This architecture is based on the client-server model, in which the proxy captures the user's requests and the content server's responses. The adaptation decision mechanism implements the adaptation policy. If the adaptation policy defines the need for the CCFS, the proxy will send an ICAP request to the Classification and Filtering Server (CFS).
The CFS was designed to allow for the easy integration of new Classification modules. The Classification and Filtering Management module manages the Classification modules and, using ICAP and including the ICAP and HTTP headers, manages the communications with the Content Adaptation Proxy. It also filters the content based on the information sent by the Classification modules. The profiles were implemented using the *Composite Capability /Preference Profile (CC/PP)* (W3C, 2004a). Figure 5 shows a fragment of the user profile.

```
<rdf:Description rdf:ID="UserProfile">
<ccpp:component>
    <rdf:Description rdf:ID="Identification">
        <usr:UserName>mlobato</ usr:UserName>
        <usr:Gender>Male</ usr:Gender>
        <usr:Age>21</ usr:Age>
    </ rdf:Description>
</ ccpp:component>
<ccpp:component>
    <rdf:Description rdf:ID="Preferences">
        <usr:ImageGrayScale>0</ usr:ImageGrayScale>
        <usr:Filter_Profile>001</ usr:Filter_Profile>
        <usr:UrlDB>001</ usr:UrlDB>
        <usr:KWDB>005</ usr:KWDB>
    </ rdf:Description> ....
```

Fig. 5. Fragment of the user profile

The adaptation rules were implemented as clauses stored in a database, and they use the Prolog inference mechanism to deduce the actions to be taken as a function of the conditions to be met. Each adaptation executing point is represented at the rules base by a different functor, allowing the rules of a given executing point to be processed. Figure 6 illustrates an example of adaptation rule implementation to be invoked at the executing point 3.

```
Point_three(Ret,UserID.DeviceID,SLAID,Content):-
        contentIsText(Content),
        userPayforFilter(ContractID),
        =(Ret,' content-filter.com filter').
```

Fig. 6. Example of adaptation rule

In this adaptation rule the user identification (*UserID*), device identification (*DeviceID*), service level agreement (*SLAID*), and content type (*Content*) are provided. If they met, the action is stored in the variable *Ret*, which receives the values of the *contentfilter.com* and *filter*.
Figure 7 illustrates the sequence of a content adaptation. Starting from an HTTP request from the user (1), the access provider sends the HTTP request to the adaptation proxy together with the user identification (2). The adaptation decision mechanism pulls the user profile and SLA from its database and verifies that the user chose a filtering service, which

needs the requested content and the content profile. Failing to locate this content in its cache, the proxy sends a request to the origin content server (3) and, upon receiving a response (4), dynamically creates the content profile. Since the requested content is of text type, all the requisites of CFS's rule are met. Then, the decision mechanism creates an ICAP request, attaching the user's preferences (e.g., icap://adaptation.com/filter?*filter_profile=001 &urldb=001&kwdb=005&append*) and the content received from the Web server, and sends them through the proxy to the adaptation server (5). The latter executes the requested adaptation and returns the result to the proxy (6), which in turn sends it to the user (7).

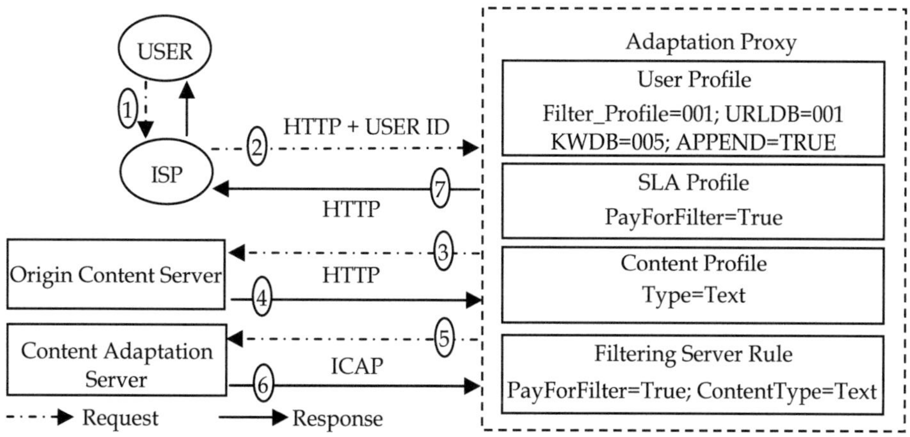

Fig. 7. Sequence of a content adaptation

An ICAP request encapsulates the ICAP header, the HTTP request header, the HTTP response header and the requested page body, the last two only when operating in *respmod*. When this request reaches the CFS, the following information is extracted from the ICAP header: the categories of content to be blocked (e.g., *filter_profile=001*); the URL databases and categorized domains that will be used (e.g., *urldb=001*); and, if the adaptation is in *respmod*, the database of keywords (e.g., *kwdb=005*). The domain and URL page requested by the user are extracted from the HTTP request header. In *respmod* the requested content will be extracted (*body*), allowing for classification by keywords. Figure 8 shows the states model of this ICAP request.

2.4 CCFS evaluation

For the CCFS performance evaluation three computers were employed: the first executing Linux Fedora Core 2 (2Ghz - 256MB) and the others Windows 2000 (700Mhz - 256MB). Because the variations in the response times of the Origin Servers, including those due to the Internet throughput, could interfere on this evaluation, an Apache 2 server was installed. This enabled the tested pages to be cloned, restricting the data flow to the computers involved in the case study. The software described in (Forte et al., 2007) was employed for the content adaptation proxy implementation, with the addition of specific CCFS profiles and rules, and was installed on the Linux platform. The CFS and its database, containing 651,620 categorized sites and 29 keywords, were installed on a Windows 2000 platform. Five predefined links have been accessed: two links were not blocked by the filter, one was blocked because of its address domain and another because of its URL address, and the last

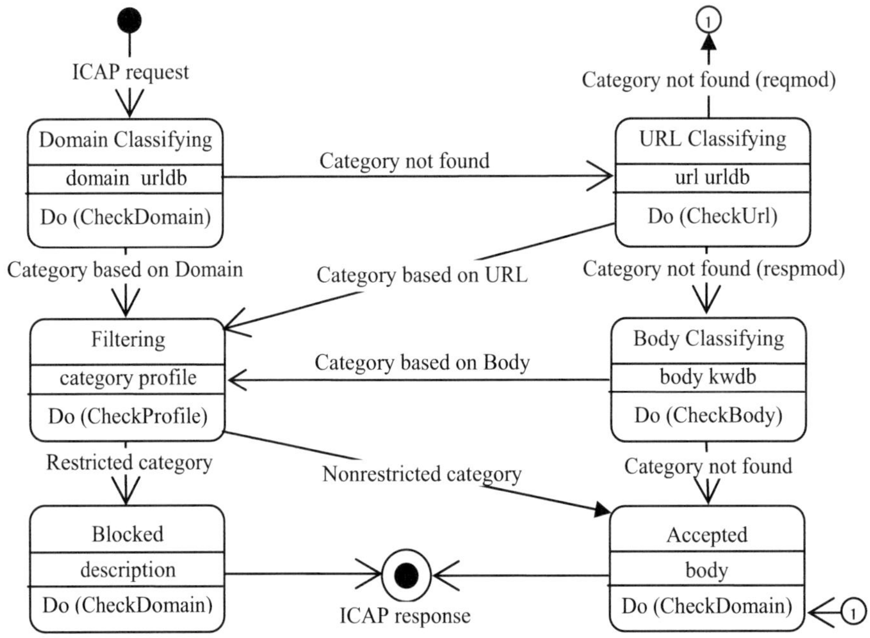

Fig. 8. States model of an ICAP request for CCFS

was blocked due to a restricted keyword. The load was progressively increased, adding one user every 1.5s up to the limit of 200 users, each user accessing a link every 5s. Figure 9 shows the results of these scenarios. The difference between the response times in *reqmod* and *respmod* is due to the addition of the content classification routine based on keywords.

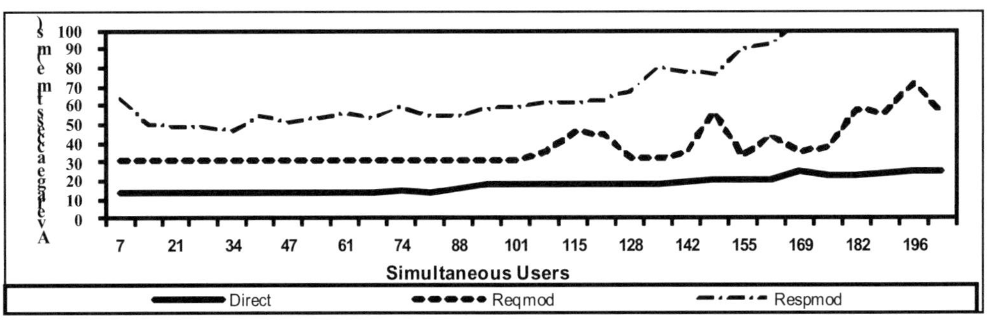

Fig. 9. Average response time *versus* number of users

For the CCFS efficiency evaluation the CFS and the Squid proxy (SourceForge, 2002) were used in a Brazilian university administrative network, and in an informatics laboratory of this university. During 48 hours 1,215,854 requests (6.8 GB) from the administrative network and 409,428 requests (2.8 GB) from the laboratories' network were checked. To minimize the interference on the response time of the employees' and students' accesses, only the *reqmod* was used by the adaptation server. Figure 10 depicts the results of this evaluation.

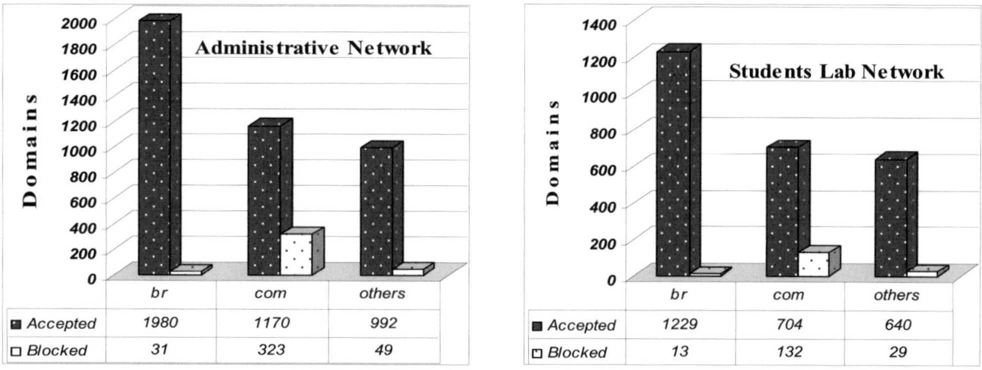

Fig. 10. CCFS efficiency evaluation

Considering all the domains classified in the two networks, 3 were incorrectly classified in restricted categories (*over-blocking*), and 22 were not classified passing incorrectly through the filter (*under-blocking*). Among those that passed incorrectly through the filter, 19 belonged to .br domains, which demonstrates the lower efficiency of *blacklists* produced in other countries. These 22 domains were tested again, with CCFS operating in *respmod* and using keywords for the content analysis, and 16 were correctly categorized.

3. Frameworks for content adaptation

In the mid-90s most of the content adaptations were done in the proxy (Bharadvaj et al., 1998; Smith et al., 1998). Since this approach tends to overload the proxy, services networks were developed for intercepting the content delivery and adapting this content, and these networks were mainly based on the Open Pluggable Edge Services (OPES) model (Tomlinson et al., 2001). Since OPES distributes adaptations among dedicated servers, it became feasible to build a single architecture offering several types of adaptation.

The OPES WG also developed the languages Intermediary Rule Markup Language (IRML) and P for the specification of content adaptation rules. IRML is based on eXtensible Markup Language (XML), and was designed to express service execution policies and to reflect the interests of the origin server and user on a content transaction (Beck & Hofmann, 2003). P is based on Smalltalk and C++, it is interpreted and has the following qualitative aspects: exactness, flexibility, efficiency, simplicity, security and hardiness (Beck & Rousskov, 2003).

Several requirements must be considered when offering adaptation services. For instance, to avoid overloading the proxy in a service network, it is important to distribute the adaptation services among dedicated servers. Based on such requirements, the ideas of service networks, and using the OPES model, some important works have been done.

(Beck & Hofmann, 2001) presents an architecture for executing content adaptations that contains a decision-making mechanism based on a condition set. These conditions and related actions constitute the adaptation rules, which are specified in IRML. However, these conditions do not employ information related to the adaptation environment. (Ravindran et al., 2002) proposes a framework to manage personalization of services, whose adaptation policy is based on a combination of user preferences, device constraints, and content characteristics. (Marques & Loureiro, 2004) presents an adaptation architecture specifically designed for mobile devices, which offers image, audio, and text compression adaptations, and uses access network information to decide the best adaptation to be carried out.

Unlike the aforementioned works, we developed the Internet Content Adaptation Framework (ICAF) (Forte et al., 2007), an extremely flexible framework thanks to the reuse of its components. Moreover, this framework contains an adaptation policy based on the user, device and SLA profiles, and based on the access network and content information.

3.1 Internet Content Adaptation Framework (ICAF)

ICAF has two main packages: Adaptation Proxy and Adaptation Server. The User and Origin Server actors interact with the Adaptation Proxy through content requests and responses. The Adaptation Proxy analyzes these interactions based on an adaptation policy and uses the available services at the Adaptation Server, which in turn adapts the transmitted content. Figure 11 illustrates the components of the Adaptation Proxy package. *Content Transfer Protocol* is responsible for the communications between User and Origin Server. It is generic enough to support most of the used protocols for content transmission on the Internet, including: Hypertext Transfer Protocol (HTTP), Real-time Transport Protocol (RTP), Simple Object Access Protocol (SOAP), and File Transfer Protocol (FTP).

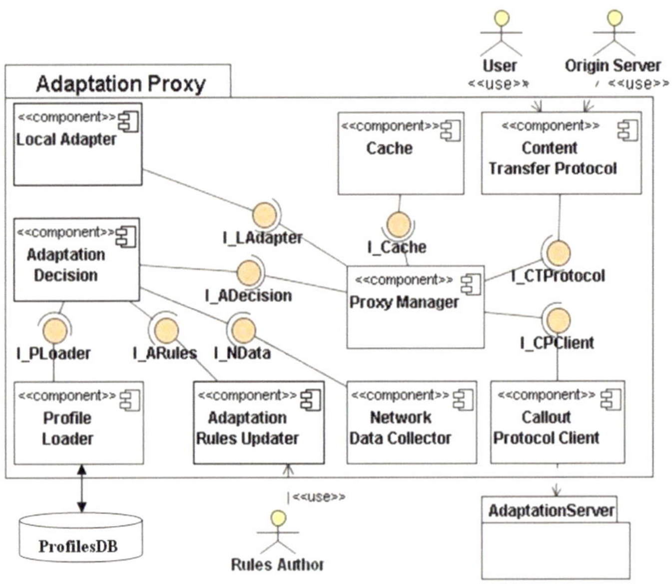

Fig. 11. Components of the Adaptation Proxy package

Since the Adaptation Proxy requests remote adaptations to an Adaptation Server using communication protocols, the *Callout Protocol Client* was defined for doing the remote adaptation calls. This component supports different protocols, including those especially created for this communication: ICAP, and OPES Callout Protocol (OCP) (Rousskov, 2005).

Cache was built to improve the ICAF's performance. It temporarily stores requested contents on the Internet, as well as Web pages, videos and images. Before requesting content to the Origin Server, the Adaptation Proxy checks whether it is already in the *Cache*. If so, a request to the Origin Server is avoided, speeding up the content delivery to the User.

Although it uses adaptation service modules, ICAF can do content adaptations locally via the *Local Adapter*. As this component employs the proxy resources, its wide-scale use may affect the Adaptation Proxy performance, and delay the content delivery to the User.

The Adaptation Proxy data flow is controlled by the *Proxy Manager*, which receives, through the *Content Transfer Protocol*, the User requests and the Origin Sever responses. Using the information carried in these communication primitives, the *Proxy Manager* asks for an adaptation analysis to the *Adaptation Decision*. If adaptation is needed the *Proxy Manager* invokes locally or remotely this service. To avoid an unnecessary content request, the *Proxy Manager* checks if this content is already in the *Cache*.

The ICAF's adaptation policy takes into account the user's interests and preferences, device capabilities and constraints, access network conditions, content characteristics, and SLA for building the adaptation rules. It is implemented through the *Adaptation Decision*, *Profile Loader*, *Adaptation Rules Updater* and *Network Data Collector* components.

The *Profile Loader* gets the user, device and SLA profiles in the ProfilesDB database. For inserting these profiles in this database an Internet interface must be available, which could be a Web page with a form where the user fills out the data related to these profiles. The SLA profile could be inserted in the same way by the system administrator.

The ICAF policy is controlled by the *Adaptation Decision* that receives: the access network conditions from the *Network Data Collector*, which monitors the network parameters; the profiles stored in the ProfilesDB from the *Profile Loader*; and the content to be analyzed from the *Proxy Manager*. Based on this information set, the *Adaptation Decision* uses the adaptations rules to decide what adaptations will be done, which servers (local and/or remote) will execute these adaptations, and the order in which they will be executed.

To prevent processing of outdated rules, the *Adaptation Rules Updater* inserts, removes and updates the adaptation rules implemented in the *Adaptation Decision*. The Rules Author carries out these updates using an interface provided by the *Adaptation Rules Updater*.

The Content Adaptation Server is responsible for doing the content adaptations requested by the Adaptation Proxy. Since different types of adaptation services can be offered, we adopted the Component-Based Development approach to define a generic structure for the Adaptation Servers, which includes the components illustrated in Figure 12. The *Callout Protocol Server* handles the communications with the Adaptation Proxy, supporting several protocols (e.g., ICAP, HTTP), analyzes the adaptation requests received from the *Callout Protocol Client*, and defines the action to be taken and its parameters. Based on this information, which is sent in the header of the appropriated protocol message, the *Callout Protocol Server* asks for the requested adaptation to the *Remote Adapter*.

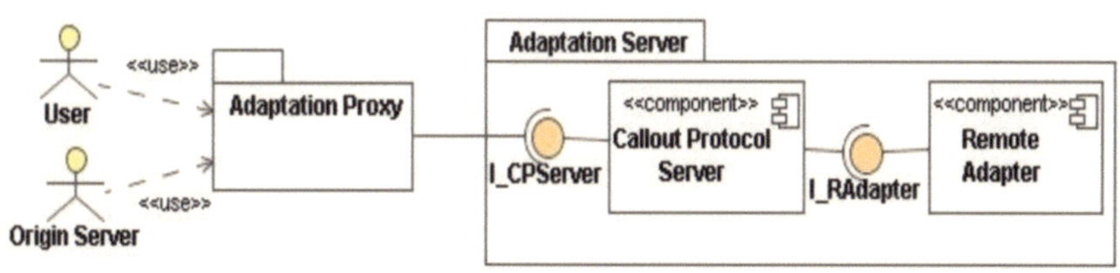

Fig. 12. Components of the Adaptation Server package

The *Remote Adapter* executes the content adaptations, its internal structure can vary according to the type of adaptation offered by the Adaptation Server, and it carries out the same functions of the *Local Adapter* but does not use the processing resources of the Adaptation Proxy. The decision-making process of adapting the content locally or remotely must consider the ratio between the execution times of the Callout Protocol and the content

adaptation. The lower the ratio the more the decision will be in favor of the remote adaptation. A design example of the *Remote Adapter* was presented in section 2.3.
ICAF was built to support the same ICAP operating modes and the same execution points defined in section 2.2. It was also developed to offer a basic structure for creating Internet content adaptation applications through the reuse of its components.

3.2 ICAF reuse and evaluation

Figure 13 shows the components used in a case study, where the following components were reused by ICAF direct instantiation: *Local Adapter, Remote Adapter, Proxy Manager, Cache, Adaptation Rules Updater, Network Data Collector*, and *Profile Loader*.
ICAF's adaptation policy takes into account adaptation rules and information related to the adaptation environment. Since there are several ways of implementing this policy, including by a procedural language algorithm, several ICAP components were customized and new components were added to this framework.

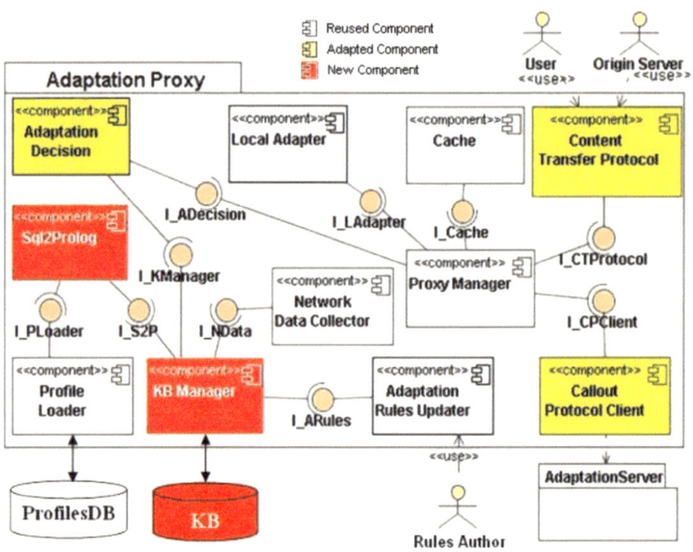

Fig. 13. ICAF reuse example

The *Adaptation Decision* is responsible for the decision-making process of the ICAF's adaptation policy. For this case study, this component was customized to perform with an inference mechanism, based on adaptation rules and environment's information, for defining the adaptation services to be executed. The *Adaptation Decision* decides the adapter (local or/and remote) that will perform an adaptation and, if multiple adaptations are required, decides the sequence of them. The inference mechanism was introduced through a Prolog Knowledge Base (KB) for giving more flexibility to the ICAF´s adaptation policy, and for giving some "intelligence" to the decision-making process.
To handle KB, the *KB Manager* was added to ICAF. It receives the updated adaptation rules from *Adaptation Rules Updater*, translates these rules to Prolog, stores this translation in KB and, when requested by the *Adaptation Decision*, carries out a query for retrieving information on users, devices and access network. KB answers this query based on the user, device and SLA profiles, and based on the access network and content information. Since

KB is implemented in Prolog and ProfilesDB in SQL, the *SQL2Prolog* component was added to ICAF for enabling KB to receive and analyze profiles stored in ProfilesDB.

Three components were customized with specific interfaces, characterizing the reuse through specialization. *Content Transfer Protocol* was specialized for transmitting content requests and responses through HTTP, which consists of two fields: the header and the payload (i.e., content). The content is modified by an HTTP parser, which identifies the semantic actions of this protocol. *Callout Protocol Client* and *Callout Protocol Server* were specialized to allow for ICAP communication between the Adaptation Proxy and the Adaptation Server. Upon receiving a service request, *Callout Protocol Client* encapsulates the actions, parameters and content in an ICAP request and sends it to *Callout Protocol Server*. This latter component retrieves the information for doing a semantic analysis of this request, and asks the requested service to the *Remote Adapter*. After receiving the adapted content from the *Remote Adapter*, *Callout Protocol Server* encapsulates this content in an ICAP response for returning it to the Adaptation Proxy.

ICAF was developed having in mind the definition of an adaptation policy with a short processing time, and the offer of adaptation services without degradation of the Internet's infrastructure performance. In this case study, these requirements were evaluated measuring the adaptation policy and content adaptation execution times on a network with five computers: one Adaptation Proxy, three Adaptation Servers and one User. The Adaptation Proxy implementation was based on (SourceForge, 2003), the implementations of the Image Adapter (IA) and Virus Scan (VS) servers were based on (Network, 2001), and the implementation of the Content Filter (CF) server was based on the CFS presented in section 2.3. The Origin Servers were accessed directly from Internet content servers.

For the performance evaluation of this case study, the model described in (Mastoli et al, 2003) was employed, and the temporal collecting points T_0 to T_7 were defined for measuring: the origin server response time T(Origin Server); the processing time of the adaptation policy T(Analysis); the adaptation time consumed by the ICAP protocol and by the content adaptations T(Adaptation); and the delivery time of the content to the user after executing all adaptations T(Delivery). Figure 14 depicts these points and measuring times.

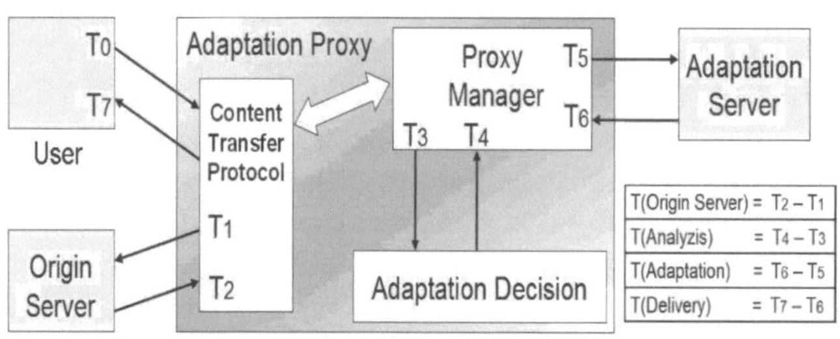

Fig. 14. Temporal collecting points and measuring times

For this evaluation 1,000 requests for www.folha.com.br were executed with five different kinds of adaptation on this Web page: no adaptation (NA), using each one of the Adaptation Servers (VS, IA, CF) independently, and combining these servers (VS+IA+CF). Figure 15 shows the T(Origin Server), T(Analysis), T(Adaptation) and T(Delivery) average times.

The origin server response times are by far the longest ones, and the adaptation policy processing times are similar for all adaptations. Without adaptation (NA) it was consumed 121 ms, corresponding to 103 ms of origin server response time, 17 ms of adaptation policy

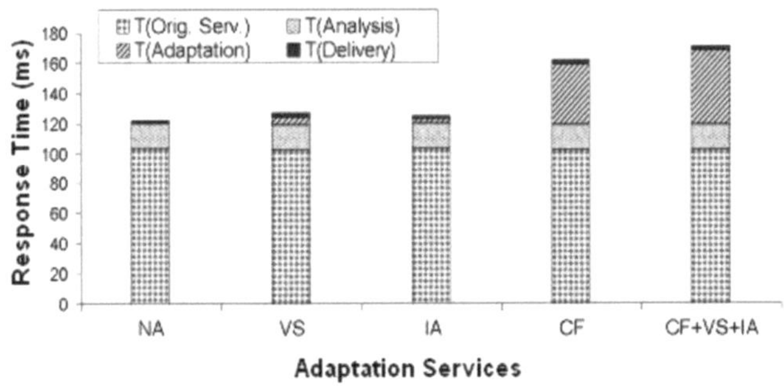

Fig. 15. Measuring times *versus* adaptation services

processing time, and only 1 ms of delivery time. Therefore, the relatively short delay (17ms) introduced by the inference mechanism can be considered satisfactory. With the VS and IA servers the adaptation times were 5.3 ms and 2.5 ms respectively, and the delays introduced by these servers can be also considered satisfactory. However, with the CF server the adaptation time was 40 ms, and the delay introduced by this server is relevant.

4. Ontologies and Web services for content adaptation

To achieve interoperability among heterogeneous systems executing applications of a given domain, it is essential to be able to share information, with a common and unambiguous understanding of the terms and concepts used by these applications. In this context, ontologies are important artifacts for making feasible the treatment of this heterogeneity.

Berners-Lee proposed the Semantic Web (Berners-Lee et al., 2001) as an evolution of the traditional Web to allow for the manipulation of content by applications with the capacity to interpret the semantics of information. The Web content can thus be interpreted by machines through the use of ontologies, rendering the retrieval of information from the Web less ambiguous and providing more precise responses to user requests.

The World Wide Web Consortium (W3C) guides the development, organization and standardization of languages to promote interoperability among Web applications. These languages include the Resource Description Framework (RDF) (W3C, 2004b), and the Ontology Web Language (OWL) (W3C, 2004c).

OWL is a markup language used for publication and sharing of ontologies in the Web. In this language, ontology is a set of definitions of classes, properties and restrictions relating to the modes in which these classes and properties can be used.

Web services have been for years the basis of service-oriented architectures, but begun to show deficiencies for service description, discovery, and composition due to the lack of semantic support in Web Services Description Language (WSDL) (W3C, 2007), and in the mechanism of storage and discovery services of Universal Description Discovery and Integration (UDDI) (UDDI Spec TC, 2004). To integrate semantic Web to Web services the Ontology Web Language for Services (OWL-S) (Martin et al., 2006) was developed.

OWL-S allows for the discovery, composition, invocation and monitoring of services, it has a larger number of Application Programming Interfaces (APIs), and inherits tools from OWL and from the Semantic Web Rule Language (SWRL) (Horrocks et al., 2003). OWL-S combines elements of WSDL, OWL's semantic markup and a language for rules description (e.g., SWRL). The OWL-S model is composed of three parts: Service Model for describing how a Web service operates; Service Grounding for describing the access to a Web service, and Service Profile for describing what the Web service does.

Service Model specifies the communication protocol, telling what information the requester must send to or receive from the service provider at a given moment of the transaction. This module distinguishes two types of processes: atomic and composite. The first one supply abstract specifications of the information exchanged with the requester, corresponding to operations the supplier can directly execute. The latter is employed to describe collections of processes (atomic or composite) organized through some type of flow control structure.

Service Grounding describes how atomic processes are transformed into concrete messages, which are exchanged via a network or through a procedure call. A "one-on-one" mapping of atomic processes for WSDL specifications is defined.

Service Profile is a high level specification of the service provider and service functionalities, including: contact information of a provider/service (e.g., *serviceName, textDescription, contactInformation*); categorization attributes of the offered service (e.g., *serviceParameter, serviceCategory*); and service functional representations in the form of *Inputs, Outputs, Preconditions,* and *Effects* (IOPEs). IOPEs are described by the properties *hasParameter, hasInput, hasOutput, hasPrecondition,* and *hasEffect.*

Since descriptions of OWL-S services are based on OWL, the OWL domain model can be employed to structure the service descriptions, facilitating the reuse of OWL ontologies already developed. In this sense, we extended ICAF for allowing the use of ontologies and Web services in the development of content adaptation applications (Forte et al., 2008).

4.1 Adaptation policy specification with ontologies and Web services

One major challenge in Ubiquitous Computing is the description of the delivery context, which is as a set of attributes that characterizes aspects related to the delivery of Web content. For content adaptation the delivery context must contain even more information that can be described in a set of profiles. For the CCFS development, presented in section 2, these profiles were implemented using CC/PP, and the adaptation rules were implemented as clauses stored in a database and the Prolog inference mechanism was employed. In this section we propose to specify the same profiles in OWL, and to employ semantics in the adaptation rules description for facilitating their extension and the addition of new rules.

To make available an infrastructure of adaptation servers over the Internet, we propose to use Web service technology, since it offers a large number of tools, and well-defined standards. Moreover, the use of ontologies and the inclusion of semantics in these standards help the migration from the proprietary solutions, for the discovery and composition of services, to an open distributed architecture based on the semantic Web.

The following information about the adaptation servers is essential: characteristics; communication needs (e.g., protocols, addressing); and the conditions, for the execution of their services, which are described by the adaptation rules. We propose to make available this information via the adaptation server profile and to specify it in OWL, and the services information via the service profile and to specify it in OWL-S.

All ontology models for the OWL profiles are based on the EMF Ontology Definition Metamodel (EODM) (IBM, 2004), which is derived from the OMG's Ontology Definition Metamodel (ODM) and implemented in the Eclipse Modeling Framework (EMF). These models use the following OWL components: *Classes* that are the basic building blocks of an OWL ontology; *Individuals* that are instances of classes; *Object properties* to relate individuals to other individuals; and *Datatype properties* to relate individuals to data type, such as integers, floats, and strings. OWL supports six main types of classes: *named, intersection, union, complement, restrictions,* and *enumerated.*

The *UserAgent* field of the HTTP header is employed to identify the user's access device and to look up the device profile stored in the database. Figure 16 depicts an ontology model for a device profile, describing the following characteristics: supported image formats (*Supported_image* class); display information, including resolution (*Display_Resolution* class) and colors (*Color* class); supported audio and video streaming (*Streaming* class); markup languages supported by the device's browser (*Supported_Markup* class), including their properties (*WML_UI, XHTML_UI* and *CHTML_UI* classes); model and manufacturer (*Product_Info* class); and security (*Security* class). One OWL characteristic present in this model is the restriction insertion that helps the consistency checking and the validation of this profile. For instance, *Supported_ImageRestriction* defines that the class *Supported_Image* can only be instantiated with the individuals declared in the enumerated class *Image_Format.*

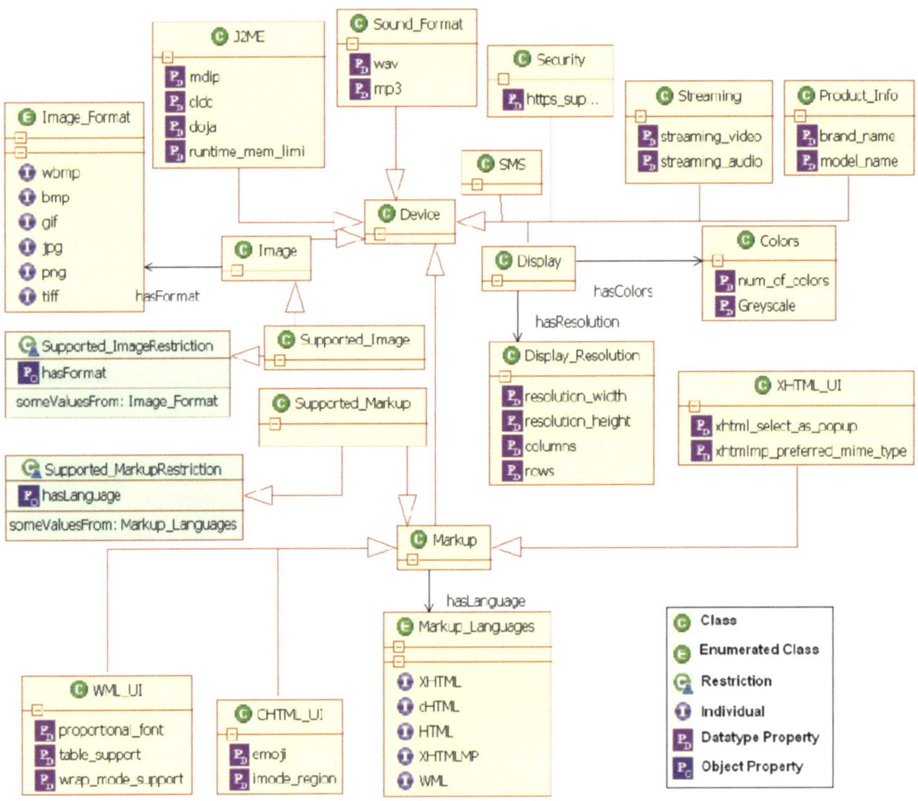

Fig. 16. Ontology model for a device profile

Figure 17 depicts an ontology model for a user profile. This model represents the *User* class that encloses the *Info* and *Service_Preferences* subclasses. *Info* holds the following properties: *ID* for retrieving the user's information from the database, and *FirstName/LastName* for identifying the user's name. *Service_Preferences* contains the specifications of the adaptation service properties, which can be configured by the user according to his/her preferences.

ID_Required defines that the class *Person* has exactly one value for the property *ID* inside *Info*. Three adaptation services are represented in this model: *Antivirus*, where the user can choose to check or not viruses using a script language on a Web page; *Image_Adapter*, where the user can define the action to be taken if a low throughput is detected (e.g., color and/or resolution reductions, conversion to black and white); *Classification_and_Filtering*, where the user can define the content types to be blocked (e.g., sex, shopping, games) and which URLs (*URLDB*), databases, and keywords (*KWDB*) will be used for the classification.

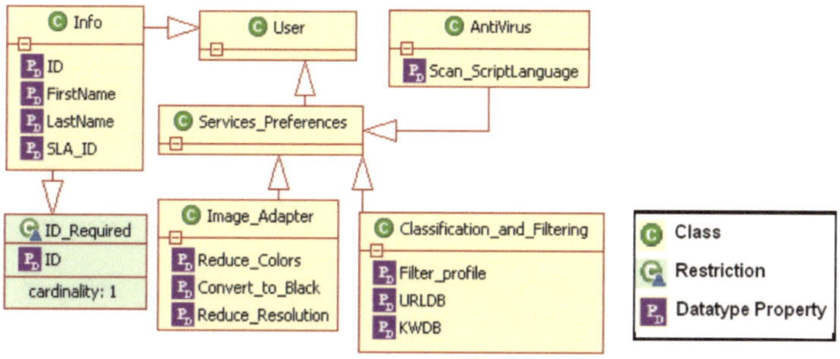

Fig. 17. Ontology model for a user profile

The network profile is built dynamically using the agents that monitor network parameters. The information in this profile is used to guide some adaptation processes (e.g., images, video and audio on demand), for the optimization of the content adaptation as a function of the network current conditions. Figure 18 depicts an ontology model for a network profile.

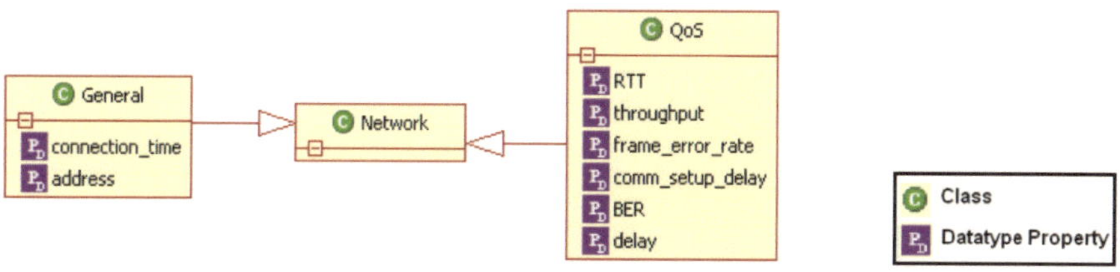

Fig. 18. Ontology model for a network profile

The content profile is built dynamically using the characteristics of the requested content. The needed and applicable adaptations to the content depend on information extracted from the HTTP header (e.g., the content has text and/or image, language) and depend on content metadata, if available. Figure 19 depicts an ontology model for a content profile.

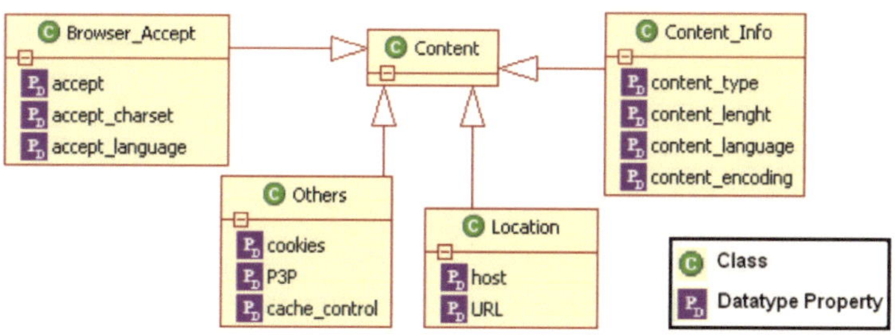

Fig. 19. Ontology model for a content profile

The terms of the agreement between the access provider and the user are described in the SLA profile. These providers offer to their users a variety of plans, including bandwidth, connection time and several added value services, enabling the user to choose the plan that best meets his/her needs. Figure 20 depicts an ontology model for a SLA profile.

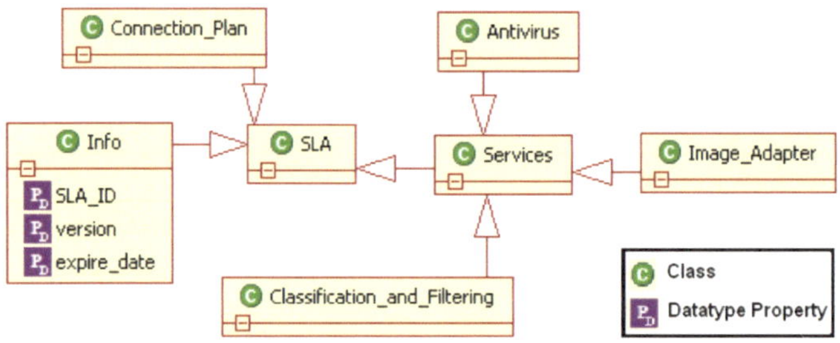

Fig. 20. Ontology model for a SLA profile

Some characteristics described in the adaptation server profile are related to the Quality of Service (*QoS*), including the server's *Availability* and *Reliability*, the last characteristic for evaluating the successful execution rate. This information, allied to *MaxProcessTime*, *RequiredBandwidth* and *Cost*, helps the decision-making process when the service discovery finds more than one service provider satisfying the delivery context needs. This profile also defines the communication protocol between the proxy and the adaptation server. Figure 21 shows an ontology model for an adaptation server profile, where *Supported_Execution_Points* specifies four execution points for processing adaptation rules, with exactly the same meaning found in section 2.2. To help in consistency checking and validation of this profile, it is inserted *Supported_ProtocolsRestriction*, restricting *Supported_Protocols* to be instantiated with individuals declared in *Protocols*, and *Supported_Execution_PointsRestriction*, restricting *Supported_ExecutionPoints* to be instantiated with individuals declared in *Exec_Points*.

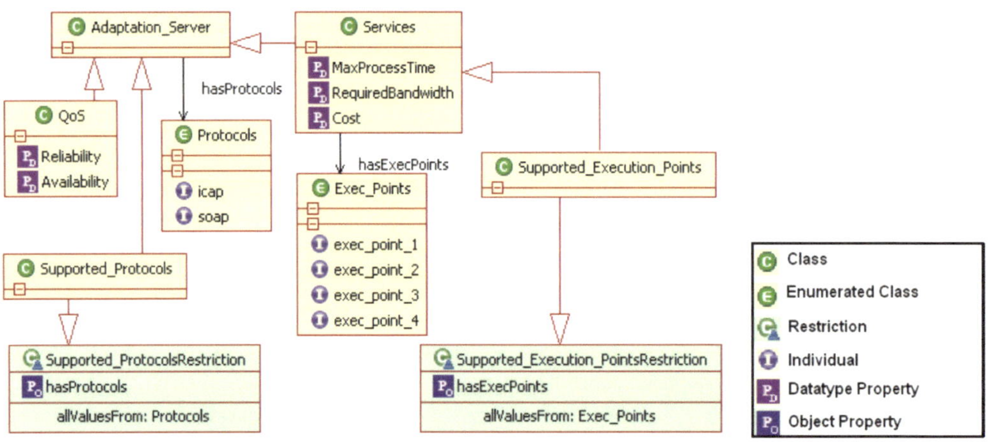

Fig. 21. Ontology model for an adaptation server profile

Service characteristics, including the necessary conditions for its execution, can be associated to the adaptation process, represented by the *Inputs* and *Outputs*, or associated to the service, represented by the *Preconditions* and *Effects*, which help the adaptation policy deciding whether or not to execute a given service. Figure 22 depicts these associations.

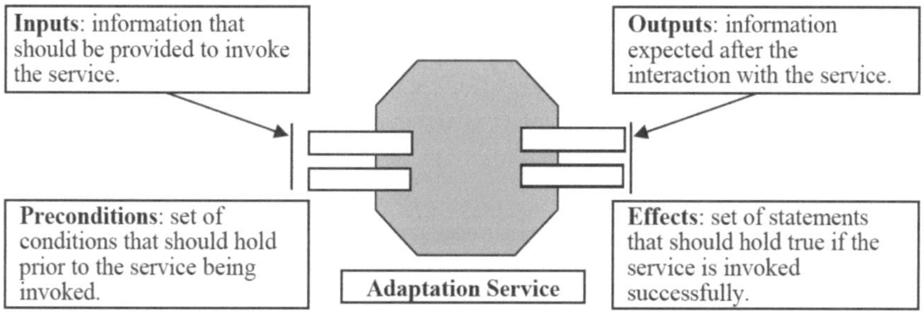

Fig. 22. Associations of service characteristics

The service profile has the service characteristics and some exclusive functions that must be specified in OWL-S. The main one is the mapping of OWL semantic specifications of other profiles into WSDL syntactic specifications, allowing for the integration of ontologies and Web services. The service profile also imports semantic specifications contained in other profiles or other OWL ontologies to facilitate their reuse and to avoid ambiguities.

Figure 23 shows the OWL-S specification skeleton of a Markup Language Translation Service (MLTS) profile. The Ontologies, to be imported to include the semantic information needed for this service, are defined, the public ontology *semwebglossary.owl*, which specifies terms of the semantic Web for avoiding ambiguous definitions, the *content.owl* profile, and the *device.owl* profile are reused (1). *SupportedMarkupLanguage* class (2) and *canBeConvertedTo* property (3), which will be used for defining the possible conversions to be carried out by the service (4), are defined. The *InputMarkupLanguage* parameter indicates the markup language to be converted (5), which is obtained from the *Content_Type* class of the content profile, previously instantiated with information about the requested content. The *OutputMarkupLanguage* parameter indicates the desired markup language that is defined in the *Supported_Markup* class of the device profile, which in turn informs the supported languages (6). The inputs, outputs, preconditions and effects are defined in the process *MarkupConverterProcess* (7). The precondition *SupportedTranslation* is based on a SWRL rule (8), which returns *true* when the needed translation belongs to the list defined in (4).

If it is not found a Web service that meets all the needs of a given adaptation, those needs may be met by an appropriate composition of Web services, which should be identified. Let $S = \{S_1, S_2, \ldots, S_n\}$ be a Web service set, where each S_i is defined by a quadruple

$$\left(I_s^i, O_s^i, P_s^i, E_s^i\right) \tag{1}$$

with its elements representing the sets of *Inputs, Outputs, Preconditions* and *Effects* of the service S_i. Let $G = \{G_1, G_2, \ldots, G_m\}$ be a goals set, where each goal G_j is defined by a quadruple

$$\left(I_g^j, O_g^j, P_g^j, E_g^j\right) \tag{2}$$

with its elements representing the sets of *Inputs, Outputs, Preconditions* and *Effects* required by the goal G_j. If there is at least one S_i that satisfies

$$\bigcup_{i=1}^{n} I_s^i \subseteq \bigcup_{j=1}^{m} I_g^j \text{ and } \bigcup_{i=1}^{n} P_s^i \subseteq \bigcup_{j=1}^{m} P_g^j \text{ and} \tag{3}$$

$$\bigcup_{i=1}^{n} O_s^i \supseteq \bigcup_{j=1}^{m} O_g^j \text{ and } \bigcup_{i=1}^{n} E_s^i \supseteq \bigcup_{j=1}^{m} E_g^j \tag{4}$$

```
...
<!ENTITY gloss "http://www.personal-reader.de/rdf/semwebglossary.owl">
<!ENTITY device "http://www.adaptationsrv.org/device.owl">                    (1)
<!ENTITY content "http://www.adaptationsrv.org/content.owl">
...
<owl:Class rdf:ID="SupportedMarkupLanguage">
  <owl:oneOf rdf:parseType="Collection">
    <factbook:Language rdf:about="&gloss;#HTML"/>
    <factbook:Language rdf:about="&gloss;#XHTML"/>
    <factbook:Language rdf:about="&gloss;#XML"/>                               (2)
    <factbook:Language rdf:about="&gloss;#CHTML"/>
    <factbook:Language rdf:about="&gloss;#WML"/>
  </owl:oneOf>
</owl:Class>
<owl:ObjectProperty rdf:ID="canBeConvertedTo">
  <rdfs:domain rdf:resource="#SupportedMarkupLanguage"/>                       (3)
  <rdfs:range rdf:resource="#SupportedMarkupLanguage"/>
</owl:ObjectProperty>
<rdf:Description rdf:about="&gloss;#HTML"><canBeConvertedTo rdf:resource="&gloss;#WML"/></rdf:Description>
<rdf:Description rdf:about="&gloss;#HTML">< canBeConvertedTo rdf:resource="&gloss;#XHTML"/></rdf:Description>
<rdf:Description rdf:about="&gloss;#HTML">< canBeConvertedTo rdf:resource="&gloss;#XML"/></rdf:Description>        (4)
<rdf:Description rdf:about="&gloss;#HTML">< canBeConvertedTo rdf:resource="&gloss;#cHTML"/></rdf:Description>
<rdf:Description rdf:about="&gloss;#XML">< canBeConvertedTo rdf:resource="&gloss;#XHTML"/></rdf:Description>
...
<process:Input rdf:ID="InputMarkupLanguage">
  <process:parameterType  rdf:datatype="&xsd;#anyURI">&content;#Content_Type   (5)
  </process:parameterType>
</process:Input>
<process:Input rdf:ID="OutputMarkupLanguage">
  <process:parameterType  rdf:datatype="&xsd;#anyURI">&device;#Supported_Markup   (6)
  </process:parameterType>
</process:Input>
...
<process:AtomicProcess rdf:ID="MarkupConverterProcess">
  <process:hasInput rdf:resource="#InputMarkupLanguage"/>
  <process:hasInput rdf:resource="#OutputMarkupLanguage"/>
  <process:hasInput rdf:resource="#InputString"/>
  <process:hasOutput rdf:resource="#OutputString"/>                            (7)
  <process:hasPrecondition rdf:resource="#SupportedTranslation"/>
  <process:hasEffect rdf:resource= ="#MarkupLanguageConverted"/>
</process:AtomicProcess>
...
<expr:SWRL-Condition rdf:ID="SupportedTranslation">
  <rdfs:label>canBeConvertedTo(InputMarkupLanguage, OutputMarkupLanguage)</rdfs:label>
  <expr:expressionLanguage rdf:resource="&expr;#SWRL"/>
  <expr:expressionObject><swrl:AtomList><rdf:first>
      <swrl:IndividualPropertyAtom>
        <swrl:propertyPredicate rdf:resource="#canBeConvertedTo"/>             (8)
        <swrl:argument1 rdf:resource="#InputMarkupLanguage"/>
        <swrl:argument2 rdf:resource="#OutputMarkupLanguage"/>
      </swrl:IndividualPropertyAtom>
    </rdf:first></swrl:AtomList></expr:expressionObject>
</expr:SWRL-Condition>
...
```

Fig. 23. OWL-S specification skeleton of a MLTS profile

then S_i is put in the services list that provides the required content adaptation. Otherwise, if there is at least one S_i that satisfies (3), there is no service to carry out alone the adaptation, the composition algorithm is activated. Otherwise, the adaptation cannot be carried out.
One of the techniques used for the services composition is *forward chaining* (Lara et al., 2005). Starting from a goal G_j, where an S_i is found that satisfies (3), a new goal is defined

$$G_k = \left(I_g^k, O_g^k, P_g^k, E_g^k\right) \tag{5}$$

where

$$I_g^k = O_s^i \text{ and } P_g^k = E_s^i \tag{6}$$

This process is repeated until (4) is satisfied, otherwise the adaptation cannot be carried out.

4.2 Extended Internet Content Adaptation Framework (EICAF)

ICAF was extended to deal with ontologies and Web services. Figure 24 shows the EICAF component model, where the following ICAF components were reused: *Local Adapter, Cache, Content Transfer Protocol, Network Data Collector* and *Remote Adapter*. The components *Callout Protocol (Client* and *Server), Proxy Manager* and *Service Profile Updater* were modified to include new interfaces and functionalities for using semantic profiles and new protocols. *Matching and Composition, Ontologies Manager* and *Reasoner* are new components, introduced for managing the ontologies and for processing the adaptation policy.
Callout Protocol Client and *Callout Protocol Server* support ICAP and SOAP. The first, already supported by ICAF, was kept to allow for communication with the servers previously developed. The second was introduced to provide compatibility with Web services.

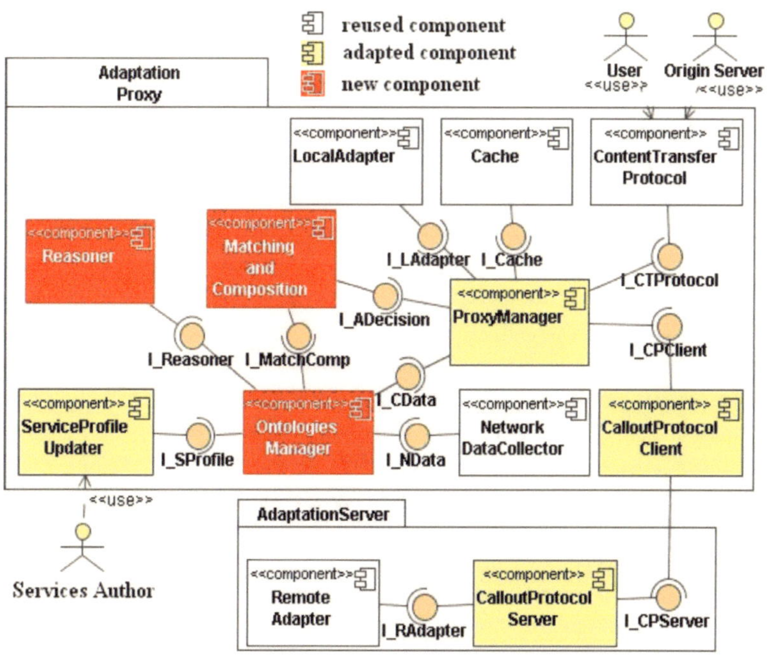

Fig. 24. EICAF component model

Ontologies Manager handles the storage, retrieval and processing of the static ontologies (device, user, SLA, adaptation server and service profiles) that are stored in a relational database. This component also treats the service profiles that are inserted through *Service Profile Updater*. The stored dynamic ontologies are generated on demand, from the information obtained by the *I_NData* interface, for the network profile generation, and by the *I_Cdata* interface, for the content profile generation.
To help the addition of new service profiles, *Service Profile Updater* provides a Web interface, where the service author can insert information related to the adaptation services to be converted to an OWL-S specification. Figure 25 shows some pages of this interface.

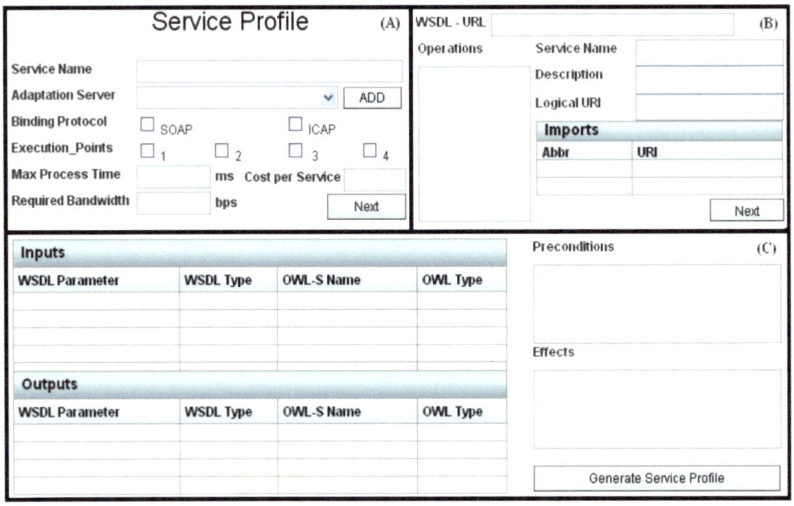

Fig. 25. Web interface for the insertion of service profiles

Initial page (A) is for insertion of service general information, mainly on the used protocol and the execution points for invoking the service: if ICAP is used, then this will be the only page available; if SOAP is used, then page (B) will be loaded. The operations are listed on this page, starting with the URI insertion of service WSDL specification, whose information will be converted in an OWL-S Service Grounding. Information about service profile URI is also inserted on page (B), and the ontologies to be imported are defined. On page (C) the mapping table of OWL semantic descriptions for WSDL parameters is filled out with the parameters inserted from information kept in WSDL file. The SWRL rules are specified in the *Preconditions* and *Effects* text boxes, and *Generate Service Profile* generates this profile.
EICAF was implemented in Java using several public APIs. The API OWL-S and the relational database MySQL were used in *Ontologies Manager*. The API Pellet was used in *Reasoner*, and the SPARQL module of the API OWL-S was used in *Matching and Composition*. This component makes requests based on SPARQL, using information contained in profiles and information inferred by the *Reasoner*, to locate the services that have inputs and outputs compatible with the delivery context. The results of these requests are filtered to check their conformity to preconditions and effects and, if a services composition is needed, *Matching and Composition* will manage the execution order of them. Next, this component sends to *Proxy Manager*, via the *I_ADecision* interface, the information regarding the services to be invoked. *Proxy Manager* forwards this information, via the *I_CPClient* interface, to *Callout*

Protocol Client that asks the services to the appropriated *Adaptation Servers*, which in turn execute these services. Last, *Proxy Manager* sends the adapted content to the *User*.
Figure 26 illustrates the tasks of the Web services composition mechanism by means of a delivery context example in which the user accesses the Web via a mobile phone. The notation *profile.class - context information* indicates the profile name, the class name, and the context information to be stored in this class. Since the user hired CCFS, the *Pay_for_Filtering* property of the SLA profile was configured as *true*. Once this profile information has been collected, the initial goal G_1 = *(HTML, XHTML, Pay_ for_Filtering, _)* is established, and the search for services to carry out this service is started. *Matching and Composition* discovers that the CCFS S_1 = *(HTML, HTML, Pay_for_Filtering, _)* meets the *Inputs* and *Preconditions*, but does not support the *Output XHTML*. Since the goal G_1 was only partially achieved, a new goal G_2 = *(HTML, XHTML, _ , _)* is established. A new search discovers that the MLTS S_2 = *(HTML, XHTML, _ , _)* meets completely this new goal, ending this composition process.

User.Filter_Profile - 001	**Network**.WAN - GPRS
SLA.Services - Pay_for_Filtering	**Network**.RTT - 10
Device.DisplayResolution - 320x200	**Content**.Type - HTML
Device.Supported_Markup - XHTML	**Content**.URL - www.test.com

Fig. 26. Example of a delivery context

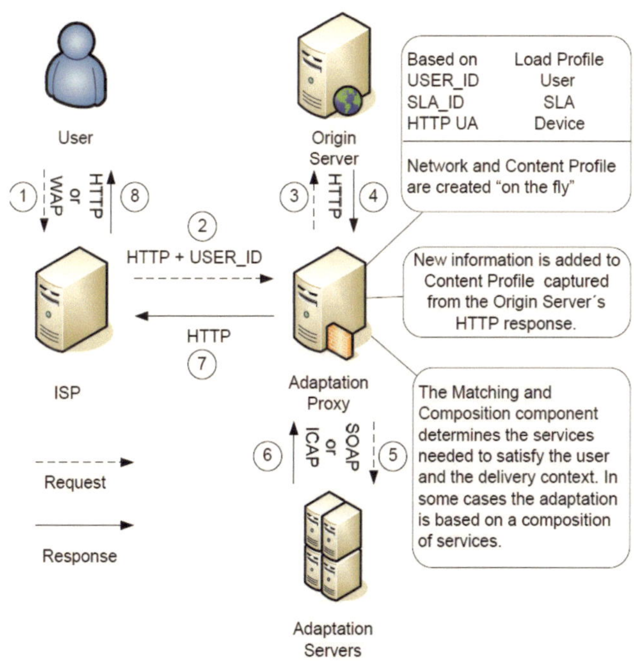

Fig. 27. Execution sequence of a content adaptation

Figure 27 illustrates the use of profiles and rules by means of an execution sequence of a content adaptation. Based on a user HTTP or WAP request (1), Internet Service Provider (ISP) sends the HTTP request to the Adaptation Proxy with the User identification (2). The *Ontology Manager* of the Adaptation Proxy employs the *USER_ID* for retrieving the user's profile, the *SLA_ID* of the user's profile for retrieving the SLA profile, and the *HTTP User_Agent* for retrieving the device profile. The need for executing a content adaptation on the user's request is verified (*exec_point_1* and *exec_point_2* of the adaptation server profile). If so, the required services for this adaptation are executed (5)(6). If the requested content is not in the *Cache* of the Adaptation Proxy, it sends a request to the Origin Server (3), which responds with the content (4). *Ontology Manager* extracts information from this content to complete the content profile. It is verified if the content of the Origin Server response needs to be adapted (*exec_point_3* and *exec_point_4* of the adaptation server profile). If so, the required services for this adaptation are executed (5)(6). Lastly, the duly adapted content is sent to the ISP (7), which forwards it to the User (8).

4.3 EICAF evaluation

A case study was conducted involving the configuration illustrated in Figure 28: computers (1) and (2) were configured with Windows XP (700Mhz/256MB, 3Ghz/1GB) and computer (3) with the Linux Fedora Core 2 (2Ghz/256MB). The Apache JMeter was installed in computer (1) to simulate user access, and the Adaptation Proxy with the CCFS and MTS profiles was installed in computer (2). Because the variations in the response times of the Origin Servers, including those due to the Internet throughput, could interfere on this evaluation, an Apache 2 server with the virtual hosts resource was installed in computer (3). This enabled the tested pages to be cloned, restricting the data flow to the computers involved in the case study. A Tomcat/Axis server with the respective *Remote Adapters*, which played the role of Adaptation Server, was also installed in computer (3).

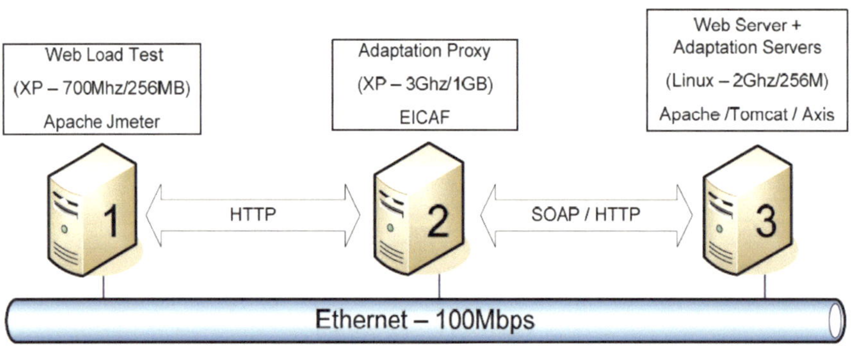

Fig. 28. Configuration in the case study

Five predefined links have been accessed for 5 minutes with three of these links blocked by the domain addresses. They were accessed using desktops and mobile phones, distributed randomly among the users, so that in some cases the MLTS would have to be used. The load was progressively increased, adding one user every 1.5s up to the limit of 20 users, each user accessing a link every 5s. To simulate different devices, 20 samplers were configured with the JMeter, each containing a different User-Agent.

Two test scenarios were defined: using ontologies, and carrying out the discovery and composition services on demand, an average response time of 425 ms was obtained; without using ontologies, and defining the discovery and composition services manually, an average response time of 38 ms was achieved. The difference of 387 ms between these two average response times can be attributed: 38.4% to the OWL-S API initialization, including all its dependencies (e.g., Jena); 25.6% to the ontologies load and validation, corresponding to the dynamic and static profiles; and 36% to the matching and composition function. These values were obtained with the IDE Netbeans profiler tool. Figure 29 indicates an increase in response time and in processing demand caused by the use of ontologies in EICAF.

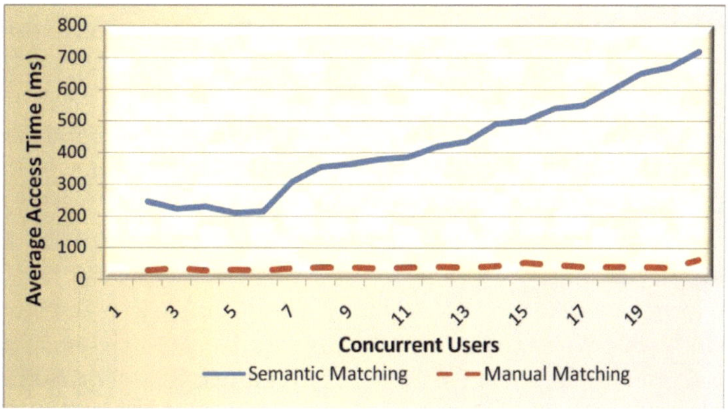

Fig. 29. Average Response Time *versus* Number of Users

From a qualitative standpoint, should be considered the enhanced flexibility and precision resulting from the use of semantics in the discovery and composition mechanism that aids the service authorship, and gives the user a high degree of satisfaction. It should also be considered that this response time tends to decrease with the semantic APIs improvement.

5. Conclusion

Applications involving multimedia usually require a certain level of QoS and, if this quality cannot be guaranteed over the Internet, these applications should be able to adapt to the available quality. ICAP defines the syntax and semantic for exchanging the content between the ICAP client and the ICAP server, but it does not define any adaptation policy. In this sense, we proposed a general architecture that considers a set of elements described in a set of profiles, which affect the quality of the content delivered to the user, for controlling the adaptation functions provided by the ICAP server. This architecture was employed in the development of a CCFS. We also proposed ICAF, a component-based framework that provides a flexible infrastructure for the Internet content adaptation domain, and we described an experiment reusing this framework. Finally, we proposed the use of ontologies and Web services to facilitate the development of content adaptation applications. To this end, ICAF was extended to allow for the use of ontologies and Web services, existing components were reused and adapted, and new components were introduced, thus broadening the range of applications that can be developed from EICAF.

6. References

Beck, A.; Hofmann, M. & Condry, M. (2000). Example Services for Network Edge Proxies, *Internet-Draft*, The Internet Society, http://standards.nortelnetworks.com/opes/non-wg-doc/draft-beck-opes-esfnep-01.txt

Beck, A.; Hofmann, M (2001). Enabling the Internet to Deliver Content-Oriented Services, In: *Web Caching and Content Deliver*, A. Bestavros & M. Rabinovich (Eds), pp. 109-124, Elsevier, ISBN 0-444-50950-X, The Netherlands

Beck, A. & Hofmann, M. (2003). IRML: A Rule Specification Language for Intermediary Services, *Internet-Draft*, The Internet Society, http://tools.ietf.org/html/draft-beck-opes-irml-03

Beck, A. & Rousskov, A. (2003). P: Message Processing Language, *OPES Internet-Draft*, The Internet Society, http://tools.ietf.org/html/draft-ietf-opes-rules-p-00

Berners-Lee, T.; Hendler, J. & Lassila, O. (2001). The Semantic Web. *Scientific American*, May 2001, http://citeseerx.ist.psu.edu/viewdoc/download?doi=10.1.1.115.9584&rep=rep1&type=pdf

Bharadvaj, H.; Joshi, A. & Auephanwiriyakul, S. (1998). An Active Transcoding Proxy to Support Mobile Web Access, *Proceedings of the 17th Symposium on Reliable Distributed Systems*, pp. 118-123, ISBN 0-8186-9218-9, West Lafayette-IN (USA), October 1998, IEEE Computer Society, USA

Buchholz, S. & Schill, A. (2003). Adaptation-Aware Web Caching: Caching in the Future Pervasive Web, *Proceedings of the 13th GI/ITG Conference Kommunikation in verteilten Systemen (KiVS)*, pp. 55-66, ISBN 3-540-00365-7, Leipzig (Germany), Februray 2003, Springer-Verlag, Germany

Forte, M.; Souza, W. L. & Prado, A. F. (2006). A content classification and filtering server for the Internet, *Proceedings of the 21st Annual ACM Symposium on Applied Computing*, Vol. 2, pp. 1166 - 1171, ISBN 1-59593-108-2, Dijon (France), April 2006, ACM, USA

Forte, M.; Claudino, R. A. T.; Souza, W. L.; Prado, A. F. & Santana, L. H. Z. (2007). A Component-Based Framework for the Internet Content Adaptation Domain, *Proceedings of the 22nd Annual ACM Symposium on Applied Computing*, Vol. 2, pp. 1450-1455, ISBN 1-59593-480-4, Seoul (Korea), March 2007, ACM, USA

Forte, M; Souza, W. L. & Prado, A. F. (2008). Using ontologies and Web services for content adaptation in Ubiquitous Computing, *Journal of Systems and Software,* Vol. 81 , No 3, March 2008, pp. 368-381, ISSN 0164-1212

Elson, J. & Cerpa, A. (2003). Internet Content Adaptation Protocol (ICAP), *Request for Comments 3507*, The Internet Society, http://www.icap-forum.org/documents/ specification/rfc3507.txt

Hansmann, U.; Merk, L.; Nicklous, M. S. & Stober, T. (2003). *Pervasive Computing*. Springer-Verlag, ISBN 3-540-00218-9, Germany

Horrocks, I. et al (2003). SWRL: A Semantic Web Rule Language Combining OWL and RuleML, DAML, http://www.daml.org/2003/11/swrl/

IBM (2004). IBM Integrated Ontology Development Toolkit, http://www.alphaworks.ibm. com/tech/semanticstk

ICOGNITO Technologies Ltd (2002). Dynamic Filtering of Internet Content: An Overview of Next Generation Filtering Technology, http://www.icognito.com

Lara, R. et al. (2005). D2.4.2 Semantics for Web Service Discovery and Composition, *KnowledgeWeb*, http://knowledgeweb.semanticweb.org/semanticportal/ deliverables/D2.4.2.pdf

Marques, M. C. & Loureiro, A. F. (2004). Adaptation in Mobile Computing, *Proceedings of the 22nd Brazilian Symposium on Computer Networks*, pp. 439-452, Gramado-RS (Brazil), Mai 2004, Brazilian Computer Society, Brazil

Martin, D. et al. (2006). OWL-S: Semantic Markup for Web Services. DAML, http://www.ai.sri.com/daml/services/owl-s/1.2/overview/

Mastoli, V.; Desai, V.; Shi, W (2003). SEE: a service execution environment for edge services, *Proceedings of the Third IEEE Workshop on Internet Applications*, pp. 61-65, ISBN 0-7695-1972-5, San Jose-CA (USA), June 2003, IEEE Computer Society, USA

Network Apliance Inc (2001). Demo ICAP-Server by Network Appliance, http://www.icap-forum.org/icap?do=resources&subdo=specification

Ravindran, G.; Jaseemudin, M. & Rayhan, A (2002). A Management Framework for Service Personalization, In: *Management of Multimedia on the Internet*, Lecture Notes in Computer Science (LNCS) 2496, Kelvin C. Almeroth & Masum Hasan (Eds), pp. 276-288, Springer-Verlag, ISBN 3-540-44271-5, Germany

Rideout, V.; Richardson, C. & Resnick, P. (2002). See No Evil: How Internet Filters Affect the Search for Online Health Information, *The Henry J. Kaiser Family Foundation*, http://www.kff.org/entmedia/20021210a-index.cfm

Rousskov, A (2005). Open Pluggable Edge Services (OPES) Callout Protocol (OCP) Core, *Request for Comments 4037*, The Internet Society, https://tools.ietf.org/html/rfc4037

Smith, J.; Mohan, R. & Li, C. (1998). Content-based Transcoding of Images in the Internet, *Proceedings of the 1998 IEEE International Conference on Image Processing*, Vol. 3, pp. 7-11, ISBN 0-8186-8821-1, Chicago-IL (USA), October 1998, IEEE Computer Society, USA

SourceForge (2002). Squid Web Proxy as ICAP Client, http://icap-server.sourceforge.net/ squid.html

SourceForge (2003). Shweby Proxy Server, http://shweby.sourceforge.net/

Tomlinson, G.; Chen, R. & Hofmann, M. (2001). A Model for Open Pluggable Edge Services, *Internet- Draft*, The Internet Society, http://tools.ietf.org/html/draft-tomlinson-opes-model-00

UDDI Spec TC (2004). UDDI Version 3.0.2, OASIS, http://www.uddi.org/pubs/ uddi_v3.htm

W3C (2004a). Composite Capability/Preference Profiles (CC/PP): Structure and Vocabularies 1.0, http://www.w3.org/TR/CCPP-struct-vocab/

W3C (2004b). RDF/XML Syntax Specification (Revised), http://www.w3.org/TR/REC-rdf-syntax/

W3C (2004c). OWL Web Ontology Language Overview, http://www.w3.org/TR/owl-features/

W3C (2007). Web Services Description Language (WSDL) Version 2.0 Part 1: Core Language, http://www.w3.org/TR/wsdl20/

5

Caching in Ubiquitous Computing Environments: Light and Shadow

Mianxiong Dong, Long Zheng, Kaoru Ota, Jun Ma, Song Guo, and Minyi Guo
School of Computer Science and Engineering, University of Aizu
Japan

1. Introduction

The word ubiquitous [1] means an interface, an environment, and a technology that can provide all benefits anywhere and anytime without you are aware of what it is, and the ubiquitous computing is the term which is a concept to let computer exist everywhere in the real world [2]. In recent years, ubiquitous devices such as RFID, sensors, cameras, T-engine, and wearable computer have progressed rapidly and have begun to play important roles at everywhere and at any time in our daily life [3-5]. Although there are potential ubiquitous applications in nearly every aspect of our world, it is not so easy to build such an application over infrastructure-less networks.

As our earlier research, we proposed a ubiquitous computing scenario which consists of many heterogeneous processing nodes, named Ubiquitous Multi-Processor (UMP).We introduced a basic framework of multiprocessor simulator system based on a multi-way cluster for the research of heterogeneous multiprocessor system with both high scalability and high performance [6]. The objective of [6] is to organize a basic simulator system framework. Furthermore, as the next step, we proposed and implemented a double-buffered communication model to improve communication speed keeping independence from each processor model on the system. The proposed model showed over 50% system performance improvement rate compared with the basic framework integrated with the single-buffered model [7]. As the further stage of the hardware simulation, we implemented a ubiquitous multi-processor network based pipeline processing framework to support the development of high performance pervasive application [8]. In [8], we also developed a distributed JPEG encoding application successfully based on the proposed framework. Based on these previous researches, the next work would be improving the performance of the UMP system. In the research of the evaluation of the network transmission speed [13-14], we focused on the performance of the network communication part of the UMP system. Through our experiment, we have found the best way to decide the packet size of the UMP network.

Continuously to [13-15] in this article we evaluated four algorithms of the UMP system which the purpose is to find an optimal solution considering the loading balance of the Resource Router, total execution time, execution efficiency and task waiting time (delay).

2. An overview of the ubiquitous multi-processor system

The final goal of the UMP project is to provide a network framework for the coming ubiquitous society. In the ubiquitous society, services could be likened the air, i.e., they will exist everywhere and anytime to meet each user's request. In order to fill such requests, computing resources are necessarily provided under two conflicting conditions: higher performance and lower power consumption. To this end, we have proposed the UMP system which is introduced in detail in this section.

2.1 Software architecture of UMP system

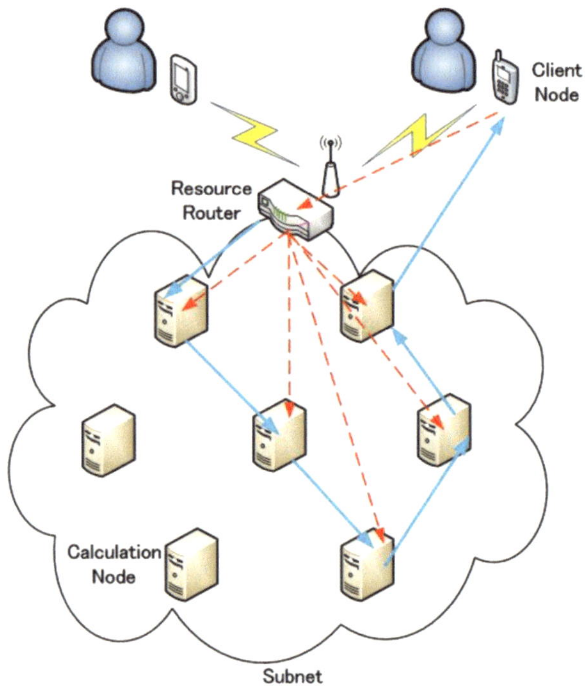

Fig. 1. UMP system overview

Fig. 1 is an overview of the UMP system. In our system, there are three kinds of nodes. One is the Client Node which works instead of the mobile users. This node requests tasks through mobile terminals on a wireless network. The other is the Resource Router (RR) which is a gateway of the system. There exists only one node of RR in one subnet. This node received task requests from the Client Nodes. Then, the node manages a list of tasks and determines which tasks should be executed currently on the subnet. The last one is the Calculation Node which actually executes tasks requested from the Client Nodes. Every task is allocated by the RR on the subnet. When a task is executed, several Calculation Nodes are connected to each other like a chain. For example, to encode a bitmap file into JPEG file, the whole steps are six. So it means the chain has six Calculation Nodes. Combination of the Calculation Nodes is always unique so that actions of tasks can be changed flexibly by the demands of the Client Nodes. We call the Calculation Nodes as Processing Elements (PEs) afterwards.

2.2 Motivation of our work

As a case study of the UMP system, we implemented a prototype application of the JPEG encoding [8]. The application is developed to convert bitmap format image to JPEG format image. At that stage, the implementation was simple and the algorithm of the processing schedule was not considered enough. The scale of the prototype system was small; it couldn't server a large request of tasks. In the real world, many users will request the service/task at simultaneously to the UMP system. So, it is obviously optimizing the time efficiency, loading balance of the RR, reducing the delay of task execution, total execution time of the whole task are pressing needs. Of course, there is a trade off between these factors. How to design the UMP system to meet the providing of the real service is a challenge thing. Generally speaking, processing speed would be quite faster than network speed in usual. One of benchmarks of network performance is the network overhead [9]. In [13-14], we compared processing time of using stand-alone application to processing time of using UMP system. The result shows the difference between processing time of the former and later is network overhead time. So, increasing the usage of each PE is one way to generate the good performance. In other words, assign tasks as much as possible under the limitation of the processing ability and reducing the communication cost.

3. Resource allocation algorithms for the resource router

In this section, we introduce two resource allocation algorithms for the RR to find single PE whose state is idle. Resource allocating should be optimized since time consumption for that is not trivial over total execution time. We propose an optimized algorithm and evaluate it by probability analysis. Resource allocation algorithms with multi PEs are also introduced in the following section 4.

3.1 Basic algorithm for the RR to search idle PEs

The RR has a role to look for a PE necessary to execute a task as the following steps.

1. The RR searches an idle PE randomly and sends a PE a message to check its state.
2. The PE sends the RR an answer of idle/busy.
3. After the RR gets the answer of idle, it finishes the search. If the answer is busy, back to (1) and continue.

Firstly, the RR randomly searches a PE in a state of the idle by sending a message to ask a PE whether the PE is in an idle state or a busy state. The PE replies to the RR with its current state when it receives the message. When a response from PE is an idle state, the RR sends the PE a message to request execution of the task. Otherwise, the RR looks for other available PE. It keeps retrieving idle PEs until the execution of all tasks ends.

We can consider two possible scenarios for the RR to search an idle PE: the best case and the worst case. The best case means the RR successfully finds an idle PE at the first search, i.e., the first retrieved PE is in the idle state so that the RR no longer looks for other PE. In contrast, the worst case means the RR finds an idle PE after searching every PE on the subnet, i.e., it retrieves the idle PE at last although the all other PEs are busy.

In the basic algorithm, the RR looks for an available PE at random. Therefore, the best case can be not always expected and the worst case cannot be avoided. One reason for the worst case is there exist PEs being often in the busy state. A long delay can be generated if the RR keeps retrieving such a busy PE instead of other idle ones.

We consider that if the RR omits such PEs to retrieve, it can find an idle PE quickly and efficiently. The basic idea can be described as follows: 1) firstly making a group of PEs being often in a busy state, and 2) the RR does not retrieve any PE from the group. A concrete method is needed for finding such busy PEs and presented in the following subsection.

3.2 Optimized algorithm

In the optimized algorithm, firstly the RR searches an idle PE randomly and checks each PE's state. After the RR repeats this procedure many times, it makes a group of busy PEs based on a history of each PE's state the RR checked. In the next search, the RR tries to find an idle PE excluding from the group. If the RR cannot find any idle PE, it searches an idle PE from inside and outside of the group. This algorithm is based on an assumption that there exists at least one idle PE of all. Details of the algorithm are described as the following steps.

---

1. The RR secures a storage region of each PE to save its degree of idle state, which starts from 0.
2. The RR searches an idle PE randomly and sends a PE a message to check its state.
3. The PE sends the RR an answer of idle/busy.
4. If the RR gets the answer of idle from the PE, it finishes the search and the PE's degree of busy state is decremented by 1. If the answer is busy, the PE's degree is incremented by 1 and the RR searches the next PE.
5. If repeating from Step 2 to Step4 s times, the RR looks into each PE's storage. If a PE's degree of busy state is more than a threshold, the PE is regarded as ``PE with high probability of busy''
6. After the end of looking into storages, the RR makes a group of PEs with high probability of busy.
7. The RR searches an idle PE again expect for PEs belonging to the group t times. If the RR cannot find any idle PE, it begins to search for an idle PE including inside of the group.
8. Step5-7 are repeated until the entire search ends.

In the optimized algorithm, we can also consider the best case and the worst case for the RR to spend time for searching an idle PE. The best case can occur when the RR finds an idle PE at the first search like the best case of the basic algorithm. On the other hand, the worst case is the RR firstly searches an idle PE from outside of the group but all PEs are in the busy state. Hence, the RR starts to look for an idle PE from the group and then it finally finds an idle PE after the all other PEs in the group are queried by the RR.

3.2 Probability analyses and discussion

As the first stage, we evaluate the optimized algorithm with probability analyses using probabilities of finding an idle PE in the best case and the worst case with the basic algorithm and the optimized algorithm respectively. Both probabilities depend on probabilities of a PE in an idle state and a busy state respectively.

We use the queuing theory \cite{11} to obtain the probabilities of a PE in an idle state and a busy state. The queuing theory is used to stochastically analyze congestion phenomena of queues and allows us to measure several performances such as the probability of encountering the system in certain states like idle and busy. Here, we consider one PE as on one system and then its queuing model can be described as M/M/1(1) by Kendall's notation. That means each PE receives a message from the RR randomly and deals with only one task at once. Hence, when a PE processes a task and at same time a message comes from the RR, the message is not accepted by the PE because of the busy state.

P_0	Probability that a PE is in an idle state where $0 \leq P_0 \leq 1$.
P_1	Probability that a PE is in a busy state where $P_1=1-P_0$.
n	The total number of PEs in a subset.
m	Number of PEs in the group (regarded as a PE with high probability of busy).
P'_1	Probability that a PE in the group is busy.
λ	Average arrival rate of a message from the RR to a PE.
μ	Average task execution rate of a PE.
ρ	Congestion condition.
ρ'	Congestion condition of the group

Table 1. The notations used in equations

Before the analysis, some notations are defined in Table 1. Equation (1) and (2) show the probabilities of finding an idle PE from one subnet in the best case and the worst case respectively when the basic algorithm is used.
In the best case of the probability of finding an idle PE:

$$P = P_0 \tag{1}$$

In the worst case of the probability of finding an idle PE:

$$P = P_1^{(n-1)} \tag{2}$$

On the other hand, Equation (3) and (4) show the probabilities of the best case and the worst case respectively when the optimized algorithm is used. Here, we have new notations as follows.
In the best case of the probability of finding an idle PE:

$$P = P_0 \tag{3}$$

In the worst case of the probability of finding an idle PE:

$$P = P_1^{(n-m)} * P_1'^{(m-1)} \tag{4}$$

The best case is just the same as the one using the basic algorithm since the RR finds an idle PE at the first search in the both algorithms. Therefore, we consider only the worst cases to comparing the optimized algorithm with the basic algorithm.
The range of m in the worst case, since PEs in the group is a part of all PEs in the subnet, can be $0 \leq m \leq n$. In the case of $m=0$ or $m=n$, it is just the same as the worst case using the basic

algorithm. Moreover, we assume $P_1 < P'_1$ since PEs in the group are regarded as PEs with high probability of busy and should encounter a busy state more than else PEs in the subnet. From the queuing theory,

$$P_1 = \rho(1-\rho) \tag{5}$$

$$P_1^{'} = \rho'(1-\rho') \tag{6}$$

A notation ρ can be calculated as

$$\rho = \lambda / \mu \tag{7}$$

And ρ' in Equation (6) shows the congestion condition of a PE in the group. We also assume $\rho < \rho'$ from the condition $P_1 < P'_1$ as mentioned before.

Here we can consider ρ as each PE's degree of busy state, since the RR classifies PEs based on the degree by comparing with a threshold decided beforehand. Therefore, ρ' of all PEs in the group should be more than or equal to the threshold, so that $\rho < threshold$ for other PEs. To always keep these conditions, we assume $\rho' = threshold$ and simply fixed the relation between ρ' and ρ as follows.

$$\rho' = \rho + 0.1 \tag{8}$$

where $0.1 < \rho < 0.9$ and $0.2 < \rho' < 1.0$ with considering possible values of threshold in a practical use.

Based on the assumption, we obtain the probabilities of the worst case in the basic algorithm and the optimized algorithm using the Equation (2) and the Equation (4) respectively. Fig. 2 shows the probabilities with changing n, the total number of PEs in a subnet, from 10 to 100. In each case of n, we also change m, the number of PEs in the group, from 0% to 50% of n. When m is 0% of n, i.e., $m=0$ in Fig. 2, that means the basic algorithm is applied since there is no PE in the group. For example, Fig. 2(a) shows the probabilities of the worst case for each m from 0 to 5 with $n=10$.

In Fig. 2, we focus on the three parameters which are ρ, n, and m for discussion of the results. Firstly, when $0.4 < \rho < 0.8$, the probabilities where $m>0$ become lower than one where $m=0$ in most cases, so that the threshold of ρ should be set to more than 0.5 and less than 0.9 to avoid the worst case using the optimized algorithm.

Secondly, the more the total number of PEs n, the bigger difference of the probabilities between the basic algorithm ($m=0$) and the optimized algorithm ($m>0$) as shown in Fig. 2. Therefore, we can conclude the optimized algorithm has less risk of the worst case than the basic algorithm as the total number of PEs is larger.

Finally, the number of PEs in the group m gives less impact on results comparing to other two parameters. However, in Fig. 2, we can see slightly less probabilities of the worst case as m is larger.

As a result, using the optimized algorithm encounters the worst case less than using the basic algorithm if the following conditions are met; (1) the threshold to make a busy group by checking of each PE ranges from 0.6 to 0.8, and (2) the total number of PEs in a subnet is relatively large. Considering these two conditions in implementation, effective performance using the optimized algorithm can be expected.

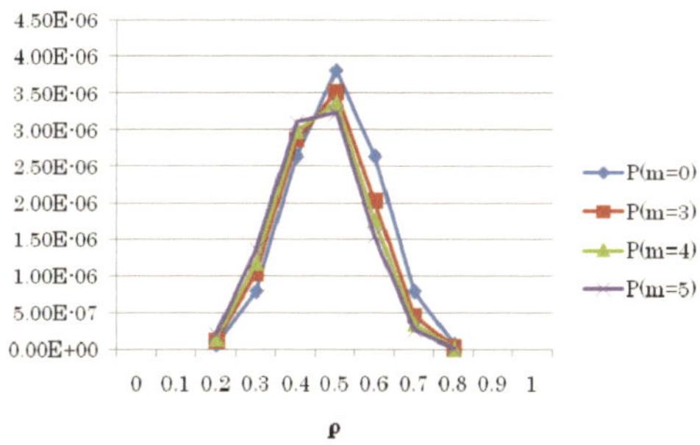

(a) When the total number of PEs n is 10

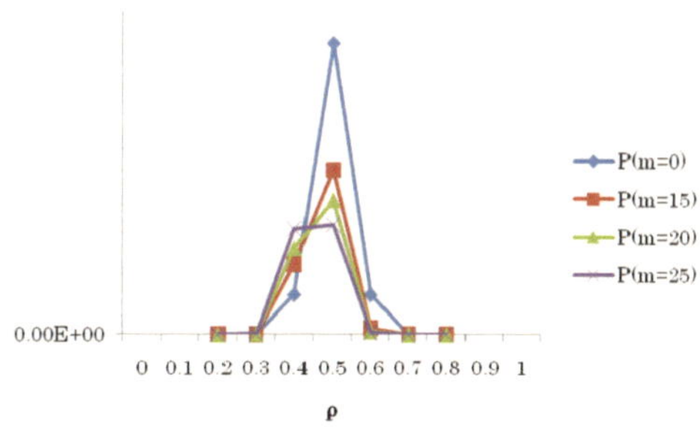

(b) When the total number of PEs n is 50

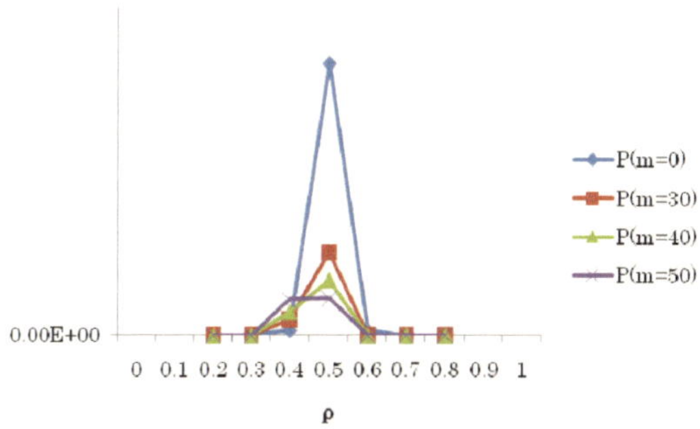

(c) When the total number of PEs n is 100

Fig. 2. The probabilities of the worst case with diverse values of m

4. Resource allocation algorithms with chained PEs

In practical use, multiple PEs are used to complete one task at most of time. In this section, we introduce four resource allocation algorithms to find multiple PEs all who are in idle state.

In this chapter, we use JPEG encoding as an archetypal example to test the proposed algorithms. There are six stages to encode a bitmap file into JPEG image. They are reading bitmap file, RGB to YCbCr, down sampling translator, processing Discrete Cosine Transform, Huffman Encoding, and JPEG image writer. When a user requests a task of JPEG encoding, the RR will first reserve six PE as a chain for the whole processing. After the user connected to the first PE, the chain processing will be started. When the last PE finished its sub-task, the user can get the result and the RR change the entire PEs chain to a standby status. Due to the user side is assumed as a mobile client, the battery life-time is a very important factor in the system design. To reduce the energy consumption of user side, we fix the first PE and the last PE to provide the frequently access from user to search the last PE. Thus, all the optimization process is effect to the middle PEs in the whole process chain. Therefore, the algorithm can be described as follows.

4.1 Current Algorithm (CA)

When task comes, RR will reserve the whole PEs which will be needed to process the task until the task is finished. During the processing time, even some PEs are free, they cannot be used by other tasks.

The characteristic of the current resource allocation algorithm can be analyzed into two parts:

i. Mean delay:

$$d = \frac{1}{n}\left(m \cdot \sum_{i=1}^{\lfloor n/m \rfloor} (i-1)t + (n - \lfloor n/m \rfloor m) \cdot \lfloor n/m \rfloor t \right) \tag{9}$$

where m is the number of tasks RR can handle at one time, t is the time to handle m tasks. So the first m tasks wait 0 time, the second m tasks wait t time, the i-th m tasks should wait $(i-1)t$ time.

We can also get task execution efficiency as follows:

ii. Task Execution Efficiency:

$$f = \sum_{i=1}^{n} e_i \bigg/ \left(\sum_{i=1}^{n} e_i + \sum_{i=1}^{n-1} c_{i,i+1} \right) \tag{10}$$

Where e_i $(1 \le i \le n)$ is the execution time in i-th PE, $c_{j,j+1}$ is the communication time between j-th PE and $(j+1)$-th $(1 \le j \le n)$ PE.

In our simulation, we assume the communication time between any two PEs is the same, i.e. $c_{j,j+1} = c_{m,n} = c \forall i,j,m,n \in N$, N is the natural number set. Hence,

$$f = \sum_{i=1}^{n} e_i \bigg/ \left(\sum_{i=1}^{n} e_i + (n-1) \cdot c \right) \tag{11}$$

Abstract of the CA is described as follows.

---

1. Router retrieves a new task from the task queue. If there is no task in the task queue, then ends.
2. Router generates a PE chain which is used to process a task. Set the PEs in the PE chain as busy, which means these PE can not do any other task until they are released.
3. Router sends the PE chain information and task to PE1.
4. PE1 finishes its work and follows the PE chain information to transfer the task to PE2.
5. PE2 finishes its work and follows the PE chain information to transfer the task to PE3.
6. PE4 finishes its work and follows the PE chain information to transfer the task to PE5.
7. PE5 finishes its work and follows the PE chain information to transfer the task to PE6.
8. PE6 finishes its work and sends the processed task back to router.
9. Router sets all PEs in the PE chain as idle.
10. Remove the task from the task queue. If there is no task left in the task queue, then terminates. Otherwise go to Step (1).

4.2 Randomly Allocating Algorithm (RAA)

The biggest limitation of the current policy is that if the RR allocates the PEs to the users once, the all PEs are reserved until the whole task will be finished. This is obviously a big useless of the computational resource. To regard as this point, we apply a randomly distribute algorithm to the UMP system. The concept of RAA is after the PE finished the execution of the process, the PE will ask the RR for the next phase of PE. The usage rate of PE is quite high, but the load balance is heavy for the RR. We can get task execution efficiency as follows:

i. Task execution efficiency:

$$f = \sum_{i=1}^{n} e_i \Bigg/ \left(\sum_{i=1}^{n} e_i + \sum_{i=1}^{n-1} cr_i + \sum_{i=2}^{n} c_{i-1,i} \right) \tag{12}$$

where $e_i 1 \leq i \leq n$, is the execution time, $c_{i-1,i} 2 \leq i \leq n$ is the communication time between *i*-th PE and RR, $cr_i 1 \leq i \leq n$ is the communication time between *(i-1)*-th PE and *i*-th PE.
Abstract of the RAA is described as follows.

---

1. Router retrieves a new task from the task queue. If there is no task in the task queue, then ends.
2. Router finds an idle PE1 and any PE6 and then transfers the task to this PE1.
3. After getting the task from router, this PE1 sends a busy status message to router.
4. After processing the task, this PE1 send an idle status message to router and meantime ask the router for the next PE.
5. Router finds an idle PE2, and then tells the PE1.
6. PE2 sends the status busy to router; PE1 transfers the task to PE2, and sends idle status message to router.
7. PE2, PE3, PE4 act the same.
8. After PE5's processing the task, PE5 transfers the task the PE6 which is decided by router at Step 2.
9. After PE6's processing the task, transfer the processed task back to router.
10. Remove the task from the task queue. If there is no task left in the task queue, then terminates. Otherwise go to Step (1).

4.3 Randomly Allocating Algorithm with Cache technology (RAA-C).

To improve the RAA, we introduce a cache concept of the resource allocating algorithm. For every PE, we assign a cache for them to memorize the next stage's PE. When they finished their sub-task, they will search the next phase of PE in their cache. If the all PEs in the cache are at the busy status, it will ask RR to assign one free PE as the next phase PE.
We can get task execution efficiency as follows:

i. The best case of task execution efficiency:

$$f = \sum_{i=1}^{n} e_i \Bigg/ \left(\sum_{i=1}^{n} e_i + \sum_{i=2}^{n} (3c_{i-1,i}) \right) \tag{13}$$

where $e_i 1 \leq i \leq n$ is the execution time, $c_{i-1,i} 2 \leq i \leq n$ is the communication time between (i-1)-th PE and i-th PE. The best case means each (i-1)-th PE can access each i-th PE memorized in their cache because i-th PE is not busy. (i-1)-th PE is supposed to have communication with i-th PE three times in total. As the first communication, (i-1)-th PE asks i-th PE whether or not it is busy currently. Then, i-th PE replays to (i-1)-th PE in the second communication. Since this is the best case so that i-th PE's answer must be "available", (i-1)-th PE starts to send data to i-th PE in the third communication.

ii. The worst case of task execution efficiency:

$$f = \sum_{i=1}^{n} e_i \Bigg/ \left(\sum_{i=1}^{n} e_i + \sum_{i=2}^{n} (3c_{i-1,i}) + \sum_{i=1}^{n-1} cr_i \right) \tag{14}$$

where $e_i 1 \le i \le n$ is the execution time, $cr_i 1 \le i \le n-1$ is the communication time between *i*-th PE and RR, $c_{i-1,i} 2 \le i \le n$ is the communication time between *(i-1)*-th PE and *i*-th PE. The worst case means each *(i-1)*-th PE cannot access each *i*-th PE memorized in their cache because *i*-th PE is busy. Therefore, each *(i-1)*-th PE has to ask RR for a free PE.
Abstract of the RAA-C is described as follows.

---

1. Router retrieves a new task from the task queue. If there is no task in the task queue, then ends.
2. Router finds an idle PE1 and any PE6 and then transfers the task to this PE1.
3. After getting the task from router, this PE1 sends a busy status message to router.
4. After processing the task, this PE1 sends an idle status message to router.
5. Find the idle PE from its cache.
6. If the PE1 finds an idle PE2, then send a request message to verify whether the PE2 is truly idle or not.
7. If the response from PE2 is yes, then go to step 10; or send a request message to router, by which router will look for an idle PE2 without restriction of PE1's cache.
8. If router finds one, then tell PE1, otherwise, repeat steps from Step (5).
9. Router finds an idle PE2, and then tells the PE1.
10. PE2 send the busy status message to router; PE1 transfers the task to PE2, and then sends the idle status message to router.
11. PE2, PE3, PE4 act the same, besides updates the information of cache of PE1, PE2, PE3, respectively.
12. After PE5's processing the task, PE5 updates the information of cache of PE4; and then transfers the task the PE6 which is decided by router at Step 2.
13. After PE6's processing the task, transfer the processed task back to router.
14. Remove the task from the task queue. If there is no task left in the task queue, then terminates. Otherwise go to Step (1).

4.4 Randomly Allocating Algorithm with Grouping method (RAA-G).

The RAA-G is slightly different from RAA-C. We use a grouping method to group the PEs. The difference between the RAA-G and RAA-C is the restriction of jumping to the PEs which is out of the cache that current PE has. That means when a certain PE finished its sub-task and the whole PEs in the cache (group) are busy, the PE will not ask RR to assign a free PE out of the cache. For example, assume every cache at each phase has four PEs. When a certain PE at one stage finished the sub-task, it can search the next phase PE in the same cache. If the next phase PE is all busy status, it has to wait. This is the biggest difference between RAA-C and RAA-G. And the Efficiency of RAA-G in the best case is the same to RAA-C. Here, the best case means each *(i-1)*-th PE succeeds to find the next phase PE in only one access without asking all PE members in the cache.

i. The worst case of task execution efficiency:

$$f = \sum_{i=1}^{n} e_i \Bigg/ \left(\sum_{i=1}^{n} e_i + \sum_{i=2}^{n} \left(\sum_{j=1}^{l} 2c_{i-1,j} + c_{i-1,i} \right) \right) \tag{15}$$

where $e_i 1 \le i \le n$ is the execution time, $c_{i-1,i} 2 \le i \le n$ is the communication time between (i-1)-th PE and i-th PE, $c_{i-1,ij} 2 \le i \le n, 1 \le j \le l$ where l is the number of PEs in one group, is also the communication time between (i-1)-th PE and i-th PEs in the group. The worst case means each (i-1)-th PE asks all next phase PEs in a group at every stage. It is because (i-1)-th PE checks whether or not PE in the group is busy one by one in order to seek one available PE.
Abstract of the RAA-G is described as follows.

1. Router retrieves a new task from the task queue. If there is no task in the task queue, then ends.
2. Router finds an idle PE1 and any PE6 and then transfers the task to this PE1.
3. After getting the task from router, this PE1 sends a busy status message to router.
4. After processing the task, this PE1 sends an idle status message to router.
5. Find the idle PE from its cache.
6. If the PE1 finds an idle PE2, then send a request message to verify whether the PE2 is truly idle or not.
7. If the response from PE2 is yes, then go to step 10; or waits a particular time, then go to step 5.
8. PE1 transfers the task to PE2.
9. PE2, PE3, PE4 act the same, besides updates the information of cache of PE1, PE2, PE3, respectively.
10. After PE5's processing the task, PE5 updates the information of cache of PE4; and then transfers the task the PE6 which is decided by router at Step (2).
11. After PE6's processing the task, transfer the processed task back to router.
12. Remove the task from the task queue. If there is no task left in the task queue, then terminates. Otherwise go to Step (1).

4.5 Performance evaluation and discussion

We built a simulation system to evaluate the 4 algorithms. We used the Poisson Distribution to generate the tasks because the Poisson Distribution arises in connection with Poisson processes. It applies to various phenomena of discrete nature (that is, those that may happen 0, 1, 2, 3, ... times during a given period of time or in a given area) whenever the probability of the phenomenon happening is constant in time or space.
After run the generator, we got 291 tasks for the evaluation. And we set 240 PEs. Each processing needs 6 PEs, therefore the total chains of PEs are 40. We also set the network delay as 100. Table 2 shows the environment of the simulation.
Fig. 3 shows the loading balance of RR from the simulation result. We can see the sum loading balance of CA and RAA-G perform a good result because the algorithms their self restrict the communication with RR. And it is naturally the RAA had worst result, because almost every time the PE should ask RR to know the next phase PE which should be connected to.

OS	Windows Vista Business (32-bit)
CPU	AMD Athlon64 3200+
Memory	DDR SDRAM 2GB
Language	JAVA 1.5
Network	Localhost

Table 2. The experiment environment

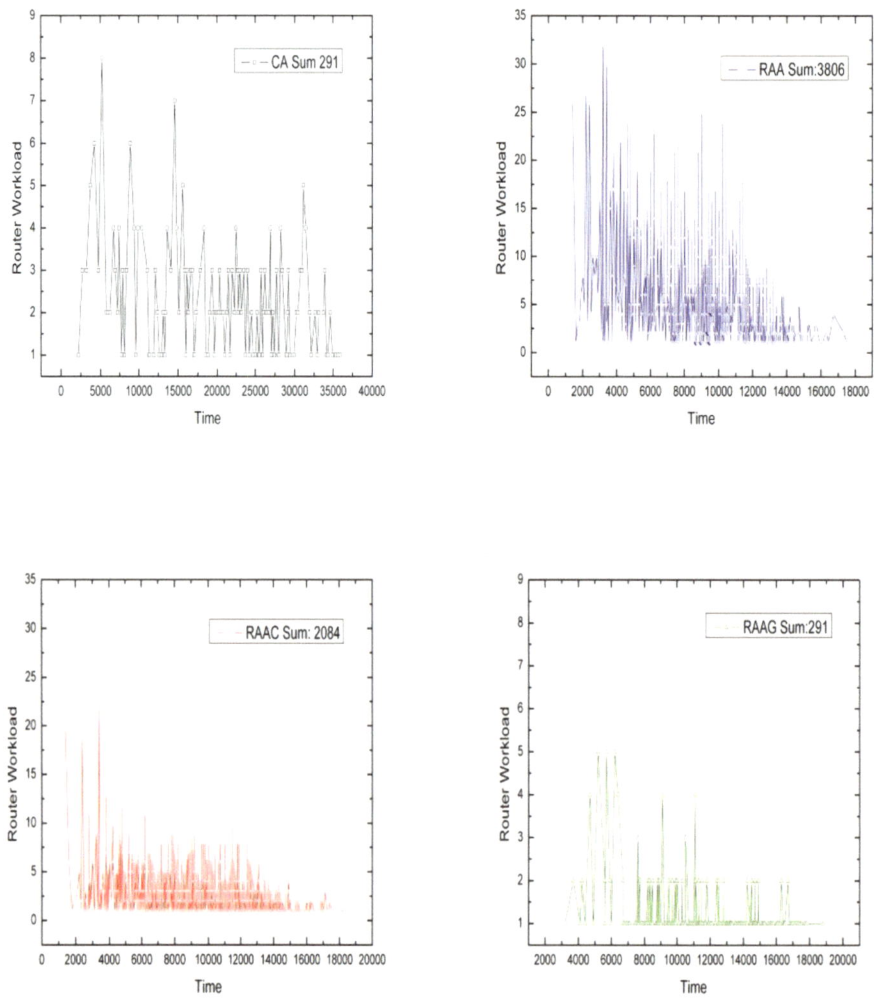

Fig. 3. The loading balance of RR of four algorithms

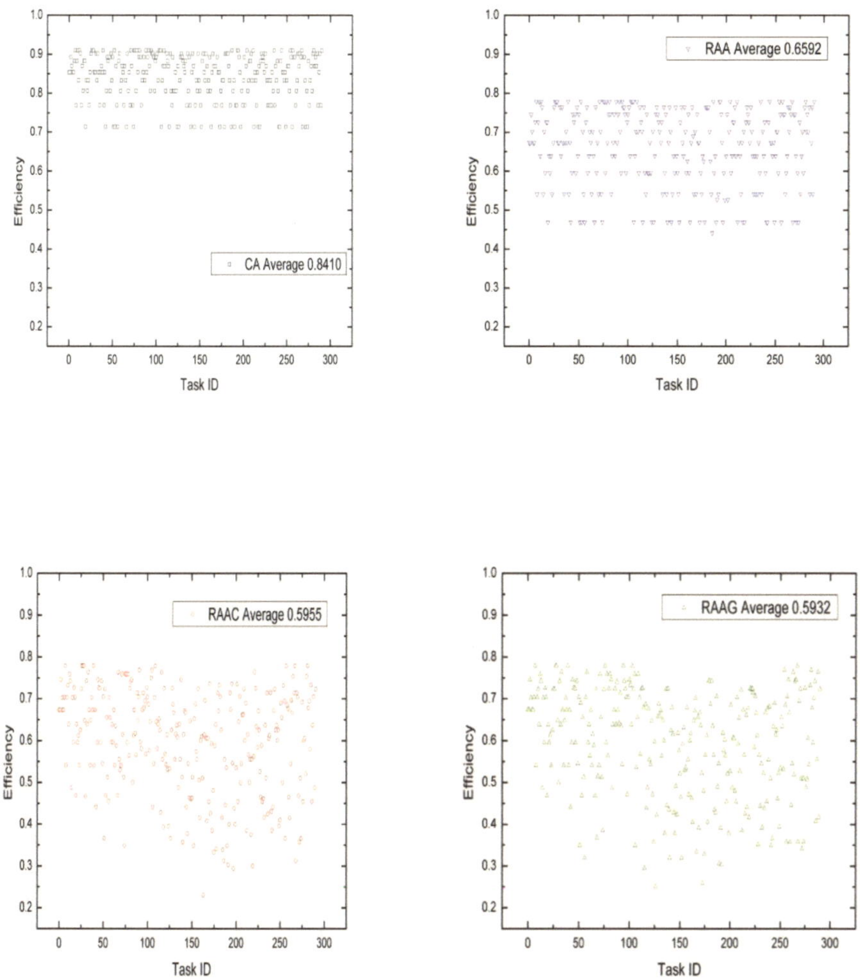

Fig. 4. The efficiency of tasks

Fig. 4 is a distribution view of efficiency of tasks. Because the efficiency is highly related with the communication cost, CA shows a best result as well as it doesn't have much communication with RR and the other PEs. The average efficiency of RAA-C and RAA-G are almost the same, it is perfect matching the mathematic model we have described above. RAA also has a better result than RAA-C and RAA-G. But consider the loading balance of RR it is still not acceptable.

From the left part of Fig. 5, we can see the proposed algorithms have a significant improvement compared with the current implementation. Also, from the right part of Fig. 5, we can see the RAA-G and RAA-C are slightly performing a good result than RAA.

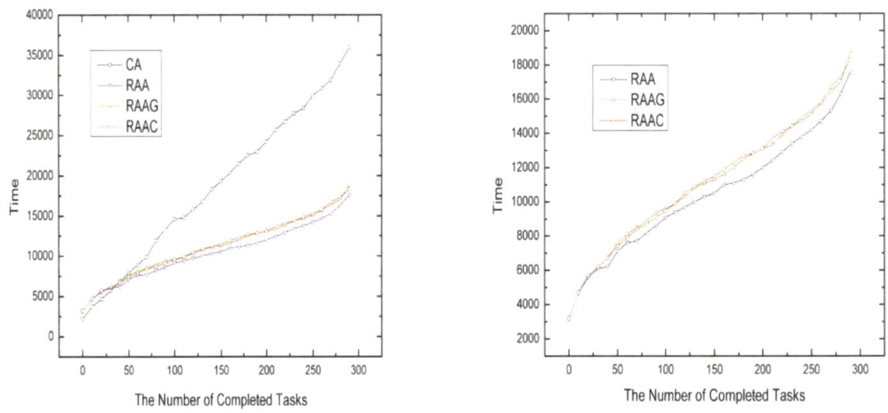

Fig. 5. The total processing time of the tasks

5. Conclusion

In this chapter, we propose an optimized algorithm for resource allocation to a processing node, which can improve the overall performance of the UMP system. Using the optimized algorithm, the RR can effectively find a single PE in an idle state, which actually can process an assigned task. As a result, the RR saves the time to search for an idle node so that total performance of resource allocation can be improved. Finally, we evaluated the optimized algorithm with probability analyses and figured out conditions for the optimized algorithm to be better than the basic algorithm.

Also, as the further step our previous works, we evaluated the performance with four different resource (PE) allocating algorithm for multiple PEs and analyzed these algorithms from three points of view. Though these huge experiments, we have successfully proofed our proposed algorithms are meaning while. Considering those three key factors (the time efficiency, loading balance of the RR, and total processing time of the whole task), each algorithm has its merit and demerit. There is always a trade off between these factors. Taking into account the balanced point of all factors, we found the RAA-G is the best algorithm to allocating resources (PEs) when the condition is the system has many users and many task to process. The next better algorithm is RAA-C, following by RAA. For other cases, it is difficult to say which algorithm is the best, because it is truly case by case. One more things we have realized through the experiments are we can set the allocating policy flexibly answering to the user's request. Maybe that is the best solution to design the UMP system. In the future, we will focus on the above layer of the UMP system - the service layer, to deal with the context information from users, resources and environments.

4. Acknowledgment

This work is supported in part by Japan Society for the Promotion of Science (JSPS) Research Fellowships for Young Scientists Program, JSPS Excellent Young Researcher Overseas Visit Program, National Natural Science Foundation of China (NSFC) Distinguished Young Scholars Program (No. 60725208) and NSCF Grant No. 60811130528.

5. References

[1] M. Weiser, "The Computer for the 21st Century," Scientific Am., pp. 94-104, September, 1991.; reprinted in IEEE Pervasive Computing, pp. 19-25, January-March 2002.

[2] Wikipedia, the free encyclopedia, http://ja.wikipedia.org/wiki/

[3] M. Satyanarayanan, "Pervasive Computing: Vision and Challenges", IEEE Personal Communication, pp. 10-17, August 2001.

[4] S. R. Ponnekanti, et.al, "Icrafter: A service framework for ubiquitous computing environments", In Proc. of Ubicomp 2001, pp. 56–75, Atlanta, Georgia, October 2001.

[5] V. Stanford, "Using Pervasive Computing to Deliver Elder Care", IEEE Pervasive Computing, pp. 10-13, January-March, 2002.

[6] A. Shinozaki, M. Shima, M. Guo, and M. Kubo, "A High Performance Simulator System for a Multiprocessor System Based on a Multi-way Cluster", Advances in Computer Systems Architecture, Lecture Notes in Computer Science vol. 4186, pages 231-243, Springer Berlin/Heidelberg, September, 2006.

[7] A. Shinozaki, M. Shima, M. Guo, and M. Kubo, "Multiprocessor Simulator System Based on Multi-way Cluster Using Double-buffered Model", Proceeding of AINA 2007, Niagara Falls, Canada, May 2007, pp. 893-900.

[8] M. Kubo, B. Ye, A. Shinozaki, T. Nakatomi and M. Guo, "UMP-PerComp: A Ubiquitous Multiprocessor Network-Based Pipeline Processing Framework for Pervasive Computing Environments", Proceeding of AINA 2007, Niagara Falls, Canada, May 2007, pp. 611-618.

[9] Wikipedia, the free encyclopedia, "Computational overhead", Available: http://en.wikipedia.org/wiki/Computational overhead.

[10] Wikipedia, the free encyclopedia, "Maximum transmission unit", http://en.wikipedia.org/wiki/Maximumtransmissionunit.

[11] Microsoft, "Default MTU Size for Dierent Network Topology", Knowledge Base Article, ID.140375.

[12] Lawrence S. Husch and University of Tennessee, Knoxville, Mathematics Department, "Horizontal Asymptotes", http://archives.math.utk.edu/visual.calculus/1/horizontal.5/.

[13] M. Dong, S. Guo, M. Guo and S. Watanabe, "Design of the Ubiquitous Multi-Processor System Focusing on Transmission Data Size", In Proc. of HPSRN, pp. 158-166, Sendai, Japan, March 2008

[14] M. Dong, S. Watanabe, and M. Guo, "Performance Evaluation to Optimize the UMP System Focusing on Network Transmission Speed", In Proc. of FCST, pp. 7-12, Wuhan, China, November 2007

[15] M. Dong, M. Guo, L. Zheng, S. Guo, "Performance Analysis of Resource Allocation Algorithms Using Cache Technology for Pervasive Computing System", in Proceedings of ICYCS 2008, pp. 671-676, November 2008

Part 2

Privacy and Security

6

Security Analysis of the RFID Authentication Protocol using Model Checking

Hyun-Seok Kim, Jin-Young Choi, and Sin-Jae Lee
Korea University
Republic of Korea

1. Introduction

In RFID security(Gildas), few mechanisms focus on data protection of the tags, message interception over the air channel, and eavesdropping within the interrogation zone of the RFID reader(Sarma et al.a)(Weis et al.). Among these issues, we will discuss two aspects on the risks posed to the passive party by RFID , which have so far been dominated by the topics of data protection associated with data privacy and identity authentication between tag and reader.

Firstly, the data privacy problem states that storing person-specific data in an RFID system can threaten the privacy of the passive party. This party might be, for example, a customer or an employee of the operator. The passive party uses tags or items that have been identified as tags, but the party has no control over the data stored on the tags.

Secondly, the authentication will be carried out when the identity of a person or a program is checked. Then, on that basis, authorization takes place, i.e. rights, such as the right of access to data are granted. In the case of RFID systems, it is particularly important for tags to be authenticated by the reader and vice-versa. In addition, readers must authenticate themselves to the backend, however in this case there are no RFID-specific security problems.

There have been some approaches focusing on the RFID privacy and authentication issues, including killing tags at the checkout, renaming the identifier of the tag, physical tag password, hash encryption, random access hash and hash based ID variation. The last three approaches of these will be discussed in detail in this chapter. We will not discuss the remaining approaches in this chapter as they are physical solving approaches. The last three approaches are security protocols(Ryan & Schneider) that play the essential role of minimizing the burden of privacy and authentication problems. As with any protocol, the security protocol comprises a prescribed sequence of interactions between entities, and is designed to achieve a certain end. Security protocols are, in fact, excellent candidates for rigorous analysis techniques: they are critical components of distributed security architecture, very easy to express, however, extremely difficult to evaluate by hand.

Formal methods play a very critical role in examining whether a security protocol is ambiguous, incorrect, inconsistent or incomplete. Hence, the importance of applying formal methods, particularly for safety critical systems, cannot be overemphasized. There are two main approaches in formal methods, logic based methodology (Gong et al.), and tool based methodology (Hoare)(Lowe)(FDR). In this chapter, we specify hash based RFID security protocols(Sarma et al.a) as the previous work that employs hash functions to secure the RFID

communication using Casper (A Compiler for Security Protocol Analyzer)(Lowe) specifying tool. Then we verify whether or not it satisfies security properties such as secrecy and authentication using the FDR (Failure Divergence Refinement) model checking tool(FDR). After running the FDR tool, we reconfirm the existence of known security flaws in this protocol and propose the schemes of two security protocols for secure RFID communication. The contribution of this chapter is in analyzing the secure authentication protocols and designing new security protocols that could be widely researched in RFID systems. Therefore we provide a way for all methods, specifically Casper and FDR, which have been developed over the last decade by the theoretical community for the analysis of cryptographic protocols to be able to analyze RFID privacy and authentication problems. This especially applies to the new security protocols proposed in this chapter, which require read access control. If a reader requests a tag's ID, then the tag has to firstly identify that the reader is authenticated. In the process of authentication, the tag sends out a random number. The reader then responds to the tag with a function value of the random number and its own ID. The reader's output for each query changes, meaning that even if the output is eavesdropped, the adversary can not pass the authentication in the next query. The random number based authentication can prevent spoofing and man-in-the-middle attacks.
This chapter is organized as follows. In brief, Section 2 describes related work on RFID privacy and authentication schemes. Section 3 describes how RFID security protocols can be modeled in CSP (Communication Sequential Processes)(Hoare), generated by using Casper. Our analyzed results of the protocols will be described in Section 4. The proposed hash based and challenge response based security protocols are presented in Section 5. Finally, the conclusion and future work are addressed in the last section.

2. Background

2.1 The components of RFID system

RFID systems(Sarma et al.a)(Weis et al.) are made up of three main components, that we briefly describe as follows:

1. ***Transponder or RFID Tag*** In an RFID system, each object will be labeled with a tag. Each tag contains a microchip with some computation and storage capabilities, and a coupling element, such as an antenna coil for communication. Tags can be classified according to two main criteria: - The type of memory: read-only, write-once read-many, or fully rewritable. - The source of power: active, semi-passive, and passive.
2. ***Transceiver or RFID Reader*** RFID readers are generally composed of an RF module, a control unit, and a coupling element to interrogate electronic tags via RF communication. Readers may have better internal storage and processing capabilities, and frequently connect to back-end databases. Complex computations, such as a variety of cryptographic operations, may be carried out by RFID readers, as they usually do not suffer from the same limitations as those found in modern handheld devices or PDAs.
3. ***Back-end Database or Host*** The information provided by tags is usually an index to a back-end database (pointers, randomized IDs, etc.). This limits the information stored in tags to only a few bits, typically 96, which is a sensible choice, due to severe tag limitations in processing and storing. It is generally assumed that the connection between readers and back-end databases is secure, because processing and storing constraints are not as constrained in readers, and therefore common solutions such as SSL/TLS can be used.

2.2 Related work with security problem in RFID

There have been many papers in the literature that attempt to address the security concerns raised by the use of RFID tags in RFID system. The last three approaches outlined below are discussed in details in this chapter. We will not discuss the remaining approaches since they are physical solving approaches.

2.2.1 Kill tag

The Auto-ID Center explicitly designed the EPC(Electronic Product Code) (EPCGLOBAL INC.) kill command as a pro-privacy technology. The designers realized that EPC tags might be irretrievably embedded in consumer devices and consumers might not want to be tracked. They viewed killing EPC tags at the point-of-sale as an easy way out of the apparent privacy dilemma. The underlying principle is that "dead tags don't talk". As an alternative to killing EPC tags, tags can also be attached to a product's price tag and discarded at the point-of-sale.

2.2.2 Renaming approach

Even if the identifier emitted by an RFID tag has no intrinsic meaning, it can still enable tracking. For this reason, merely encrypting a tag identifier does not solve the problem of security. An encrypted identifier is itself just a meta-identifier. It is static and, therefore, like any other serial number, is subject to tracking. To prevent RFID-tag tracking, it is necessary that tag identifiers be suppressed, or that they change over time.

2.2.3 Tag password

Basic EPC(EPCGLOBAL INC.) RFID tags have sufficient resources to verify PINs or passwords. At first glance, this appears to be a possible vehicle for privacy protection: A tag could emit important information only if it receives the right password. The paradox here is that a reader doesn't know which password to transmit to a tag unless it knows the tag's identity. Passwords might still prove useful in certain environments. For example, retail stores could program tags at checkouts to respond to a particular password permitted by the RFID network in a consumer's home. This would protect consumersąŕ privacy between a store and their homes. If consumers want to use RFID tags in multiple environments, however, they would face a challenging password management problem.

2.2.4 The hash lock scheme

A reader defines a "Lock" value by computing lock = hash(key)(Sarma et al.a) where the key is a random value. This lock value is sent to a tag and the tag will store this value into its reserved memory location (i.e. a metaID value), then the tag will automatically enter into the locked state. To unlock the tag, the reader needs to send the original key value to the tag, and the tag will perform a hash function on that key to obtain the metaID value. The tag then has to compare the metaID with its current metaID value. If both of them match, the tag unlocks itself. Once the tag is in unlocked state, it can respond with its identification number such as the EPC(EPCGLOBAL INC.) to readers' queries in the forthcoming cycles. This approach makes it simple and straightforward to achieve data protection, i.e. the EPC code stored in the tag is being protected. Only an authorized reader is able to unlock the tag and read it, then lock the tag again after reading the code. This scheme will be analyzed in this chapter in detail in Section 4.1.

2.2.5 The randomized hash lock scheme

This is an extension(Weis et al.) of the hash lock(Sarma et al.b3) scheme based on Pseudo Random Functions (PRFs). An additional pseudo-random number generator is required to embed into tags for this approach. Presently, tags respond to reader queries by a pair of values (r, hash(IDk || r)) where r is the random number generated by a tag, IDk is the ID of the k-th tag among a number of tags in ID1, ID2, . . ., IDk, . . ., IDn. For reader queries, the tag returns two values. One is the random number. The other is a computed hash value based on the concatenation(||) on its own IDk and r. Once the reader gets two values, it retrieves the current N number of ID (i.e. ID1, ID2, . . ., IDn) from the backend database. The reader performs the above hash function on each ID from 1 to n with r until it finds a match. When the reader finds a match, the reader is able to identify that tag k is on its tag's ID list (i.e. tag authentication). The reader will then send the IDk value to the tag for unlocking it. This scheme also will be analyzed in detail in Section 4.2.

2.2.6 The hash based ID variation scheme

Henrici-M*ü*ller(Henrici & Muller) propose a 4-round protocol for low-cost RFID systems based on a one way hash function and a random number generator. The protocol begins as the reader queries the tag, and the tag responds with its hashed identification and current transaction number. The response is forwarded by the reader to the back-end server for validation. To identify the tag, the server checks the validity of the identifying information of the tag. The server then concludes by sending a random number to the tag so that the tag's identification is refreshed and synchronized. This scheme also will be analyzed in detail in Section 4.3.

3. Modeling RFID security protocols in CSP

In this section we describe how the security protocol of the RFID system is modeled using CSP(Communication Sequential Processes)(Hoare) and how this model allows us to reason about it. We denote R as Reader, T as Tag and m as Message, for figuring out the RFID system.

3.1 The message datatype

The datatype Message represents the messages exchanged between the different agents. It is based on a set of atoms called Atom where the set of Key (contains session keys used in RFID), Nonce and Text(for Authenticating between Reader and Tag) are defined as subsets of the atom set (Key $\subseteq$ Atom, Text $\subseteq$ Atom and Nonce$\subseteq$Atom). In addition, we define HashFn to be the set that contains all the available cryptographic hash functions. The datatype Message is composed of encrypting, hashing, sequencing and the atomic value in the Atom and is defined by:

Message ::= Encrypt.Key.Message | Hash.HashFn.Message | Sq.Message* | Atom.Atom

In this chapter we use the Casper notation of writing $\{m\}k$ for Encrypt.k.m. We use H(|m|) for Hash.H.m and abbreviate Sq.$<m_1,\ldots,m_n>$ to $<m_1,\ldots,m_n>$. For example, we denote the construct Encrypt.k.(Sq.$<a,n_a>$) by $\{a,n_a\}_k$.

3.2 Trustworthy agents

Every agent taking part in the protocol is modeled as a CSP process. (An agent can also be internalized in the intruder deduction set (Broadfoot & Roscoe), but for now we assume that all honest agents are implemented as CSP processes). We define the process P_R, denoting agent R, using the following events:

- *send*.R.T.M - symbolizes agent R sending message M to agent T.
- *receive*.T.R.M - symbolizes agent T receiving message M apparently from R.

In addition, we define the following events for delineating specifications for the protocol we want to analyze. (See (Lowe) for more details, on how these events are used to express properties of security protocols)

- *claimSecret*.R.T.M symbolizes that R thinks that message M is a secret shared only with agent T.
- *running*.R.T.M_1,. . . ,M_n symbolizes that R thinks he started a new run of the protocol with T where M_1,. . . ,M_n represent some details of this run.
- □*nish*.R.T.M_1,. . . ,M_n symbolizes that R thinks he has just finished a run of the protocol with T where M_1,. . . ,M_n represent some details of this run.

For more information regarding the translation of a protocol description to a CSP representation see (Ryan & Schneider).

3.3 Modeling the intruder and putting the network together

Based on the Dolev-Yao model (Dolev & Yao), we allow the intruder to have the following abilities when attacking a set S of trusted agents: (i) overhearing all messages flowing through the network, (ii) intercepting messages, (iii) faking messages based on what he knows limited only by cryptography, and (iv) behaving as would any agent outside of S. We first define the rules that allow the intruder to construct new messages. The definition is based on the relation $\vdash$, which characterizes deduction rules by which the intruder can deduce new messages. We say that $B \vdash M$ if message M can be deduced from the set of messages B.

member $B \in M \Rightarrow B \vdash M$
sequencing $B \vdash \{M_1, \ldots, M_n\} \Rightarrow \{M_1, \ldots, M_n\}$
splitting $B \vdash <\ldots, M, \ldots> \Rightarrow B \vdash M$
encrypting $B \vdash M \wedge B \vdash \text{Atom } K \wedge K \in \text{Key} \Rightarrow B \vdash \{M\}K$
decrypting $B \vdash \{M\}K \wedge B \vdash \text{Atom } K^{-1} \Rightarrow B \vdash M$
hashing $B \vdash M \wedge H \subseteq \text{HashFn} \Rightarrow B \vdash H(|M|)$

Informally, the intruder can conduct encryption when he knows the message and the key. He can decipher an encryption for which he knows the inverse of the key, create a reference to a key that he knows, hash every message he knows and can both break up and form sequences. Since by using the Dolev-Yao model, the intruder should be able to overhear, intercept and block each message, the intruder process also models the communication medium. The process representing the intruder is parameterized by **X**, which ranges over subsets of Message, and represents all the facts the intruder has learned. In this model the intruder gets every message sent by the honest agents or by the server via the *send* channel. He then can pass it to the agents via the appropriate *receive* channel unless he decides to block it or fake a new message instead.

$$\text{Intruder}(X) \mathrel{\hat{=}} \Box_{M \in Message} \text{send?R?T!M!} \rightarrow \text{Intruder}(X \cup \{M\})$$
$$\Box_{M \in Message, X \vdash M} \text{ receive?R?T!M!} \rightarrow \text{Intruder}(X)$$
$$\Box_{M \in Message, X \vdash M} \text{ leak.M} \rightarrow \text{Intruder}(X)$$

The initial state of the intruder is IIK(Intruder Initial Knowledge). The complete system is then:[1]
SYSTEM $\widehat{=}$ $(|||_{A \in Honest} P_A)$ || INTRUDER(IIK)

3.4 Specifying protocol requirements

The requirements of the protocols are encapsulated by *trace speci cations*.
Secrecy As mentioned in Section 3.2, secrecy is when agent R performs the event *claimSecret.R.T.Secs*, and that we believe, at this point in the protocol run, that the values in the set *Secs* are secret and shared only with agent T. It expresses the expectation that the intruder cannot be in possession of values from *Secs*, i.e. the intruder should not be able to perform *leak.M* where M $\in$ *Secs*.
Authentication We first introduce the *nish* and *running* events (See (Ryan & Schneider) for more details)[2]. The *nish* event is performed by the honest agents when they complete a protocol run and the running event should be performed before the last send event. We will use the following definition which is one of the more common forms of authentication:

> If Reader thinks he has completed a run of the protocol with Tag, then Tag has previously been running the protocol, with Reader, both agents agreed on the roles they took, both agreed on the values of the variables $v_1, \ldots, v_n$, and there is a one-to-one relationship between the runs of Tag and the runs of Reader.

The following specification corresponds to this definition[3]:

Agreement$_{AgreementSet}$(tr) $\widehat{=}$
$\forall$ R $\in$ Agent;T $\in$ Honest;Ms $\in$ AgreementSet $\bullet$ tr $\downarrow$ *nished*.R.T.Ms $\leq$ tr $\downarrow$ *running*.T.R.Ms

4. Analyzing hash based protocols

In this section we specify hash based protocols introduced briefly in Section 2 using Casper and describe the result of verification. In particular, we obtained each CSP model of hash based protocol through the process of code generation from Casper.
Message Datatype, Trustworthy Agents and Intruder Model specified in Section 3 are applied in hash based protocols as identical models in this section and Protocol Requirements are applied in analyzing the verification of each of the protocols.

- **The message datatype in hash based protocols** The *metaID*(in Fig.1) datatype represents the metaID messages that are sent and received by the agents. Similar to the Message datatype, *metaID* will be based on the Atom set, where Key $\subseteq$ Atom, and on HashFn, the set that contains all cryptographic hash functions. In addition, we define % notation as *metaID*. The % notation is used so that the metaID can be forwarded to other participants. This is why a reader can not construct the metaID, since the other reader does not know the value of the hash function, where m is a message and v is a variable, denoting that the recipient of the message should not attempt to decrypt the message m, but should instead store it in the variable v. Similarly, v % m is written to indicate that the sender should send the message stored in the variable v, and the recipient should expect a message of the form

[1] For clarity this model is abstracted. In the model generated by Casper each fact is modeled as a process paralleled with the entire fact space. This technique reduced dramatically the state space that FDR needs to explore (see (Ryan & Schneider) for more details).
[2] notice that (Ryan & Schneider) refers to these events as *Running and Commit*
[3] The binary operator $\downarrow$($tr \downarrow e$) represents the number of occurrences of event e in a trace tr.

given by m. Therefore, *metaID* could not be known the result value of the hash function for tag by first receiver.

- **Trustworthy Agents** In hash based protocols, every agent taking a part in the protocol sends and receives in the communication channel as described in Section 3.2
- **The Intruder** The Intruder's definitions in the hash based protocol models are the same as the one in the RFID model in Section 3.3 and is still based on the basic six deduction rules presented in Section 3.3.

T	RF tag's identity
R	RF reader's identity
DB	Back-end server's identity that has a database
Xkey	Session Key generated randomly from X
metaID	Key generated from reader using hash function
ID	Information value of tag
Xn	A random nonce generated by X
H	Hash function

Table 1. The Hash Lock Scheme Notation

4.1 Hash unlocking protocol

Message 1. R $->$ T : Query
Message 2. T $->$ R : (H(Rkey)) % metaID
Message 3. R $->$ DB : metaID % (H(Rkey))
Message 4. DB $->$ R : RKey, ID
Message 5. R $->$ T : RKey
Message 6. T $->$ R : ID

Fig. 1. The hash unclocking protocol

The general overview of the above protocol(Fig.1) was already described in Section 2.2.4(Sarma et al.a).
To unlock the tag, in the first line, the reader needs to send a query to the tag and the tag sends the metaID to authenticate with the reader (Message 1,2). The reader forwards this metaID to DataBase to confirm his identity (Message 3). The DataBase compares the metaID with its current metaID value and ,if both of them match, it lets the reader know the key and ID of the tag (Message 4). The reader authenticates his identity with the tag sending key received from the database (Message 5). As a result, if both of them match, the tag unlocks itself. Once the tag is in an unlocked state, it can respond with its identification number(*ID*) to queries of readers in the forthcoming cycles (Message 6).

4.1.1 Protocol requirements and verification results

We describe the properties, i.e *Secret* property associated with data privacy and *Agreement* property associated with authentication between tag and reader, then show verification results of the safety specifications of the hash unlocking protocol in the hash lock scheme, using traces refinement provided in the FDR tool. In particular, we focus on the Session key(Rkey), ID for tag and communicating messages to verify the requirements.
After running the FDR model checking tool, this protocol does not satisfy the *Secret* and *Agreement* requirements and the testing result of the protocol can be described in CSP as below.

1. $Secret_{R,T}$(tr) = ∀ m • signal.*Claim_Secret.R.T*.m in *tr* ∧ R ∈ Honest ∧ T ∈ Honest ⇒ (*leak.Rkey* in tr)

   For all message m, through trace specification(tr), the message Rkey was leaked by an intruder. Therefore, T cannot ensure the *key(Rkey)*. That is, in message 2, the confidentiality of the Rkey cannot be ensured due to the sniffed metaID(H(Rkey)) value. This makes a replay and man-in-the-middle attack possible.

2. $Secret_{R,T}$(tr) = ∀ m • signal.*Claim_Secret.R.T*.m in *tr* ∧ R ∈ Honest ∧ T ∈ Honest ⇒ (*leak.ID* in tr)

   For all message m, through trace specification(tr), T's data(ID) was leaked by an intruder. It is possible to be sniffed a identity easily by an intruder in message 4. The privacy problem of the user will be brought out.

3. $Agreement_{AgreementSet}$(tr) $\widehat{=}$ R ∈ Honest ⇒ *signal.Running_Initiator.T.R.ID.Rkey* precedes *signal.Commit_Responder.R.T.ID.Rkey*

   If agreement is required on some or all of this information, then the signal event at the end of the responder's run should be *signal.Commit_Responder.R.T.ID.Rkey* and it should follow an event *signal.Running_Initiator.T.R.ID.Rkey* in the initiator's run. It means that the responder is not even in possession of all information until receipt of the last message, so the only possible for the commit message is right at the end of the protocol. Similarly, if the initiator is not in possession of all the information until just before its final message, the *Running* signal should either precede or follow that message. However, in this protocol, we cannot guarantee that the corresponding Running signal has occurred, provided we assume that the responder is honest: that *R* ∈ *Honest*. The intruder can capture messages and modify them. This may result in a failed key agreement between two agents.

Through debugging the counter-example trace events, we confirm that the hash unlocking protocol may be susceptible to a sniff and spoof attacks by an intruder due to the unsecured communication channel between reader and tag. A general attack scenario that could be found in this protocol is described below; *I _ Agent* means an intruder who can sniff messages and spoof his identity.

```
1.    Tag      ->  I_Reader  : H(RKey)
2. I_Mallory  ->   DataBase  : H(RKey)
3.  DataBase  -> I_Mallory   : RKey, ID
```

An intruder may obtain the current metaID value(H(RKey)) by querying a tag. The intruder replays the obtained metaID value and broadcasts it to any readers nearby, to get the specific random key for this metaID value if any reader responds to his replay. Therefore, the intruder may have a chance to get the key to unlock the tag and obtain its data.

4.2 The randomized hash unlocking protocol

This is an extension of the hash unlocking protocol. In the randomized hash unlocking protocol (Sarma et al.a), the tag makes a random number, and then sends it to the reader as a response on every session. For reader queries, the tag returns two values. One is the random number (Rn). The other is a computed hash value based on the concatenation(||) of its own IDk and Rn. Once the reader gets two values, it retrieves the current N number of ID (i.e. ID1, ID2, . . ., IDn) from the backend database. The reader will perform the above hash function on each ID from 1 to n with Rn until it finds a match. When the reader finds a match, the reader is able to identify that tag k is on its tag's ID list (i.e. tag authentication). The reader will then send the IDk value to the tag for unlocking it. Fig. 2 shows the process of the randomized hash unlocking protocol.

Message 1.	R	$->$ T	: Query
Message 2.	DB	$->$ R	: ID1, ID2, ..., IDk , ..., IDn
Message 3.	T	$->$ R	: Rn, H(IDk ‖ Rn)
Message 4.	R	$->$ T	: IDk

Fig. 2. The randomized hash unlocking protocol

4.2.1 Protocol requirements and verification results

After running the FDR model checking tool, this protocol satisfies the first *Secret* requirement regarding the *RKey* in Section 4.1.1 because this protocol does not use the session key in the communication channel. However this protocol does not satisfy the other two requirements, as follows;

1. $Secret_{R,T}$(tr) = ∀ m • signal.*Claim_Secret.R.T*.m in *tr* ∧ R ∈ Honest ∧ T ∈ Honest ⇒ (*leak.IDk* in tr)

   For all message m, through trace specification(tr), the message IDk was leaked by an intruder. That is, IDk is sent to the tag through the insecure channel. Therefore, the tag can be tracked. In addition, the protocol is vulnerable to a replay attack since the attacker can masquerade as the right tag when the attacker overhears the tag's response(Rn, H(IDk ‖ Rn)) then sends it to the reader.

2. $Agreement_{AgreementSet}$(tr) $\widehat{=}$ R ∈ Honest ⇒ *signal.Running_Initiator.T.R.Rn.H(IDk ‖ Rn)* precedes *signal.Commit_Responder.R.T.Rn.H(IDk ‖ Rn)*

   However, in this protocol, we cannot guarantee that the corresponding Running signal has occurred with Rn and H(IDk ‖ Rn), provided we assume that the responder is honest: that *R ∈ Honest*. The intruder can capture messages and modify them. This may result in a failed key agreement between two agents.

4.3 The hash based ID variation protocol

The hash-based ID variation protocol (Henrici & Muller) exchanges the ID as a tag's identification information on every session like the hash-chain protocol(Ohkubo et al.). This protocol is secure against replay attacker since the tag's ID is renewed by random number R and LT and LST are updated. LT means the last transaction number and LST means the last successful transaction number. Fig. 3 shows the process of the hash-based ID variation protocol. In message 2 and 3, these messages are the same as the hash unlocking protocol and R means the public identity of the Reader in the channel. Message 4 and 5 can be described in the same ways as message 2 and 3.

Message 1.	R	$->$ T	: Query
Message 2.	T	$->$ R	: (H(ID), H(LT (+) Id))%metaID, △ LT
Message 3.	R	$->$ DB	: metaID%(H(ID), H(LT (+) ID)), △ LT
Message 4.	DB	$->$ R	: R, (H(R (+) LT (+) ID))%metaID2
Message 5.	R	$->$ T	: R, metaID2%(H(R (+) LT (+) ID))

Fig. 3. The Hash based ID Variation protocol

4.3.1 Protocol requirements and verification results

After running the FDR model checking tool, this protocol satisfies the first and second *Secret* requirement in Section 4.1.1 because it also does not use any key in the communication channel and the ID can be updated using △LT (LT = LST - LT). However this protocol does not satisfy the third requirements as below;

1. $\text{Agreement}_{AgreementSet}(\text{tr}) \mathrel{\widehat{=}} \text{R} \in \text{Honest} \Rightarrow$ *signal.Running_Initiator.T.R.LT* precedes *signal.Commit_Responder.R.T.LT*

   The attackers can be authenticated when the attacker disguises the reader and receives H(ID),H(LT (+) ID),△ LT from the tag then sends them to the reader as a response before the tag performs the next authentication session. In this time, if the attackers don't transmit the information described in message 5 in Fig. 3, the tag classifies that the information as lost and the tag doesn't update its ID. Therefore the attackers can track the location of the tag since H(ID) is fixed, before the tag performs the next authentication session and updates its H(ID). The IDs of the back-end database and tag are updated on every session. Therefore this protocol isn't suitable for a ubiquitous computing environment with distributed databases.

4.4 Summary of possible attacks

We can summarize the verification results of the above protocols using model checking. We find that the previous protocols are vulnerable to the spoofing attack and replay attack and can be tracked by an attacker. The attacker performs the following attack.

1. Security against the spoofing attack : The attacker masquerades as the reader, then sends Query to the tag. The attacker gets the tag's response value due to not ensuring the response value of the hash function from this attack.
2. Security against the replay attack : After the reader transmits Query to the tag, the attacker eavesdrops on the response value from the tag.
3. Security against traffic analysis and tracking: To receive responses, the attacker masquerades as the reader then transmits a fixed Query and reads the tag or eavesdrops on the information sent between the reader and the tag. The attacker can therefore analyze the response from the tag.

5. The proposed security protocols for RFID system

The most threatening attacks are spoofing, replay attack, tracking and eavesdropping attacks, as these attacks affect all participants. To protect from these attacks, this section proposes two effective countermeasures.

5.1 Modified hash based protocol

Firstly, modified hash based protocol is the extended version of hash unlocking protocol using hash and exclusive-or algorithm, and can be used in the environment that requires lower burden of communication load with hand-held device reader.

We propose a modified protocol(Kim et al.a) (Fig.4) to ensure secure channel between DB and Reader, and Reader and Tag, using agent's nonce and exclusive-or technique in Casper, as follows;

In this protocol, we assume that the communication channel between Reader and DataBase is secure and the description of the protocol is as follows;

Message 1.	T	− > R	: Tn, H(Rkey(+)Tn) % metaID
Message 2.	R	− > DB	: Tn, metaID % H(Rkey(+)Tn)
Message 3.	DB	− > R	: DBn, H(Rkey(+)DBn) % auth
Message 4.	R	− > T	: DBn, auth % H(Rkey(+)DBn)
Message 5.	T	− > R	: ID, H(ID)

Fig. 4. The modified hash based protocol for secure RFID systems

In message 1, we add *Tn* to metaID and use the exclusive-or(+)technique with Rkey, where it is originally stored in the hash-lock protocol and would be sent with nonce(Tn) to the Reader. In message 2, the Reader will forward metaID to DB with Tn to let the DB know who sent this message and to compare it with Tn in metaID. In message 3, DB sends another value *auth* to Reader including Rkey and DBn, using exclusive-or and hash function with DBn. This message is forwarded from Reader to Tag in message 4. Finally, the Tag unlocks itself after checking the Rkey when the Tag receives message 4 and sends the ID to the Reader.

5.1.1 Protocol analysis and verification result

In this chapter, the main ideas of our modified protocol to correct the problems in previous protocols are as follows;

1. To ensure the data privacy and freshness of tag's behavior over a number of requests from the reader and authentication between Tag and Reader, we introduce the *Tag's nonce(Tn) and DataBase's nonce(DBn)*.For this, a tag needs to have a Random Nonce Generator(PRN). Although there is literature indicating that a PRN needs greater computation capability, it is mandatory that there exists at most one PRN, to protect against replay and tracking attacks.
2. To ensure the confidentiality of data between agents, we add the *exclusive-or(+)technique* into this protocol.
3. To establish a secure channel between the reader and the tag, we introduce an *Auth* value, which consists of Rkey and DBn similar to metaID. This makes it possible for the protocol to be protected against spoofing attack.

After running the FDR tool, we confirm that our modified protocol overcomes the security weaknesses in hash-lock protocols and this protocol satisfies the Secret and Agreement requirements in whole Casper script and the testing result of the protocol can be described in FDR as below(Fig.5). The "$\surd$" marks in ahead of each statements show the satisfaction of the properties(i.e. two *Secrets* and *Auth1* : each statement means secrecy property and authentication property in Casper script) if the properties do not satisfy then the "X" mark would be shown.

5.2 Challenge response based protocol

Secondly, this protocol is based on the security algorithm employed in Yahalom protocol (Gong et al.) and can be used in the environment that user uses a more sophisticated secret to calculate the response to a challenge issued by the network requiring higher complex capability like fixed reader for warehousing and out of a ware-house of inventory systems.
The proposed protocol(Kim et al.b)(Fig.6) must guarantee the secrecy of the session key: in message 4 and 5, the value of the session key (Skey) must be known only by the participants playing the roles of Tag and Reader. Reader and Tag must be also properly authenticated to the DB. In this protocol, we use the *Server Key* and *Tag's Nonce(Tn)* to minimize the burden of

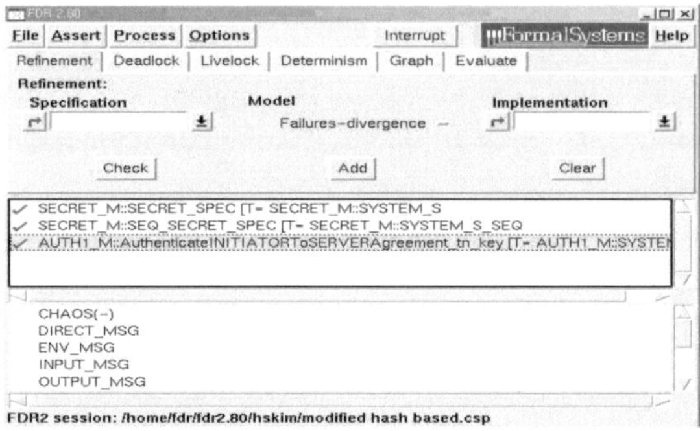

Fig. 5. The verification result of modified hash based protocol using FDR

Message 1.	T	− > R	: Tn
Message 2.	R	− > DB	: {T, Tn, Rn}{ServerKey(R)}
Message 3.	DB	− > R	: $(\{R, Tn, Rn, ID, Skey\}\{ServerKey(T)\})$%metaID
Message 4.	R	− > T	: metaID%({R, Tn, Rn, ID, Skey}{ServerKey(T)})
Message 5.	DB	− > R	: {Skey}{ServerKey(R)}
Message 6.	T	− > R	: {ID}{Skey}

Fig. 6. The challenge response based protocol for secure RFID systems

the Tag and to ensure authentication between Tag and Reader. The functions can be defined to take in an input parameter and return an output. It resembles a functional programming language in this aspect. The definition of a function called *ServerKey*, which takes in the name of an *Agent* and returns a *ServerKey*, could be given as shared : *Agent* → *ServerKey*. In message 1, we design that Tag makes random nonce Tn and sends it to the Reader. This makes simple challenge-response easy. Therefore, in message 2, through *T, Tn, Reader's Nonce(Rn), and Server Key*, Reader can ensured authentication from DataBase. In message 3 and 4, DB encrypts all of the *R (Reader's identity), Tn, Rn, ID and Skey(Session key)* received from Reader and sends these to Reader. Then Reader forwards this metaID to the Tag for letting the Reader authenticate securely using a session key in message 6. In message 5, the DB also sends *Skey* to Reader for him to decrypt Tag's ID in message 6. In message 6, Tag can send his *ID* securely using Skey received in Message 4.

5.2.1 Protocol analysis and verification result

We describe the main ideas of our challenge-response protocol to correct the problems in previous protocols as follows;

1. Shifting all data except the ID to the backend : This is also recommended for data management. (i.e. the ID for the Tag existing at the backend database will be shifted to protect spoofing and eavesdropping attacks securely on the Tag through the database when the Reader sends a request. This means that the Tag originally does not have the an ID value).

2. Encoding data transfer : We support encryption of the data transmission to ensure authorized access to the data of concern and to protect against replay attack and tracking.

3. When a tag receives a "get challenge(query)" command from a Reader, it generates a random number Tn and sends it to the Reader. The Reader in turn generates a random number Rn and generates an encrypted data block that includes Tag's identity and Tn on

the basis of an encryption algorithm with *Serverkey(R)*. The data block is then returned to the database to authenticate the reader. Both Reader and Tag use the same encryption algorithm and since the server key is stored on the Tag, the Tag is capable of decrypting the *Serverkey(T)*. If the original random number Tn and the random number Tn in message 4, which has now been decrypted, are identical, then the authenticity of the Tag is ensured. Vis-a-vis the Reader has also been proved.

In addition, we verify the proposed authentication protocol based on a challenge-response authentication mechanism, which establishes a secure channel between Tag and Reader and confirms that our protocol satisfies the Secret and Agreement requirements in whole Casper script and the testing result of the protocol can be described in FDR as below(Fig.7).

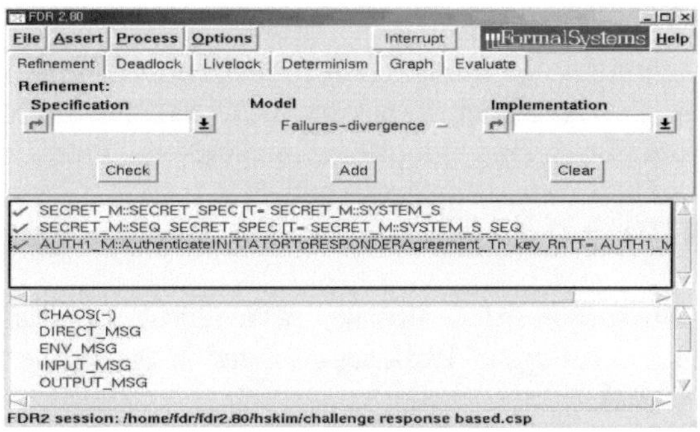

Fig. 7. The verification result of challenge-response protocol using FDR

6. Conclusions

Mobile and ubiquitous computing based on the RFID tag is defined as environments where users can receive network services for anytime and anywhere access through any device, with the tag connected via a wired and wireless network, to information appliances, including the PC. In this environment, there are many security threats that violate user privacy and interfere with services. It would be ideal if we could overcome RFID system's privacy and authentication threats by making minor modifications to the technology itself. Technical solutions have great appeal, implementation and testing costs are fixed and up-front, and once developed, the solutions can be directly integrated into the product. Further these solutions generally require little user education or regulatory enforcement.

Therefore, as an approach to solve the security problems using security protocol at the design level before implementation, we focus on safety analysis of the protocols and propose security protocols that can be widely researched in RFID systems using Casper and FDR. In verifying our protocols with the FDR tool, we were able to confirm that our protocols protect against some of the known security vulnerabilities that are likely to occur in RFID systems.

7. References

[Sarma et al.a] Sarma, S.; Weis, S. & Engels, D. (2003). RFID systems and security and privacy implications.*Proceedings of Workshop on Cryptographic Hardware and Embedded Systems(CHES 2002)*, pp. 454-469, LNCS No. 2523.

[EPCGLOBAL INC.] http://www.epcglobalinc.org.

[Gong et al.] Gong, L.; Needham, R. & Yahalom, R. (1990). Reasoning about Belief in Cryptographic Protocols. *Proceedings of the 1990 IEEE Symposium on Security and Privacy*, pp. 18-36.

[Sarma et al.b3] Sarma, S. E.; Weis, S. A. & Engels, D. W.(2003). Radio-frequency-identification security risks and challenges. *Security Bytes*, Vol. 6(1).

[Henrici & Muller] Henrici, D. & Muller, P. (2004). Hash based Enhancement of Location Privacy for Radio-Frequency Identification Devices using Varying Identifiers. *Proceedings of PerSecař04 at IEEE PerCom*, pp. 149-153.

[Juels] Juels, A. (2004). Minimalist cryptography for low-cost RFID tags, *Proceedings of the Fourth International Conf. on Security in Communication Networks*, LNCS, Springer-Verlag, September.

[Gildas] Gildas, A.(2005). Adversarial model for radio frequency identification.

[Weis et al.] Weis, S.; Sarma, S.; Rivest, R. & Engels, D. (2003). Security and Privacy Aspects of Low-Cost Radio Frequency Identification Systems, *Proceedings of the 1st Intern. Conference on Security in Pervasive Computing(SPC).*

[Hoare] Hoare, C.A.R.(1985). *Communicating Sequential Processes.* Prentice-Hall, Englewood Cliffs. NJ.

[Broadfoot & Roscoe] Broadfoot, P.J & Roscoe, A.W. (2002). Internalising Agents in CSP Protocol Models, *Proceedings of Workshop in Issues in the Theory of Security(WITS '02)*, Protland Oregon, USA.

[Dolev & Yao] Dolev, D and Yao, A.C. (1983). On the Security of Public-key Protocols. *Communications of the ACM*, 29(8), pp. 198-208

[Lowe] Lowe, G. (1997). Casper: A compiler for the analysis of security protocols. *Proceeding of the 1997 IEEE Computer Security Foundations Workshop X*, IEEE Computer Society. Silver Spring. MD, pp. 18-30.

[FDR] *Formal Systems Ltd.* FDR2 User Manual. Aug, 1993.

[Ryan & Schneider] Ryan, P. Y. A.; Schneider, S. A. (2001). *Modelling and Analysis of Security Protocols: the CSP Approach.* Addison-Wesley.

[Ohkubo et al.] Ohkubo, M.; Suzuki, K. & Kinoshita, S. (2004). Hash-Chain Based Forward-Secure Privacy Protection Scheme for Low-Cost RFID. *Proceedings of the SCIS 2004.* pp. 719-724.

[Kim et al.a] Kim, H.S.; Oh, J.H. & Choi, J.Y. (2006). Analysis of the RFID Security Protocol for Secure Smart Home Network, *Proceedings of the International Conference on Hybrid Information Technology*, pp. 356-363.

[Kim et al.b] Kim, H.S.; Oh, J.H. & Choi, J.Y. (2006). Security Analysis of RFID Authentication for Pervasive Systems using Model Checking, *Proceedings of the thirtieth Annual International COMPSAC*, pp. 195-202.

7

On Modeling of Ubiquitous Computing Environments featuring Privacy

Vivian C. Kalempa, Rodrigo Campiolo, Lucas Guardalben,
Urian K. Bardemaker, João Bosco M. Sobral
Federal University of Santa Catarina - UFSC
Computer Science Program - PPGCC
Distributed Mobile Computing and Network Security Research Group - DMC & NS
Brazil

1. Introduction

This chapter discusses a metamodel suitable for ubiquitous computing environments Weiser et al. (1999), Weiser (1993). It includes a way to pervasive computing and includes the aspects of mobility for resources and people. The pervasive computing explores the increasing integration of computing devices in our physical world, while mobility is studied in the context of mobile computing, which exploits the connectivity of the devices which move within the world of people.

However, there are still technical challenges that prevent ubiquitous computing be consolidated in people's lives. Currently, research has been done by focusing on technical matters, such as the connection of devices and the building of applications for these environments. Issues such as security and privacy are still poorly treated. In this article, the challenges to ensuring privacy in ubiquitous computing environments are explored. A metamodel that aims to several aspects of ubiquitous computing is extended to the aspects of privacy. For instance, the degree of anonymity provided by an environment may be achieved.

The chapter approaches on privacy. This one is a right of every person and many nations have laws in their constitutions that guarantee to the citizen the right to possess it. However, privacy can not be guaranteed only by laws, especially when it comes to digital data. This problem has been tackled in conventional computing for some time and the solution that has been used is cryptography. This solution has been satisfactory for the current paradigm, the personal computing. The ubiquitous computing is a new paradigm where the environments have sensors and computing devices capable of computing and communication. The user can communicates with such environments through their personal devices and vice versa. In ubiquitous computing, privacy has achieved new dimensions, which were often idealized by books and movies, but in modern times are becoming reality.

This chapter presents and discusses the dimensions of privacy in the context of ubiquitous computing, the issues being addressed by the scientific community and provides a model for addressing some of these issues in environments closed. This model is then simulated through a simulator and a metric Diaz et al. (2002) is used to measure the degree of anonymity achieved.

In the follow, section 2 presents foudations and the methods. The section 3 describes a metamodel for ubiquitous computing environments. The main issues surrounding the privacy (services and restrictions) in ubiquitous environments are describes in section 4. Section 5 presents an extension to the metamodel developed by Campiolo (2005) to describe ubiquitous environments, with features to ensure privacy in such environments. In section 6 is presented a case-study, which was developed using the metamodel proposed and which was simulated. Section 7 contains important conclusions of this the work.

2. Foundation and methods

In this section the base concepts and the methods used for developing the specification are shown. It describes the entities, requirements and features of the environments and the formal language used at the specification process as in Campiolo (2005).

2.1 Entities

Entity refers to all of the instances that somehow collaborate for the formation and definition of a ubiquitous computing environment. In the current context, entities are people, devices, softwares and communication medias. People engage to the environments through the relation with other entities and behaviors. Devices with communication and/or computing capacity are the foundation for the existence and the growing ascension of pervasive computing. Softwares provide mechanisms for programming and to control devices. Finally, the communication medias, in special, wireless communication, are responsible for establishing connectivity among all entities that compose ubiquitous computing environments.

2.2 Features

Features define properties and important requirements for composition of the environments and must be respected by elements and in the modeling process. The most important are:

- Invisibility: it is the disappearance of user perception on the technology used;
- Intelligent environments: presence of saturated environments with electronic devices and defined frontiers, with capacity of computing and communicating to itself and other devices that present to them;
- Context awareness: awareness of location of the devices in pervasive world to use information on managing and communications in the environment;
- Security and privacy: to assure security of information and of the physical devices and to assure privacy in an environment with constant interactivity and connectivity.

3. The elements of a metamodel

In this section the model got though formal specification of the elements and features of ubiquitous computing environments is shortly presented as in Campiolo (2005) and Campiolo et al. (2007). Modeling aspects are presented, detailed and discussed informally, through explaining sentences, and formally, through the model in Object-Z Spivey (1989) and Duke et al. (1991).

3.1 Common features

In Figure 1 several properties of the physical elements that compose the scenarios of a ubiquitous computing environment are common. By using the concept of inheritance, the common features were extracted and aggregated within a single class. A *ModelBase* class defines common properties of four elements of the model: people, objects, entities and spaces. An identification property exists to represent uniquely a physical object whereas the class and description properties allow to specify object details. A position property defines the absolute spatial location of a physical entity in the scenario. Every element that has this feature can be located through coordinates. The emittedSignal property has the function to aggregate and represent the set of signals that an element can transmit.

ModelBase

$ClassType : \{Person, Object, Entity, Space\}$

$identification : \mathbb{N}$
$class : ClassType$
$description : TEXT$
$position : \mathbb{N} \times \mathbb{N} \times \mathbb{N}$
...
$emittedSignal : \mathbb{F} Signal$

Fig. 1. Features of the *Model Base* Class

3.2 People

The whole essence of the representation of a person can be modeled for who is in a ubiquitous environment. A POSITIONAL type defines people positions in the environment and the characteristics that relate to position, such as velocity, direction and orientation. A PHYSICAL type represents physical characteristics, such as gender, age, size, among other. A PSYCHOLOGICAL type type represents abstract characteristics like emotions, interests, temper, at last, characteristics related to psychological.

3.3 Objects

Objects are all elements that do not have computing and communication, unless they are aggregated or embedded to them.

An initialState property is a set of state variables and defines the object initial state. The possibleState property is a set of state variables and defines all possible and valid values for composition of any object state. The changeState property is an association function among the events that change the object states with the transition relationship between the current values and the new values of the state variables changed by the event. Finally, the associations property allows the association of elements to objects.

3.4 Entities

An entity is the basis for the specifications of sensors, actuators and devices. These ones have common features and need a structure to restrict access to determined properties. The result is the creation of an abstract structure named Entity.

An enabled property defines if the entity is active or inactive. The connections, communication and channel properties specify with which entities the connections, protocols and physical communication channels are maintained.

3.5 Communication

Connectivity in ubiquitous computing environments is essential. Connectivity is provided by an *Entity* class which can be described. It defines for an entity the relation among the physical environment, protocol and connection. The physical mean is specified through a *CommunicationChannel* class, the protocol by the PROTOCOL basic type and the connection by a pointer to an entity. Despite an *Entity* and *CommunicationChannel* classes specify properties to represent and control communications, they are not enough to represent active communications and to a possible simulation management. To help on these issues, must exists a class named *CommunicationController.*

3.6 Events and signalings

Events and signalings in the model are represented by three classes: *Signal, Event and Command*. These classes represent respectively signals, events and commands. In this case, signals are information emitted by any element of the pervasive world; events are notifications issued by entities, in special, devices; and commands are orders and parameters to change object states. The common features of these classes are represented by *Trigger* base class. Common properties like event identification and content representation are provided by this class.

3.7 Location

Through the location information of people, objects and entities, environments manage resources and interactions among the elements present in the spaces. For the model, location information must support the features defined for real environments and even, provide practical mechanisms to manage this information. Absolute location of all elements is defined by the *ModelBase* class. The *SymbolicLocation* and *RelativeLocation* classes specify symbolic and relative location, respectively. They are aggregated by the *Location* class. As it is complex to maintain the location of the entities using location symbolic or relative, every element that uses that location type it should be registered in the location controller. To manage the location of all objects there is the LocationController class.

3.8 Situations

Occurrences or events generated in real world, or even in a simulation, are not all time-dependent. Some of them have relationship with time just by running in a random instant. Besides the existence of random events, there is a subset dependent on a collection of states of given elements. The term used in this paper for these events is situation-based events. Formally, they are event triggered when a finite event set is reached or activated and originate a determined situation. The *SituationController* class is a structure that aggregates the states of interest of a determined situation, associates and triggers events when states are activated.

4. On Ubiquitous environments

In ubiquitous computing, the technology is very close to people and lives in various scenarios that might be considered real. According to this paradigm, the computing elements should be invisible or to induce the minimum of distraction to the user. Based on this idea, is not acceptable that users are often interrupted with alerts and options to configure, accept or reject any type of intrusive action. In this section, we present services that can be intrusive in ubiquitous computing environments, the issues to be considered and the restrictions that may be imposed on these services.

4.1 Services

Most services in ubiquitous computing are not yet widespread or applied in real environments Aoyama (2008). Below are described some of these services and their implications for privacy:

- **Service of product identification:** Through this service it is possible count and track a product that a consumer is buying. The implications are the lack of control of the types and use of information being collected and the possibility of an external entity track the contents of the purchase outside the shop;
- **Service of warning proximity:** This service informs when a known and registered person with your device is close to its physical location or in a common environment. The problem is that people do not always want to be located in certain situations or times;
- **Advertising service:** This service sends advertisements of products to user devices when they are close to their shops. In this case, there are some issues to be considered: (a) How to define policies to restrict the advertising? (b) How to avoid the stressful protocols to obtain this informations? (c) How to map the interests of a client? (d) How to define the limits to achieve this mapping?

4.2 Restrictions

The services introduced to ubiquitous computing aims to facilitate the implementation of tasks of the user. However, the services must comply with certain restrictions that do not become intrusive.
A classification for these restrictions is presented below Myles et al. (2003):

- **Temporal**: it determines the time periods in which the service is available or disabled. For example, a user does not like to be located in the time for lunch;
- **Localization**: this restricts access to informations or to the device based on the user's location. For example, in a restaurant the user can allow a service to obtain its name for a personalized treatment;
- **Organization**: it defines who and when a person can be located. For example, an employee of a company want to be found only when he is in the physical limits of the company;
- **Service**: this defines what services a client device can access. For example, when entering an environment with ad services, you can restrict what is allowed to access;
- **Order**: it defines what informations may be disclosed for a given service. For example, to complete a registration the client defines what data are relevant to be transmitted from your device to the register;
- **Situation**: this defines the situations in which policies defined for a service may be overlapping. This type of service requires a level of intelligence for the device. For example, a user does not want to access any service, while he is in the room with your boss;
- **Group**: it defines a common group that can access a set of user information. This restriction applies to devices from other users. For example, a user wants to share work information with all in their sector;

- **Interest**: this determines whether services or information transmitted to the device are of interest to the user. For instance, a user may wish to receive results of football matches, then he can set as interest this type of information.

5. Privacy model

This section presents an extension of the metamodel for ubiquitous environments created in Campiolo (2005) by presenting the aspects related to privacy Langheinrich (2001), Jiang & Landay (2002), Cheng et al. (2005), Bhaskar & Ahamed (2007). These aspects are presented and discussed informally, through explanatory sentences, and formally, through the model in Object-Z. In addition, the mathematical notations such as those that can be used in Object-Z are usually adopted, therefore accurately describe the properties of a computational system Duke et al. (1991).

In closed ubiquitous computing environments[1] the issue of privacy can be ensured internally by a local system. Thus, privacy violations and the problems caused by the communication must be protected in the environment.

Based on this assumption, in this research are considered the issues involving the environment and the individuals within the limits of that environment. Therefore, the interaction between devices of different individuals in the environment is not addressed.

One of the initial problems is about the user's device communication with devices of the environment. Additionally, all communication between devices consumes energy. Therefore it is necessary to avoid stressful protocols and repeated attempts at communication.

The metamodel presented in Campiolo (2005) does not allow specifying the problems relating to privacy on ubiquitous environments. The Figure 2 shows all classes built in Campiolo (2005) and within the red rectangle are created three classes that are appropriate and based on the concepts of (1) anonymity Pfitzmann & Köhntopp (2001), (2) the use of pseudonyms Beresford & Stajano (2004), (3) the user's preference profile Lederer et al. (2002) and (4) the creation of mixing zones Beresford (2005), if necessary the existence of these in the ubiquitous environment.

The *Service* class represents the services in ubiquitous environment and are detailed in Figure 3. These services are provided by devices and sensors and, as discussed in section 4.1. They can be intrusive and annoying that may pose serious threats to privacy of such environments.

The property *identification* uniquely identifies a service on the environment. The property *description* can provide some information sufficient enough to describe the features of the service. Finally, the property created has the record of the date and time of creation of the service.

What can threaten the privacy of individuals in ubiquitous environments are abusive services, e.g. the sending of ads and ads that are not user interest, user location monitoring, collection of information without permission and unauthorized identification.

To prevent any service has access to personal information of people of a particular environment ubiquitous, class *PrivacyPolicy* (Figure 4) for which an individual can specify which services may have or not have access to your information.

The property *identification* of class *PrivacyPolicy* allows to specify only one privacy policy in the model. To inform about which service is the privacy policy, can be created the property

[1] Closed ubiquitous computing environments are that are physically delimited and where the communication and computing are restricted to those limits

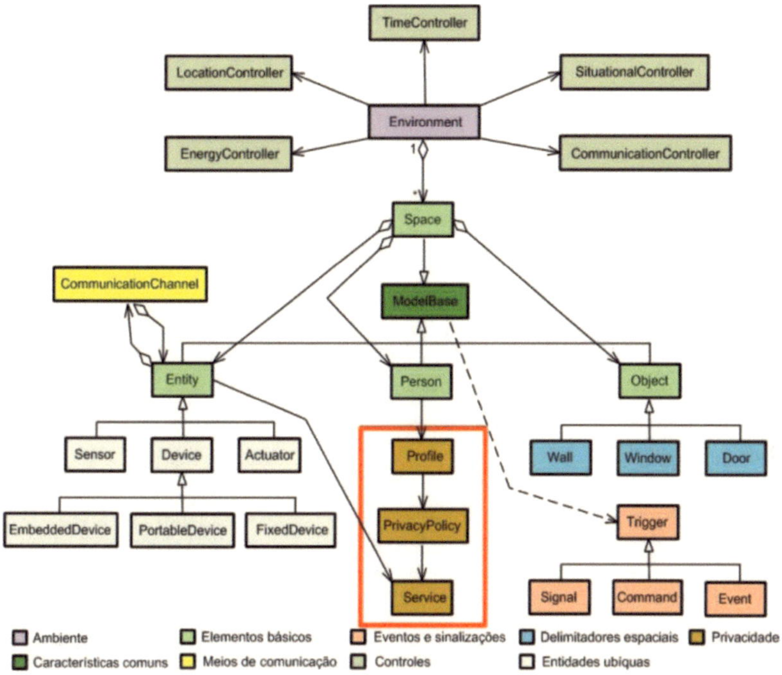

Fig. 2. Main components of the specification

Service

ServiceState

$identification : \mathbb{N}$

$description : TEXT$

$created : TimeStamp$

$\forall x, y : identification \bullet x \neq y$

CreateService

$\Delta(identification, description, created)$

$identification? : \mathbb{N}$

$description? : TEXT$

$created? : TimeStamp$

$identification' = identification?$

$description' = description?$

$created' = created?$

Fig. 3. Characteristics of the class *Service*

service. The *serviceProvider* property allows us to enter a partial set of service providers. For the execution of the service provided by these providers, the *defaultMode* property should be consulted about their modes such as: *allow*, *deny* or *ask*. If a provider is not listed,

PrivacyPolicy

$MODE ::= allow \mid deny \mid ask$

PolicyState

$identification : \mathbb{N}$
$service : Service$
$serviceProvider : \mathbb{P} \downarrow Entity$
$defaultMode : MODE$
$unknownMode : MODE$
$temporalConstraint : \text{seq}(TIME \times TIME)$

Fig. 4. Characteristics of the class *PrivacyPolicy*

the model allows to specify which default mode of execution of the service through the property *unknownMode*. If the mode is *allow* all unknown services have access to personal information, if it is *deny* all unknown services will not have access and, finally, if "ask", the user will have to be consulted about the new service provider and so can determine whether or not to share your information. Finally, based on the section 4.2, it is created the property *temporalConstraint*, which determines which periods of time in which the service will be available or not.
So that the model has a more complete specification of the personal information of users and their preferences, the class *Profile*, Figure 5 has been prepared.

Profile

ProfileState

$identification : \mathbb{N}$
$pseudonym : TEXT$
$personalProperties : \mathbb{P}(TEXT \times \mathbb{F}\, TEXT)$
$servicePolicies : \mathbb{P}\, PrivacyPolicy$
$mixingRate : \mathbb{N}$

$\forall x, y : pseudonym \bullet x \neq y$

Fig. 5. Caracteristicas of the class *Profile*

In the class *Profile*, the property *identification* uniquely identifies a user's profile. Using the concept of mixing Beresford (2005), the property *pseudonym* stores the pseudonym used to identify the user's device and allow the mixing. The property *personalProperties* allows to specify personal preferences such as, for instance, in the category of sports, for instance: soccer, volleyball, basketball; and in the category of movies, for example: action, comedy, romance. The property *servicePolicies* relates the User Profile to their privacy policies, that is, the set of services that may or may not access the information in your personal profile. Finally, *mixingRate* defines a minimal rate of individuals which must be present to occur a mixing. If the rate is zero, this means the user does not want to participate in the mixing. Moreover, to integrate aspects of privacy to the modeling in Campiolo (2005) has been created the property *profile* in the class *Person* which allows to assign the class *Profile* to a person; likewise the property *offeredServices* in the class *Entity*, which allows inform which services are provided by a particular entity.

6. The simulation of an environment

This section presents the application of the metamodel presented in section 5 for the scenery of a shopping center. The choice for this application is due to the fact that a shopping center is a sufficiently complex scenery, because it is composed of several other open and closed sceneries (for instance shops, exhibition areas, salons, escalators) and these are well defined from the physical structure shopping.
The goal is to highlight the importance and applicability of metamodel drafted, as well as discuss the various problems leading in this scenario, in the sense to propose some viable solutions. Only the main classes are presented in this section. In addition, in the end of the section is presented a scenery of the shopping center modeled and analyzed in a simulation tool.

6.1 The scenario

As previously presented in Campiolo (2005), the shopping center (Figure 6) corresponds to a scenario consisting of a large amount of people with their devices and several closed and open spaces, clearly delimited physically by the structure of shopping center. There are sensors and distributed devices, monitoring and providing services to individuals within the limits of the internal environment. The services are intended to conquer and provide convenience to users. These services must not be intrusive, i.e. not transgress, the environment because it has an infrastructure to protect the privacy of its users.

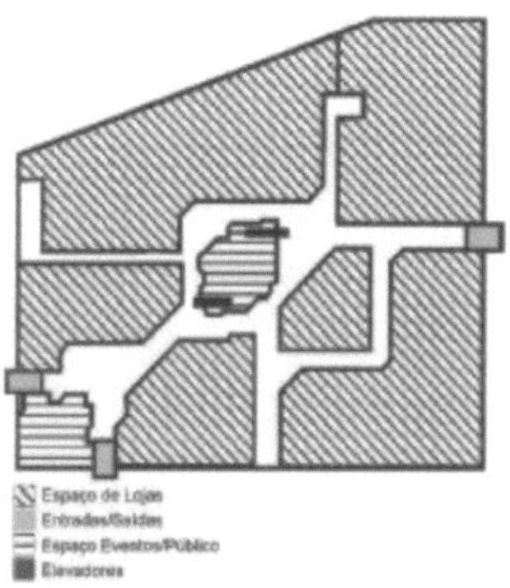

Fig. 6. Illustration of the shopping scene. Source: Campiolo (2005).

The devices and sensors can be located in the stores. They can communicate internally in the store, that is, a client device is detected within the limits of the store, or to communicate a certain distance outside the store. The same principle is valid for the sensors. In addition, sensors and devices can be property of the shopping and can be distributed in other points, being shared by several stores.

6.2 Specific problem

The following scenario illustrates a specific privacy problem in the environment studied. Alice has a profile that is composed of two parts: a set of propositions provided by Alice (profile

A) and a set of propositions inferred by the system or by other entities (Profile B). Alice can determine how to the profile A can be used by the system, in whole or for a particular purpose. On the profile B, his control is very limited, because Alice can not know of its existence. For example, consider that Alice prepares the profile indicating that likes of action movies, gymnastics and self-help books, as shown in Figure 7. The structure named **alice** is the specification of the class *Person* that instantiates Alice in the environment. In this case, the identification **alice** was used as the value of the property *pseudonym*, because Alice had opted out of mixing (property *mixingRate* is zero), i.e., she does not want to maintain your anonymity. This issue will be again discussed in the section 6.5.

Profile : *profile_A*

$identification = 14$
$pseudonym = alice$
$personalProperties = \{sports, \{gymnastics\}\},$
$\{films, \{action\_movies\}\}, \{books, \{self\_help\}\}$
$servicePolicies = marketing\_policy$
$mixingRate = 0$

Fig. 7. Profile A provided by Alice

The Figure 8 presents the privacy policy of Alice, where she determines that your informations are used by advertising service (**marketing_service**), should not be passed to third parties, only to the L and M libraries. In addition, through the property *temporalConstraint*, Alice has defined a temporal restriction alleging that want to be addressed by these services only in time from 8h to 18h.

PrivacyPolicy : *marketing_policy*

$identification = 16$
$service = marketing\_service$
$serviceProvider = sen\_bookstore\_L, sen\_bookstore\_M$
$defaultMode = allow$
$unknownMode = deny$
$temporalConstraint : (8h00m00s, 18h00m00s)$

Fig. 8. Privacy policy for the advertising service

Now, suppose that Alice perform some purchases of books about travel in the bookstore L, one or more times per month for a period of six months. It can be assumed that these books are for herself, it is difficult to be present (unless Alice knows several friends who like to travel and make birthday in this period). Thus, this bookstore is able to create a second profile for Alice, the profile of Figure 9, which is a copy of the profile provided by her, with an additional value in the property *personalProperties*, saying that she likes travel books, fact which she did not reveal personally.
It is important to consider that this information is produced without the knowledge of Alice, it does not fit in the constraint, it will not be provided to third parties and it is a profile more accurate than the profile provided by herself.

Profile : profile_B

$identification = 15$
$pseudonym = alice$
$personalProperties = \{sports, \{gymnastics\}\},$
$\{films, \{action\_movies\}\}, \{books, \{self\_help, traveling\}\}$
$servicePolicies = marketing\_policy$
$mixingRate = 0$

Fig. 9. Profile B inferred by system

Now, suppose Alice goes shopping porting a handheld with your unambiguous identification and your profile A stored. At the entrance, Alice is identified, the profile A is read and profile B is rescued by the system. Passing next to the bookstore M, Alice receives a message from some promotion of travel books. This can be approached from various points of view. Alice did not put the information that she likes of travel books in the profile A, because personally prefer to search when she has a specific need. Suppose she travels a lot for work, but can not determine her destination previously. In this case, it is not useful to receive promotion notices. Alice knows that the information placed on your profile A are used for different companies can make customized offers. On the other hand, these offers may be interesting to Alice, they may be more in line with their interests, and provide a good economy in some cases. In any case, the goal of the companies is to sell, which does not necessarily satisfy completely Alice, neither respect your wishes.

6.3 Model and architecture of the environment

The physical structure of the environment remains the same as shown in Figure 6. In this case, are added only new sensors and devices in some areas of the environment. In the inputs and outputs of the environment, are the sensors responsible for collecting the privacy policies of the user. These sensors are called I/O sensors. Only the I/O sensors collect privacy policies. Therefore, it is required an entity to store these policies. The entity responsible for storing security policies is the central server. This server receives from the I/O sensors the information gathered from the user's device. The sensors and local devices access the privacy policies of a client through a connection with the central server.

Thus, the communication protocols with the devices become less stressful and saves the battery from the client device. The same effect is achieved with the collection of the privacy policy file at the entrance. The collection is performed by wireless communication (radio). The distance between the collecting device and client device is small. Therefore, the energy expended and packet loss are much smaller. The I/O sensors must be isolated and have a range of extension, i.e. they must not allow an external sensor retrieve or disrupt privacy policies collection and should ensure that the client device to remain in the range of transmission until the end of the protocol. The last architecture element added are the mixing zones, where none of the users can be located by services. In the environment studied, mixing zones are in the central region and in the exposure environments of the shopping center because, in this places, there is a constant movement of people.

6.4 Understanding the protocols

To facilitate comprehension, the implications and operation of the protocols, these are described based on possible situations that a client is entering into an closed environment of ubiquitous computing.

6.4.1 Entry of a client/user

A client, upon entering the environment carrying his ubiquitous computing device initiates communication with the I/O sensors. The privacy policy file and the client identification are transmitted. The server generates a pseudonym for client registration, which serves as a key to recovery policies. The client device receives this unique identifier and stores it in the corresponding field. The communication is closed.

6.4.2 Detection of a client by a sensor

Upon detecting the presence of a device, the sensors of the environment or establishment, through a simple protocol, gets its pseudonym. After this, consult the central server to determine the privacy policies of user's device. If it is registered the interest of an user for any service provided, a protocol starts to assist him.

6.4.3 Client terminates the communication with a device

A customer, when leaving an establishment or range of a sensor or device, ends links and a mixing mark is redefined. Therefore, while trasiting through a mixing zone, this device will receive a new pseudonym and its mark of mixing again will be redefined.

6.5 Applying the model to a problem

In this section, the problem of Alice (section 6.2) is resumed and the situations described in the problem are applied to the proposed model. The generation of profile B, where is recorded the interest of Alice by travel books, it is inevitable, once that to purchase, Alice is identified, either through credit or otherwise, as the memory of seller or even facial recognition systems used in security cameras in the store.

Given the inevitability of the generation of a profile B, the solution to maintain the privacy of Alice is dissociate her from your profile B. This can be done by assigning a pseudonym to Alice that will be used to identify her. Thus, when passing by the sensors of the store, Alice will not be identified and, therefore, not linked to your profile B. Starting from the idea that Alice wants to have anonymity, the new profile A of Alice with his new pseudonym automatically generated by the central server is shown in Figure 10.

Profile : profile_A

$identification = 14$
$pseudonym = 4fasd452$
$personalProperties = \{sports, \{gymnastics\}\},$
$\{films, \{action\_movies\}\}, \{books, \{self\_help\}\}$
$servicePolicies = marketing\_policy$
$mixingRate = 1$

Fig. 10. Profile A provided by Alice

However, there are situations in which Alice should be identified, for example, to make a payment by credit card. At this moment, the systems can locate Alice, because she is related to the alias pseudonym. The solution is to change your pseudonym again. Forcing a user to leave and re-enter the environment to change the pseudonym is not something plausible. To do this, mixing zones exist, in which Alice can literally mix the crowd, emerging from this zone with a new pseudonym untraceable by commercial establishments. Thus, even in cases where Alice's identity can be inferred by their habits (habits like visiting specific shops in a certain order in a given time), just that Alice passes through a mixing zone to stay anonymous. In the case of shopping center, mixing zones are central points that the user always pass, whether to change level, or to see other stores. Thus, the chances of identification and tracking become very low, except in circumstances where mixing rates are too low.

6.6 The OPNET network simulator

The OPNET (*Optimized Network Engineering Tool*) *Modeler*[2] allows to design and study communication networks, devices, protocols and applications. The models in OPNET are hierarchical. At the lowest level, the behavior of an algorithm or protocol is encoded by a finite-state diagram with embedded code based on C/C++ language. At the intermediate level, discrete functions such as processing, transmission and reception of data packets are executed by separate objects, which behave as defined in a process model. These objects, called modules, are connected to form the network model that, in the hierarchy, is the highest level model. This model, finally, is what defines the scope of a simulation.

6.7 The environment represented in OPNET

For the simulation was considered a simplified environment of the shopping center described in section 6.1. In the simulated environment there are two bookstores, represented by the sensors **Bookstore L Sensor** and **Bookstore M Sensor**; 3 sceneries: the first with 50 users, the second with 100 users and third with 300 users which are represented by their mobile devices; the central server or **Server**; a mixing zone represented by **Mix Sensor** and a I/O sensor that is **IO Sensor**. This elements are presented in the OPNET network model, in the Figure 11 .

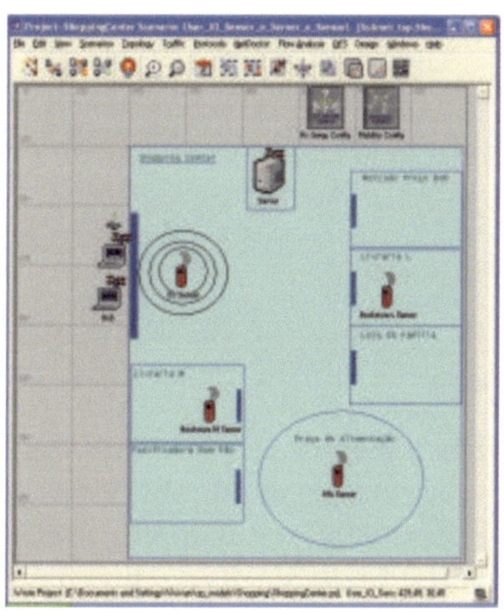

Fig. 11. Shopping center scenario in Opnet.

[2] www.opnet.com

The following describes the exchange of messages as well the element modules of the shopping center.

6.8 Packages for exchange of messages

For the exchange of messages between the elements of the shopping center were developed the following packages:

- shopping_sensor_requests_pck or request package;
- shopping_profile_pck or profile package;
- shopping_pseudonym_pck or pseudonym package;
- shopping_new_pseudonym_pck or new pseudonym package, created by mixing sensor and useful only for users who wish to participate in the mixing;
- shopping_service_policies_of_user_pck or service policies of user package;
- shopping_mixing_pck or mixing package;
- shopping_marketing_pck or marketing package.

6.9 Model of I/O sensor node

Each network node represented in OPNET consists of a *node-model* and a *process-model*. The model of the I/O sensor node is shown in Figure 12. It is possible perceive that there are two input flows (**stream 0** and **stream 1**) and one output flow.

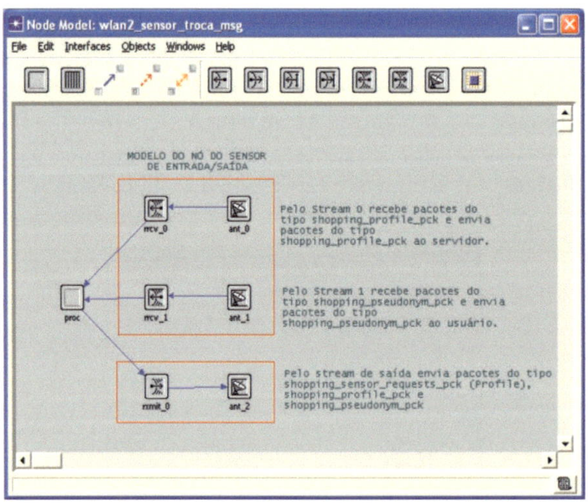

Fig. 12. Model of I/O sensor-node

The sensor-node is responsible for capturing user information and forward it to the server, and vice-versa. The sensor-node periodically sends request packets or **shopping_sensor_requests_ pck** of type *Profile* to the new shopping users to start exchanging messages. If a user responds to these requests, it is by the flow 0 that the sensor will receive the packets of type **shopping_profile_pck** from the user and will send by the output flow to the server. The server then generates a pseudonym for this user and send it to the I/O sensor. It is by flow 1 that the sensor will receive the packages of type **shopping_pseudonym_pck** from the server and it sends by the output flow to the user.

The Figure 13 presents the process-model of the I/O sensor. There are four states: **start**, **send**, **wait** e **end**. The state **start** loads a structure variable called **Address**, with IP values informed in the node interface. The I/O sensor node, as all other environmental sensors, works with two BSS: 0 and 1. The BSS 1 is for communication with the user and the BSS 0 is for communication between the sensors and the server.

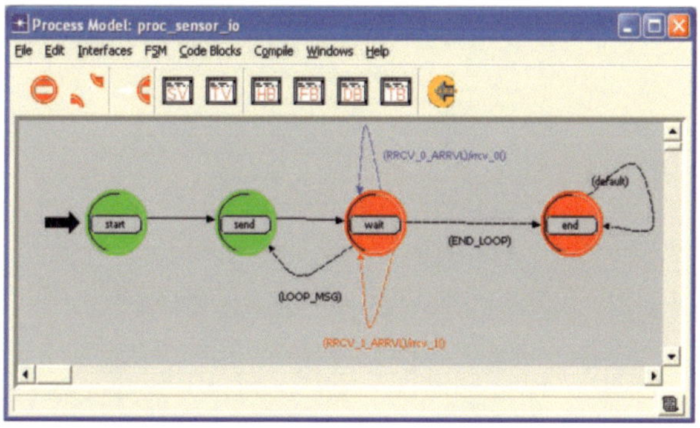

Fig. 13. Process model of I/O sensor.

The state **send** is what sends request packets to new users of the shopping, which are packages **shopping_sensor_requests_pck** of type **Profile**. After send this request, the state machine assumes the State **wait**. In this state the sensor waits packages from the user (flow 0) or from the server (flow 1). This state can also return to the state **send** to send new requests (transition **LOOP_MSG**) or go to the final state **end** with the transition model.
The user-node model is the most important, because it represents the key element of this work, which is the user and how to maintain your privacy. As shown in Figure 14, the user's device has six input flows (**stream 0**, **stream 1**, **stream 2**, **stream 3**, **stream 4** e **stream 5**) and a output flow.
By the flows 0, 1 and 4, the user receives request packets, which are packets of type **shopping_sensor_requests_pck** of the I/O sensor, bookstore sensor and mixing sensor, respectively. After receiving request packets from the I/O sensor, the user sends the packet with your profile **shopping_profile_pck** to the sensor, so that the user can receive a pseudonym. As explained in section 6.9, the sensor sends this packet to the server, which generates a pseudonym for the user, and that is sent by the I/O sensor. The pseudonym is received by user through the flow 2. Upon receiving the pseudonym the user's device writes in its internal memory the value that can be used in other communications during their stay at the shopping.
After receive the pseudonym, the user is able to answer the requests of the bookstores sensors, which are the requests made by flow 1. Then, the bookstore sensor will query the server to check the permissions to send advertisements to the user and to find out the user preferences. If it is possible to send out advertisements, the user will receive by the flow 3, and if there is any promotion that is of interest, certainly, he will go to the bookstore.
If the user walks near an mixing zone, they receive, by flow 4, a request about your mixing rate for the mixing zone sensor determine if the user wants or not join the mixing. Your mixing rate value is sent in the **shopping_mixing_pck** packet. If the value of mix rate is 1, the sensor will request the server a new pseudonym that is sent to user. This new pseudonym is received by flow 5 in the packet **shopping_new_pseudonym_pck**. This causes any parallel profile generated by the stores is lost and only the user-generated profile is respected, maintaining so

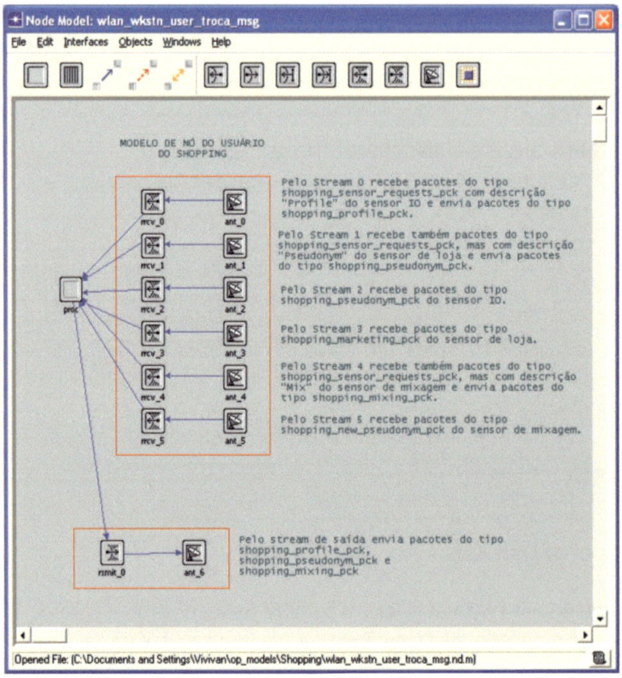

Fig. 14. Users node model.

your privacy.
In addition to the user-node model, there is also a process-model, shown in Figure 15 . There are two states: **start** e **wait**. The state **start** loads internally the user's IP adress and the state **wait** is responsible for waiting the communications in all flows described above.

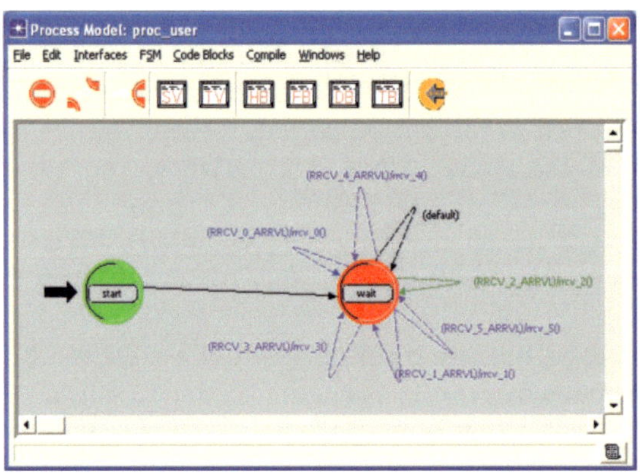

Fig. 15. User node model.

6.10 Server-node model

The server-node model is responsible for storing the user's profile and generate a pseudonym for this user, as soon as he enters in the shopping. The server-node model has three input flows and a output flow.

By flow 0, the server receives the user's profile from the I/O sensor through the packets **shopping_profile_pck** and it stores in your user list. After store the user, the server generates a pseudonym, store it in the user registration and sends it to the user by the I/O sensor in the packet **shopping_pseudonym_pck**. The flow 1 is for communications between the sensors of bookstores with the central server. The bookstore sensor sends to the server the pseudonym of the user, to locate your personal preferences, privacy policies are used and checked if the sensor has permission to send an ads to the user. If it has permission, the server sends the personal preferences and user privacy policies in the packet **shopping_service_policies_of_user_pck**. The flow 2 is for the server receive requests from mixing sensor to generate new pseudonyms for the shopping clients who wish to participate in the mixing. In this case, the incoming packet is the **shopping_sensor_ requests_pck** of type **New Pseudonym**, and the server sends the new pseudonym to mixing sensor in packet **shopping_new_pseudonym_pck**.
As in the user-process, the server process has two states: **start** and **wait**. In **start** state, the server's IP variable is loaded and int the state **wait**, the server waits for packets to establish a communication with the sensors.

6.11 Sensor-node model of bookstores

The bookstore sensor-node is interested in obtaining the user's personal information to send advertising services. Its sensor-node model has two input flows and one output flow.
The sensor-node periodically sends pseudonym request messages, which are the **shopping_sensor_requests_pck** packets, to the users who are nearby. The response to this request is received in the flow 0, in the packet **shopping_pseudonym_pck**. This pseudonym is sent to the server to the sensor obtain the preferences and service policies provided by the user. So this informations are received by the flow 1, in the packet **shopping_service_policies_of_user_pck**. At receive this packet, the sensor verifies the advertisements that can interest the user and sends in the packet **shopping_marketing_pck**.
The process-model of the bookstore sensor-node is similar to I/O sensor and has four states: **start**, **send**, **wait** and **end**. The state **start** loads the sensor's IP adress internally. The state **send** sends request packet of the type **shopping_sensor_requests_pck**, and wait the response of this requests in the state **wait**. Finally, the **end** state finishes the processing.

6.12 Mixing zone

The mixing zone is represented in the environment by the mixing sensor. It checks which users are interested in change his pseudonym, avoiding that he is associated with any secondary profile created by stores, as explained in section 6.5.
The mixing sensor periodically sends **shopping_sensor_requests_pck** packets of type **Mix** to the near users, to response with its mixing rate. The packet **shopping_mixing_pck** is received by the input flow and processed. If the mixing rate is 1, the mixing sensor sends the user pseudonym to the server, to create a new pseudonym. This request is made sending the packet **shopping_sensor_requests_pck** of type **New Pseudonym** to the server. After receive the new pseudonym generated by the server in flow 1, the sensor in packet **shopping_new_pseudonym_pck**, sends to the user, who wants to join the mix.

6.13 Anonymity measures

Anonymity is the state of being not identifiable within a set of subjects, that is: the anonymity setPfitzmann & Köhntopp (2001). For the shopping example, the definition given by

Nussbaumer (2007) clarifies what is the set of anonymity: the group of people visiting a mixing zone during the same period. The higher the number, the greater the degree of anonymity offered. When the anonymity set is reduced to one element, the user is fully exposed and loses all its anonymity. However, the user can deny the information of his location to an application until the mixing zone offers a minimum level to anonymity. This procedure was not implemented in the shopping scenario. According to Toth et al. (2004), the first studies were aimed to quantify the anonymity level provided, as the size of anonymity set Berthold et al. (2000). However, this is not a good measure of anonymity, by considering that the probabilities might not be uniformly distributed.

With the need to measure the degree of anonymity, Serjantov and Danezis Serjantov & Danezis (2002) introduced the entropy degree as a measure of anonymity. The following model was presented by them:

Definition 1: Given an attack-model and a finite set of all users Ψ, be $r \in R$ a function for an user (R = sender, address) with respect to a message M. Let U the probability of the user $u \in \Psi$ being attacked having a function r with respect to M. With this definition, the measure of anonymity of the sender and of the receiver can be defined as:

Definition 2: The size S of a probability distribution U of the anonymity r is equal to the entropy of the distribution. In other words:

$$\boxed{S = - \sum_{u=1}^{\Psi} p_u \log_2 p_u} \qquad (1)$$

where $p_u = U(u, r)$.

This type of entropy is known as simple entropy Toth et al. (2004). In Diaz et al. (2002) was followed a different approach, where only the anonymity of the sender is considered. A represents the set of anonymity of a certain message M, i.e. $A = \{ u \mid (u \in \Psi) \wedge (p_u > 0) \}$. In addition, let N the anonymity set size, i.e. $N = |A|$.

Definition 3: The anonymity degree provided by the system is defined by:

$$\boxed{d = \frac{H(X)}{H_M}} \qquad (2)$$

Where $H(X) = S$ e $H_M = log_2 N$. For a particular case with one user, d is assumed to be zero. This measure is known as normalized entropy. In both cases, zero means no anonymity, ie, the attacker knows 100% the sender of the message.

In the simple case of entropy, the maximum anonymity is achieved when $S = log_2 N$ and in normalized when $d = 1$ Toth et al. (2004). In this chapter will be used the normalized entropy metric, since the major interest is in the anonymity of the sender, i.e. of the shopping user and not the other elements.

6.14 Scenarios for simulation

To obtain the maximum degree of anonymity of the shopping were considered 3 scenarios: one with 50 clients, one with 100 customers and, finally, a scenario with 300 customers. This represents the number of users that may be present in the mixing zone, but not necessarily want to join the mix. For each scenario, some situations were simulated, by varying the number of users who wish to join the mix, as shown in Table 1.

The attack-model for these scenarios is similar to that presented by Diaz et al. (2002), for the *Onion Routing* case. In this model, N is the size of the anonymity set, and the maximum entropy for this N users is:

Users in mix zone	Users participating in the mix
50	1
	2
	10
	25
	40
	50
100	1
	2
	20
	50
	80
	100
300	1
	2
	60
	150
	240
	300

Table 1. Situations for simulation.

$$H_M = log_2 N \quad (3)$$

In the case of shopping, N is the number of users that are in the mixing zone of shopping, not even having the desire to participate in the mixing zone. In this case, the attack is characterized as a sensor of the stores trying to associate the identity of a client with a secondary profile for this. The set that contains only users interested in participating in the mix is called set A, where $1 \leq A \leq N$. In this case, the probability distributions for the users A are uniform:

$$p_i = \frac{1}{A}, 1 \leq i \leq A; p_i = 0, A+1 \leq i \leq N \quad (4)$$

So that, the entropy and the degree of anonymity are defined as:

$$H(X) = log_2 A, d = \frac{H(X)}{H_M} = \frac{log_2 A}{log_2 N} \quad (5)$$

To apply this attack-model to the presented scenarios, we are considering various sizes for the set A, as previously shown in Table 1. The degree of anonymity obtained for each scenario is presented in Table 2.
The results obtained with the simulations of the three scenarios were summarized and compared in Figure 16. In all situations where there is only one client, there is no guaranteed anonymity for the client. Even with two users, the degree of anonymity achieved is very low. In Diaz et al. (2002) is suggested an intuitive value to the minimum degree of anonymity for a system to provide adequate anonymity. This value is $d \geq 0{,}8$. The situations for the samples of sets A being approached, which gives a degree of anonymity $\geq 0{,}8$ are the situations where $A \geq 25$, for the scenario where $N = 50$ users, $A \geq 25$, for $N = 100$ users and $A \geq 150$, where there are 300 users. In addition, the maximum degree of anonymity is obtained when $N = A$.

Set N	Set A	p_i	$log_2 N$	$log_2 A$	d
	1	1,0000	5,6439	0,0000	0,0000
	2	0,5000	5,6439	1,0000	0,1772
50	10	0,1000	5,6439	3,3219	0,5886
	25	0,0400	5,6439	4,6439	0,8228
	40	0,0250	5,6439	5,3219	0,9430
	50	0,0200	5,6439	5,6439	1,0000
	1	1,0000	6,6439	0,0000	0,0000
	2	0,5000	6,6439	1,0000	0,1505
100	20	0,0500	6,6439	4,3219	0,6505
	50	0,0200	6,6439	5,6439	0,8495
	80	0,0125	6,6439	6,3219	0,9515
	100	0,0100	6,6439	6,6439	1,0000
	1	1,0000	8,2288	0,0000	0,0000
	2	0,5000	8,2288	1,0000	0,1215
300	60	0,0167	8,2288	5,9069	0,7178
	150	0,0067	8,2288	7,2288	0,8785
	240	0,0042	8,2288	7,9069	0,9609
	300	0,0033	8,2288	8,2288	1,0000

Table 2. Degree of anonymity obtained for the scenarios

Based on the results presented in Figure 16 , can say that the degree of anonymity of an environment increases as the number of elements in the set A increases. That is, the more users want to participate in the mix, harder for an attacker to discover the identity of a user.

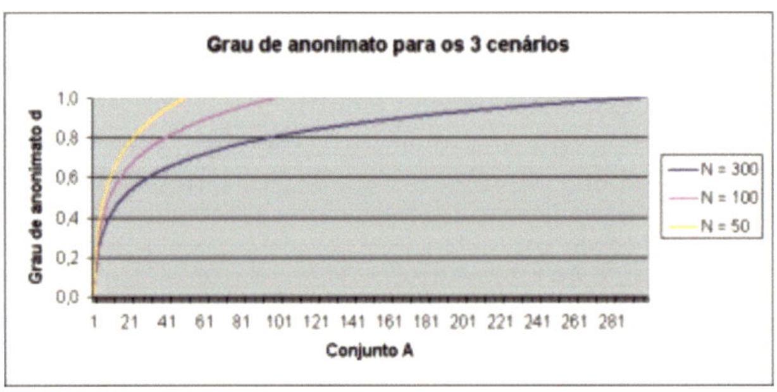

Fig. 16. Comparison between the 3 scenarios.

A problem found in metric of calculation of the degree of anonymity is that, when considering an environment where $N = 2$ and $A = 2$, there is $d = 1$. That means that we obtained the maximum degree of anonymity for that environment, considering $p_i = 0,5$. However, in practice, it is known that $N = 2$ does not guarantee the anonymity of these two users, even with $A = 2$. For this reason, it is important always consider higher values for N and A. An alternative could be to set a minimum value for the size of A, and the user only accept participate of the mix when the minimum number of users for the set A is reached.

7. Conclusion

The model developed for dealing with privacy issues in closed ubiquitous computing environments presents a solution, based on service constraints through user-defined privacy

policies. This is satisfactory to solve the problems of privacy invasion caused by services offered in such environments.
The model of architecture and data developed satisfies the requirements, avoiding unnecessary packet traffic and wasting battery of client devices.
The discussion of privacy issues led to a reflection on which future concerns and precautions that users and applications should consider for the use of devices and ubiquitous computing environments.

8. References

Aoyama, T. (2008). A new generation network - beyond ngn, *Innovations in NGN: Future Network and Services. First ITU-T Kaleidoscope Academic Conference* pp. 3–10.

Beresford, A. R. (2005). Location privacy in ubiquitous computing, *Technical Report UCAM-CL-TR-612*, University of Cambridge, Computer Laboratory.

Beresford, A. R. & Stajano, F. (2004). Mix zones: User privacy in location-aware services, *Pervasive Computing and Communications Workshops, IEEE International Conference on* 0: 127–131.

Berthold, O., Federrath, H. & Kpsell, S. (2000). Web mixes: A system for anonymous and unobservable internet access, *Designing Privacy Enhancing Technologies*, Springer-Verlag, pp. 115–129.

Bhaskar, P. & Ahamed, S. I. (2007). Privacy in pervasive computing and open issues, *ARES '07: Proceedings of the The Second International Conference on Availability, Reliability and Security*, IEEE Computer Society, Washington, DC, USA, pp. 147–154.

Campiolo, R. (2005). *Aspectos de modelagem de ambientes de computação ubíqua*, Master's thesis, Universidade Federal de Santa Catarina.

Campiolo, R., Cremer, V. & Sobral, J. B. M. (2007). On modelling for pervasive computing environments, *in Proceedings of 10th International Symposium on Modelling, Analyses and Simulation of Wireless and Mobile Systems - MSWiM 2007* pp. 3–10.

Cheng, H. S., Zhang, D. & Tan, J. G. (2005). Protection of privacy in pervasive computing environments, *ITCC '05: Proceedings of the International Conference on Information Technology: Coding and Computing (ITCC'05)*, Vol. 2, IEEE Computer Society, Washington, DC, USA, pp. 242–247.

Diaz, C., Seys, S., Claessens, J. & Preneel, B. (2002). Towards measuring anonymity, *in* R. Dingledine & P. Syverson (eds), *Proceedings of Privacy Enhancing Technologies Workshop (PET 2002)*, Springer-Verlag, LNCS 2482, pp. 54–68.

Duke, R., King, P., Rose, G. & Smith, G. (1991). The object-z specification language: Verson 1, *Technical Report 91-1*, University of Queensland.

Jiang, X. & Landay, J. A. (2002). Modeling privacy control in context-aware systems, *IEEE Pervasive Computing* 1(3): 59–63.

Langheinrich, M. (2001). Privacy by design — principles of privacy-aware ubiquitous systems, *j-LECT-NOTES-COMP-SCI* 2201: 273–??

Lederer, S., Dey, A. K. & Mankoff, J. (2002). A conceptual model and a metaphor of everyday privacy in ubiquitous computing environments, *Technical Report UCB/CSD-02-1188*, EECS Department, University of California, Berkeley.
URL: *http://www.eecs.berkeley.edu/Pubs/TechRpts/2002/5464.html*

Myles, G., Friday, A. & Davies, N. (2003). Preserving Privacy in Environments with Location-Based Applications, *IEEE Pervasive Computing* 2(1): 56–64.

Nussbaumer, M. (2007). Location privacy.
URL: *www.sec.informatik.tu-darmstadt.de/pages/lehre/SS07/sem_misc/papers/nussbaumer.pdf*

Pfitzmann, A. & Köhntopp, M. (2001). Anonymity, unobservability, and pseudonymity - a proposal for terminology, *Designing Privacy Enhancing Technologies*, Springer-Verlag, pp. 1–9.
URL: *http://dx.doi.org/10.1007/3-540-44702-4_1*

Serjantov, A. & Danezis, G. (2002). Towards an information theoretic metric for anonymity, *Proceedings of Privacy Enhancing Technologies (PET2002)*, Springer-Verlag, pp. 41–53.

Spivey, J. M. (1989). *The Z Notation : A Reference Manual*, Prentice Hall.

Toth, G., Hornak, Z. & Vajda, F. (2004). Measuring anonymity revisited, *in* S. Liimatainen & T. Virtanen (eds), *Proceedings of the Ninth Nordic Workshop on Secure IT Systems*, Espoo, Finland, pp. 85–90.

Weiser, M. (1993). Some computer science issues in ubiquitous computing, *Communications of the ACM* 36(7): 75–84.

Weiser, M., Gold, R. & Brown, J. S. (1999). The origins of ubiquitous computing research at parc in the late 1980s, *IBM Systems Journal* 38(4): 693–696.

Part 3

Integration Middleware

8

WComp, a Middleware for Ubiquitous Computing

Nicolas Ferry*, Vincent Hourdin, Stéphane Lavirotte, Gaëtan Rey, Michel Riveill and Jean-Yves Tigli
I3S/Université de Nice-Sophia-Antipolis
France

1. Introduction

Ubiquitous computing relies on computers present everywhere, at any times and in any things. Indeed with recent years advance in mobile communication technologies and the miniaturization of computer hardware, processing units are becoming invisible and a part of the environment. Middlewares for ubiquitous computing have to manage three main features specific to their environment: devices' *mobility*, devices' *heterogeneity* and environment's *dynamicity*. The devices' *mobility*, due to motion of users and their associated devices, forbids to assume that entities are known and will always be available. The second concept, entity's *heterogeneity*, outlines the diversity between devices' capabilities and functionalities provided by new smart objects. Finally, the environment high *dynamicity* illustrates the ubiquitous world entropy with the appearance and disappearance of devices. Devices used to create applications are thus unknown before discovering them. Then, ubiquitous computing must deal with such a dynamic software environment (called software infrastructure afterwards). As a result, future ubiquitous computing architectures must take into account those three constraints to solve ubiquitous computing challenges.

Our model of middleware WComp is based on three parts: a software infrastructure, a service composition architecture, and a compositional adaptation mechanism.

To manage the dynamicity and heterogeneity of entities in the software infrastructure, we highlight the use of Web Service Oriented Architecture for Device (WSOAD). This will be discussed in section 2. Ubiquitous applications are then based on a set of Web services for devices that must interact with each other. Consumers can not edit these services. Therefore, in order to add new functionalities to the system, an application has to be a composition of services for devices. Such an application, and thus such a composition, must be modifiable at runtime.

The second part of the WComp middleware enables us to make such applications by *dynamically* composing services from the software infrastructure. To allow reusability of newly created functionalities, and for scalability purposes, such composition can be encapsulated as a composite service. This part of the system will be presented in Section 3. Moreover, the infrastructure of ubiquitous computing applications evolves dynamically led by appearances and disappearances of objects or devices. The variation of this infrastructure is dynamic due to arbitrary node *mobility*, failures or energy constraints. The service composition must be as relevant as possible according to the underlying software infrastructure. Managing these

*also supported by CSTB (Centre Scientifique et Technique du Bâtiment)

compositions musn't lead to an administrative overhead but must be self-adapted at runtime, in a transparent way.
The third part of the WComp middleware proposes to address this issue using Aspect of Assembly (AA). AA is an approach for composition adaptation particularly well-suited to tune a set of composite services in reaction to a particular variation of the infrastructure or changing preferences of the users. AA will be introduced in Section 4. Finally in the last section of the chapter we will present some experimental results about performances of our composition and adaptation mechanisms.

2. Web services for device infrastructure

According to (MacKenzie et al. (2006)) "Service Oriented Architecture (SOA) is a paradigm for organizing and utilizing distributed capabilities that may be under the control of different ownership domains. It provides a uniform means to offer, discover, interact with and use capabilities to produce desired effects consistent with measurable preconditions and expectations.". They were originally used to design distributed applications and to deploy them easily. SOA allows to build dynamic applications using a set of basic entities called services. A service is defined as the way to connect consumers and providers capabilities.
SOA are a way to manage a set of independent software applications and to handle the infrastructure of a set of interrelated services. Each of them being accessible through standardized interfaces and protocols. They define an interaction between software entities as an exchange of messages between service consumers (clients) and service providers (Papazoglou (2003)).
A third entity exists: the registry. Thanks to the registry the system is able to discover available services providers and consumers (FIG. 2) (Champion et al. (2002)). Generally, it stores the service description, and not only a reference to the provider.

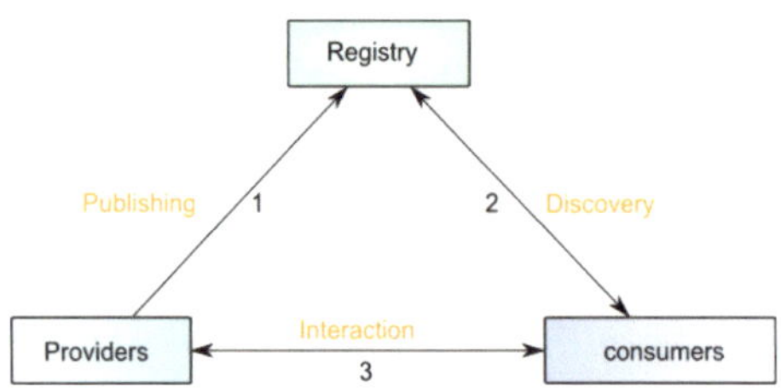

Fig. 1. Service oriented architecture

Here are services main features (Breivold & Larsson (2007); MacKenzie et al. (2006)) and commonalities with ubiquitous computing devices that lead us to the use of SOA as software infrastructure for ubiquitous applications:

- *Encapsulation*: any functionality can be encapsulated in a service and thus be part of available services creating applications. All entities of the system represented by a similar standard of service will be accessible through the same infrastructure. SOA thus provides a logical consistency. Devices also provide a set of functionalities; it is possible to encapsulate them in services at the functional level.
- *Loose coupling and autonomy*: services have no direct dependencies between them. The absence of a service does not prevent others from fulfilling their functions. Services are independent and control their internal logic without any external intervention. This is also a property of devices, for instance a light does not require shutters to operate.

- *Contracts and abstraction*: services describe the functionalities they offer using *contracts*. Services must comply with these contracts. It is the only way for consumers to obtain information about their functionality, as well as their non-functional concerns and meta-data. Services are black boxes, only their contract is known. The way they are implemented is unknown and cannot be edited. This is also true for devices. Reuse of services is facilitated by the fact that service providers are not designed for a specific consumer. At launch time, service providers publish their contracts into the registry to become an available entity of the system.
- *Dynamic discovery*: services are discovered according to some criteria and can be replaced during runtime. Service consumers send a request to the registry to find providers in line with their criteria. They get the provider's contract, and a reference to contact it, generally an URL.
- *Composability*: services can be coordinated and composed to create new composite applications or services. Such a composition is not involved in services, but is organized by an external entity. The content of the composite service may be changed at runtime and the black box abstraction is not fulfilled anymore. Composite services can be seen as gray boxes.

All these properties, common to services and devices, and their adoption in other works (Bottaro et al. (2007); Chakraborty et al. (2005); Vallée et al. (2005)), lead us to consider the use of SOA as infrastructure for ubiquitous computing. In such a case, devices and information systems are represented by services. Applications are compositions of these services. They are continuously observing changes of the infrastructure (appearance or disappearance of services) and react to them if needed FIG. 2.

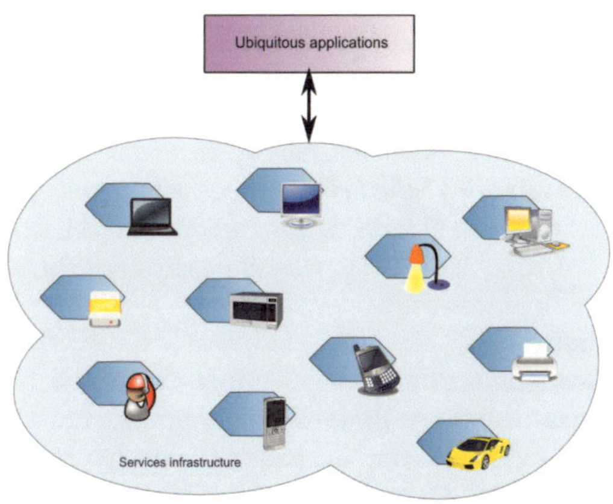

Fig. 2. Using SOA to represent the software infrastructure in ubiquitous computing

To validate the use of services as an infrastructure for ubiquitous computing, we will now investigate if they allow to consider the properties described in the introduction: heterogeneity, reactivity and frequent disconnections due to mobility. Since their creation, SOA have evolved in several directions: Web, information systems, mobile and ubiquitous computing. Despite these different directions, a new type of services oriented architecture, including all these evolutions is born: Web Services Oriented Architecture for Devices (WSOAD).

2.1 Interoperability

In classical SOA, the choice of a programming language, a data representation, or a communication protocol should be done by designers of consumers and producers jointly in order to be compatible. To partially resolve the problem, distributed applications were usually designed by a same working group. But two kinds of interoperability must be guaranteed. First, the interoperability of platforms, in which all entities that want to provide a service must be based on a virtual machine. This is the case of JINI (Arnold et al. (1999)) which is Java-based. The second type of interoperability is at the level of communication protocols. This is proposed by CORBA (Vinoski & Inc (1997)) or Web services. Using Web services (Champion et al. (2002)), designers of providers do not know how their service will be used. They will probably use some hardware platforms and languages that are different from those of future consumers.

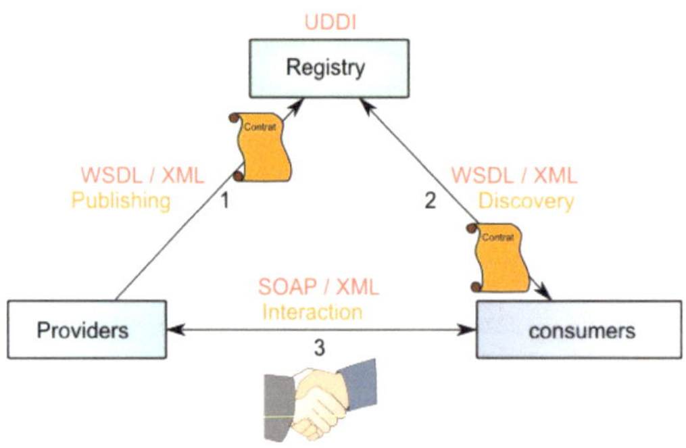

Fig. 3. Web services oriented architecture

From the perspective of the use for devices infrastructures, Web services standards provide a great benefit to handle their heterogeneity. Then, interoperability, as provided by Web services, is an essential feature for ubiquitous computing.

Web technologies have brought to SOA interoperability at several levels. WSOA allows to create applications based on services executing with heterogeneous programming languages, and on various hardware architectures. This evolution of services was required in order to use SOA as infrastructure for ubiquitous computing, because of the heterogeneity of involved devices or applications.

2.2 Evented communications

Mobile computing applications are reactive. Frequent disconnections must be addressed promptly. Indeed, because of battery limitations, programs have to be effective and use eventing rather than *polling*. Moreover, human-machine interactions must be as fast as possible. Processing capabilities of mobile devices are reduced, in terms of processing time, memory and duration of use, because of the battery power. Processes should be as effective and relevant as possible. Using systems based on queue or complex mechanism of publish/subscribe is hardly suitable.

Services for devices (Hourdin et al. (2006)), which are SOAD providers, are lightweight services using evented communications. Evented communications enable applications based on devices an effective use of hardware interruptions. Moreover, they provide loose coupling between services. As an example, considering a smart switch, when activated, a hardware interruption is raised. Thanks to events, a notification will be immediately sent to consumers. The dynamics and efficiency of the application are then maximal. Without the use of events, the switch should keep a state variable up to date, until consumers request its value. Since

these calls are done periodically, there is a risk of missing a change of state if many occur before the end of the period.
Evented communications add to classical services the dynamicity required for interactions between devices that may be involved into some ubiquitous systems.

2.3 Appearance and disappearance

As we have seen previously, in the field of ubiquitous computing, the infrastructure of an application is highly variable due to node mobility. Users' mobility, and then devices' mobility, must lead to frequent disconnections and network changes. The topology of such infrastructures cannot be known *a priori*. Moreover, in a mobile network, we cannot know in advance the address of service registries, or even assume that one exists. To build applications based on these entities, a middleware must know the entities that are in this infrastructure. SOAD proposes to address this issue.
When a service provider enters or leaves a network, it broadcasts a notification across the network. Those appearances or disappearances by announces are asynchronous, and provide the property of dynamicity to the software infrastructure. If a provider is disconnected abruptly, or undergo a programming error, the announcement of their disappearance will not be sent. To overcome these problems, providers use a lease mechanism which involves periodic notifications of their presence.
Thanks to these mechanisms of announcements, network entities are then able to know the entities in their network dynamically and to see them appear and disappear. This mechanism makes sense when coupled with a decentralized dynamic mechanism of discovery.

2.4 Decentralized discovery

Another evolution of SOA provided by SOAD impacts the discovery mechanism. This evolution aims to enable considering network, consumers and providers unknown in advance. The entities that will be present to create an application are not known and must be discovered dynamically.
When a registry is used, consumers send a request based on some criteria (a service type, a name or some more complex expressions (Hourdin et al. (2006))). Some architectures provide a second type of interaction between registries and consumers. Consumers can subscribe to an entry on the registry in order to be notified when a relevant provider (according to the entry) is registred (Bustamante et al. (2002)). When consumers get a reference to the provider, generally a URL, they perform a query to get the service contract. Then, they will be able to interact with the service at a functional level. This contract describes the technical characteristics of the service. Thanks to the interpretation of this contract the service can be discovered.
Then, mechanisms of decentralized search emerged in industry standards (SLP (Guttman (1999)), Jini (Arnold et al. (1999)), Bluetooth SDP [1], Salutation [2], Bonjour [3]) and in many research projects (Chen et al. (2000); Huang et al. (2002); Preuß (2003); Sedov et al. (2003); Ververidis & Polyzos (2008); Zhu et al. (2005)). They allow consumers to find providers without using a centralized registry. In fact, the search mechanism is introduced into providers and consumers so that they communicate directly with each other. Then, the discovery phase uses the mechanisms of appearance / disappearance previously described.

[1] Bluetooth Service Discovery Protocol, in *Specification of the Bluetooth System. Core*, version 1.1. 2001.
[2] the *Salutation Consortium* no longer exists.
[3] Bonjour is used in Mac OS X to discover printers and to share data.

This mode is centered on consumers. As in architectures using services registries, consumers can process a search request, but the request is broadcasted across the network.
In the figure (FIG. 4), the dotted lines represent communications by broadcasting, while those in solid lines are point to point ones.

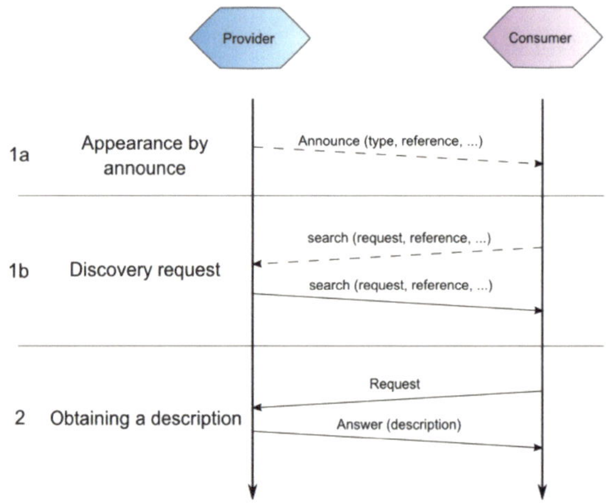

Fig. 4. Dynamic decentralized discovery : discovery and search protocols

However, for some efficiency or safety issues, various protocols (SLP, Jini) use some broadcasting mechanism to discover a service registry. In mobile environments, wireless communications are often expensive in term of energy consumption. A registry allows consumers to consider a single contact and then send point to point request. They are considered as mandatory to scale to large networks (Ververidis & Polyzos (2008)). Such a registry built its database from announces of appearance and disappearance of service providers.
Discovery is the first step in creating applications from a service infrastructure. In ubiquitous computing, it is especially the case because the environments in which they are created are not known a priori. *Dynamic discovery coupled with decentralized mechanisms of appearance/disappearance allows to discover services without knowing them* a priori *and without relying on a static entity.*

2.5 Web services for devices oriented architecture (WSOAD)

We have seen the major evolutions of classical SOA:

- *Web Service Oriented Architecture*: the use of web technologies addresses the issue of interoperability between services (2.1).
- *Service Oriented Architecture for Device*: decentralized discovery (2.4) and appearance/disappearance (2.3) mechanisms allow to discover services in mobile environment that are not known *a priori*. Evented communications (2.2) introduce some dynamic interactions between consumers and providers. Moreover, it adds a loose coupling between services.

WSOAD (*Web Service Oriented Architecture for Device*) is born of the combination of these evolutions. They benefit from all the advantages of SOAD, on which is added interoperability from WSOA. Currently there are two implementations of WSOAD: UPnP[4] and DPWS [5].

[4] Universal Plug and Play
[5] Devices Profile for Web Services

WSOAD provides the properties needed for software infrastructures of ubiquitous systems. Since the code of these entities is not editable, to create some new ubiquitous applications we must enable interactions between services. We must compose them together. There are two majors types of service composition: orchestration and choreography (Singh & Huhns (2005)). Orchestration is based on a centralized entity. This entity performs all the methods calls on the various services of the application by relaying their messages. On the other hand, choreography consists in a decentralized approach. Indeed, the choreography implies that services are able to organize themselves independently to communicate with each other. It is more complex to implement. In fact it implies that each service knows each other. Moreover, any adaptation mechanisms must then be embedded in each service.
Thus orchestration seems more suited to ubiquitous computing, since the frequent changes in the infrastructure would be complex to manage in each services (Cardoso & Issarny (2007)). The orchestration of services is usually described by defining workflows or abstract processes, such as BPEL (Business Process Execution Language). In the next section, we will present more in detail how to achieve such compositions in the field of ubiquitous computing.

3. Dynamic service composition

Ubiquitous applications are based on a set of Web services for devices that interact with each other. These services are non-editable software entities. Therefore, an application is a composition of services for devices that has to be adapted at runtime because of the dynamicity of the software infrastructure. If services propose to address the issue of interoperability, components offer high dynamicity and reusability. As explained in (Brønsted et al. (2007)): "The ability to seamless compose services from various devices in a more or less ad-hoc manner is a frequently emphasized feature of ubiquitous computing.".
They are created thanks to some components factories into containers. Containers provide non-functional properties to components. Components factories define the type of component to be instantiated. They can be instantiated and manipulated easily by a developer. Conversely, services on devices are fixed and sustained. However, services could be deployed on nodes of a controlled network, but they would not provide the same benefits of dynamicity. This is due to interface connections and because services are stateless and cannot be instantiated by the developer. Therefore, we base ourselves on services to communicate with various entities in the environment, devices included, and on components for their adaptation capability.
To address this issue of dynamicity, the proposed architecture is based on two paradigms:

- *Events:* they are taking place in the model as well as at the services level, with Web services for devices for example, than in lightweight assemblies of components. Their advantages are twofold: they promote reactivity of systems, increase the loose coupling between entities, and thus dynamicity of applications.
- *Lightweight components assemblies :* composite Web services are created from a dynamic assembly of black box components, executing in a local container, which doesn't provide mandatory non-functional services. Dynamicity of applications is then provided, and reusability is increased.

LCA (*Lightweight Component Architecture*) (Tigli et al. (2009a)) thus defines a compositional architecture model based on events, to design lightweight components assemblies, and increment the cooperation graph of services and applications. The environment consists of mobile users interacting with the world or other users with wearable or mobile devices.

We see them as some services momentarily available in the infrastructure. Components assemblies are a suitable way to orchestrate them.

3.1 Web service for device composition : LCA

The component model LCA is a model derived from Beans (Englander (1997)), adapted to other programming languages, with concepts of input, output ports and properties.
These components are called "light" for several reasons. The first is that they execute in the same memory addressing space, and in the same process (Clarke et al. (2001)), so their interactions are reduced to the simplest and the more efficient, the function call. The second reason, which stems from the first, is that they don't embed non-functional code for middleware or other non-mandatory technical service in this local environment. Their memory footprint is then reduced and they can be instantiated and destroyed quickly (Tigli et al. (2009b)). A container is not limited to one type of components but may contain all components of an application. To finish, they don't contain any reference between them at design-time, and respect black box and late-binding concepts. The dynamicity of the model is thus maximal, since they use events to communicate between them, components are fully decoupled, and highly reactive.

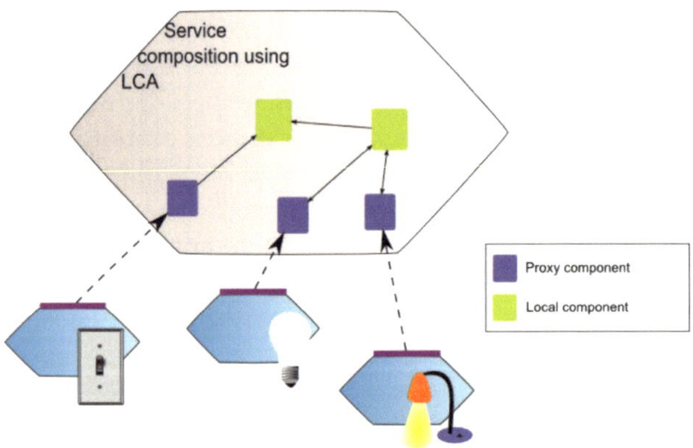

Fig. 5. Composing Web services for devices using lightweight components assemblies based on evented communications

The only non-functional code present in the components event management and properties accessing. Higher level programming languages define these operations; component code is then a simple object, like JavaBeans or .NET components, not overloaded with code injection for any purpose. The container does not provide technical services easing the programmer work, but consequently allows the creation of components with various requirements, like components needing to access hardware and thus low-level functions. Adding non-functional properties, like security, journaling, or persistence of messages can be made by adding components in the assembly, guaranteeing scalability of the model.
As described in the LCA model (Fig. 3), components have an interface, defined by the component's type. This interface is a set of input ports (methods), and output ports (events), each one being typed by its parameters, and having a unique identifier. Interactions between components are bindings. They link an output port of a component to one or more input port of components. Ports being explicit, no code has to be generated, nor studied by introspection to know what to modify in components to change the target of a binding at run-time. When an event is emitted, the control flow is passed to recipients in an undefined order, but this can be

fixed adding sequence components. When limiting to unique bindings, and using sequence components, the control flow managing the application is fully deterministic. Not having indirections, due to technical services of the framework, gives a full control on control flow, and eases their debugging.

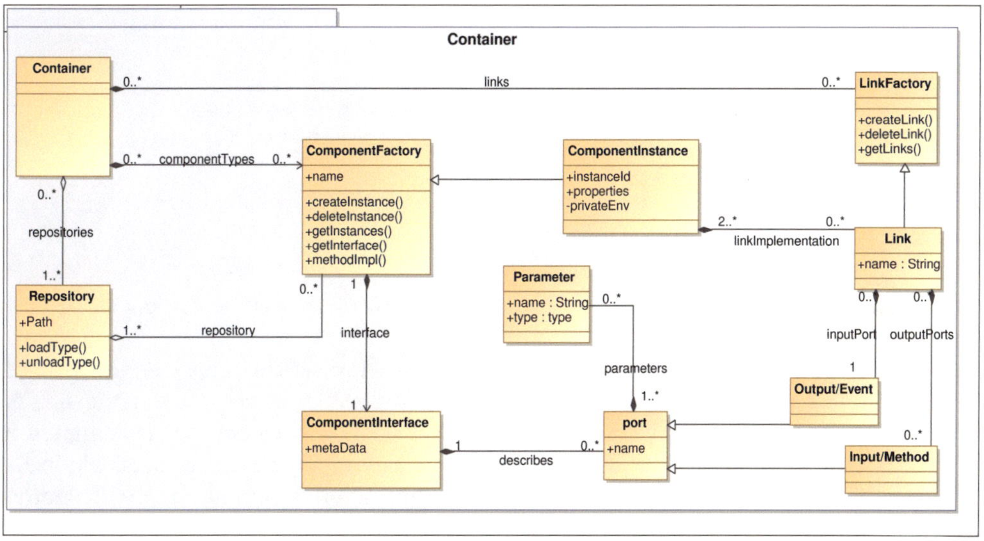

Fig. 6. LCA meta-model: lightweight components

When a service is discovered, a specific component, called *proxy* component, is generated from the description (contract) of the services. Then, the component type will be loaded and instantiated in order to be a part of the component assembly. *Proxy* components will enable communication with services of the environment.

Composing Web services for devices using LCA, the lightweight components model, allows to dynamically create new applications from services that are available in a software infrastructure. However, newly created functionalities are only available locally creating a specific application. It is then necessary to add reusability to the model, and to export the new functionalities created by a component assembly as a new service for device in the infrastructure.

3.2 Distributed composition: SLCA

Multi-paradigms systems have emerged, like new SOA 2.0, which use services and events, or SCA (Service Component Architecture) (Chappell (2007)), dedicated to service composition or iPOJO (Escoffier & Hall (2007)).

SCA defines a component and service architecture, using components to manipulate services orchestrations, and create composite services.

SLCA (*Service Lightweight Component Architecture*) (Hourdin et al. (2008)), is a model of architecture for service composition based on an assembly of lightweight components, inspired by SCA. The SLCA model relies on a software and hardware execution environment evolving dynamically. We define this environment as a set of resources, which are all software/hardware entities that undergo appearing or vanishing from the infrastructure. It's not the application that drives this process. SLCA is based on a Web service for device infrastructure using events, and dynamically discoverable in a distributed way. They

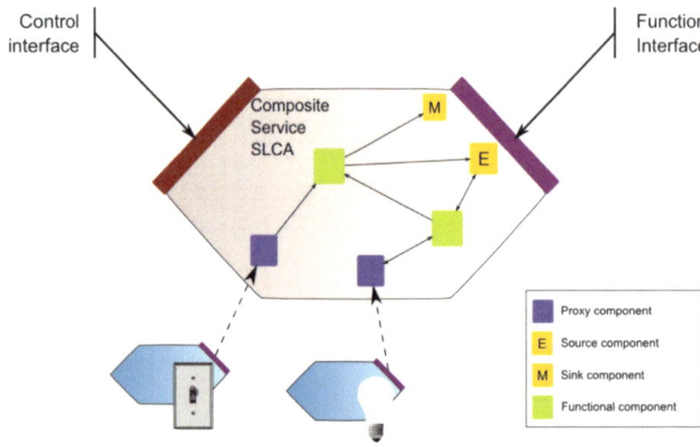

Fig. 7. Composite web service with evented communications

represent devices used in ambient computing applications, as well as composite services created by SLCA.

Applications are designed by service composition mashup, assembling components. A composite service then contains an LCA assembly of components, in a container encapsulated into a service for device. Proxy components to other Web services are thus instantiated in the container of a composite service, and create applications from services available in the environment. Composite service can then create an application communicating with another composite service. It can be seen as a gray box, since it is possible to alter the assembly and access to some functionalities of the components assembly.

A *composite service* provides two service interfaces (FIG. 7). The first one, the dynamic functional interface, allows publishing and accessing functionalities provided by the composite Web service; the second one, the control interface, allows dynamic modifications of the internal component assembly which provides these new functionalities.

The *functional interface* allows to export events and methods of the internal component assembly to the service infrastructure. Then composite services will be part of the graph of the software infrastructure (FIG. 8). The interface is dynamic and exports events and methods of the internal component assembly using *probe components*. Adding or removing a probe component dynamically modifies the functional interface and its description in the corresponding composite service. Adaptation to environment variations can be made by modifying the interface of a composite service, without stopping its execution.

Two types of probe components exist (FIG. 9): *sink*, which adds a method to the composite service interface, and which, in the internal component assembly, has only an output port. The invocation of the method from the service interface thus emits an event in the component assembly. The second type of probe is the *source*, which adds an event to the composite service interface, and has only an input port. The invocation of the method from the component interface thus emits a Web service event.

The *control interface* addresses dynamic modifications of the internal component assembly. It provides methods for adding or removing component instances, types, or bindings, and also to get information about the assembly. Therefore, another client, which can be a composite service using a proxy component for this service, can act on the structure of a composite service. The structural adaptation of composite services and applications is thus possible in the model, by its own entities.

This interface also provides events in order to notify subscribers when structural changes occur into the composite service. Thanks to this mechanism we can adapt composite services

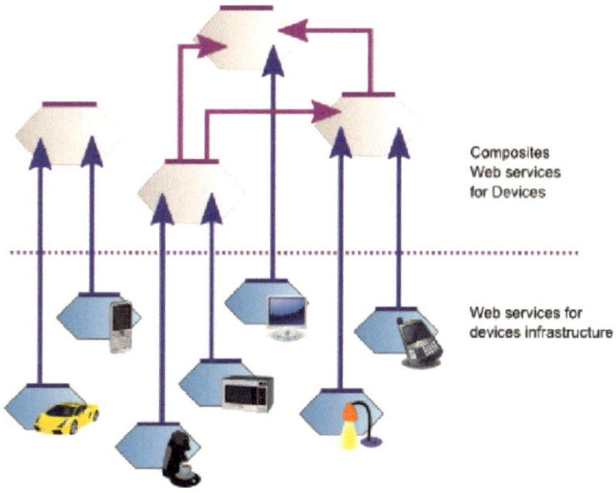

Fig. 8. Graph of Web services with evented communications

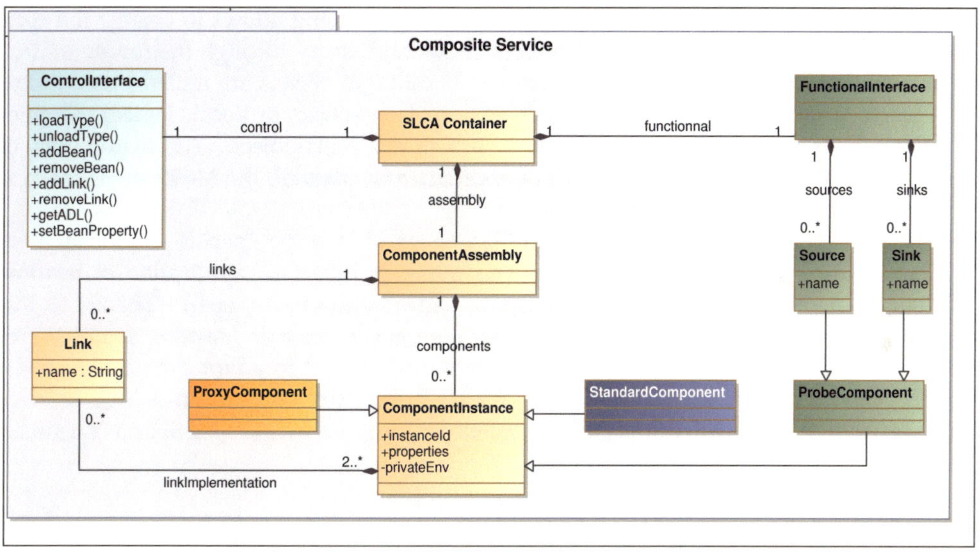

Fig. 9. SLCA Metamodel : composite services interfaces

in a reactive way. Then, we can imagine many sorts of mechanisms of adaptations, and tools to create applications. They are called *designers*. Designers are service consumers for which the control interface of composite services is a required interface. They enable the viewing or modification of a component assembly of composite services using various formalisms and representations. Among these designers, we can mention three that are most often used in the design of ubiquitous computing applications: a designer to visualize an assembly, a designer to dynamically generate proxy components for Web services for devices of the infrastructure, and the Aspect of Assembly designer.

The Aspect of Assembly designer aims to adapt a composite service. It is based on the composite service's control interface to manage a set of adaptation rules. They are triggered when a change occurs in the assembly of the composite service. We will study this mechanism in the next section.

3.3 Synthesis

SLCA composite services are a mean to create fully dynamic applications from a services infrastructure, particularly web services for devices based on communication events.
This dynamicity of the model is available in both (1) setting up applications thanks to functionalities exported in the software infrastructure and (2) the control of composite services. Various tools exist or can be created to consider various concerns of application adaption, such as availability of infrastructure entities, or users' needs.

4. Dynamic application adaptation to the infrastructure evolution

We have seen that ubiquitous systems must be able to consider changes occurring in their environment. And since these changes occur continuously, this must be done at runtime. Reflection is a mechanism that offers such a possibility. Reflection is itself based on two mechanisms: (1) intercession which is the ability for a system to modify itself and (2) introspection which is the ability for a system to observe itself.
Thus reflection through the use of object-oriented programming allows to change the code of objects in their interpretation. It introduces some modularity through the representation of data and their relationships (inheritance ...). At runtime, objects are reified into editable meta-objects (a representation of the said object) and meta-object protocols (MOP) (Kiczales et al. (1999)) ensure the consistency between object and meta-object. The possibilities of intercession and introspection offered by this approach are maximal. But MOPs use languages that are too generic for ubiquitous systems.
Aspect-Oriented Programming (AOP) is a way to provide some specific abstractions for some crosscutting concerns. Dynamic aspects allow to adapt an application at runtime while encapsulating the adaptation into aspects(Zambrano et al. (2004)). Thanks to this encapsulation, adaptation mechanisms can be more easily reused. Aspects applied over components can be seen in two ways: (1) aspects can be used to adapt components code, (2) aspect can be used to adapt structurally components assemblies. Because Web services for device from the software infrastructure cannot be modified by the system as a consumer; components have to be seen as blackboxes.

4.1 Aspect oriented programming principles

AOP has been proposed by Kiczales *et al* in 1997 (Kiczales et al. (1997)). It allows to define software abstractions that will be woven (applied) on a base application. Originally, AOP appeared to tackle the following problem: *despite all efforts to achieve it, there is still a strong coupling between functional concerns and crosscutting concerns (security, monitoring ...).* The idea of AOP is to separate, into aspects, the representation of crosscutting concerns. Then, the code described in an aspect is injected in the base application thanks to the aspect weaver.
Aspects are composed of *pointcuts* and *advices*. Pointcuts point out "where" to inject the code to adapt the application while advices describe the code to be injected, "what" functionality will be added.
Pointcut genericity allows an aspect to be woven in many parts of the application. AOP allows to minimize code dispersion, grouping it into reusable entities. Joinpoints represent all hooks of applications where advices can be woven. Classically, the aspect language provides mechanisms for adding behavior to pointcuts thanks to operators *after*, *before* and *around*. Thus an advice whose pointcut specifies the *before* keyword will be executed before the execution of the jointpoint matching the pointcut; and inversely with *after* advices. An advice *around* allows to replace or to execute some code before and after the pointcut. The genericity offered

by pointcuts provides an abstraction that reduces the complexity of use of reflection, allowing a high reusability of aspects and a good separation of concerns. According to the paradigm on which is based AOP, the nature of joinpoints can change (objects, components, code ...) but AOP still offers a good separation of crosscutting concerns (Charfi & Mezini (2004)).

```
public aspect Aspect_Name {
pointcut Method_Name() : // code

//// Advice
before():Method_Name() {
        // code
} }
```

Fig. 10. Aspect model in AspectJ

The weaver is the mechanism that takes as input a set of aspects and an application in order to produce an augmented application. Initially, weavers were static and were involved at compile-time as in AspectJ (Kiczales et al. (2001)). The code described into advices is woven into the application code to generate a new source file (eg *.java* or bytecode with AspectJ). So that, the separation of concerns introduced by aspects is no longer relevant at runtime. Aspects are not always independent of each other, some interactions may occur between them. In classical approaches, there is no support offered to resolve these interactions, this must be done by developers. Therefore, weavers have evolved in order to adress these issues. As an example EAOP (Event-based AOP) (Douence & Sudholt (2002)) proposes a dynamic weaving triggered according to some events related to the execution of the base application. Moreover, these works propose mechanisms to resolve interactions between aspects. One approach is to explicitly compose advices relying on a same joinpoint. The second approach is to encapsulate aspects into aspects. In the latter, the weaver intends to evaluate events and, according to this evaluation, execute the corresponding advice.
Finally some works were interested in the implementation of aspects on components, such as SAFRAN (David & Ledoux (2006)), CAM/DAOP (Pinto et al. (2005)) or on services such as AO4BPEL (Charfi & Mezini (2004)). These approaches provide the required modularity for adaptation of applications based on components, with respect to the component's blackbox property.
SAFRAN introduces a new type of triggering mechanism of aspects. Aspects can be triggered on the occurrence of endogenous events (events from the system) or on the occurance of exogenous events (events from outside); adaptation composition is external. CAM/DAOP proposes some mechanisms for concurrency checking of aspects, their composition is external. In CAM/DAOP aspects are components; to improve aspects reusability their pointcuts are separated from advices. AO4BPEL proposes to use aspects to extend BPEL (Business Process Execution Language) in order to increase its modularity and to enable its dynamic adaptation. Accordingly, this approach does not consider changes occurring in the software infrastructure of the application.
In the following sections we will present an example of persistent structural adaptation mechanism based on aspects triggered on changes occurring in the software infrastructure of the application. Those aspects will be merged in case of aspects interactions. This approach allows, in a modular and declarative way, system self-adaption as well as creating applications from scratches.

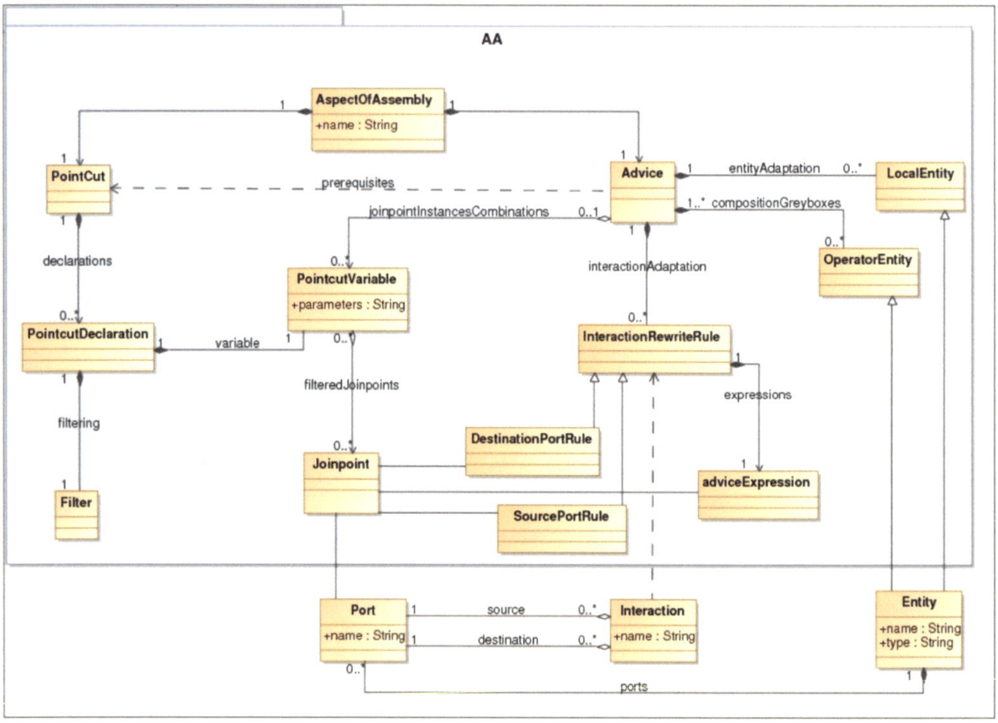

Fig. 11. Aspect of Assembly meta-model

4.2 Crosscutting adaptation

Aspects of Assembly (AA) are an original concept, based on aspect oriented programming. They define some structural reconfigurations of an application that are triggered in response to events from the software infrastructure. Events inform of the appearance / disappearance of devices in the software infrastructure. These rules are woven and composed according to a well-defined logic in case of conflict. They are applied on components assemblies which are not necessarily known *a priori*. Various languages and composition rules can be defined according to the type of applications on which they will be applied. So, Aspect of Assembly can be used to adapt applications based on a component model using evented communications (Cheung-Foo-Wo (2009)). AA are based on a non-invasive model and respect the blackbox property of components.
In the following section we will present the main concepts of Aspects of Assembly as modelized in Figure 11: the joinpoint model(4.2.1), the pointcut model (4.2.2), the advice model (4.2.3), and the weaver (4.2.4).

4.2.1 Joinpoint

Joinpoints are all entities of the assembly that structurally represent the application, on which changes will take place: components and their ports. This allows to consider messages related to ports.

4.2.2 Pointcut

Pointcuts are defined as a set of filters on joinpoints. In fact, they are filters on joinpoint's meta-datas (port name, types ...). Those filters produce some combination of *instantiated joinpoints* (FIG. 12). AA may use various strategies to perform the pointcut matching, the most common one is based on a pattern matching language. Instead of identifying elements of code, since AA describe structural changes, they identify components and ports thanks to their meta-datas like their name. Pointcuts allow to introduce into an application some crosscutting concerns described in their associated advice without knowing the assembly on which they will be applied. At runtime, they interface a real assembly with some abstract advices to produce some real configurations to be incorporated in the application. These configurations are called instances of advice. An advice produces many instances of advice when many combinations of instantiated joinpoint are matched by pointcuts.

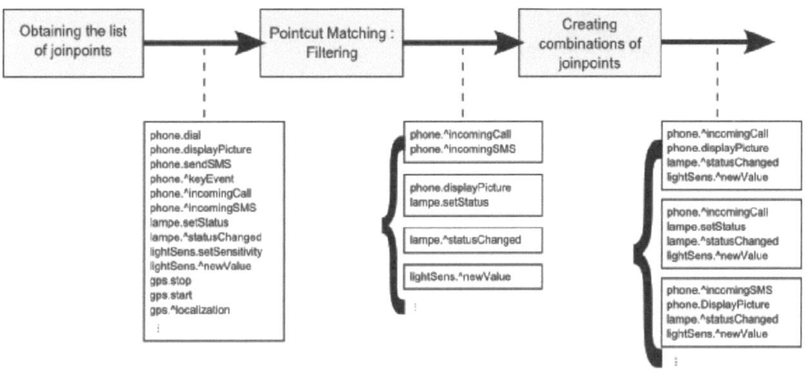

Fig. 12. Example of pointcut matching process

Some others mechanisms for pointcut matching than pattern matching can be studied. For instance, if an AA defines an adaptation related to a switch, rather than processing a pattern matching as `switch*`, a semantic matching would be more appropriated. Indeed, one of the ideas that we stand for in ubiquitous computing is the separation of features offered by devices into more basic features. As an example a phone is designed to make call or send messages, but could act as a display, a switch, etc... The French national project Continuum[6] is working on such an extension of AA.

Pointcut are evaluated when an AA is selected or when a change occurs in the software infrastructure (appearance/ disappearance of devices) of the application to be adapted (FIG. 18). When at least one joinpoint is satifying each pointcut rule, some combinations of joinpoints are generated and the AA is now in the state : *applicable*. Then, it can be woven on the application assembly.

Therefore, pointcuts define the prerequisites to weave AA; even if they are selected by users to adapt an application, AA cannot be woven unless the application assembly is in a state compatible with its poincut (i.e. it contains the entities and ports required for adaptation).

4.2.3 Advice

Because AA modify the structure of components assemblies, adaptations consist in a set of basic structural changes: adding a component or a connection between ports to the base assembly. The removal of components or interactions is performed too if an AA is withdrawn.

[6] ANR CONTINUUM — ANR-08-VERS-005. http://continuum.unice.fr/

Links additions are usually done by rewriting the existing ones, for adaptations that fit with an existing application, rather than redefining the application. Any change can be seen as a transformation from an assembly to a new assembly (FIG. 16).
A specific language is also used to express advices. In traditional aspects, advices are often code written in the same language as the language of the targeted application. In AA, entities are added and their code is not dependent of the advice's expression; an advice must describe the integration of these new entities in the existing assembly. The specific language of AA's advices is not fixed by the model and designers can define their own language according to the type of adaptation expected.
The various keywords, or operators of a language allow a designer to define how will be composed advices. In the following section we will study the ISL4WComp language, that is used in our works in the field of ubiquitous computing. Thanks to this language, we can describe advices based on events streams.

4.2.3.1 Components used in advices

As explained previously, advices describe changes that must be done in a component assembly. Those changes consist in adding components or bindings between components.
The added entities must be defined and available in the system to manage the component assembly during AA weaving.
Among components that can be instantiated by AA, we can distinguish two types of components: blackbox components and greybox components.
Blackbox components encapsulate functionalities that are only accessible through their ports (Szyperski et al. (1999)). Only the way they interact can be managed. The entities explicitly added to provide a new functionality in the adaptation described by an advice are blackbox components. When several advices involving blackbox components are composed, we talk of external weaving. As a consequence the weaver cannot process some internal merging between those components since only their interface is known. Entities explicitly added by advices are also called local entities. They are represented as `LocalEntity` in the AA meta-model presented in (FIG. 11).

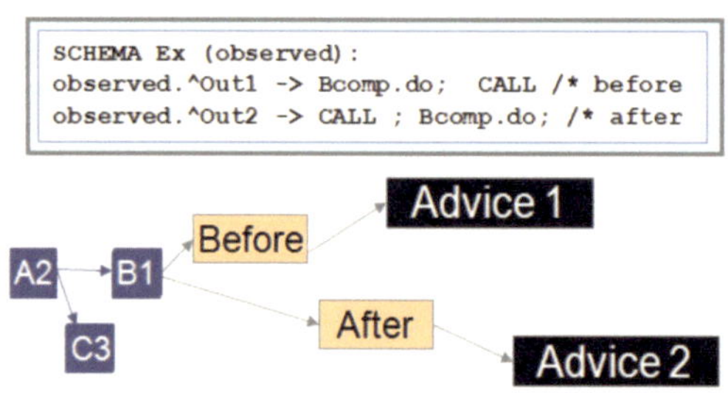

Fig. 13. Blackbox components

As an example, considering and adaptation whose aims to filters one of two messages between two components. This adaptation will add a component to do this. Such a component is a blackbox, only its interface is known by the weaver. It will be added in place of the former interaction. Two new interactions will be created to link the input port of the primary interaction.
Greybox components, conversely, partially explain their semantics, either using an interface description or reflectivity, either it is at least partly known by the weaver. From this knowledge, it is possible to work on a way to compose them manually or automatically. Such

a process is called *composition* or *merging* process (Cheung-Foo-Wo (2009)) of greybox advices. Then, thanks to this mechanism the system is able to manage interactions between various instances of advice from various AA. Greybox components are instanciated by the weaver when some advice language operators are used or when the weaver has to manage some interactions between instances of advice.

```
SCHEMA Ex (observed, timeout):
    observed.^Out ->
          (  IF ( timeout.Check ) CALL )
    timeout.Check ->
          (  timeout.Start ; CALL      )
```

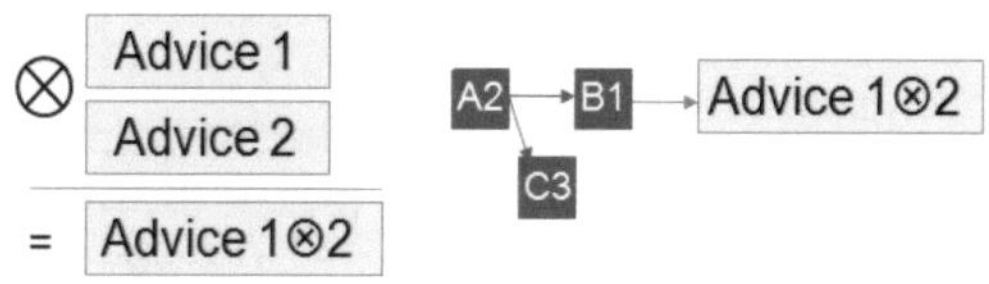

Fig. 14. Greybox components

As an example, an advice rule can specify that when two interactions from a same component are created from various instances of advice, a *sequence* type greybox component will be introduced to establish a priority between those two interactions.

4.2.3.2 ISL4WComp : A language for advices

ISL4WComp is based on the ISL Interaction Specification Language that describes interactions patterns between independent objects (Berger (2001)). ISL4WComp adapts these specifications to consider interactions based on messages or events between components. This language is composable: multiple instances of advice can be composed and merged into a single assembly combining their respective behavior. The merging mechanism, embedded into the weaver, ensures the property of symmetry (associativity, commutativity and idempotency) (Cheung-Foo-Wo, Blay-Fornarino, Tigli, Lavirotte & Riveill (2006)) in the weaving operation of various AA. This means that, the order in which aspects are woven is not important. It implies that the result of a weaving cycle will not be the base assembly given as input to the next cycle (Ferry et al. (2009)). Hence, there is no history of AA appliance. This property is ensured for AA's weaving operation because the operators of the language are symmetrical. This means that the order in which rules are merged is not important. This property is a major point since the application assembly changes dynamically, lead by devices appearance or disappearance. Because of the unpredictability of these changes, the order in which adaptations must be woven cannot be known. So the order in which AA are woven must not be important.

Advices written using ISL4WComp are based on three types of rules: (1) the addition of blackbox components, (2) rewriting links between components of the assembly and (3) the creation of new links. Rewriting involves components ports, it consists in : forwarding an input port or redirecting a message (output port). These rules are identified thanks to two key words, ':' for blackbox components instanciation and '$\rightarrow$' for rewriting and creating links.

An advice describes a set of adaptation rules to be applied on variable components defined in pointcut. Some specific language operators as `call` and `delegate` allow to control how the composition of instances of advice will be done. These keywords, associated to sequence and parallelism operators are similar to classical AOP keywords : *before*, *around* and *after*.

	Keywords / Operators	Description
port types	*comp.port*	'.' is to separate the name of an instance of component from the name of a port. It describes a provided port.
	comp.^ port	'^ ' at the beginning of a port name describes a required port.
Rules for structural adaptations	*comp : type*	To create a blackbox component
	comp : type (prop = val, ...)	To create a blackbox component and to initialize properties
	provided_port → (required_port)	To create a link between two ports. The keyword → separate the right part of the rule from its left part
	provided_port → (provided_port)	To rewrite an existing link by changing the destination port
Operators (symmetry property, conflicts resolution)	... ; ...	Describe the sequence
	... || ...	To describe that there is no order (parallelism)
	`if (condition) {...} else {...}`	`condition` is evaluated by a blackbox component
	`nop`	Nothing to do
	`call`	Allow to reuse the left part of a rule in a rewriting rule
	`delegate`	Allow to specify that an interaction is unique in case of conflict

Table 1. ISL4WComp operators and keywords

4.2.3.3 A sample of ISL4WComp based advice

To illustrate the concepts previously presented, we will now study an example of advice based on ISL4WComp. First we define an independent adaptation schema for a domotic application. It aims to link a switch to any kind of light in order to control the light using the switch. Both light and switch proxy components are generated into the components assembly. The advice presented below proposes to adapt this behavior by adding an energy saving concern. To be applied, it takes into account a brightness sensor, therefore allowing to switch on the light when the brightness is under a defined threshold. Moreover, the new assembly sends a message to give a feedback to the user when it tries to switch on the light while the brightness is too high.

The advice is called `brightness_light`. The three variables `light`, `brightness` and `switch`, defined at the first line, describe the joinpoints (eg components) identified by the pointcut matching that will be used in the advice. They will be replaced by the instantiated joinpoint identified at weaving time. This AA highlights the three types of rules previously presented. At line 3,4 and 5, some blackbox components are added. The *threshold* component is instantiated with the property threshold up to 10. A property is a public variable from a component accessible through its interface. Line 7 defines a rewriting rule for input ports. All links connected to the input port (method) 'SetState' will be rewritten. Line 10 and 12 describe a creation rule for interactions from output ports (event).

```
1 advice brightness_light ( light, brightness, switch ) :
2
3 Emitter : 'BasicBeans.PrimitiveValueEmitter'
4 threshold : 'BasicBeans.Threshold' ( threshold = 10 )
5 t1,t2 : 'System.Windows.Forms.TextBox'
6
7 light.SetState -> (
8       if (threshold.IsReached) {Emitter.FireValueEvent}
9       else {call})
10 Emitter.^EmitStringValue -> (
11      t1.set_Text)
12 brightness.^Value_Evented_NewValue -> (
13      threshold.set_Value ; t2.set_Text)
```

Fig. 15. Sample of ISL4WComp advice

Among all the operators found in this example, the more complex is `call` (line 9). The `if` block describes that if the brightness threshold is reached the system must sent an error message. Otherwise, the `call` operator is replaced with the left part of the rule, by the original method call that is being rewritten. This means that when this adaptation is woven into the base application, if a link to the input port `lumiere.SetState` was previously defined, the interaction already defined will still be implemented.

ISL4WComp is well-defined to describe reactive adaptations to create ubiquitous applications. Its operators can define more complex behavior than a structural reconfiguration. Moreover, it guarantees that the result of the weaving of several behaviors is idempotent, associative and commutative.

4.2.4 The weaver

The weaver is the program responsible for aspects weaving. It builds a unique component assembly from a base assembly and a set of Aspect of Assembly. The base assembly of an application is the assembly without any AA applied. The weaver manages all the processes that are required to weave some adaptations (FIG. 16). The weaving process can be decomposed into three steps. First, the pointcut matching is a function that has a set of components, from the base assembly, and pointcuts, from a set of selected AA, as input. Its goal is to find the joinpoints on which advices will be woven. The second step is called the advice factory. It then generates instances of advices, replacing variable components in advices of selected aspects by joinpoints obtained during the first step. Instances of advices describe modifications to be woven in the actual base assembly of components. Finally, the composition engine merges all instances of advices with the initial assembly. It generates a single instance of advice that will be woven as the final assembly. In the next section, we will present more in details those processes.

4.2.4.1 Pointcut matching and advice factory

The weaver has a list of aspects of assembly that have been selected by users for the adaptation of an application. Their weaving in the target assembly depends on the evaluation of pointcuts. When a joinpoint is identified for each pointcut rules of an AA, it becomes *relevant*. (FIG. 18). Then the advice factory generates instances of advices, replacing variable components in advices of selected aspects by joinpoints obtained during the weaving. Several strategies are possible when several joinpoints are identified for a same rules (FIG. 12). An example can help to understand the different options: let us consider an application composed of a pair of switch and a pair of lights. A first strategy would create two combinations: the

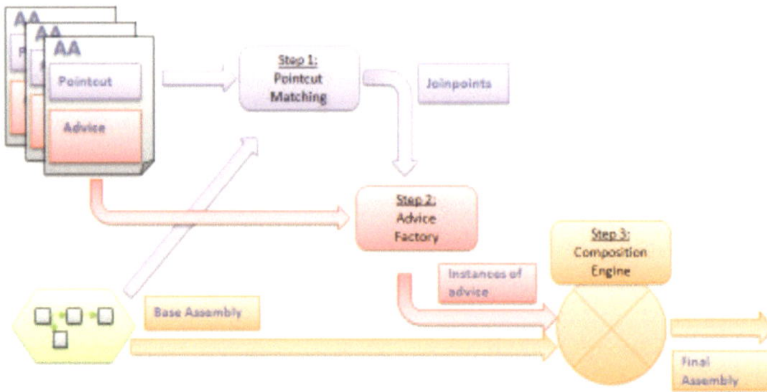

Fig. 16. The weaving process

first containing the first switch and the first lamp, and the second consisting of the second switch and the second lamp. An ''all combination'' strategy would create the combinations of all pairs of switches and lights. The choice of a strategy is up to the designer.

4.2.4.2 Conflict identification

Two instances of advice are conflicting (interacting) when they have at least one joinpoint in common. So, when several instances of advice and the base assembly are composed, some conflicts may occur. They have to be detected and considered by the weaver. Some operators in the advice language can define how conflicts should be managed. As an example, using ISL4WComp, the `call` and `delegate` operators are replaced by conflicting rules, but do not define any order when there are more than two rules conflicting.

4.2.4.3 Instances of advice composition

As we have seen, several AA can be applied on the same application. In the ISL4WComp language (4.2.3.2), operators are based on a set of logical rules that ensure the property of *symmetry* to the instance of advice composition. This property is composed of three subproperties: *associativity*, *commutativity* and *idempotency*. These logical rules are grouped in a matrix of composition operators ensuring the three subproperties. AA composition is an implementation of formal works on the composition of logical rules (Cheung-Foo-Wo, Blay-Fornarino, Tigli, Déry, Emsellem & Riveill (2006)). According to those logical rules, the weaver is able to resolve AA's rules conflicts while ensuring the symmetry property of the weaving operation. So that the order in which rules are merged is not important and neither is the order in which instances of AA are woven.

4.2.4.4 Adaptations Triggering

In the manner of automatons cycles, consisting of a phase of acquisition (storage of inputs), then processing and finally writing outputs, we're talking about weaving cycle (Figure 3). Inputs are AA and an assembly, processing is the weaving process and output is a new assembly, a new application. In order to be reactive, the weaver can be triggered in two ways:

User-driven by changing the set of AAs given as input to the weaver. This can be done by selecting/deselecting or adding/removing aspects of assembly at runtime. When the set of AA is modified, the weaver is triggered, leading to adaptation if an added AA can be applied or if an AA has been removed.

Infrastructure-driven when a new device appears or disappears in the environment, a new component communicating with the device, is dynamically instantiated in or removed from the assembly. The adaptation process is triggered and only AAs that can be woven according to newly available components are applied. AA over SLCA benefits from the dynamicity of such an architecture. They can be triggered when a proxy appears into a container since it sends a notification trough its structural interface when a new component is instantiated.

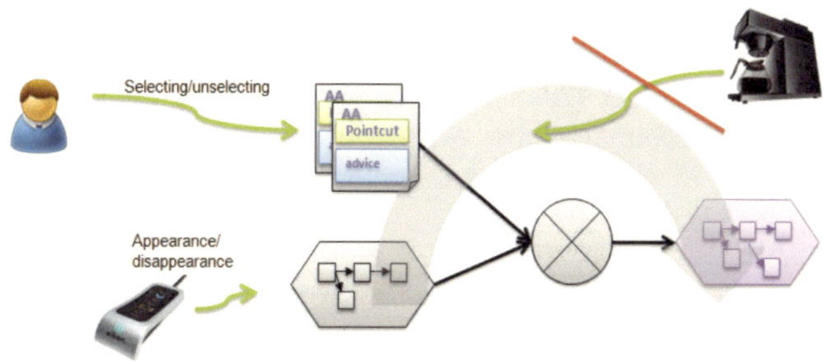

Fig. 17. Triggering mechanisms

An important point for the reactivity of such a mechanism is that the system doesn't require any information about the state of the software infrastructure. With a dynamic of its own, the infrastructure imposes its pace. However, during a weaving cycle, the system does not tolerate other disruptions (FIG 17).
Therefore, the life-cycle of an AA passes through various states (FIG 18). Originally an AA is in an *unselected* state. This means that the user does not want to apply it. In such a case, its pointcuts are not even evaluated. When an AA is selected, its pointcuts are evaluated. They will be evaluated for each modification of the assembly on which will be applied the AA. If some joinpoints are satisfying all the pointcut rules of an AA, it becomes *relevant* before being woven. AA that were not relevant may become, unless a new component appears in the application assembly. Similarly, those that have been woven can become disapplicated and still *selected* if an entity identified by their pointcut disappear.

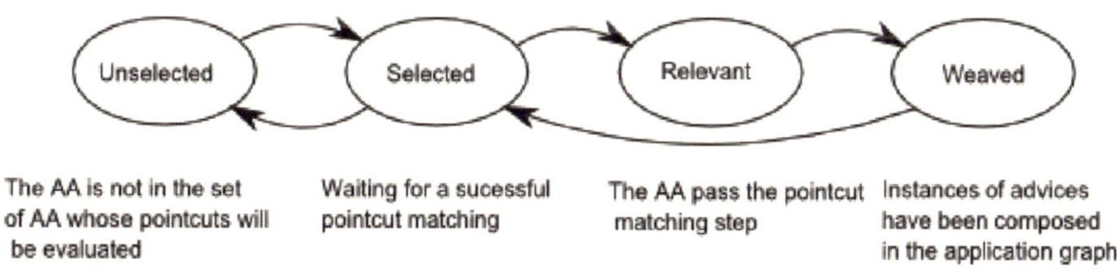

Fig. 18. AA life cycle

4.3 Synthesis

Aspect of Assembly are a model of compositional adaptation mechanism triggered by events from the software infrastructure. The model is generic enough to allow its use in various fields and for various concerns. According to the language used to express AA, various adaptations policies and composition policies can be defined. The ISL4WComp language helps building safe adaptations thanks to the property of symmetry and the respect of components blackbox properties.

5. Experiments

To validate our works in term of performances some experiments on service composition and adaptations have been made. First, we will present some results on the creation time of basic components in a composite service. Second, we will describe some results on the major step of the adaptation process and for the overall process.

5.1 Experiments on service composition

The SLCA model has been projected into an implementation called SharpWComp 2.0, which was deposed as copyrighted software in France, used and developed in three programs of the French National Research Agency (ANR). Service composition in pervasive computing needs to be reactive to take into account changes of the infrastructure quickly and to adapt to users' needs. We measured time of creation and destruction of components in a composite service in SharpWComp 2.0 (FIG. 21).

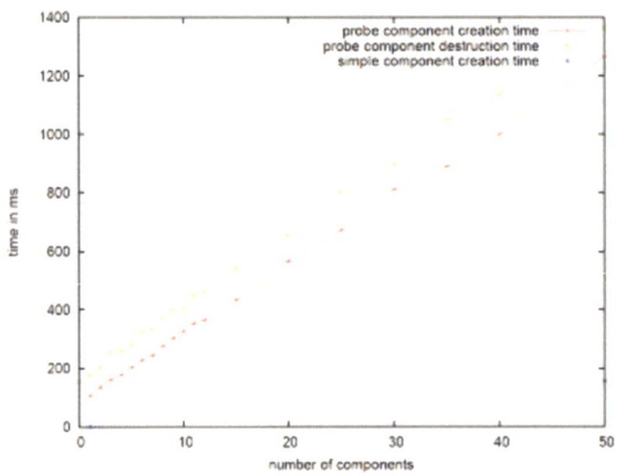

Fig. 19. Component creation and destruction time measures.

The creation time of basic components, as well as proxy components, is constant, around 3ms. Therefore, to create n components, $3 \times n$ ms are needed. The removal of such components couldn't have been measured, because we are in a managed memory environment. This is equivalent to dereference the instance of the component, and remove it from the container's list, which was too fast to be measured. Link creation and destruction time are also too simple operations and could not be measured. These measures correspond to the Lightweight Component Architecture (LCA). For probe components, that rely, in SharpWComp 2.0, on Intel's C# UPnP stack, the creation and destruction time are more important. This is due to the fact that when changing the service interface of a composite service, service advertisements are sent to inform that the previous interface is no longer valid, and then they are reissued with the new interface. With UPnP, an advertisement has to be made for each existing service, so if we consider that a probe component creates a service, every new probe will correspond to sending one more message each time. This is why adding the fortieth probe will take nearly one second

The generation time for proxy component is an important factor in our model. We measured it for a standard light device, containing ten methods divided into two services and two evented variables: the average value is 140.6ms. Thus, the time elapsed from the appearance of a service on the infrastructure to the adaptation of a composite service can be calculated. It will be a sum of the proxy component generation time (140.6ms), the component instantiation time (3ms), the adaptation of the composite service time, depending on how many new components are created, especially probe components and their number in the former assembly.

5.2 Experiments on assembly adaptation

We validate our approach in term of reactivity with some experiments on components assemblies randomly generated. Weaving cycles can be divided into three categories, each with its own cost in time.

1. Selection of AAs and pointcut matching
2. The advice factory
3. Composition and potentially merging of advice instances.

Those experiments were conducted on a standard personal computer (Athlon x2 1,8GHz processor). For this purpose various types of components have been instantiated randomly.
The advice factory step is a low cost process in term of duration. Experiments have shown that for an assembly including about 300 joinpoints and 2 AA, the duration of the process is between 2 or 3 ms.
Some experiments have been made on pointcut matching duration. They have involved a pointcut consisting of three rules, and a set of joinpoints ranging from 0-300. Several experiments have been made, the curve presented in Figure 20 is an average of these series and the standard derivation between the values obtained. We can conclude that the pointcut matching process is not time consuming.
The curve presented in Figure 20 shows the experimental results of the merging mechanism with a conflict probability about 0.5 for the red curve and about 0.33 for the blue curve. These evaluations highlight the high cost of the merging mechanism which is about 85 percents of the total cost of the weaving process. Then the probability of conflict between several instances of advice also plays a major role in the duration of the conflict resolution mechanism.

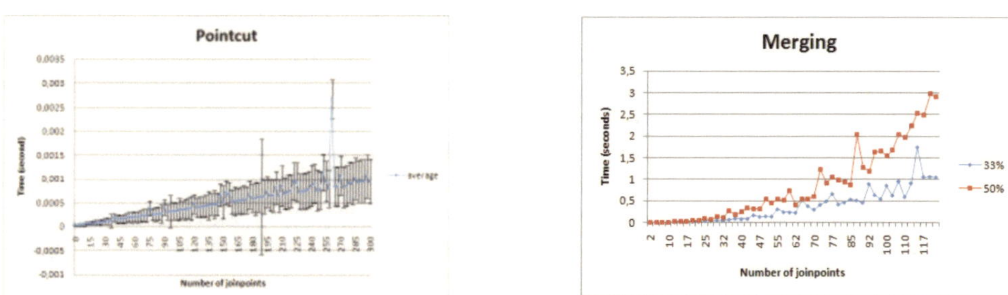

Fig. 20. Pointcut matching and merging time measures.

Figure 21 presents the duration of a weaving cycle according to the number of joinpoints in the base assembly. We consider that all these joinpoints are satisfying the pointcut matching and all combinations between all those joinpoints are generated.
In the field of human computer interactions, it is considered that the user latency at most is about 100ms. Then, Bérard in (Crowley et al. (2000)) propose that the latency for highly tied interactive systems must be twice lower than user latency : 50ms. Under this bound, we are able to compose about 30 components together. On the other hand, ubiquitous computing

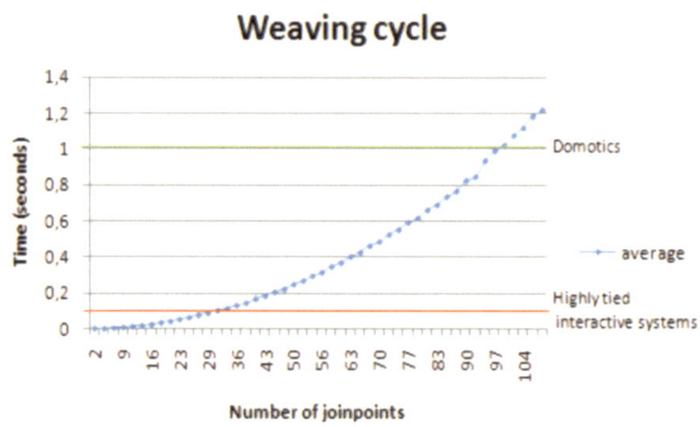

Fig. 21. Weaving time measures.

does not necessarily require such a response time. In the field of domotics, a bearable latency is about 1 second. Under this bound we are able to compose about 100 joinpoints.

6. References

Arnold, K., Scheifler, R., Waldo, J., O'Sullivan, B. & Wollrath, A. (1999). *Jini Specification*, Addison-Wesley Longman Publishing Co., Inc.

Berger, L. (2001). *Mise en Œuvre des Interactions en Environnements Distribués, Compilés et Fortement Typés : le Modèle MICADO*, Thèse de doctorat, Université de Nice-Sophia Antipolis - Faculté des sciences et techniques, École doctorale STIC - Informatique.

Bottaro, A., Gérodolle, A. & Lalanda, P. (2007). Pervasive service composition in the home network, *Advanced Information Networking and Applications, 2007. AINA'07. 21st International Conference on*, pp. 596–603.

Breivold, H. & Larsson, M. (2007). Component-Based and Service-Oriented Software Engineering: Key Concepts and Principles, *Software Engineering and Advanced Applications, 2007. 33rd EUROMICRO Conference on*, pp. 13–20.

Brønsted, J., Hansen, K. & Ingstrup, M. (2007). A survey of service composition mechanisms in ubiquitous computing, *Second Workshop on Requirements and Solutions for Pervasive Software Infrastructures (RSPSI) at Ubicomp*.

Bustamante, F., Widener, P. & Schwan, K. (2002). Scalable directory services using proactivity, *Proceedings of Supercomputing 2002*.

Cardoso, R. S. & Issarny, V. (2007). Architecting Pervasive Computing Systems for Privacy: A Survey, *Proceedings of the Sixth Working IEEE/IFIP Conference on Software Architecture*, IEEE Computer Society, p. 26.

Chakraborty, D., Joshi, A., Finin, T. & Yesha, Y. (2005). Service Composition for Mobile Environments, *Mobile Networks and Applications* 10(4): 435–451.

Champion, M., Ferris, C., Newcomer, E. & Orchard, D. (2002). Web services architecture, *W3C working draft* .

Chappell, D. (2007). Introducing SCA, *David Chappell and Associates* .

Charfi, A. & Mezini, M. (2004). Aspect-oriented web service composition with AO4BPEL, *Lecture Notes in Computer Science* pp. 168–182.

Chen, H., Chakraborty, D., Xu, L., Joshi, A. & Finin, T. (2000). Service discovery in the future electronic market, *Proc. Workshop on Knowledge Based Electronic Markets, AAAI2000, Austin*.

Cheung-Foo-Wo, D. (2009). *Adaptation Dynamique par Tissage d'Aspects d'Assemblage*, PhD thesis, Université de Nice - Sophia Antipolis.

Cheung-Foo-Wo, D., Blay-Fornarino, M., Tigli, J., Lavirotte, S. & Riveill, M. (2006). Adaptation dynamique d'assemblages de dispositifs dirigée par des modèles, *2ème journées sur l'Ingénieurie Dirigée par les Modèles (IDM)*.

Cheung-Foo-Wo, D., Blay-Fornarino, M., Tigli, J.-Y., Déry, A.-M., Emsellem, D. & Riveill, M. (2006). Langage d'aspect pour la composition dynamique de composants embarqués, *RTSI - L'Objet* 12(2-3): 89–111.

Clarke, M., Blair, G., Coulson, G. & Parlavantzas, N. (2001). An efficient component model for the construction of adaptive middleware, *Proceedings of the IFIP/ACM International Conference on Distributed Systems Platforms Heidelberg*, Springer-Verlag, pp. 160–178.

Crowley, J., Coutaz, J. & Bérard, F. (2000). Perceptual user interfaces: things that see, *Communications of the ACM* 43(3).

David, P. & Ledoux, T. (2006). An aspect-oriented approach for developing self-adaptive fractal components, *Lecture Notes in Computer Science* 4089: 82.

Douence, R. & Sudholt, M. (2002). A model and a tool for Event-based Aspect-Oriented Programming (EAOP), *LMO'03* .

Englander, R. (1997). *Developing Java Beans*, O'Reilly & Associates, Inc.

Escoffier, C. & Hall, R. (2007). Dynamically adaptable applications with iPOJO service components, *Lecture Notes in Computer Science* 4829: 113.

Ferry, N., Lavirotte, S., Tigli, J.-Y., Rey, G. & Riveill, M. (2009). Context Adaptative Systems based on Horizontal Architecture for Ubiquitous Computing, *International Conference on Mobile Technology, Applications and Systems (Mobility)*.

Guttman, E. (1999). Service Location Protocol: Automatic Discovery of IP Network Services, *IEEE Internet Computing* 3: 71–80.

Hourdin, V., Lavirotte, S. & Tigli, J.-Y. (2006). Comparaison des systèmes de services pour dispositifs, *Technical Report I3S/RR-2006-25-FR*, Laboratoire I3S, Sophia Antipolis, France.

Hourdin, V., Tigli, J.-Y., Lavirotte, S., Rey, G. & Riveill, M. (2008). SLCA, composite services for ubiquitous computing, *Proceedings of the 5th International Conference on Mobile Technology, Applications and Systems(Mobility)*, p. 8.

Huang, P., Lenders, V., Minnig, P. & Widmer, M. (2002). Mini: A minimal platform comparable to Jini for ubiquitous computing, *International Symposium on Distributed Objects and Applications (DOA), Irvine*.

Kiczales, G., Bobrow, D. & des Rivieres, J. (1999). *The art of the metaobject protocol*, MIT press.

Kiczales, G., Hilsdale, E., Hugunin, J., Kersten, M., Palm, J. & Griswold, W. (2001). An overview of AspectJ, *ECOOP 2001 - Object-Oriented Programming* pp. 327–354.

Kiczales, G., Lamping, J., Mendhekar, A., Maeda, C., Lopes, C., Loingtier, J.-M. & Irwin, J. (1997). Aspect-oriented programming, *ECOOP*, SpringerVerlag.

MacKenzie, M., Laskey, K., McCabe, F., Brown, P. & Metz, R. (2006). Reference model for service oriented architecture 1.0, *Technical Report wd-soa-rm-cd1*, OASIS. **URL:** *http://www.oasis-open.org/committees/tc_home.php?wg_abbrev=soa-rm*

Papazoglou, M. (2003). Service-oriented computing: Concepts, characteristics and directions, *Web Information Systems Engineering, 2003. WISE 2003. Proceedings of the Fourth International Conference on*, pp. 3–12.

Pinto, M., Fuentes, L. & Troya, J. (2005). A dynamic component and aspect-oriented platform, *The Computer Journal* 48(4): 401.

Preuß, S. (2003). JESA Service Discovery Protocol: Efficient Service discovery in ad-hoc networks, *Lecture notes in computer science* pp. 1196–1201.

Sedov, I., Preuss, S., Cap, C., Haase, M. & Timmermann, D. (2003). Time and energy efficient service discovery in Bluetooth, *Vehicular Technology Conference, 2003. VTC 2003-Spring. The 57th IEEE Semiannual*, Vol. 1.

Singh, M. & Huhns, M. (2005). *Service-oriented computing: semantics, processes, agents*, John Wiley & Sons Inc.

Szyperski, C., Bosch, J. & Weck, W. (1999). Component Oriented Programming, *Lecture Notes in Computer Science* 1743: 184–184.

Tigli, J.-Y., Lavirotte, S., Rey, G., Hourdin, V. & Riveill, M. (2009a). Lightweight Service Oriented Architecture for Pervasive Computing, *International Journal of Computer Science Issues (IJCSI)* 4: 1–9.

Tigli, J.-Y., Lavirotte, S., Rey, G., Hourdin, V. & Riveill, M. (2009b). Lightweight Service Oriented Architecture for Pervasive Computing, *International Journal of Computer Science Issues (IJCSI)* 4.

Vallée, M., Ramparany, F. & Vercouter, L. (2005). Flexible composition of smart device services, *The 2005 International Conference on Pervasive Systems and Computing(PSC-05).*

Ververidis, C. & Polyzos, G. (2008). Service Discovery for Mobile Ad Hoc Networks: A Survey of Issues and Techniques, *IEEE Communications Surveys and Tutorials* .

Vinoski, S. & Inc, I. (1997). CORBA: integrating diverse applications within distributed heterogeneous environments, *IEEE Communications Magazine* 35(2): 46–55.

Zambrano, A., Gordillo, S. & Jaureguiberry, I. (2004). Aspect-based adaptation for ubiquitous software, *Mobile and Ubiquitous Information Access* pp. 136–140.

Zhu, F., Mutka, M. & Ni, L. (2005). Service discovery in pervasive computing environments, *IEEE Pervasive Computing* 4(4): 81–90.

9

Semantically Enriched Integration Framework for Ubiquitous Computing Environment

Habib Abdulrab, Eduard Babkin and Oleg Kozyrev
[1]*LITIS laboratory, INSA de Rouen*
[2]*State University – Higher School of Economics*
[1]*France*
[2]*Russia*

1. Introduction

Miniaturization, reduced costs of electronic components, and advanced information technologies now open practical possibilities to design, develop and deploy thousands of the coin-sized sensors and mechanical devices at multiple locations. This kind of software-hardware systems, pervasively available to the user in everyday activities, is named Ubiquitous Computing Environment (UCE) (Abowd & Mynatt, 2000; Niemelä & Latvakoski 2004), or even - Ubiquitous Smart Space (Jeng, 2004 ; Kawahara et al., 2004). Establishing *ad hoc* communication via wireless media numerous elements of the UCE provide the user with real-time global sensing, context-aware informational retrieval, and enhanced visualization capabilities. In effect, they give extremely new abilities to look at and interact with our habitat. Many researches made a contribution to developing of Sensors and Actuators Networks (SANET), which became a foundation of UCE. There are tiny hardware devices available in practice for building SANET, embedded operating systems, wireless network protocols, and algorithms of effective energy management (Misc.Tinyos, 2010; Feng et al., 2002; Tilak et al., 2002; Crossbow, 2010). Now researchers' community demonstrates growing interest to resolving the next important problem that will be faced by the developers and the users of UCE since a short time. That is the problem of semantic interoperability in the joint context of SANET, existing IT-infrastructure and people society.
Resent results (Branch et al., 2005 ; Curino et al., 2005 ; Tsetsos et al., 2005; Ahamed et al., 2004; Tokunaga et al., 2004 ; Chan et al., 2005) show applicability of the middleware paradigm for the solution of that problem, and provide for approaches facilitating integration of SANET on the application level of enterprise systems.
However in the case of actual wide-area UCE, multiple SANETs spread across administrative borders, enterprises, and even social cultures. Deep involving of tiny computing devices in our everyday activities requires closer coincidence of computer interfaces with people's way of perception and mental world models. As activities and social experience are different, the mental world models also differ. So, interfacing with the same sensors can be absolutely dissimilar in respect with the style, modality and informational contents. The same raw data collected by sensors can be interpreted differently and can be applied in absolutely divergent contexts. This simple fact breaks a "closed world" assumption, and requires shedding light of researcher's attention on such

issues as explicit meta-data representation, and formal modelling of system properties and interfaces to achieve semantic interoperability.

In our research we explore ways to extend existing partial middleware solutions in UCE with a consistent model-driven methodology for semi-automated design and development of semantic integration components called "Ontology Mediators". The main purpose of Ontology Mediator is communication with SANETs, data integration and seamless fusion of diverging real-world concepts and relationships in accordance with information needs of certain single user or a small user's group. Depending on specific conditions and requirements, implementation of Ontology Mediator varies from specialized middleware components to reconfigurable hardware devices. Tailored for local *ad hoc* requirements Ontology Mediator provides strong support for the claim (Herring, 2000) "…that computer products now eventually progress from large, general-purpose, impersonal static forms to portable, personal, flexible, market-targeted forms. Personalization, flexibility, and quick time to market dictates a 'quick turn' design approach."

During domain modelling, design, and development of Ontology Mediators different end-user tools, component libraries and algorithms should be used. No doubt, the best results can be achieved when all these elements are combined into the vertical framework supporting all stages of the methodology. We have designed architecture of such semantic interoperability framework suitable for loosely coupled distributed systems like SANETs, and developed a number of software and hardware prototypes to evaluate benefits and afford proof of Ontology Mediator and the design methodology. This framework supports semi-automated design and development of Ontology Mediators, as well as it allows for designing and establishing coherent information flow between different components on the basis of coordinated ontology transformation activities. In the course of the prototype implementation we applied RDF-model transformations in order to provide semantic interoperability and semantic validation, and explored different kinds of software technologies (the JavaSpace, JMS Messaging, and CORBA). Altogether, these contributions are used for rapid development of highly customized Ontology Mediators in UCE.

In this work we describe most important characteristics of the proposed framework as follows. In Section 3 our motivation is explained using a specific use case of semantic integration. Section 3 gives a short description of foundations and relevant topics to our research. Section 4 contains explanation of major steps in our methodology of Ontology Mediator's design. The general architecture of the supporting framework is presented in Section 5. Sections 6 and 7 give a detailed view on the most important components of the framework: the Transformation Engine (T-Engine) and the extensible hardware platform. We summarize obtained results and compare them with other known approaches in the conclusion (Section 8).

2. Motivation

In order to support necessity of a specific methodology for design and development of Ontology Mediators we propose to concern a case study of their application in the context of wide-area UCE. In this case study modern seaports were chosen for consideration due to significant role of sea transportation in economics and its great impact on environmental safety and security.

Since last thirty years seaport infrastructure became an extremely complex system where multiple physical objects with interfering properties, abstract logical concepts and normative procedures are tightly coupled to support 24-hour cargo operations, transportation logistics, custom and security checking. Although a usual seaport provides for different services like containers import-export, oil terminals and passengers transportation, the former kind of services plays a major role. Different authors estimate amount of container operations from 80 to 90 percent of total world cargo throughput. And most of these operations are concentrated at a relatively small number of huge ports. For example, in 2003 the total European container throughput was 50 million TEUs (Twenty-foot Equivalent Units, standard container volume measure); more than half of containers were processed on the Hamburg-Le Havre range ports (25.4 million TEU). It is expected that over the next 20 years, demands on seaport capacity will double. However, most major seaports cannot grow larger, so increase in capacity and port productivity can be achieved mostly in result of elaborate business process reengineering and broad application of advanced IT-solutions which obviously include UCE.

To show applicability of UCE and needs for continuously evolving mediation of ontologies we concern a typical port with berths at the dock facility, a container terminal with gantries, a container yard with cranes and forklifts, an oil terminal, an extensive land transportation network including railroads and truck routes and gates. In such complex heterogeneous environment IT-infrastructure of the seaport should support continuous operations of different own and third party employees, effective supply chain management, logistic and highest level of security within maritime and ground port areas as well as surrounding territories. Apart from internal client-server or service-oriented information systems IT-infrastructure also includes external information sources and three different kinds of SANETs spreading across the seaport territory and nearest regions. The sensors of the first SANET (SANET#1) monitor such environmental conditions as temperature, humidity, biological and chemical contamination levels. The sensors of the second network (SANET#2) precisely track container and other objects movement with the help of RFID and GPS technologies within the seaport. The third network (SANET#3) supports surveillance, personal identification and access control. At last the wide-area sensors network (SANET#4) gathers information about traffic conditions for the main regional routes.

Among multiple participants of seaport business-processes we select only three groups of individuals with specific informational interests for further analysis and assign to them certain roles: the truck driver (TD-User), the security officer (SO-User), and the manager of the long-distance goods delivery service (DM-User). Table 1 contains the key issues each user usually faces in the context of business activities.

Except differences in the world models the users also employ different software application models. DM-USER has a stable location and primarily uses a desktop application with service-oriented architecture. SO-USER and TD-USER are equipped with mobile special terminals; we can say that they are "immersed" into the UCE and should directly interact with the sensor networks.

Although the world concepts are seemed to be absolutely different for three concerned users, construction of these concepts requires access to the same sensors measurements at the lowest level of abstraction.

For example, the world model of TD-USER consists of such high-level concepts as distances, container dimensions, speed limits, map directions, goods damage risks. For such the model raw RFID and GPS data acquired by SANET#2 should be transformed, analytically processed and integrated with traffic and weather condition information of SANET#1 and SANET#4. While TD-USER remains inside the sea port the sensors of SANET#3 provide for

TD-USER	The shortest and safe route to the uploading position and estimated queuing time. Average speed of transportation with respect to road conditions, traffic level and specifics of the goods to be transported. Import-export declaration for transported goods.
SO-USER	Access privileges for a particular area in the port and privileges assignment policies. Destination and intermediate checkpoints of vulnerable goods. Location of the next container for security inspection and the list of necessary screening and inspections procedures. Possible threats and security risks with respect to global security alerts, the current situation in the port and weather conditions. Where in some proximity to a given location specific goods can be found. Impact of certain kinds of cargo on nearly located materials and goods. Consequences of port accidents and their influence on surrounding areas. Risk mitigation routines adapting to the actual situation and environmental conditions.
DM-USER	Estimated quality of goods in accordance with past and present storage conditions, duration of travel and other circumstances. The list of the goods that can be shipped or stored together to reduce costs of operations. Probable delays in cargo operations due to night-time, weather or other restrictions. Average time of delivery to the city local storage, demands of remote customers, estimations of supply levels, schedules of connection between local carriers and airlines.

Table 1. Subjects of interest for different groups of the users

access control information needed for quickest route determination. For SO-USER following concepts are necessary: trucks and ships entering the port, results of radiation, chemical, biological monitoring, oil leakage facts, loading level of oil terminals, number of tankers at the berths, weather conditions, and permissions violation accidents. For building this model measurements of SANET#1, SANET#2 and SANET#3 as well as external security information sources are necessary. Finally DM-USER needs aggregated information in terms of storage conditions from SANET#1 to predict critical delivery dates. At the same time that user performs analysis of delivery delays in terms of maximum safe truck speed and cargo operations limitations (e.g. oil change delays, capacity of oil terminal). These characteristics can be calculated on the basis of operational data from information systems, local weather conditions and traffic level measured by SANET#1 and SANET#4.

The described conceptual models and data representation formats are very specific and sensitive to peculiarities of user's activities. Proper implementation of these models requires seamless integration of multiple heterogeneous software and hardware components operating within different restrictions (e.g. user interfaces and protocols supported, failover capabilities, battery life, protection class, etc). At the same time continuous and uncorrelated changes in legal regulations, regional environment, seaport business processes and underlying infrastructure lead to permanent evolution of integration algorithms, data structures and communication technologies.

The later condition makes impractical development of a centralized middleware system responsible for data acquisition and semantic transformation: each time when the user's requirements are changed the structure and algorithms of the system are changed dramatically. Maintenance and integration costs of the centralized approach overcome practical abilities. Analyzing another extreme of modern distributed information systems, the service-oriented architecture, we can point to relatively poor reusability capabilities: for any new combination of hardware and software platform a considerable amount of efforts is needed to design and implement an isolated service, even if mapping principles between different information models are already known on a conceptual level.

In this situation a whole family of semi-automatically generated Ontology Mediators becomes a more convenient solution. The family of Ontology Mediators includes middleware components as well as end-user oriented devices located near sources of raw data. Despite differences in hardware and software design all members of the family of Ontology Mediators have certain common features: conceptual modelling with the same modelling tools, reusable hardware and software components, and similar formal foundations of semantic transformations.

Altogether they play a role of semantic filters that provide only valuable information for the user or for other information systems in terms of the recipient's world model. In our seaport example we can recognize at least four Ontology Mediators supporting users' activities:

- the software Ontology Mediator that feeds the seaport information system with information needed for DM-USER;
- the hardware Ontology Mediator combined with the mobile terminal of TD-USER;
- the hardware Ontology Mediator combined with the mobile terminal of SO-USER.

Design, development and continuous maintenance of Ontology Mediators involve many participants with different skills, roles and administrative responsibilities. We believe that in order to support the described scenario and facilitate rapid replacement, re-design and deployment of different kinds of Ontology Mediators an advanced methodology of automated or semi-automated design should be applied.

3. Formal foundations

From a conceptual point of view our research is related with knowledge engineering and knowledge integration techniques specialized for pervasive computations (Chen et al., 2004; Zhou et al., 2005; Hönle et al, 2005). In this area the concept of ontology plays now the leading role for knowledge representation. It is became a good breeding to refer to the Gruber's pioneer definition of ontology as "a specification of a conceptualization" (Gruber, 1995). According to (Sowa, 2000) ontology serves for strong support in detailed study of all potentially possible entities and their interrelations in some domain of discourse shared by multiple communities; ontology also enables conceptualization and forming categories of the entities committed by those communities. This direct connection of the ontology technique to integration is pointed out by Y. Kalfoglou: "An ontology is an explicit representation of a shared understanding of the important concepts in some domain of interest. (Kalgoglou, 2001)" In (Dragan et al., 2006) one can see a good collection of more recent cross-references, all of them underline ontology support for achieving interoperability: "Ontology ... can be seen as the study of the organization and the nature of the world independently of the form of our knowledge about it."

To build the formal foundations for our methodology of Ontology Mediator's design we apply a well-defined and elegant mathematical theory of ontology developed at the University of Karlsruhe (Ehrig, 2007). That theory defines a core ontology (the intentional aspect of the domain of discourse) as a mathematical structure $S = \langle C, \leq_C, R, \sigma, \leq_R \rangle$, where

C – is a set of concept identifiers (concepts for short).

R – is a set of relations identifiers (relations for short).

$\leq_C$ – is a partial order on C, called concept hierarchy or taxonomy.
σ – a function $R \rightarrow C \times C$ called signature, such that σ I= ⟨domI, ranI⟩, where $r \in R$, domain domI, range ranI.
$\leq_R$ – is a partial order on R, called relation hierarchy, such that $r_1 \leq_R r_2$ if and only if $\mathrm{dom}(r_1) \leq_C \mathrm{dom}(r_2)$ and $\mathrm{ran}(r_1) \leq_C \mathrm{ran}(r_2)$.
Domain-specific dependencies of concepts and relations in S are formulated by a certain logical language (e.g. first-order predicate calculus) which fits a rather generic definition:
Let L be a logical language. An L-axiom system for a core ontology is a pair A = $<AI, \alpha>$,where
AI – is a set of axioms identifiers.
α – is a mapping $AI \rightarrow$ L
The elements of A are called axioms.
Extensional definition of the domain of discourse (assertions or facts about instances and relations) is given by description of the knowledge base KB. KB is the following structure:
KB = $\langle C, R, I, \iota_C, \iota_R \rangle$, where
C – is a set of concepts.
R – is a set of relations.
I – is a set of instance identifiers (instances for short).
ι_C – is a function $C \rightarrow \mathrm{P}(I)$ called concept instantiation.
ι_R – is a function $C \rightarrow \mathrm{P}(I^2)$ called relation instantiation; it has such properties:
$\forall\, r \in R,\ \iota_R \mathrm{I} \subseteq \iota_C(\mathrm{domI}) \times \iota_C(\mathrm{ranI})$.
The theory provides also names for concepts and relations calling them signs, and defines a lexicon for ontology:
Lex = $\langle G_C, G_R, G_I, Ref_C, Ref_R, Ref_I \rangle$, where
G_C – is a set of concepts signs.
G_R – is a set of relations signs.
G_I – is a set of instances signs.
Ref_C – is a relation $Ref_C \subseteq G_C \times C$ called lexical reference for concepts.
Ref_R – is a relation $Ref_R \subseteq G_R \times R$ called lexical reference for relations.
Ref_I – is a relation $Ref_I \subseteq G_I \times I$ called lexical reference for instances.
In summary, a complete ontology O is defined through the following structure:
O = $\langle S, A, KB, Lex \rangle$, where
S – is a core ontology.
A – is the L-axiom system.
KB – is a knowledge base.
Lex – is a lexicon.
Such strict mathematical theory of ontology along with other similar approaches formed a solid foundation for machine-readable representation of ontologies in modern information systems and facilitated their practical applications. For example, the research line known as Semantic Web pays great attention to various practical aspects of ontology manipulation for information heterogeneity resolution in the Internet. Recent examples of XML language application in coordination frameworks (Niemelä & Latvakoski, 2004 ; Tokunaga et al., 2004) illustrate that Semantic Web solutions can be successfully adopted and applied in many different domains. It seems for us that potential usefulness of the Resource

Description Framework (RDF) and the RDF Scheme (RDFS) standards (Jeng, 2004), proposed initially for semantic enrichment of WEB contents, is much greater. In order to achieve semantic interoperability for UCE we suggest applying RDF standards as the basic technique for the interoperable description of the knowledge base KB. Fusion of the formal theory of ontology together with RDF allows representing the knowledge base in the single frame of semi-structured data models. In (Abiteboul, 1995) semi-structured data are defined as data that is neither raw, nor strictly typed as in conventional database systems. A convenient approach to represent semi-structured data uses such edge-labeled graph structures which contain both type definition and actual data elements (fig.1).

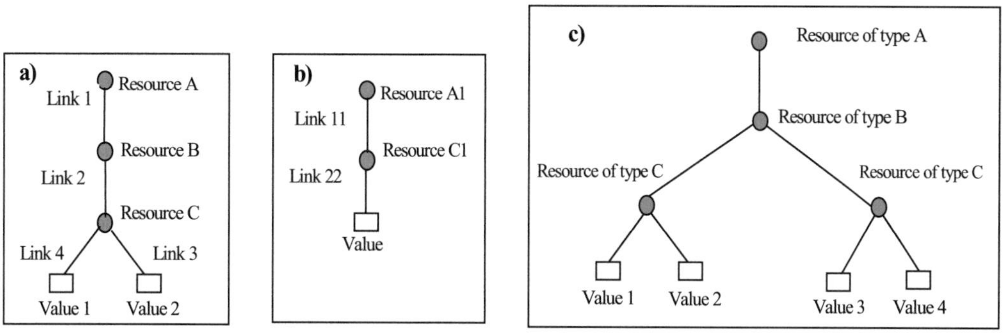

Fig. 1. Three different kinds of semi-structured data

Describing this case, P. Buneman says about "blurring the distinction between schema and instance" and proposes a suitable formalism for modelling and querying such structures (Buneman et al., 1996; Buneman, 1997). In accordance with the Buneman's approach a semi-structured database is represented in a form of a rooted edge-labelled graph, and a schema is a rooted graph whose edges are labelled with formulas. A database SDB conforms to a schema SS if there is a correspondence between the edges in SDB and SS, such that whenever there is an edge labelled a in SDB, there is a corresponding edge labelled with predicate p in SS such that $p(a)$ holds.

We can naturally set a correspondence between elements of the RDF semi-structured database SDB and the knowledge base KB: the set of concepts C and the set of instances I become the nodes of the graph, and the set of relations R maps to the graph's edges. In this context the general problem of achieving semantic interoperability can be looked at as the task of graph-based ontology transformation. The source graph of the semi-structured database comprises messages from the sensors networks, and corresponds to the ontology of IT-infrastructure. Another ontology expresses the user's domain of discourse in terms of the knowledge base, and defines permitted structure of the destination graph. Applying the formal approach and visual cues of graph transformations (Rozenberg, 1997; Hoffmann & Minas, 2000) we may define a transformation workflow process with the aim to produce the destination graph of semi-structured database expressed in terms of user's ontology. The definition of the transformation workflow process consists of two different kinds of operations: the data transformation and the structure transformation. The data transformation uses leaf's values of the source graph, namely the literals of the RDF model, to produce values of the destination graph, namely literals of another RDF model. The data transformation is described as a sequence of interrelated data processing operations that can include elementary RDF literals' transformation functions as well as access operations to external databases and Commercial Out-of-Shelf Software. The structure transformation uses location information of different subparts of the source graph to build the corresponding subparts of the destination graph.

4. Description of methodology

Concerning implementation and design issues we share the opinion (Oliver, 2005; Volgyesi & Ledeczi, 2002), which says that software engineering knowledge representation, its transformation and automation of systems design can be achieved by application of formal model-driven approaches examining hierarchies of UML-based meta-models, models and ontologies. In our approach to consistent design and development of the Ontology Mediators' family, we apply a few foundation principles for unification of work activities and formal methods. First of all, the consistent three-level UML modelling paradigm is used to create all information models and ontologies. At the top level 'M3' UML Meta-Object Facility provides for a single consistent meta-meta-model; at the middle level 'M2' UML profiles play a role of meta-models and specify domain languages for various aspects descriptions; at the level 'M1' a collection of UML models represents formal description of IT-infrastructure, business view and architecture concepts of Ontology Mediator. The second distinctive feature of our methodology is coupled consideration of classes together with instances during modelling of IT-infrastructure and Enterprise business aspects. It allows for application of formal methods of heterogeneous models and ontologies mapping based on Information Flow theory (Barwise & Seligman, 1997). At the same time simultaneous working with classes and instances facilitates natural application of semi-structured data models. Representation of domain concepts and actual data in the context of the same semi-structured data model gives as an opportunity to employ a powerful technique of graph-oriented transformations in order to define rules of ontology transformation and methods of mapping between different models.

Fig.2. illustrates general principles of the proposed design methodology, in which three main tracks of modelling and design activities can be recognized. All three tracks begin from conceptualization of correspondent domains of discourse. Conceptualization activities of the first track produce UML models with architecture concepts of Ontology Mediator. The architecture models describe reusable software and hardware components and define extensibility interfaces for future use. The second track includes analysis of Enterprise business aspects and producing whole enterprise ontology. Based on Ontology UML profiles, that ontology describes structure and behaviour of the appropriate knowledge domain, expressed in form of appropriate UML concepts (classes and logic constraints). The third track starts from conceptualization of underlying IT-infrastructure in terms of specialized UML models.

Following our methodology the designer should perform Core Activities (conceptualization of IT-infrastructure, Enterprise business aspects and architecture of Ontology Mediator) only for the first time of methodology's application in new domain. But specification of UML-based user's domain ontology is the repetitive activity and it precedes development of any new Ontology Mediator device. In terms of the produced ontology shared instances are classified and matching between enterprise ontology and user's ontology is performed. In the result the developers can select necessary elements of IT-infrastructure to communicate with, and they can design a correspondent source semi-structured data model in terms of IT-infrastructure models. By a similar way, the destination semi-structured data model is developed in terms of the user's ontology. Once the source and destination models are produced all three tracks are joined, and mutual design of a semantic transformation model is performed. In terms of specialized UML profiles this model describes a workflow transforming the source model to the destination model. In fig.3 a fragment of the correspondent transformation profile is represented.

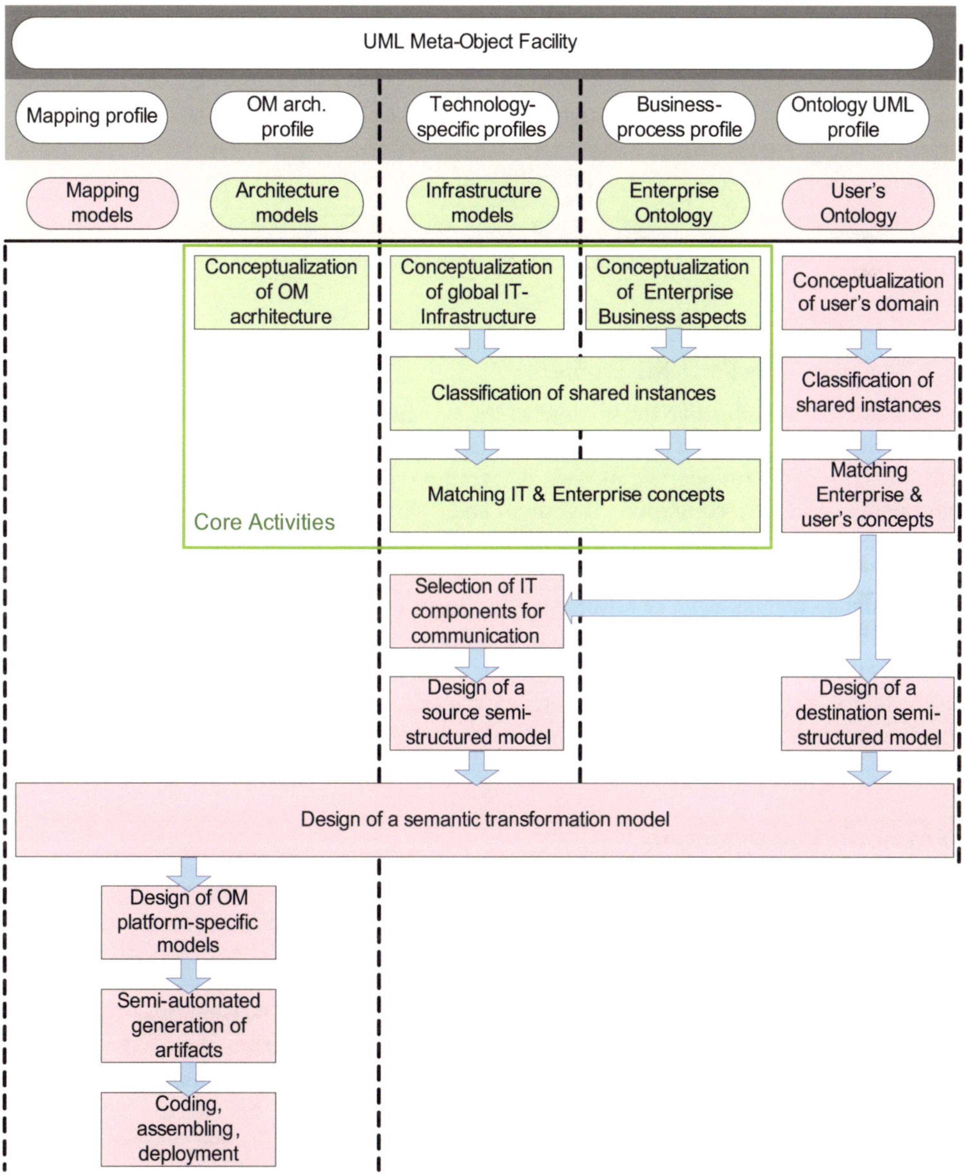

Fig. 2. Proposed methodology of Ontology Mediator's design and implementation. Dotted filling denotes initial core activities; dark colour defines repeatable activities during design of specific Ontology Mediator. UML models of the level 'M1' are the results of activities of the correspondent track

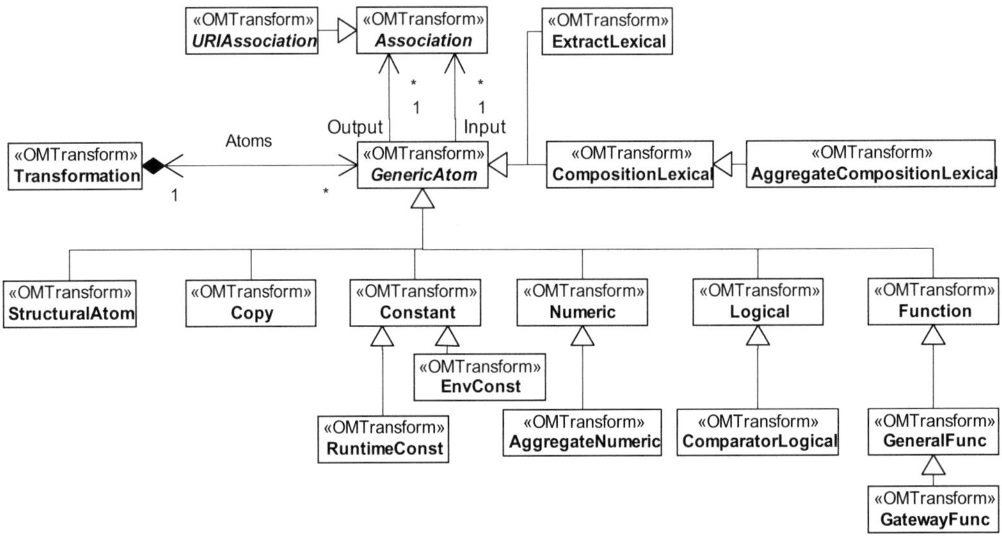

Fig. 3. The Transformation UML Profile

As soon as the users approve the content of the semantic transformation model it becomes a basis for design of platform specific models describing a concrete instantiation of Ontology Mediator. The platform-specific models determine which reusable hardware and software components will be combined together and which extension interfaces should be implemented during manual coding. Once the platform-dependent models have been produced the platform designers apply generation algorithms, which produce a skeleton of source code, as well as a list of additional hardware components and recommendations for selection of suitable base hardware modules. During final assembly of Ontology Mediator the programmers write small portions of glue code extending the generated skeleton, and the hardware engineers equip base hardware modules with additional components. This stage finishes process of Ontology Mediator development and the ready end-user product is shipped to the customer or is deployed in to the existing IT-infrastructure.

5. Framework architecture

According to the proposed methodology we developed a consistent ontology-based framework supporting design and development of Ontology Mediators. The framework has client-server architecture, and consists of front-end and back-end components promoting team work (fig.4).

The graphical front-end supports design of ontologies and UML-models for semantic transformations. Based on the Rational Software Architect platform by IBM and Eclipse Modelling Framework, the front-end adds several plugins, which implement a new visual modelling principle called Semantic Transformation Lasso (SETRAL), and provide interfaces to the framework back-end. SETRAL is extremely useful when modern Tablet PC and Visual Interactive Desks can be used during conceptualization and matching different ontology's concepts. For the user SETRAL offers a special smart graphical tool - Semantic Lasso (SL). That is a closed shape with arbitrary smooth boundaries. The user can draw a free-hand fragment of the SL boundary (the path) on top of the source UML class model to select certain classes to be matched. SETRAL automatically closes the path has been drawn

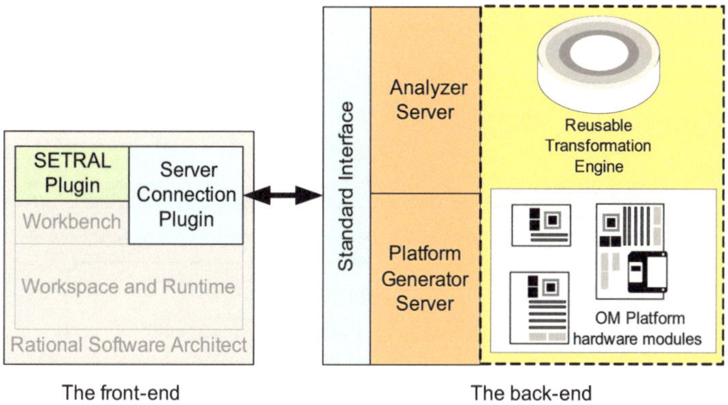

Fig. 4. Ontology-based framework for design and development of Ontology Mediators

and makes it smooth as necessary. Additionally SETRAL analyzes the source model and the meta-model to detect other entities (classes) that are semantically closely related to the entities inside the SL, but were not manually selected by the user. SETRAL proposes to include related entities with automatic extension of the SL's shape as needed. As soon as the source content of the SL was defined, SETRAL performs semantic mapping of the source entities inside the SL to the correspondent entities of the destination model. The result is displayed inside the SL as a fragment of the destination UML model. The level of transparency inside the SL can be adjusted interactively, so the user sees either two models or only one of them. Inside the SL the user can select entities of the destination model and switch to another editors to see the complete result of the matching. She/he has a possibility to easily return to the original editor with the active SL. SL tool can be used also for comprehensive analysis of the class instances. In this case after definition of the classes inside the SL, the user can run special SETRAL algorithms that will automatically generate instances with populated attributes.

The framework back-end contains the Analyzer Server and the Platform generator Server. The former server is closely related with the mapping design GUI. That component implements mathematical models of ontologies matching and models transformations as well as provides interfaces for loading core meta-models, domain models, domain-specific constraints in terms of OCL, as well as specifications of target software and the hardware platform. In accordance with loaded models the Analyzer Server automatically finds correspondent classes and attributes, returning results to the design GUI for further analysis by experts. The Platform Generator Server adopts basic principles of Model-Driven Architecture and automatically generates software artefacts for the selected target transformation platform. Each kind of the supported target platform uses the same library of software components (T-Engine). T-Engine contains algorithms for runtime semi-structured data transformation and business process enactment. Components of T-Engine can be deployed into the application server, the multi-agent system, or into the embedded platforms. In the later case our own specialized hardware platform is used.

6. T-Engine: architecture and implementation concepts

T-Engine is parted into four architectural layers, providing for different aspects of semantic interoperability: the External Communication Media layer, the RDF-mediation layer, the Internal Communication Media layer, and the Semantic Transformation layer (fig.5).

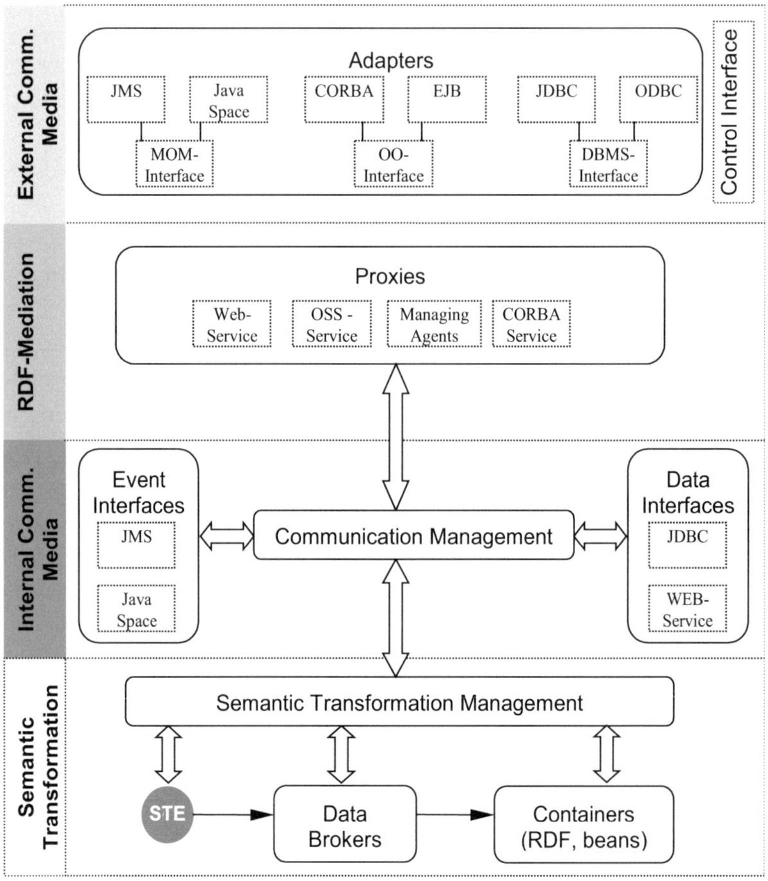

Fig. 5. Detailed architecture of T- Engine

The External Communication Media layer gives the implementation-neutral interface to outer distributed components of UCE. This layer comprises three unified operational interfaces to deal with major classes of modern distributed technologies (namely, Message-Oriented Middleware, remote calls of object's methods, Database Management Systems), as well as so-called adapters. Each adapter implements certain operational interface by means of concrete libraries and vendor-specific tools. A separate part implements control and management interface of T-Engine.

The RDF-Mediation layer provides for encapsulation of heterogeneous data structures and communication algorithms in accordance with a single message-oriented paradigm. Following this paradigm the correspondence is set between every communication act with an external component and a message of the certain type. Interacting with external components the RDF-Mediation Layer creates one or many message instances, and passes them to the Internal Communication media Layer for further use. Similar to the adapters, at the RDF-Mediation Layer a special component called Proxy takes responsibility of messages' production for a certain technology.

The produced message consists of actual data embodied in the form of RDF, and internal meta-information (e.g. type qualification, message's timestamp or a message's producer). The type of the message poses restrictions on its possible data structure. These restrictions are expressed in the form of the RDF schemata and define allowable atomic fields and sub-structures for any valid message instance of this type. Thus the message type can be concerned likely a micro-ontology, and it can be created and modified in the framework front-end during designing the source semi-structured model. Generalization of information interchange in the form of message's flows promotes uniform representation of UCE component's behaviour and data inside the underlying layers: components play roles of message consumers or producers and their interaction can be represented as modification, creation or transformation of message's instances.

The Internal Communication Media layer supports asynchronous message-based communication between the layers and provides for transaction management. Interacting with the Communication Management module, different modules of T-Engine subscribe to messages of particular type. Being notified of occurrence of new messages, the modules-subscribers fetch the messages from the internal queue, transform them, and put newly produced messages back for shared use.

To improve performance and reduce the message-processing costs the Communication Management module also promotes separation of event and data flows as much as possible avoiding passing large RDF models inside the message body at the intermediate stages of the message processing. Once submitted to the Communication Management module, the message is analyzed and rearranged to store either the original RDF model or only short pragmatic instructions. In later case the module of Data Interfaces uses pragmatic instructions for the "lazy" information retrieval from external data sources in order to reconstruct the complete RDF model. In the module of Event Interfaces all intermediate message processing tasks such as routing, filtering, collecting are performed on the basis of the internal meta-information without touching upon the correspondent RDF model. Hence the creating of the content of the huge RDF model can be postponed up to the moment of its actual use, but in the case of the small RDF model its content is completely stored inside the message.

The Semantic Transformation layer plays the central role in the successful fulfilment of Ontology Mediator's activities. In particular, on this layer the Semantic Transformation Management module collects instances of input messages and fuses them into the united RDF model, which is in direct correspondence with the source semi-structured model produced as the result of our design methodology. Relating message's instances with each other, the Semantic Transformation module exploits the message's meta-information and capabilities of RDF framework to link different resources via universal resource identifiers (URI). Once all needed instances have been collected and the source RDF model has been completely composed in accordance with the specification, the Semantic Transformation Management module places the model into the container for further processing by means of so-called Semantic Transformation Entities (STE).

Each STE serves as an independent workflow process reacting on completed model's appearance in the particular container. T-Engine allows dynamic independent deployment of different STEs and later manages their concurrent execution. STEs can be organized into chains of linked semantic transformations establishing complex information processing inside Ontology Mediator. Through the interface of DataBrokers a single STE gains access to the elements of the united RDF model, and performs transformation of this model to the destination RDF model in accordance with the semantic transformation UML model. When the STE successfully finishes building of the destination RDF model, algorithms of the Semantic Transformation Management module split this model into separate RDF sub-models corresponding to distinct messages. Carrying on the information in terms of the

user's ontology, messages proceed to the External Communication Media layer. Alternatively, the messages can take part in construction another source RDF model.
The architecture of T-Engine, as it has been described in previous paragraphs, is almost technology independent. Indeed, different modern distributed technologies such as CORBA, EJB, JMS and JINI can be used for practical implementation. In the course of various software prototypes design we have found that although CORBA and EJB are more widely used, the JINI-based implementation gives many attractive features. We have found that JINI technology is the most suitable for implementation of proxies on the RDF-Mediation layer. In this case JINI Smart Proxies can be installed quickly for preparation of the RDF-model. Smart JINI proxies expose a unified interface to Event Interfaces, Control Interfaces and Data Interfaces. These proxies are available via JINI lookup service (reggie). CORBA and JMS implementations of Event Interfaces were also performed but they are not described here.

7. The extensible hardware platform for ontology mediator

Our investigations of several use cases determined major guidelines for hardware architecture of Ontology Mediators. It should have nearly the same customer properties as sensor network devices: reasonably low prices, friendly interface for installation and maintenance. These properties allow for preserving unique features of sensors networks and deploy Ontology Mediators in different locations following changing and diverse needs of the end-users. At the same time Ontology Mediator should provide for a wide range of different mediation scenarios, and, in our vision, its hardware should be principally able to support communication via any of the most popular wireless protocols as well as wired ones (Ethernet, RS232/435, CAN). Later requirement leads to broad variations in internal hardware and software architecture.
Fitting the proposed model-driven design methodology the extensible hardware platform comprises two specially designed hardware modules:

- Processing Unit - an unmodified part of Ontology Mediator, where the central processor and basic communication interfaces are installed.
- Extension Board - a customizable interface board that can be easily extended by different hardware and embedded software components (plug-ins) on demand of specific requirements.

A number of design solutions were studied and prototypes were developed in order to find the most suitable decomposition of functions and balanced costs. Our latest experimental implementation of Ontology Mediator's Processing Unit has following features (Fig.6-a):

- MCU: LPC2294 16/32 bit ARM7TDMI-S™t with 256K Bytes Program Flash, 16K Bytes RAM, 4x 10 bit ADC, 2x UARTs, 4x CAN, I2C, SPI, up to 60MHz operation.
- 4MB SRAM 4x K6X8008T2B-F/Q SAMSUNG.
- 4MB TE28F320C3BD90 C3 INTEL FLASH.
- 10Mb TP Ethernet (CS8900A).
- OS: RTOS ECOS 2.0.
- Connectors: Power supply, RJ45, HDR26F (for connection to the extension board).

For the developed Processing Unit a reduced version of the Ontology Transformation Engine was developed. In that version transformation algorithms, internal control and interfacing functions were programmed in C and C++ programming languages. Now we are at the final stage of porting Wonka Java virtual machine (Wonka, 2010) to Processing

Unit hardware platform that will allow enriching application capabilities and provide full-fledged implementation of the Engine.

(a) (b)

Fig. 6. Hardware components of the extensible platform: a- Processing Unit in the case of stand-alone usage without Extension Board; b - an experimental sensor

Fig. 7. Specialization of Ontology Mediator for telecommunication domains

During experiments with Ontology Mediators we paid attention to semantic transformation algorithms, and used multiple wired sensors to reduce implementation costs. So, now Extension Board has support of both wired and wireless protocols: I2C, two CAN, 8x30 sensors (Fig.6-b), SPI-to-UART MAX3000 transceiver for connection to wireless SANET via radio transceiver. We place to our nearest plans generalization of the board architecture and its redesigning in the framework of evolvable hardware paradigm. The final version of Extension Board will include FPGA-based evolvable hardware part and a set of free slots for drivers and transceivers.

Most of the experiments with ontology mediation algorithms employed two wired SANETs, directly connected to Ontology Mediator via RS485 interface. The first test-bed SANET with ring topology consists of 70 sensors and actuators deployed to a rail road model. Ontology

Mediator presents dynamic state of the rail road in terms of an operator and allows performing basic actions by friendly Web-based interface (Java applets). The second SANET has star topology with eight rays. Each ray is capable of supporting up to thirty sensors. This network was installed on a real test site to monitor environmental conditions. In that case, Ontology Mediator (Fig.7) provides operators with real-time information about operational conditions, as well as equipment performance degradation forecasts. For these specific purposes, specialization of Ontology Mediator includes equipping Extension Board with LCD monitor and controls buttons, developing models and ontology mapping between low-level measurements of temperature, humidity and gas contamination to high-level abstractions of equipment operators to integrate SANET with external information systems.

8. Conclusion

In this work we attracted attention to achieving semantic interoperability in the context of wide-area Ubiquitous Computing Environment. The concept of "Ontology Mediator" was offered to designate a specialized device or a software component, which goal is fusion of sensors data, their smart transformation and expression in various forms of real-world concepts by application of ontologies manipulation. The developed design methodology and supporting framework provide foundations for model-driven development of Ontology Mediators. The basis of our approach is the ontology transformation process with locally defined conditions for joining separate input messages into the united RDF model and explicitly defined rules of its transformation into the set of output RDF models. Implementation of that process was done in the library of reusable software components (T-Engine). The T-Engine's components implement original message-oriented algorithms for semantic consistency testing, consolidation and transformation. During software implementation of T-Engine different distributed technologies were exploited and the tuple space based communication paradigm based on JavaSpaces technology showed the best performance and was the most attractive one from the architecture point of view. To study effects and benefits of embedded T-Engine's implementations we developed an extensible specialized hardware platform.

In comparison with known middleware architecture approaches for sensors networks [6, 13] our solution operates on a level of meta-data and allows bridging a gap between different information object-oriented models. In fact, having interfaces to different communication protocols, Ontology Mediator can be applied for orchestrating heterogeneous middleware services when the environment consists of different sensors networks and enterprise-wide applications. Increased reusability is seemed to be another attractive feature of our approach. During the Ontology Mediator's design, the platform designer accumulates knowledge about certain application domains and patterns of behaviour for different customers and needs. It allows continuous extending library of available models; moreover third party developers and teams can share such library. At the same time application of the single meta-model for development of different models allows simplify models transformation and integration.

Despite of using the same general ontology paradigm for meta data representation proposed in (Chen et al., 2004), we contribute original design methodology and the software-hardware framework that allow implementing solutions of various scales, performing ontology transformation simulations and testing.

The generic layered approach to design allows easy adaptation of the framework for different distributed systems. Regardless of components structure's modification and evolutionary variations in semantics, the developed solution allows for maintaining the permanent information consistence among multiple components. For example in a case of modification of the underlying database schema or the interface definition it is necessary only to modify the definition of semantic transformation for some STE without touching upon the implementation of external components.

Solutions like TSpaces (IBM), MARS-X (Cabri et al., 2001) and XMIDDLE (Mascolo et al., 2001) properly illustrate trends in application of modern Internet technologies such as XML and RDF in coordination frameworks. In our opinion MARS-X has some common points of interest and can be compared with our framework. Both approaches use tuple based coordination paradigm based on JavaSpaces software implementation. In MARS-X tuples are used for the XML document storing and different software agents can extract relevant information using complex search patterns defined programmatically. In our approach tuples are used to notify about the message instance presence and components define conditions for joining messages on the basis of its properties by a declarative way. As for semantic interoperability the important restriction of MARS-X is necessity to use the same structure of XML document (share the same DTD) for all components of a distributed system. Modification of DTD will require redesign of software components that is not always possible in the loosely coupled system. In our case the declarative description of joining conditions and delegating messages collecting and transformation activities into the separate middleware service allows to separate design of component algorithms from management of semantic interoperability.

Considering implementation issues of our framework it can be mentioned that the designed software architecture allows for rapid inclusion of new software technologies on different levels without significant changes of the core. Splitting the process of the message processing from the process of huge RDF models retrieving makes Ontology Mediator more robust.

9. References

Abiteboul, S.; Hull, R. & Vianu, V. (1995). *Foundations of databases*, Addison Wesley Publ. Co., Reading, ISBN 0-201-53771-0, Massachussetts

Abowd, G.D.; Mynatt, E.D. (2000). Charting Past, Present, and Future Research in Ubiquitous Computing,. *ACM Transaction on Computer-Human Interaction*, Vol. 7, No. 1, pp. 29-58, ISSN 1073-0516

Ahamed, S.I.; Vyas, A. & Zulkernine, M. (2004). Towards Developing Sensor Networks Monitoring as a Middleware Service, *Proceedings of the International Conference on Parallel Processing Workshops (ICPPW '04)*, pp. 465-471, ISSN 1530-2016, Montréal, Québec, Canada, August 15-18, 2004

Barwise, J.; Seligman, J. (1997). *Information Flow*, Cambridge University Press, ISBN 0-521-58386-1, Cambridge

Branch, J.W. ; Davis, J. ; Sow, D. & Bisdikian, C. (2005) Sentire: A Framework for Building Middleware for Sensor and Actuator Networks, *Proceedings of the 1st IEEE International Workshop on Sensor Networks and Systems for Pervasive Computing (PerSeNS'05)*, pp. 396-400, Kauai Island, Hawaii, March 8-12, 2005

Buneman, P. (1997). Semistructured data, *Proceedings of the ACM Symposium on Principles of Database Systems*, pp.117-121 , ISBN 0-89791-910-6, Tucson, Arizona, United States, 1997, ACM, Tucson

Buneman, P.; Davidson, S. ; Fernandez, M. & Suciu, D. (1996). Adding structure to unstructured data, *Technical Report MS-CIS-96-21,* University of Pennsylvania, Computer and Information Science Department

Cabri, G. ; Leonardi, L. & Zambonelli, F. (2000). XML dataspaces for mobile agent coordination.", *Proceedings of the 2000 ACM symposium on Applied computing,* pp. 181-188, ISBN 1-58113-240-9, 2000

Chan, E., Bresler, J. ; Al-Muhtadi, J. & Campbell, R. (2005). Gaia Microserver:An Extendable Mobile Middleware Platform, *Proceedings of the 3rd IEEE International Conference on Pervasive Computing and Communications (PerCom 2005),* pp. 309-313, Kauai Island, Hawaii, March 8-12, 2005

Chen, H.; Perich, F.; Finin, T. & Joshi, A. (2004). SOUPA: Standard Ontology for Ubiquitous and Pervasive Applications, *Proceedings of the 1st Annual International Conference on Mobile and Ubiquitous Systems:Networking and Services (MobiQuitous '04)* , pp. 258-267, ISSN 0-7695-2208-4, Boston, Massachusetts, August 22-25, 2004

Crossbow Technology,Inc., In http://www.xbow.com.

Curino, C.; Giani, M. ; Giorgetta, M. ; Giusti, A.; Murphy, A.L. & Picco, G.P. (2005). Tiny LIME :Bridging Mobile and Sensor Networks through Middleware, *Proceedings of the 3rd IEEE International Conference on Pervasive Computing and Communications (PerCom 2005),* pp. 61-72, Kauai Island, Hawaii, March 8-12, 2005

Dragan, G.; Dragan, D. & Vladan D. (2006). *Model Driven Architecture and Ontology Development*, Springer-Verlag, ISBN: 978-3-540-32180-4

Ehrig, M. (2007). *Ontology Alignment : Bridging the Semantic Gap. Series: Semantic Web and Beyond, Vol. 4*. Springer-Verlag, ISBN 978-0-387-32805-8)

Feng, J.; Koushanfar, F. & Potkonjak, M. (2002). System-Architectures for Sensor Networks Issues, Alternatives, and Directions, *Proceedings of the IEEE International Conference on Computer Design: VLSI in Computers and Processors (ICCD'02)*, pp. 226, ISSN 1063-6404, Rio de Janeiro, Brazil, September 16-18, 2002

Gruber, T.R. (1995). Toward Principles for the Design of Ontologies Used for Knowledge Sharing. *International Journal of Human-Computer Studies,* No. 43(5/6), 1995, 907-928, ISSN 1071-5819

Herring, C. (2000). Microprocessors, Microcontrollers, and Systems in the New Millennium, *IEEE Micro*, Vol. 20, No. 6, Nov/Dec, 2000, 45-51, ISSN 0272-1732.

Hoffmann, B. & M. Minas, M. (2000). Towards Generic Rule-Based Visual Programming, *Proceedings of the 2000 IEEE International Symposium on Visual Languages (VL'00),* pp. 65-67, ISBN 0-7695-0840-5, Seattle, Washington, 2000

Hönle, N.; Käppeler, U.-P.; Nicklas, D.; Schwarz, T. & Grossmann, M. (2005). Benefits of Integrating Meta Data into a Context Model, *Proceedings of the 3rd IEEE International Conference on Pervasive Computing and Communications (PerCom 2005),* pp. 25-29, Kauai Island, Hawaii, March 8-12, 2005

Jeng, T. (2004). Designing a Ubiquitous Smart Space of the Future: The Principle of Mapping, *Proceedings of International Conference of Cognition and Computation (DCC '04)*, ISBN 978-1-4020-2392-7, MIT, Cambridge, 19-21 July, 2004

Kalfoglou, Y. (2001) Exploring ontologies, In : *Handbook of Software Engineering and Knowledge Engineering, Vol. 1, Fundamentals*, S.K. Chang (Ed.), 863–887, World Scientific, ISBN 978-9810249731, Singapore

Kawahara, Y. ; Minami, M.; Saruwatari, S.; Morikawa, H. & Aoyama, T. (2004). Challenges and Lessons Learned in Building a Practical Smart Space, *Proceedings of the 1st Annual International Conference on Mobile and Ubiquitous Systems:Networking and Services (MobiQuitous '04)*, pp. 213-222, ISBN 0-7695-2208-4, Boston, Massachusetts, August 22-25, 2004

Mascolo C. ; Capra, L. & Emmerich, W. (2001) An XML-based Middleware for Peer-to-Peer computing, *Proceedings of the the First Int. Conf. on Peer-to-Peer Computing (P2P'01)*, pp. 69-74, ISBN 0-7695-1503-7, Lingkoping, Sweden, 2001

Misc.Tinyos: A component-based os for the networked sensor regime. In http://webs.cs.berkeley.edu/tos/

Niemelä, E. ; Latvakoski, J. (2004). Survey of requirements and solutions for ubiquitous software, *Proceedings of the 3rd international conference on Mobile and ubiquitous multimedia*, pp. 71-78, ISBN 1-58113-981-0, College Park, Maryland, 2004

Oliver, I. (2005) Applying UML and MDA to Real Systems Design, *Proceedings of the conference on Design, Automation and Test in Europe (DATE'05)*, Vol.1, pp.70-71, ISSN 0-7695-2288-2, Munich, Germany, 7-11 March, 2005

Rozenberg, G. (ed.) (1997). *Handbook of Graph Grammars and Computing by Graph Transformations", Volume 1: Foundations*. World Scientic, ISBN 981-02-2884

Sowa, J.F. (2000). *Knowledge Representation: Logical, Philosophical, and Computational Foundations*, Brooks Cole, ISBN 0-534-94965-7, Pacific Grove, CA

Tilak, S.; Abu-Ghazaleh, N. & Heinzelman W. (2002). A Taxonomy of Wireless Micro-Sensor Network Models, *ACM Mobile Computing and Communications Review*, Vol. 6, No. 2, 2002, 28-36, ISSN 0146-4833

Tokunaga, E.; Zee, A. van der; Kurahashi, M.; Nemoto, M.& Nakajima, T. (2004). A Middleware Infrastracture for Building Mixed Reality Applications in Ubiquitous Computing Environments, *Proceedings of the 1st Annual International Conference on Mobile and Ubiquitous Systems:Networking and Services (MobiQuitous '04)*, pp. 382-391, ISSN 0-7695-2208-4, Boston, Massachusetts, August 22-25, 2004

Tsetsos, V.; Alyfantis, G. ; Hasiotis, T. ; Sekkas, O. & Hadjiefthymiades S. (2005). Commercial Wireless Sensor Networks: Technical and Business Issues, *Proceedings of the Second Annual Conference on Wireless On-demand Network Systems and Services (WONS'05)*, pp. 166-173, ISSN 0045-7906, St. Moritz, Switzerland, January 2005

Volgyesi, P.; Ledeczi, A. (2002). Component-Based Development of Networked Embedded Applications, *Proceedings of the 28th Euromicro Conference (EUROMICRO'02)*, pp. 68, ISSN, Dortmund, Germany, 4-6 September, 2002

Wonka Java VM Project. In http://en.wikipedia.org/wiki/Wonka_VM. 2010

Zhou, Y. ; Zhao, Q. & Perry M. (2005). Reasoning over Ontologies of On Demand Service, *Proceedings of the IEEE International Conference on e-Technology, e-Commerce and e-Service (EEE'05)*, pp. 381-384, ISSN 0-7695-2274-2, Hong Kong, 29 March-1 April, 2005

Part 4

Practical Applications

10

Current Challenges for Mobile Location-Based Pervasive Content Sharing Applications

R. Francese, I. Passero and Genoveffa Tortora
Dipartimento di Matematica e Informatica (University of Salerno)
Italy

1. Introduction

Web 2.0 and social software are changing the way millions of users communicate: digital citizens are not only content receptors but also contributors to content creation, collaborating in social networks or communities.

Pervasive computing can increase this process taking our contents from everyday life, providing them in the places where there is the sharing need and often in the place where they are originated.

Until a few years ago, the ability to use technology to locate people and provide them the capability of sharing formal or informal content related to their location was limited. As an example, Prante et al. proposed the "cooperative building" metaphor, describing very expensive digital furniture, such as tabletop (InteracTable), vertical displays (DynaWall), and chairs (CommChairs) with built-in displays to support collaboration (Prante et al., 2004). However, localization technologies are nowadays more common, along with mobile devices that support them, making possible the combination of computer-mediated communication and location related data.

Top-of-the-range mobile devices allow us to adopt Augmented Reality (AR) based technologies to involve users in a mixed reality, made up of real world, observed towards the device camera, and of overlapped informative contents. In particular, the usage of AR is facilitated because of the innovative characteristics of the last device generation (on-board camera, accelerometers, compass, GPS etc.), instantly combine the preview made by the video camera with the AR information.

Several prototypes and commercial systems proposed location-based services, some of them associate textual notes to specific location, others provide awareness on places and friends for increasing informal interactions (Jones and Grandhi , 2004). Some of these systems have been successfully used, although the opportunities to innovate offered by new mobile technologies have still to be investigated in depth. The new devices, in fact, give the possibility of facing with the challenges in this field, such as creating innovative interfaces for mobile systems and implementing place-based recommender algorithms that intelligently connect people to places (Jones el al., 2004; Gartner, 2010).

Location-based pervasive applications are of growing interest for the scientific and industrial communities. Indeed, according to Gartner (Gartner, 2010b), one of the ICT enterprise world leader, Location-Based Services will be in the first ten required mobile devices applications in 2012. Moreover, the request of these services will strongly increase in the next years. Gartner predicts that Location-Based users will increase from 96 millions in 2009 to 526 millions in 2012. This kind of services is second in the top ten list for the high value that they have for users. In fact, they answer to several user needs, from productivity to social network and entertainment.

New challenges concern the development of AR applications for mobile phones supporting web 2.0 features, such as the sharing of location-based multimedia annotations in outdoor and indoor environments. Exploiting these features, the real world can be labelled using the "magic lens" interface offered by mobile devices.

The application of this technology is very wide and not limited to:

- *collaborative work*: information concerning collaboration is directly acquired and submitted in the working place, aiming at favouring formal and informal collaboration;
- *tourism and cultural heritage*: tourists uploads media and label places, monuments or pictures they are visiting;
- *learning*: teachers and students share a learning experience by uploading multimedia content in the places where they learn;
- *infomobility*: location-based information concerning transport or services to the citizen can be uploaded/downloaded in the place where there is the need;
- *commerce*: customer reviews of products shown in the store, find a store item pointing on a map, advertising in augmented reality with some form of interaction.

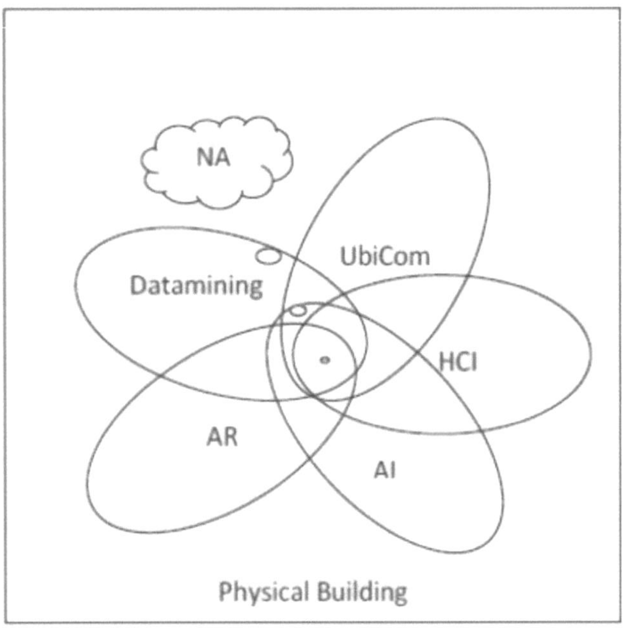

Fig. 1. Research Areas related to Location-Based Pervasive Content Applications

This chapter is organized as follows: Section 2 collects the innovative trends in the research areas related to the development of innovative mobile location-based pervasive content sharing applications, Section 3 describes some examples of this kind of applications, while Section 4 discusses how these technologies can be adopted in different application areas. Section 5, finally, concludes.

2. Research areas related to Location-Based Pervasive Content Applications

This kind of applications is very complex and has an interdisciplinary nature. Thus, this paper focuses on several research areas, as resumed in Fig. 1, all related to Location-Based Pervasive Content Sharing Applications.
In the following of this section we better detail the advanced results reached in the most relevant fields for these technologies.

2.1 Mobile AR interfaces

An important direction for the Mobile Spatial Interaction research is to investigate how spatial information should be displayed on a mobile device (Frohlich et al., 2009). To this aim new enabling technologies on mobile devices, including spatial sensors, high-end 3D graphics or augmented reality need to be considered.
Augmented Reality (AR) is a technology enabling to combine virtual information with the real world. The virtual content is superimposed to real images, and it is interactive in real time (Azuma, 1997). Mobile AR systems initially adopted a head mounted display to show virtual graphics over the real world. Innovative techniques were designed to interact with the mixed world.
As smartphones become smarter, AR degree of adoption on mobile device increases. Indeed, according to (Fitzmaurice, 93) a mobile device can be seen as a window onto a located 3D information space, enabling "to browse, interact, and manipulate electronic information within the context and situation in which the information originated and where it holds strong meaning".
Using this approach, a user acts on two information layers: the "transparent" device screen, showing georeferenced objects, and the physical surface. This interaction technique is named "magic lens" (Bier et al., 1993), "see-through interface" (Bier et al. 1994), or "magnifying glass" (Rekimoto, 95). Originally this kind of interfaces was based on GUI widgets. Actually, a magic lens interface can be used to augment the reality with 3D virtual objects and landscapes.
The first examples of AR applications for mobile phones were Mosquito Hunt and Invisible Train. In the former virtual mosquitoes are overlaid on the camera image and simple motion of the phone enables the user to fire the Mosquitoes. The Invisible Train (Wagner et al., 2005) adopts a "magic lens metaphor" as user interface. It is a mobile, collaborative multi-user AR game, enabling players to control virtual trains on a real wooden miniature railroad track. The virtual trains are shown to the players in AR modality.
Marked cards are used by (ARToolKit, 2010) together with computer vision techniques to determine the real camera position and orientation relatively to a card. In this way it is possible to overlay, in the correct perspective manner, virtual objects onto these cards. To this aim, the live video image is converted into a black and white one. Next, ARToolKit finds all the squares in the binary image, many of which are not the tracking markers. If there is a match with a marker, ARToolKit uses the known square size and pattern orientation to calculate the position of the real video camera relative to the physical marker. Starting from the real camera position, the virtual camera position is set with the same coordinates. The virtual object is then displayed by overlaying the real marker, using the OpenGL API.
Following this direction, (Popcode, 2010) combines the Popcode logo with a unique identifier. In this way, on one side the user is informed that augmented content is available, and, on the other side, the marker provides a way to access the information hosted on the

Popcode platform. A free XML language is available to developers for authoring. 3D objects, audio, and interactivity are supported.
A new research direction concerns the combination of AR with the physical manipulation of Tangible User Interfaces. In Fig. 2 (a) the user touches a virtual button to select a menu option. The camera tracks hand gestures and the device camera preview is augmented with overlaid 3D objects to provide visual feedbacks.

(a) (b) (c)

Fig. 2. Three Augmented Reality interaction approaches

(Billinghurst et al., 2009) describe the differences between interaction techniques based on the phone movement (Figure 2 (b)) and on the movement of a real object. In Figure 2 (c) the user moves the object for interacting with the application.

2.2 Methodologies for user tracking

Tracking user's position and movement in the right way is a critical aspect, especially when the content has to be displayed or created and attached considering a specific location. Indeed, the presence of an error could visualize information in a wrong place, or, if the user searches for the information, he might not find it where he expects. Thus, to take advantage of the mobility features of the new devices, wide area pose tracking systems need to be developed (Wagner and Schmalstieg, 2009).
These systems have to be capable of locating the user in a large environment, such as a building or a city. Generally, tracking is based on a model of the surrounding environment, but a big model cannot be stored in the memory of the mobile device. Thus, the model is generally maintained on a server system which has in charge the providing of localization services to the mobile devices.
Several strategies for tracking the user have been proposed in literature and they can be classified depending on if they are targeted for indoor, outdoor environments or both.
Improvements in this research area can be carried out through the usage of the sensors available on the newest devices (i.e. accelerometer, compass, camera) to provide innovative solutions and the usage of pervasive tagging (Kindberg et al., 2010).

2.2.1 Outdoor

Outdoor positioning systems are generally based on the Global Positioning System (GPS), which, recently has gained an accuracy of 10 to 20 meters.

The main advantages of this technology are that it is available everywhere outdoor and it works without a model of the world.

All the new mobile devices mount, together with the GPS, a digital compass, which provides orientation information that are useful for many mobile applications, and an accelerometer, which is a sensor measuring the acceleration applied to the mobile device.

Recently, several commercial applications such as (Wikitude, 2010), NearestTube (Acrossair, 2010) and Layar (Layar, 2010) have adopted a magic lens interface to show labels selected considering the user location, determined through GPS, accelerometers and digital compass. These applications only show labels and don't enable the user to create new labels in a web 2.0 way.

In particular, Wikitude localizes the user position using GPS and compass data and overlays Wiki information on the real camera view of the smartphone.

Layar is a free application for the Android Operating System, and is now also available for iPhone, that makes sets of data viewable on top of the device camera as the user pans around a city and points at buildings (Layar, 2010). The recent 3.0 version enables also to augment reality with 3D objects.

Layar can be seen as a new type of browser, able to provide an augmented view of the world combining virtual content and reality.

When the Layar application starts, the location of the user is automatically detected using GPS and the compass detects the orientation of the phone display. Layers are the equivalent of web-pages in normal browsers, superimposed to the reality. Real estate, banking, restaurants and other companies have already created layers of information available on the platform. Each organization identifies a set of location coordinates with relevant information, constituting a digital layer. The user easily switches between layers by tapping the side of the screen.

NearestTube allows the user to see the next tube station by tilting the phone upwards. It shows the direction in which the stations are in relation to the user location. Information concerns their distance and the tube lines they are on. If one continues to tilt the phone upwards, the application will show stacked icons representing the stations further away.

(White et al., 2009) propose SiteLens, a hand-held mobile AR system for urban design and urban planning site visits. SiteLens presents on the device screen "situated visualizations" related to the environment and displayed in situ. As an example, the environmental situation concerning smoke is mapped to density. Denser smoke represents higher ppm values. The user location and the orientation of the device camera are determined by combining ARTag fiducials, GPS, and IC3 orientation sensor. Optical markers are only used to address urban areas with limited GPS satellite visibility.

2.2.2 Indoor

In indoors environments, the GPS signal cannot be used because the signal power is too reduced to enter in buildings. An open research problem is to design an indoor location sensor providing accurate spatial information that is also not expensive, scalable, and robust. Recent indoor location sensing systems range from RFID, requiring explicit installation, to standard wireless networking hardware, or Bluetooth tags, suffering of several problems, such as long time for device discovering and passing through walls (Savadis et al., 2008).

Location sensing systems relying on standard wireless networking hardware measure signal intensity and attenuation to determine user location.

Wi-Fi location exploits existing Wi-Fi equipment on personal computers, PDAs and mobile phones. Modulated Wi-Fi transmission signals detect the devices that are visible to the network. The position of the device is then calculated by triangulating the signals received from the other access points. Wi-Fi accuracy is about 3 m - 5 m.
Another approach consists in localizing a device in its environment by analyzing in real time the video provided by the device camera to recognize objects. To this aim, a model of the world has to be created and then matched against the video stream.
As an example, the VSLAM system (Karlsson et al., 2005) concurrently builds a map and detects the location of the image on that map.
Another example is the system proposed by (Hile et al., 2008). It takes as inputs a floor plan, a rough location estimate, and an image provided by the camera phone. The image is sent to the server together with the information concerning the Wi-Fi signal strength and the floor number. The server extracts the relevant features in the image, determines the search area in the floor plan using the location estimation, searches where the image can be located on the floor considering the image features, determines the camera pose, and returns the content to be overlaid on the camera flow of the client device.

2.2.3 Hybrid

The blending of physical and virtual reality can be reached through new ways of labeling the world. Labels have a great potentiality because they can not be anymore a static label, but they can be considered as an index of an online presence (Davies, 2010). The evolution of Bar codes are two dimensional codes, such as (Quick Reference) QR codes (http://www.denso-wave.com/qrcode/qrfeature-e.html). Thanks to the second dimension, these codes can contain a large amount of data in a fixed amount of space. They carry meaningful information in the vertical direction as well as in the horizontal one. By carrying information in both directions the image is more compact than a 1D bar code. Indeed, they require about 10 percent of the space necessary for representing the same information with a 1D bar code (Ebling and Cáceres, 2010). Markers with QR code stamps may encode location coordinates and elevation value. Thus, they are useful to locate the user both in an outdoor and indoor settings.
All the recent mobile devices offer applications to easily capture and decode the code using the built-in camera.
Markers encoding positions can be placed on the walls. They can be used to support Infomobility, at the bus stop, for advertising in a shop or on a manifest, or in places as museum, public offices and everywhere.
Ten years ago QR codes became an ISO international standard, named ISO/IEC 18004. They have been largely adopted in Asia, seldom in Europe.
Esquire magazine proposed in the December 2009 an issue where six AR experiences triggered by a 2D code were printed on the cover and on several articles. To start the experience it was needed to download custom software.
Not only newspaper, but also people can be labelled. As an example, Facebook creates an application that enables a user to make a t-shirt with a custom QR code. Thus, it is possible to add a friend by shooting his/her QR code with the phone camera. Fig. 3 shows an "add-to-Friends" t-shirt.
Also Google adopts QR codes for business advertising. The service, named "Favorite Places on Google", provides the business with a windows decal showing a QR code. When scanned by the phone camera, the marker enables the user to access information on the business,

including customer reviews and also enables to write a personal review. The application does not adopt an AR interaction modality.

Fig. 3. QR code for labelling not only the world, but also people.

2.3 Usability for mobile systems in AR

New interaction approaches should be considered to effectively use augmented reality mobile applications. Indeed, it is necessary to consider that mobile device interfaces are characterized by the following aspects:

- small screen,
- limited input options (no mouse/keyboard),
- need to hold phone away from the body,
- reduced processing power (even if top-of-the range devices have this problem in reduced form).

Thus, researchers have to face the challenge of designing usable interfaces for device screens with limited dimensions and invent new interaction modalities.

To evaluate the usability of a mobile location-based AR system it is important to consider that AR representations combine rendered graphics with the real world environment and require a specific type of interaction among virtual artefacts and the real world. In particular, several factors affect the user perception of an AR system (Haniff & Baber, 2003), such as the perceived graphical resolution and rendering qualities. Image disparity is also a critical factor in augmented reality interfaces. Indeed, if the AR content reproduced on the camera is offset from the real world view, the user can be disoriented. The system lag can affect the perceived system quality and impact on the manoeuvrability.

The Magic Lens interaction pattern has several drawbacks: it requires the user focuses the information with the exclusive use of at least one hand; he/she has to move himself/herself while looking inside the phone. Thus, the user can have some problem in crowds, small spaces, or in areas with fast-moving objects or people (Lamantia, 2009).

A possible solution is to use the motion of the phone to interact with the virtual objects (Billinghurst et al., 2009). In this way it is possible to overcome the problem to interact with the application while the device is handheld (De Lucia et al., 2010b).

New research directions are studying the adoption of tangible interaction techniques.

2.4 Place-based recommender and social matching algorithms

A large amount of research work has been devoted to improve the usability of mobile applications, proposing display approaches to better present a lot of information in a very little space with too few resources. Another interesting direction is towards the research of the way to reduce the amount of information to be displayed. Recommendation systems are devoted to deal with information overload and offer personalized recommendations, content, and services to the users.

During the past and recent years, recommendation systems were developed for a series of different purposes. Recently, the rise of a large number of Web2.0 applications (blog, community forums, Web Albums, Blog and Taggings, etc.) indicates that users have the very pressing requirements of direct, rapid, useful and personalized information recommendation and sharing services (Yang and Wang., 2009).

Recommender systems start from the user preferences and item properties to discover items users are likely to take pleasure in.

According to (Gartner, 2010a), the future brands have to adopt location or profile-based information for both acquiring and retaining customers and to remain competitive in the growing mobile commerce space.

In case of location-based recommender systems, user profile analysis and context network analysis are integrated with intelligent information searching and context semantic enrichment to suggest to the user places and activities, combining his/her explicit and implicit preferences with place information.

The user preferences on places and activities can be inferred from use or openly declared.

As an example, if a user frequents a specific restaurant type (i.e. Chinese), the system could deduce that the user prefers Chinese food and recommends to him/her this type of restaurants when he/she is searching for a restaurant. Social networks are useful to find similar user profiles and to recommend restaurants and shops where other users with similar preferences are used to go. To this aim, also user ratings and comments are largely used.

The main recommendation models proposed in literature include the collaborative model, the content-based model, and the hybrid model based on both the previous ones (Yeh & Wu, 2010). In particular:

- *collaborative recommendation models* adopt data mining algorithms to group user interests collected mainly form session history;
- *content-based recommendation models* are based on semantic content classification;
- *the hybrid model* combines collaborative and content-based models. It provides a better performance because this model take care both user session history and content semantic analysis.

In many commercial situations the user judgements are implicitly collected, without explicit user input. As an example, sales transactions or pageviews can be automatically collected and considered as implicit ratings and exploited by collaborative filtering systems.

Collaborative filtering can also be based on human judgements, such as ratings and comments. These user opinions are useful to determine the proximity of users' tastes. See the suggestions provided by Amazon, such as "Users who bought the item a, also bought items b and c."

(Zanker and Jessenitschnig, 2009) propose a collaborative algorithm for determining similar users and making recommendations, based on a hybrid recommendation approach that utilizes a diverse range of input data, such as clickstream data, sales transactions and explicit user requirements.

An example of location-based recommender system based on social network is GeoLife 2.0 (Zheng et al., 2009). It exploits GPS technology to allow people to share their life experiences referring to the place they frequent. The system measures the user similarity, and makes personalized recommendation on friendship.

3. Augmented reality web 2.0 applications

Geotagging is an example of web 2.0 applications enabling to add location metadata to photo, videos, etc. World-mapping is done by powerful tools such as *Google Street View*. Thus, thanks to the innovative features of the new mobile devices, Geotagging is a very common practice for both uploads and downloads.

As discussed in Section 2.1, the most part of the AR location-based application does not support web 2.0 features, but they are limited to show location based content. This kind of features requires that the users are able to choose a 3D location, and their devices should allow them to opportunely view and add content.

(Baillot et al., 2001) proposed one of the first works on this topic, where an in-situ authoring system enabled to add virtual objects to a real scene. It also supported triangulation from different views. Augmentable Reality (Rekimoto et al., 1998) allows users to annotate an environment exposing barcode markers associated to contextual information. More recently, to obtain a better label placement considering the depth, (Wither et al., 2008) adopted a laser range finder to compute the depth information from given position and orientation.

The Sekai Camera application for iPhone is a social augmented reality application (Sekai Camera, 2010). It adopts a form of labelling that supports user communication by attaching digital contents to the real world. It is a handheld application that allows to associate media to a general location, and not to specific objects.

Recently, (Langlotz et al., 2010) present an approach for creating and exploring annotations in place using mobile phones. They adopt vision-based orientation tracking to accurately register objects overtaking the limited accuracy of the compass. Vision tracking requires an image database or a three-dimensional reconstruction, predetermined or constructed on the fly. To surmount these problems, author adopts a natural-feature mapping and tracking approach for mobile phones, allowing tracking with three degrees of freedom. It assumes the user makes pure rotational movements. The system generates a panoramic map from the live video and simultaneously uses it for tracking.

To create annotation, users move into a position where they want to create it. The application generates a panoramic image of the current environment. The user touches the display at the desired position and enters a textual description or a voice annotation. The system creates 48x48 pixel sub-image centered on the chosen point in the panorama image. This sub-image is later used for template matching. Besides the annotation itself, for finding the annotation anchor point again the system uses only the sub-image information.

In 2010 (De Lucia et al., 2010a) proposed SmartBuilding, aiming at augmenting a physical building with spatially localized areas in which users can share formal and informal multimedia documents and messages.

In particular, in SmartBuilding the screen of the mobile phone is transformed into a virtual multimedia board, where real information are overlapped with virtual information. Fig. 4 shows a screenshot of a "real" board enhanced by using a mobile phone and its camera with information concerning the course the teacher is taking in that room.

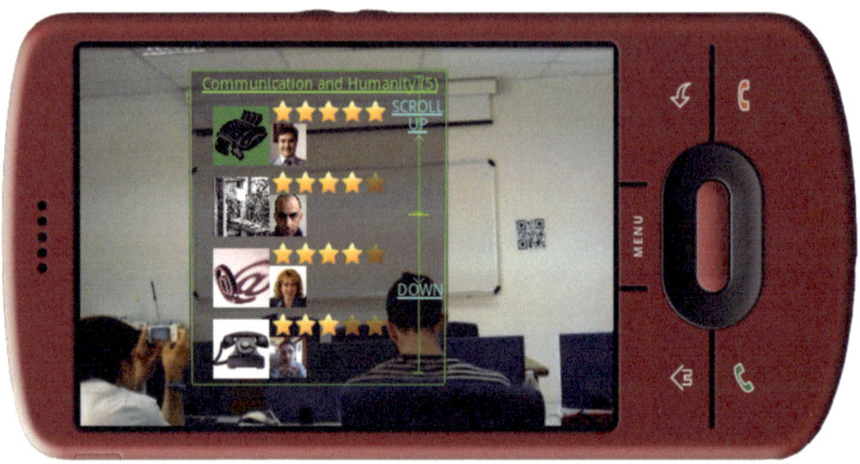

Fig. 4. An example of an Augmented Reality interface for a mobile location-based pervasive content sharing application

The user localization is performed using both QR codes and the device sensors. When a user enters into a room, he/she has to direct the camera towards the QR code by pointing a viewfinder visualized on his/her camera preview. The obtained resolution of the room marker enables us to deduct the shooting user-QR distance. In addition, the shooting angle, obtainable by comparing the shut QR side dimensions, allows us to determine more precisely the initial user position in the room. The user orientering coordinate system adopts radial orientation in the environment as main dimension and is tracked reading the Azimuth sensor, while the Roll orientation sensor is adopted, combined with the accelerometer, to detect how the camera is orientated in the space vertical dimension. The devices also communicate the current state of the Wi-Fi signals arriving from the various access points to the central server. Thus, it is possible to deduce each position variation by integrating the detected acceleration and extrapolating the new position considering the new Wi-Fi signal (Savidis et al., 2008), i.e. the strength of each access point carrier, of a user with his/her previous configurations and with those of the others. A first usability evaluation conducted in (De Lucia et a., 2010a) provides satisfying results and, in particular, verifies that system supports strong degrees of realism, thanks to the fluidity of the AR superimposed content. An innovative pagination interface enables to scroll-up and down the contribution list, using only the devices sensors.

4. Innovative trends in specific application areas

This section reports innovative trends in specific application areas of the enabling technologies.

4.1 Supporting collaboration

A research area of great interest for mobile phone based on AR interfaces is to provide support for collaborative applications. Mobile phones are already designed to support local and remote communication and thus they are a natural platform for collaboration.
According to (Szalavari et al., 1998), a collaborative AR environment provides the following features:

- *virtuality,* not existent objects are shown in the environment,
- *augmentation,* real objects are augmented with virtual information displayed considering the location,
- *cooperation,* the environment has to normally support the users interaction,
- *independence,* each user can manage an independent point of view,
- *individuality,* data can be shared but it can also be differently presented to different users.

A first form of collaboration has been provided by Invisible Train (Wagner et al., 2005). The user collaboration is performed as follows: users move around in the real world to view a virtual train set and then touches the screen with a stylus to change the position of tracks on the train set.

One of the first examples of collaboration in VR using mobile devices is the AR-Tennis game (Henrysson et. al., 2005). The application is based on ARToolkit, ported to Symbian. This game adopts the mobile phone both as an interaction tool, simulating a tennis racket, and as a display. As a consequence, the players cannot easily examine their view of the virtual world and concurrently move the device.

(Mulloni et. Al., 2008) propose a team-based competitive AR game. Players walk around the real environment to reach the goal of the game and communicate face-to-face among them.

A more recent game, Art of Defense (Nguyen Ta Huynh et al., 2010), is a strategy-based "Tower Defense" style game. Two players collaborate to defend their central tower from waves of attacking enemies. The game adopts both handheld devices and physical game pieces, creating a mixed physical/virtual game on the tabletop. The user interacts with the game trough the tangible elements. To support the control of the game, the system exploits several computer vision techniques, such as marker-based tracking and colour recognition.

For high interaction task, i.e. working together on complex independent problems, face-to-face meetings are the better way to communicate. Small group settings are generally equipped with display information technology, such as projectors, electronic whiteboards, or large monitors. Augmented Reality, location-awareness and mobile devices can be combined to share and display information for co-located collaboration.

(De Lucia et al., 2010b) proposed SmartMeeting, a component of SmartBuilding aiming at supporting group collaboration.

Each work group has assigned a Group Augmented Area, where information relevant for the group is shared. This area is permanent and represents the group reference area for formal and informal communication.

4.2 Virtual campus and collaborative learning

The rapid evolution of mobile technology enables users to communicate in very different ways. These transformations pervasively affect the way students learn: in 2005, Downes (Downes, 2005) proposed for the first time the term *elearning 2.0*. This new version of elearning principally denotes the democratization of content authoring: users are the authors and information is no longer exclusively produced by experts, structured into courses and delivered. Indeed, the students themselves produce and use content in a bottom-up fashion, with the consequent and implicit creation of learning communities. Indeed, the students of a course in Multimedia Technology provided the user requirements for mobile learning applications (Garaj, 2010). This study, among others, puts in evidence the importance of learning across contexts (i.e., to take pictures on location when students

perform a visual design activity), of uploading several content types and of combining individual and group use in a way similar to Youtube, Flickr or blogs.
Several examples of the location-based virtual campuses exists in literature, but few of them adopt mobile augmented reality interaction.
In (Liu et al., 2010) authors presented a system aiming at supporting English learning integrating the usage of 2D barcodes and Augmented Reality as follows: when approaching a zone, a student used the PDA phone to decrypt a 2D code and then obtained context-aware contents from server. The students then practiced conversation with a virtual learning partner.
(De Lucia et al., 2010c) proposed ACCAMPUS, a "collaborative campus" based on SmartBuilding, originated in the physical architectural space, exposing and downloading learning contents and social information structured as augmented virtual areas, see Fig. 3 as an example of this areas. This approach supports the creation of a virtual campus trough the definition of several types of augmented areas, such as:

- *administration areas*, representing the official bulletin board (locked), where contents are provided by the university staff, such as time tables, or teacher news on specific courses;
- *student areas*, enabling the students to communicate by uploading and commenting contents. They correspond to bulletin boards open to the student community and adopted for not strictly didactic announcements;
- *group areas*, specific for group learning approaches. During a project activity, the teacher can create an area for each group.

A collaborative learning approach exploiting the features offered by this system has also been proposed.

4.3 Tourism and cultural heritage

Location-based pervasive content sharing applications can be a powerful support for touristic promotion. It will address the users to discover Cultural Heritage in a collaborative, simple and funny way, thought the adoption of mobile technologies based on AR.
Several location-based social networks, such as MyTown, FourSquare or Gowalla, enable the user to label the places he/she is visiting and to download or retrieve virtual content, without augmenting the reality.
A first example of mobile AR application for this area is LibreGeoSocial (Zoellner et al., 2010). It provides a Cultural Heritage Layers, that uses X3D for visualizing historic multimedia content superimposed on the camera view in the right place. They use markerless tracking technologies for outdoor environments. In particular, starting from few reference images of the spot, the system analyses the images from the camera and determines if the current view is from a given spot or not. If a spot has been detected, the position of the considered object is precisely recovered and tracked, then the additional content can be appropriately superimposed to the camera view.

4.4 Face recognition based applications

Face-recognition on mobile phones is a very appealing AR location-based service. Indeed, it can be very useful when we are seeing someone but we do not remember who he is. Or, we need to get information on a person we meet for the first time. An application of this kind can access to an image database of a social network, identify the person we are shooting with the camera and report us all his public social network links. Polar Rose (http://www.polarrose.com/) proposes a facial recognition algorithm that has been adopted by several mobile applications.

Face Recognition on mobile device is a particular form of visual search. Indeed, (http://www.slideshare.net/rudydw/mobile-trends-2020 slide 55 Atanu Tanaka) it can be considered as a near future improvement of the classical web search. Searching for people is probably the first step toward an era when the users, pointing the mobile cameras in the direction of a generic object, will obtain the related information.

5. Conclusion

To better understand Mobile Location-Based Augmented Reality applications supporting content sharing, we surveyed the literature in this area. We discussed current approaches in the research areas related to the development of this kind of applications, listed some examples of this kind of applications, and described how these technologies can be adopted in different application areas.

We found that the researches on the related topics, such as usability, user tracking, collaborative filtering, collaboration and face-recognition, are still at the early stages and the interest toward this kind of applications will strongly increase.

6. References

Acrossair web page (2010) http://www.acrossair.com/acrossair_app_augmented_reality_nearesttube_london_for_iPhone_3GS.htm.

ATToolkit (2010) http://www.hitl.washington.edu/artoolkit/documentation/userintro.htm

Azuma, R. (1997) A Survey of Augmented Reality. *Presence: Teleoperators and Virtual Environments*, Vol. 6, No. 4, pp: 6(4), 355–385.

Baillot, Y.; Brown, D.; Julier, S. (2001) Authoring of physical models using mobile computers, Proceedings of ISWC 2001, pages 39–46, 2001.

Bier, E., A.; Stone, M., C.; Fishkin, K.; Buxton, W.; Baudel, T. (1994) A taxonomy of see-through tools. In *CHI '94: Proceedings of the SIGCHI conference on Human factors in computing systems*, pp. 358–364. ACM Press.

Bier, E., A.; Stone, M., C.; Pier, K.; Buxton, W.; DeRose, T., D. (1993) Toolglass and magic lenses: the see-through interface. *In SIGGRAPH '93: Proceedings of the 20th annual conference on Computer graphics and interactive techniques*, pp: 73–80. ACM Press.

Billinghurst, M.; Kato, H; Myojin, S. (2009) Advanced Interaction Techniques for Augmented Reality Applications, *Proceedings of the 3rd International Conference on Virtual and Mixed Reality: Held as Part of HCI International 2009*, pp. 13-22.

de-las-Heras-Quiros, P; Roman-Lopez, R.; Calvo-Palomino, R.; Gato, J.; Gato, J. (2010) Mobile Augmented Reality browsers should allow labeling objects. A Position Paper for the Augmented Reality on the Web W3C Workshop. http://www.w3.org/2010/06/w3car/mar_browsers_should_allow_labeling)objects.pdf

De Lucia, A.; Francese, R; Passero, I.; Tortora, G. (2010a) SmartBuilding: a People-to-People-to-Geographical-Places mobile system based on Augmented Reality, *UBICOMM 2010*, to appear.

De Lucia, A.; Francese, R; Passero, I. (2010b) A Mobile Augmented Reality system supporting co-located Content Sharing and Displaying, *in the Proc. of Information Technology and Innovation Trends in Organizations (ITAIS 2010)*, to appear.

De Lucia, A.; Francese, R; Passero, I.; Tortora, G. (2010c) A Collaborative Augmented Campus based on Location-Aware Mobile Technology (submitted)

Ebling, M.; Cáceres, R.. (2010) Bar Codes Everywhere You Look, *IEEE on Pervasive Computing*, Vol. 9, No. 2.

Davies, N. (2010) Making the Case, *IEEE on Pervasive Computing*, Vol. 9, Issue 2.

Downes, S., "E-learning 2.0", (2006) ACM eLearn Magazine, http://www.elearnmag.org/subpage.cfm?article=29-1&section=articles.

Fitzmaurice, G. (1993) Situated Information Spaces and Spatially Aware Palmtop Computers, *Communications of the ACM*, Vol. 36, No. 7.

Frohlich, P; Simon, R; Baillie, L. (2009) Mobile Spatial Interaction, *Pers Ubiquit Comput*, No. 13, pp. 251–253.

G. Fitzmaurice, "Situated Information Spaces and Spatially Aware Palmtop Computers". *Communications of the ACM*, Vol. 36, no. 7, July 1993.

Garaj, V. (2010) m-Learning in the Education of Multimedia Technologists and Designers at the University Level: A User Requirements Study, *IEEE Transactions on Learning Technologies*, Vol. 3, No. 1, pp. 24-32.

Gartner (2010a) http://www.mycustomer.com/topic/customer-intelligence/brands-must-exploit-location-based-information-remain-competitive/113589

Gartner (2010b) Gartner Identifies the Top 10 Consumer Mobile Applications for 2012, http://www.gartner.com/it/page.jsp?id=1230413

Google Favourite Places (2010)
http://www.google.com/help/maps/favoriteplaces/gallery/#los-angeles-ca

Haniff, D; Baber, C. (2003) User Evaluation of Augmented Reality Systems, *Proc. of the Seventh International Conference on Information Visualization (IV'03).*

Henrysson, A.; Billinghurst, M.; Ollila, M. (2005) Face to Face Collaborative AR on Mobile Phones, *Proceedings of the Fourth IEEE and ACM International Symposium on Mixed and Augmented Reality*, pp. 80 – 89.

Hile, H.; Borriello G. (2008) Positioning and Orientation in Indoor Environments Using Camera Phones, *IEEE Computer Graphics and Applications*, Vol. 28 , No. 4 pp. 32-39.

Jones, Q.; Grandhi, S. A. (2005) P3 Systems: Putting the Place Back into Social Networks, *IEEE Internet Computing*, 2005, pp. 38-46.

Karlsson, N.; Di Bernardo, E.; Ostrowski, J; Goncalves, L.; Pirjanian, P.; and Munich, M. (2005) The vSLAM Algorithm for Robust Localization and Mapping Published in Proc. of Int. Conf. on Robotics and Automation (ICRA).

Kindberg, T.; Pederson, T.; Sukthankar, R. (2010) Guest Editors' Introduction: Labeling the World, *Pervasive Computing, IEEE*, Vol. 9, No. 2, pp. 8 – 10.

Lamantia, J. (2009) Inside Out: Interaction Design for Augmented Reality, http://www.uxmatters.com/mt/archives/2009/08/inside-out-interaction-design-for-augmented-reality.php

Langlotz, T.; Wagner, D.; Mulloni, A.; and Schmalstieg, D. (2010) Online Creation of Panoramic Augmented Reality Annotations on Mobile Phones, *IEEE Pervasive Computing* (to appear)

Layar, http://layar.eu/. Retrieved the 20th of September 2010.

T. Liu, T. Tan and Y. Chu, (2010) QR Code and Augmented Reality-Supported Mobile English Learning System, WMMP 2008, LNCS 5960, pp. 37-52.

Mulloni, A.; Wagner, D.; Schmalstieg, D. (2008) Mobility and social interaction as core gameplay elements in multiplayer augmented reality. *In the Proceedings of the 3rd international conference on Digital Interactive Media in Entertainment and Arts*, ACM, New York, NY, USA, pp. 472–478.

Nguyen Ta Huynh, D.; Raveendran, K,; Xu, Y; Spreen, K.; MacIntyre, B. (2009) Art of defense: a collaborative handheld augmented reality board gameProceedings of the 2009 ACM SIGGRAPH Symposium on Video Games, pp. 135-142.

PopCode, http://www.popcode.info/

Prante, T., Streitz, N., Tandler, P. (2004) Roomware: Computers Disappear and Interaction Evolves. *Computer* Vol. 37, No. 12, pp. 47-54.

Rekimoto, J. (1994) The World Through the Computer: A New Human-Computer Interaction Style Based on Wearable Computers. *Technical Report SCSL-TR-94-013*, Sony Computer Science Laboratories Inc.

J. Rekimoto (1995) The magnifying glass approach to augmented reality systems. *In International Conference on Artificial Reality and Tele-Existence '95 / Conference on Virtual Reality Software and Technology (ICAT/VRST '95)*, pp. 123–132, 1995.

Savidis, A., Zidianakis, M., Kazepis, N., Dubulakis, S., Gramenos, D., Stephanidis, C. (2008) An Integrated Platform for the Management of Mobile Location-aware Information Systems, *In Proc. of Pervasive 2008*. Sydney, Australia, pp. 128–145.

Sekai Camera (2010) http://support.sekaicamera.com/en/service.

Schilit, B.; Adams, N.; Want, R. (1994) Context-aware computing applications. *In Proceedings of IEEE Workshop on Mobile Computing Systems and Applications*, pp. 85-90.

Szalavari, Z.; Schmalstieg, D.; Fuhrmann, A.; Gervautz, M. (1998) Studierstube: An environment for collaboration in augmented reality. *Virtual Reality*, Vol. 3, No. 1, pp. 137–48.

Wagner, D.; Pintaric, T.; Ledermann, F.; Schmalstieg, D. (2005) Towards Massively Multi-User Augmented Reality on Handheld Devices, *Proc. of the Third International Conference on Pervasive Computing (Pervasive 2005).*

Wagner, D.; Schmalstieg, D. (2009) History and Future of Tracking for Mobile Phone Augmented Reality, *International Symposium on Ubiquitous Virtual Reality.*

Wang, Z.; Yang, F. (2009) A Multiple-Mode Mobile Location-Based Information Retrieve System, *Fifth International Conference on Wireless and Mobile Communications, ICWMC '09*, pp. 410-415.

White, S.; Feiner, S. (2009) SiteLens: Situated visualization techniques for urban site visits. *Proc. CHI 2009*, Boston, MA, April 4-9, pp. 1117-1120

Wither, J.; Coffin, C.; Ventura, J.; and Höllerer, T. (2008) Fast annotation and modeling with a single-point laser range finder, *7th IEEE/ACM International Symposium on Mixed and Augmented Reality*, pp. 65-68.

Wither, J.; DiVerdi, S.; Höllerer, T. (2006) Using aerial photographs for improved mobile AR annotation, *IEEE/ACM International Symposium on Mixed and Augmented Reality (ISMAR 2006)*, pp. 159–162.

Wikitude (2010) http://www.wikitude.org/

Xiaofang, Z.; Jin, L. , Qi, J. (2007) Personalized Information Recommendation Service System Based on GIS, Proc. *Third International Conference on Natural Computation.*

Yang, F.; Wang, Z (2009) A Mobile Location-based Information Recommendation System Based on GPS and WEB2.0 Services, *WSEAS Transactions on Computers.*

Yeh, J; Wu, M. (2010) Recommendation Based on Latent Topics and Social Network Analysis, *Proc. of Second International Conference on Computer Engineering and Applications (ICCEA).*

Zanker, M. and Jessenitschnig, M. (2009) Collaborative feature-combination recommender exploiting explicit and implicit user feedback, *11th IEEE Conference on Commerce and Enterprise Computing (CEC),* Vienna, Austria, pp. 49-56.

Zheng, Y.; Chen, Y.; Xie, X.; Ma, W. Y. (2009) GeoLife2.0: A Location-Based Social Networking Service, *Proc. IEEE Tenth International Conference on Mobile Data Management: Systems, Services and Middleware.*

Zoellner, M.; Keil, J.; Drevensek, T.; Wuest, A.; Cultural Heritage Layers: Integrating Historic Media in Augmented Reality (2009) 2009 15th International Conference on Virtual Systems and Multimedia, pp. 193-196.

11

Case Study: The Condition of Ubiquitous Computing Application in Indonesia

Dewi Agushinta R.[1], Tb. Maulana Kusuma[1],
Bismar Junatas[2] and Deni Trihasta[2]
[1]Information System Department
[2]Informatics Department
Gunadarma University
Jl. Margonda Raya No. 100 Pondok Cina, Depok 16424,
West Java - Indonesia

1. Introduction

Generally, people, especially in developing countries, does not realize that they are in third of computer revolution era. They are in the era of ubiquitous computing, which mean that they can interact with the computer everywhere and anytime, not just sitting in front of the PC (one person many computers). Furthermore, the social and political challenges of the ubiquitous computing era will be characterized by an increasing dependence on technology, control over the information to which everyday objects are linked, and the protection of privacy. In this paper, we present the study about the condition of ubiquitous computing application in Indonesia. We divide the application of ubiquitous computing in Indonesia into three parts, i.e. ubiquitous mobile application, ubiquitous web application, and ubiquitous payment system application.

Nowadays, the next generation of computers will be embossed by ubiquitous computing (Bagci & Petzold, 2003). The computer will disappear behind daily things and people will not know that they will be faced with the computer in their day-life activities. This will make the old paradigm, where people only sit in front of the PC if they want to interact with computer, will be eliminated gradually. Unfortunately, until now it is just happened in developed countries which the infrastructure and the environment has supported to implement the ubiquitous computing. How about developing countries? In developing countries, such as Indonesia, ubiquitous computing applications are still rarely because there are many problems will be faced if the application of ubiquitous computing is going to be implemented, start from governmental support, infrastructure, finance, technological, and the professional worker. Only a few of ubiquitous computing application, which we will be explained in the next section applied in Indonesia. We will explain a few explanations about ubiquitous computing in section 2. The science aspects of ubiquitous supporting development will be introduced in section 3. Next, the application of ubiquitous computing in Indonesia will be discussed in section 4. The issues in ubiquitous computing will be presented in section 5. The last section of this paper presents the conclusion and the challenges of the application of ubiquitous computing in Indonesia.

2. Ubiquitous computing

Ubiquitous computing (ubicomp) is the method of enhancing computer use by making many computers available throughout the physical environment, but making them effectively invisible to the user (Weiser, 1993). In its development as a new technology or as a branch of computer science, Ubicomp cannot be discharged from the other computer science aspects, such as natural interfaces, context aware computing, and micro-nano technology. At this time, ubicomp become the inspiration from the development of the new paradigm of computation (off the desktop), where the interaction between humankind and the computer was natural and slowly left the paradigm keyboard/ mouse/ display from the PC generation (Widhiarta, 2007). One of the positive effects from ubicomp is people who do not have skills use the computer and people with the physical lack (the defect) could continue to use the computer for all the needs.

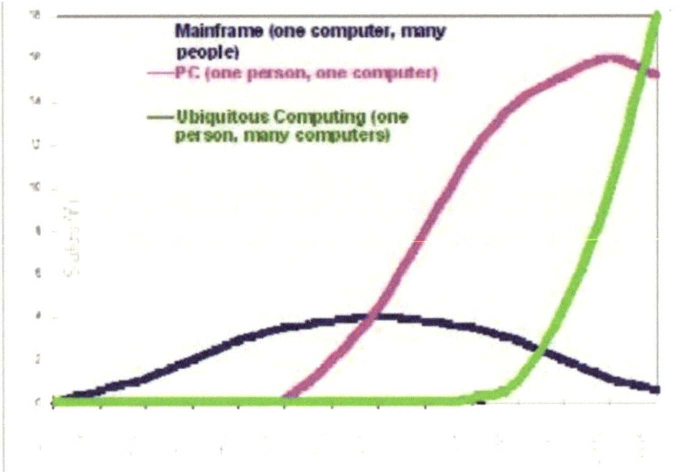

Fig. 1. The major trends of ubiquitous computing since introduced by Mark Weiser (1988) until year 2005 (*http://www.ubiq.com/hypertext/weiser/UbiHome.html*)

3. Support development aspects

As an applied technology or as a branch of computer science, ubicomp development can not be separated from other computer science aspects. Important aspects that support development of ubicomp research as follows.

3.1 Natural interfaces

Natural interface is the common parlance used by designers and developers of computer interfaces to refer to a user interface that is effectively invisible, or becomes invisible with successive learned interactions, to its users. The word natural is used because most computer interfaces use artificial control devices whose operation has to be learned. It relies on a user being able to quickly transition from novice to expert. While the interface requires learning, that learning is eased through design which gives the user the feeling that they are instantly and continuously successful. This can be aided by technology which allows users to carry out relatively natural motions, movements or gestures that they quickly discover control the computer application or manipulate the on-screen content. A common misunderstanding is that it is somehow mimicry of nature or that some inputs to a computer are somehow more 'natural' than others. In truth, the goal is to make the user feel like a *natural*.

Prior to the concept of ubicomp, we have become witnesses of various researches on natural interfaces for years, namely the use of natural aspects as a way to manipulate data. For example, voice recognizer technology or pen computing. Currently, implementation of various researches on natural inputs along with its tools became the most important aspects of ubicomp development.

The main difficulty in natural interfaces development is error prone. In natural interfaces, inputs have a wider area of form, for example the pronunciation of vowel "O" by someone can be very different from other people though with the same intent. Writing letter "A" with a pen computing can generate thousands of possible writing style that can cause computer can not recognize the input as letter "A".

Various research and new technologies in artificial intelligence is very helpful in finding a breakthrough to reduce error level. Genetic algorithm, neural networks and fuzzy logic makes into stepping technology to natural interfaces more "clever" in recognizing natural forms of input.

3.2 Context aware computing

Context aware computing is a branch of computer science who views a computing process not only focuses attention on one object to be main focus but also on its surrounding aspects. For example, if conventional computing is designed to identify who person was standing in a certain coordinate point, computer will look at that person as a single object with various attributes, such as employee number, height, weight, eye color, and so forth.

On the other hand context aware computing is not only directed its focus on human object, but also on what he was doing, where he is, what time he arrived at that position, and the reason why he was in that place.

In the simple examples above, it appears that in carrying out those instructions, conventional computing focuses only on the aspect of "who". On the other side, context aware computing is not just focusing on "who" but also "when", "what", "where" and "why".

Context Aware Computing makes a significant contribution to ubicomp. The increasing ability of a device context, the more input can be processed. This assumed for more data processed into information provided by the device.

Context aware mobile agents are a best suited host implementing any context aware applications. Modern integrated voice and data communications equips the hospital staff with smart phones to communicate vocally with each other, but preferably to look-up the next task to be executed and to capture the next report to be noted. However, all attempts to support staff with such approaches are hampered till failure of acceptance with the need to look-up upon a new event for patient identities, order lists and work schedules. Hence a well suited solution has to get rid of such manual interaction with a tiny screen and therefore serves the user with:

- automated identifying actual patient and local environment upon approach,
- automated recording the events with coming to and leaving off the actual patient,
- automated presentation of the orders or service due on the current location and with
- supported documenting the required information keying in a minimum of data into prepared form entries.

Basically such contextually well formed approach requires scheduled workflows, as all necessary preparation must refer to given orders and set schedules. Working *free hand* or *ex tempore* does not provide such qualities.

While context-aware computing aims to facilitate a smooth interaction between humans and technology, few studies of how users perceive context-aware interaction have been performed (Barkhuus & Dey, 2003). Most research focuses on the development of technologies for context-awareness as well as the design of context-aware applications.

Example applications are numerous and the level of interactivity within these varies greatly, ranging from letting the user manually define parameters on how an application should behave, to automatically providing the user with services and information that the developer finds relevant.

3.3 Micro-nano technology

The development of micro and nano technology, which led to a smaller size of microchip, becomes a major driving factor for the development of ubicomp devices now. The smaller a device will cause the smaller user focus on instrument. This is according to concept "off the desktop" from ubicomp.

Technology utilizes a variety of microchips in a kind of extremely small size of T-Engine or Radio Frequency Identification (RFID) applied in everyday life in the form of smart cards or tags, such super mini microchip illustrated in figure 2. For example someone who has a subscription bus ticket in the form of card uses this by swiping it through sensor and the balance will be directly debited according to the distance he traveled.

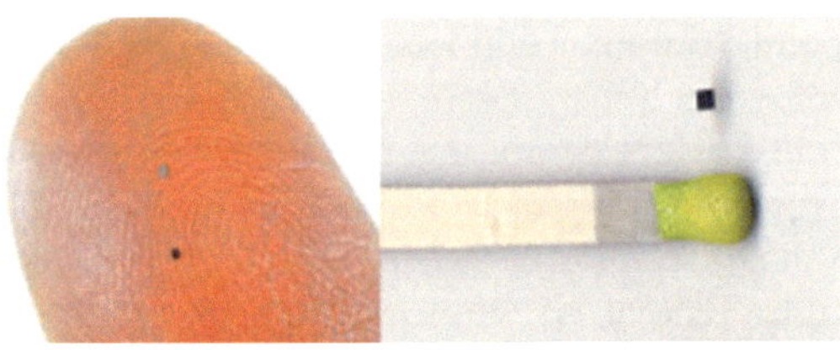

Fig. 2. Super mini microchip from Toshiba (IEEE Pervasive Computing)

In developed countries such as Japan, the current micro and nano technology has been applied to everyday life through a variety of sensors. The size of data processing tools are not seen by humans in public places as shown in figure 3.

4. Case study

How about the development and the application of ubiquitous computing in Indonesia ? As one of the developing countries, Indonesia is still developing the ICT environment, including ubiquitous computing.

Our research showed that the application of ubicomp still in the development stage. And based on our research too, we divide the use of ubiquitous computing application into three parts and will be explained as follows.

4.1 Ubiquitous mobile application

We restricted our study to the usage of mobile phones technology for Ubiquitous mobile application. And according to our observation, the amount of user of mobile phones

Fig. 3. Installed sensors in public places are very helpful for disabilities people and tourists. (IEEE Pervasive Computing)

technology have reached more than 40 million people, as shown in figure 4 *(http://www.pemberdayaan-telematika.info/wartelnet/index.php)*. Figure 4 shows graph of mobile phone user according to cellular operator usage that exists in Indonesia).

The number of mobile phone users is still continuing to improve considering that the needs of this technology are no longer become luxury requirement, but become the mandatory requirement for the Indonesia people. The new technology which is offered by the manufacturer of the mobile phone also could make the number of users of the mobile phone continue to improve.

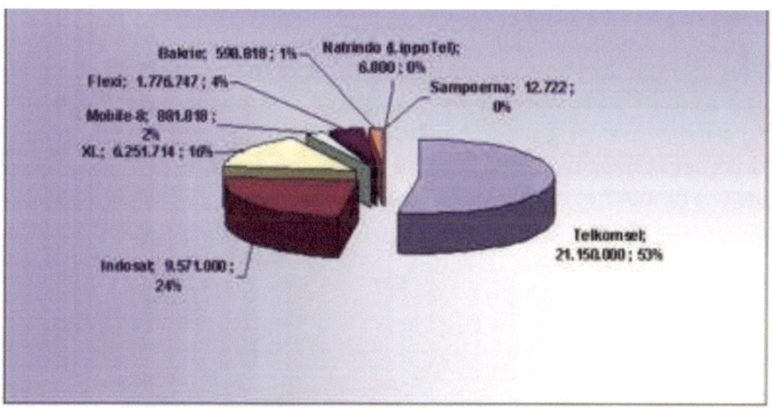

Fig. 4. Trends of mobile phone user in Indonesia

3G mobile concept has been implemented in Indonesia since 16 Aug 2006 after Singapore and Malaysia. However, 3G technology does not provide Indonesian users perfectly, because Indonesia does not have good backbone network architecture to support this technology.

Owned by PT Telekomunikasi Indonesia (Telkom) (65 percent), the largest full-service telecommunications operator in Indonesia and SingTel (35 percent), one of Asia's leading telecommunications service operators, Telkomsel provides GSM cellular services in

Indonesia through its own nationwide dual-band 900/ 1800MHz GSM network, and internationally through 244 international roaming partners in 148 countries.
The 3G phenomenon in Indonesia, especially W-CDMA-based technology, is quite interesting to observe. In comparison, its northern neighbors Singapore and Malaysia - especially since both countries launched 3G services at about the same time–have had seen starkly different uptakes in these services.

4.2 Ubiquitous web application

Web sites are evolving from repositories of (mainly) passive information to become complex applications, with operations and, sometimes, transactions available. In addition it is becoming more and more necessary to develop "families of applications", presenting the same content-services to different categories of users in different contexts.
So, what is a ubiquitous web application? A ubiquitous web application is a Web application that suffers from the anytime/ anywhere/ any media syndrome. This means that an ubiquitous web application should be designed from the start taking into account not only its hypermedia nature, but also the fact that it must run as is on a variety of platforms, including mobile phones, Personal Digital Assistants (PDAs), full-fledged desktop computers, and so on.
This implies that a ubiquitous web application must take into account the different capabilities of devices comprising display size, local storage size, method of input, network capacity, etc. New opportunities are offered in terms of location-based, time-based, and personalized services taking into account the needs and preferences of particular users. Consequently, a ubiquitous web application must be, on the one hand, context-aware i.e., aware of the environment it is running in, and on the other hand it must support personalization.
According to our study, we find that Indonesia has implemented ubiquitous web application. And we restrict our study for this ubiquitous application to the usage of internet application in Indonesia. We present the graphic of internet users in Indonesia which we have been studied at figure 5.
Figure 5 shows that the development of internet user in Indonesia is developing from year-to-year. It also shows that the people in Indonesia are aware about the benefit of Internet; know how to use the internet. Unfortunately, the use of internet at the village are still lowest than use of internet at the city. These become homework for the governance how to cast the balance of the use of internet in all area in Indonesia.

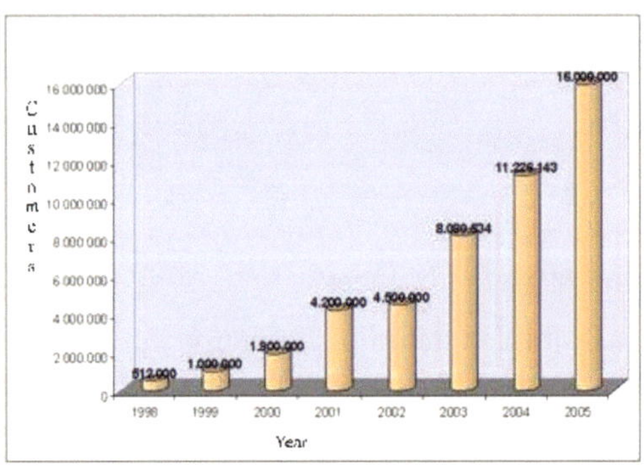

Fig. 5. The development of internet users in Indonesia (http://www.pemberdayaan-telematika.info/wartelnet/index.php)

4.3 Ubiquitous payment system application

The last part of our study about the application of ubiquitous computing in Indonesia is the use of Ubicomp for the payment system. M-payment market is in a constantly flux due to a wide variety of payment solutions, technologies, scenarios, consumer expectations, and penetration strategies of payment service providers. The systems change and are subject to a high or low market penetration according to the parties' requirements: customers, financial institutes, and merchants alike want a convenient way to perform payments, even though they have different motivations. For instance, the customer wants a convenient and trustworthy way to pay; the financial institute needs automatic and economic settlement of the payment. Based on these considerations, it would be desirable to handle different payment methods with a standardized architecture.

The customer should be able to choose his preferred device, his mobile phone or PDA, and choose the appropriate financial service (e.g. financial information or payment). Today, these services are rendered by mobile payment (m-payment) systems (Gross et. al, 2008).

M-payment can be understood as any access to payments, where at least one participant uses a mobile device. This is often a mobile phone (Krueger, 2001). Other devices are for instance personal digital assistants (PDA), or items in which transponders are integrated. This could be an identity card. The data stored on the transponder is transmitted via radio communication to a reader and passed through to a financial network.

Frost and Sullivan extracted several application areas for m-payment in a study (Legard, 2002):

- Automated point-of-sale payments (vending machines, parking meters and ticket machines)
- Attended point-of-sale payments (shop counters, taxis)
- Mobile-accessed Internet payments (merchant WAP sites)
- Mobile-assisted Internet payments (fixed Internet sites using phone instead of credit card)
- Peer-to-peer payments between individuals.

The technology of ubicomp which available in Indonesia for the payment system are RFID technology and Barcode technology. We will explain the use of both technologies in separately.

(a) Barcode Application

Barcode is an optical machine-readable representation of data. Originally, bar codes represented data in the widths (lines) and the spacing of parallel lines and may be referred to as linear or 1D (1 dimensional) barcodes or symbologies. But they also come in patterns of squares, dots, hexagons and other geometric patterns within images termed 2D (2 dimensional) matrix codes or symbologies. In spite of there being no bars, 2D systems are generally referred to as barcodes as well.

Based on our study about application of barcode, the use of this technology has been used for long time. The application of this technology could be seen at supermarket, university, library, office, etc. We can't explain when the first penetration of barcode come to Indonesia because we can't get the resource, but the usage of this technology has been developed from until now during our observation.

(b) RFID Application

The development of RFID was spurred by the need to enhance tracking and access applications in the 1980s in manufacturing and other hostile environments. This no contact

means of gathering and tracking information proved to be resilient. RFID is now an established part of specific busi- ness processes in a variety of markets.
RFID has a set of frequencies which are classified by their range which described as follows:

- Low, covering from 100 KHz to 500 KHz, has a short reading range, and Lower system costs,
- High, covering from 850 MHz to 950 MHz, has a long reading range, and High reading speeds,
- Ultra High, covering from 2.4 GHz to 2.5 GHz.

Based on our study, the implementation of the RFID technology is improved although the finance is common problem for this new technology. The implementation does not just in one place (usually at supermarket), but it has implemented in other places too, such as bus way station, KAI (Indonesia Railway Company), gas station, offices, etc. (*http://ekowahyudin.wordpress.com/tag/rfid*).
Various benefits of RFID we can feel almost in a variety of access control applications. RFID short-range has been quite widely used in Indonesia. Door access control technology is quite powerful but still it depends on the design of the security plan. Taking the example of E-toll, payments automation and highway access toll. We can learn when RFID is implemented, we do not have to worry about the queues at toll booth because all cars already automatically "pay" without waiting for officers to give receipts, less returns, money and so forth.
Further, for RFID technology, Indonesia uses RFID ISO-14443, one of RFID technology, with the frequency 13.56 MHz, in implementation of this ubicomp technology. But it is still illegal application because there is no regulation from Indonesia government and still being study by DIRJEN POSTEL Indonesia. But later, this technology will replace barcode technology because of it has more advantages than barcode technology.

5. Ubicomp issues

5.1 Security

Ubicomp increased risks to security. The use of bearer, infrared, or other wireless communication media form between input devices and data processing devices opens opportunities for other parties in hacking data. The hacker can use it for their interests. Currently, various researches on secure data transmission, including research on new protocols, became one of main focus of research on ubicomp.

5.2 Privacy

The use of devices in human causes the narrowed space on privacy. By reasons of employees time efficiency, a supervisor can ask all employees to use their tags so that it can be monitored their presence in the office. This causes the employee get no longer privacy, their rights. Their existence can be monitored at any time and accompanying data by supervisor. He can know how many his employees went to the toilet that day. In few science fiction films we have seen how government is paranoid attempt to provide citizen tags in obtaining data of national security.

5.3 Wireless speed

With a variety of ubicomp devices, the demand for speed wireless communications technology into something is absolute. Today's technology ensures this speed for one person or a group. Ubicomp is not just talking about one device for one person. Ubicomp makes someone can bring some ubicomp devices and also must be used in such a large area. This technology is not currently able to guarantee the pace for such situations because it can be ineffective if not supported with wireless technology development that can provide the required speed.

6. Conclusion

Our study shows that the application of ubiquitous computing are identified in three parts, first is ubiquitous mobile application, second is ubiquitous web application, and third is ubiquitous payment system application. For each explanation of that application, we conclude that the uses of Ubiquitous Computing technology in Indonesia are still in development stage. Further, the challenges to improve the use of ubiquitous computing in Indonesia is to provide the infrastructure and the environment of ubiquitous computing so that many application of ubiquitous computing can be available and identify in Indonesia. We also hope the research of ubicomp technology in Indonesia will improve for the next year because it is still rarely to find the paper which discuss about this technology.

7. References

Bagci, W. T. T. U. F. J. and Petzold. (2003). Ubiquitous Mobile Agent System In A P2P-Network, *UbiSys-Workshop at the Fifth Annual Conference on Ubiquitous Computing, Seattle, USA,* October 12-15.

Weiser, M. (1993). Hot topics: Ubiquitous computing, *IEEE Computer,* October.

P. A. Widhiarta, (2007). Ubiquitous Computing - Era Ketiga Dari Revolusi Komputer, *Ilmu Komputer.com.*

http://www.ubiq.com/hypertext/weiser/UbiHome.html.

http://www.pemberdayaan-telematika.info/wartelnet/index.php.

http://ekowahyudin.wordpress.com/tag/rfid.

Mattern, F.(2004). Wireless Future: Ubiquitous Computing, *Prceedings of Wireless Congress,* Munich, Germany, November.

Galloway, A. (2004). Playful Mobilities: Ubiquitous Computing In The City, *Alternative Mobility Futures Conference, Lancaster University,* January, 9-11.

Sakamura, K. *Ubiquitous Computing: Making It a Reality,* YRP Ubiquitous Networking Laboratory, University of Tokyo.

Schmidt, A. (2003). Interacting with the ubiquitous computer, University of Munich, Germany, Tech. Rep., September, 8-11.

http://www.indocashregister.com.

B. Rahardjo, (1999). Ubiquitous computing. Bandung Institute of Technology, 15 Mei.

Weiser, M. (1993). Some computer science problems in ubiquitous computing, *Communications of the ACM,* July.

Roman, M, Al-Muhtadi, J., Ziebart, B, Campbell, R., Mickunas, M. D. *System Support for Rapid Ubiquitous Computing Application Development and Evaluation,* DoCoMo Labs, USA, Department of Computer Science, University of Illinois at Urbana-Champaign.

Prince, K. Adam, B. N. B. A. (2005). Keeping Ubiquitous Computing To Yourself: A Practical Model For User Control Of Privacy, *International Journal of Human-Computer Studies,* vol. 63, pp. 228 - 253, July.

D. I. Hendrawan, *Towards the Ambient Intelligence Era: A convergence of ubiquitous computing, communication and intelligent user interfaces,* School of Electrical Engineering and Informatics, Bandung Institute of Technology.

Gross, S., Fleisch, E., Lampe, M., Müller, René. (2004). Requirements and Technologies for Ubiquitous Payment, *Multikonferenz Wirtschaftsinformatik, Techniques and Applications for Mobile Commerce.* Essen, Germany, March.

12

Using the iDTV as the Center of an Ubiquitous Environment

Orlewilson B. Maia, Nairon S. Viana and Vicente F. de Lucena Jr
Universidade Federal do Amazonas (UFAM)
Brazil

1. Introduction

The characteristics of the new interactive Digital Television (iDTV) systems are assuming a very important role in modern life. In fact, these features are being increasingly expanded, from simple signal decoders to sophisticated devices that allow the execution of interactive applications related to the content displayed, providing services of all kinds like Internet access, TV-Banking, TV-Mail, TV-Commerce, TV-Health, Games and so on. Moreover, recently, the main iDTV features have been used to integrate themselves with other consumer electronics (CE) devices in intelligent and ubiquitous environments. This new trend improves the user's experience with Digital Television and introduces several challenges for integrating heterogeneous devices, centralizing their services through a common iDTV set.

Nowadays one possible way of expanding the functionalities of a Set-Top Box (STB) is to connect it with other devices equipped with computational power such as some popular electronic equipments of a Home Network system. The firsts ideas were related to establishing a communication link between Digital TV and CE devices through one central processing unit of the Home Network, also known as Home Gateway (see Figure 1(a)). Another possibility is to integrate these two devices on a single platform, using the STB as a Home Gateway (see Figure 1(b)).

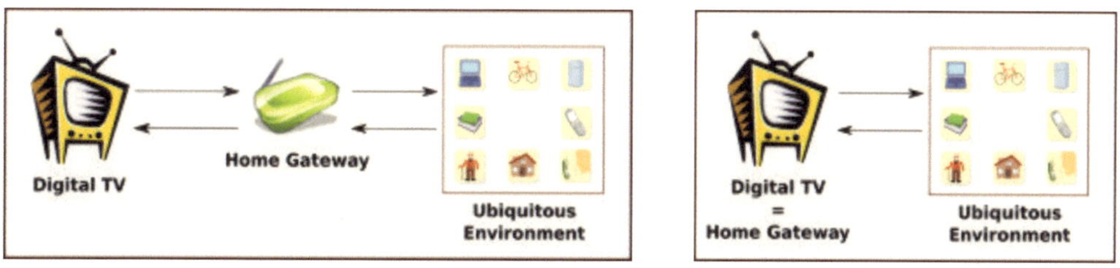

(a) Digital TV interacts with an ubiquitous environment through a Home Gateway

(b) Digital TV interacts with an ubiquitous environment directly

Fig. 1. Two ways for integrating iDTV in an Ubiquitous Computing Environment

Several scenarios can be provided by the use of Digital TV (DTV) receivers as Home Gateways. One possible example is the administration of a smart home through the iDTV, performing common tasks in the ubiquitous environment, such as the control of doors, cameras, temperature sensors and security applications. In a more specific scenario the iDTV multimedia content can be synchronized with the television program. For example, the user is able to print a document linked to a TV show or to control the environment synchronized with audio/video transmission while a he/she is watching a movie.

Indeed, based on the tecnology available nowadays, other useful real life scenarios where the iDTV set is the information center in an ubiquitous environment can be created. For example, when Maria arrives at home, the TV recognizes her through her mobile phone and recommends a list of programs that she could watch based on her known profile. After that, she chooses a movie program. A few minutes later, Maria decides to eat something and moves to the kitchen carrying her mobile phone. At this moment, she is recognized by a TV set located in the kitchen that starts automatically to show the movie she was watching in the living room.

These scenarios bring to the market new possibilities of developing convergent applications, for instance in Brazil, where most people (over 97.1 %, according to a recent research from the Brazilian National Agency of Electrical Energy, ELETROBRAS, performed from 2005 to 2007 (ELETROBRAS, 2011)) use the TV quite frequently and are large consumers of services. Additionally, the iDTV can be used not only for providing conventional services (like TV-Mail or TV-Commerce), but also for accessing services of devices in a Home Network. This allows content sharing among iDTV and mobile phones, which is another potential field in the Brazilian market (ANATEL, 2010).

The goal of this study is to present some research results about the relationship between Digital TV and electronic devices in ubiquitous environments and to describe a collaboration model between Home Networks and iDTV Systems based on the Brazilian standard. We present a platform built over a common software environment for Digital TV and Home Network applications. With this platform it is possible to create several use cases scenarios, specially those related to composed services, i.e., those who integrate services from various devices to improve the user's experience with the connected ubiquitous home. The platform considers some issues of software environments for iDTV and Home Network, and tries to offer to the programmer an appropriate environment for rapid development of applications, in a level that isolates the main software components of the two environments. This study, from the overall technologies to the specification of the platform, will be described in the next sections.

2. Overview of digital TV and home networks

2.1 Digital TV

Ever since the first TV channel (BBC London in 1936), the TV went through several changes. The first most significant occurred in 1950 with the emergence of the color TV Sets and the growing of program options to the viewers (Schwalb, 2004). In the 1980s came the first digital production islands. A consequence of this was the transmission of digital content which were decoded in devices called Set-Top Boxes (STBs) in order to enable an analog TV to show the digital content.

According to Morris & Smith-Chaigneau (2005), the Digital TV (DTV) offers many advantages, such as the delivering of more programs in the same transmission band; the improvement of audio and video quality; the absence of interference at reception; and the emergence of interactive services and applications.

2.1.1 Interactive digital TV

Originally the TV does not provide interactivity to the viewers, i.e., the viewers watch the content of the programs and there is no interaction between them; the viewers only turn on/off the TV or switch the channel. Over the years, some television programs started using telephone lines to ask the viewers their opinion about the content being watched. With the advent of the DTV, services and interactive applications are created to allow the viewers to interact with the programs through an application broadcasted with the progams. This kind of interactivity allowed the emergence of the new interactive Digital TV (iDTV).

According to Schwalb (2004) and Morris & Smith-Chaigneau (2005), the iDTV can be classified as *Enhanced TV* with texts, graphic elements and improvement of audio and video quality; *Internet on TV* where the Internet can be accessed through the TV; *personalized TV* where the TV is adapted according to the viewer's profile; *Personal Video Recorder (PVR)* where the TV content is recorded from a genre, title or schedule; *Walled Garden*, a portal from which the user can browse for some desired iDTV application; *Games*, where the viewers use the TV to play a game or to connect with other players located connected in network; *Electronic Program Guide (EPG)*, similar to the Walled Garden, but it has more details about the channels; and *Teletext* which shows information (economics, wheater, last news and so on) provided by the broadcasters in a text format.

Another issue that enables the use of interactivity for viewers is the usage of the return channel. The return channel is used to send a request from a viewer through an iDTV application (such as ordering pizza or answering a question from a quiz) to the broadcaster over the Internet or a phone line, for example. Thus, the viewers can interact with the broacasters returning a feedbak about their content programs.

2.1.2 Components of an interactive digital TV system

An iDTV System is generaly composed by the following components: the broadcaster, the receiver, the broadcast network, and the communication link (see Figure 2). These components or subsystems deal with the digital information as services, audio/video/data elementary packets that compose a program channel. The services are phisically organized as a *Transport Stream* (TS) in which some operations are performed, such as coding and multiplexing defined by ISO-IEC 13818-x (ISO, 2000).

The broadcaster is represented by a TV channel or another entity able to perform the editing, formatting and distribution of content throught the broadcast network. This process involves steps of audio/video encoding (ISO-IEC 13818-1,2), data/application insertion (Digital Storage Media Command Control standard, ISO-IEC 13818-6) (ISO, 2002) and multiplexing (ISO-IEC 13818-2). In this stage, the data that will be broadcasted is in TS format (defined by MPEG-2 Systems). The last stage is the modulation to the broadcast network which will depend on the iDTV standard assumed. The broadcast could be done by three ways: cable, terrestrial or satellite.

When the digital signal is received, the STB performs the reverse process on the TS. The signal received is demodulated, demultiplexed and delivered to the audio/video/data decodificator which processes and displays the content in a TV screen. An important feature of the STB is the support for executing interactive applications which may or may not be related to the audio/video content and allow sending information back to the broadcasters. This feature is enabled in a iDTV System by the return channel.

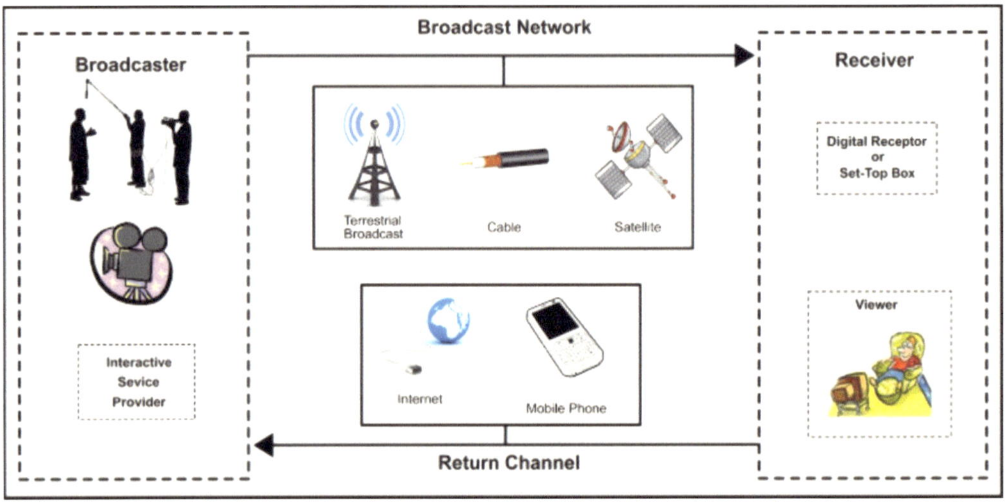

Fig. 2. General iDTV Components

2.1.3 Digital TV systems and middlewares

The main entities involved on iDTV business joined efforts to create specifications or reference models for iDTV in order to guarantee the interoperability among hardware manufactures, businesses and iDTV applications developers. Each specification has some particular caracteristic related to the regions they were developed. The main specification systems for iDTV are the American Advanced Television Systems Committee (ATSC)(ATSC, 2009), the European Digital Video Broadcast (DVB)(DVB, 2010), the Japanese Integrated Services Digital Broadcasting (ISDB)(ISDB, 2011), and more recently the Brazilian International Standard for Digital TV (ISDTV)(ISDTV, 2011).

In a generic architecture for the receiver, the main interface between the iDTV applications and the devices themselves is a component named *middleware* which consists of a set of *Application Programming Interfaces* (APIs) that provides a platform-independent execution environemt for iDTV applications. Thus, the middleware ensures portability between STBs and provides less effort for developing iDTV applications because the developers do not need to worry about how to access the low level receiver functionalities. The main existing standards for middlewares in the world are the European Multimedia Home Platform (MHP) (MHP, 2010); the American Advanced Common Application Platform (ACAP) (ACAP, 2009); the Japanese Association of Radio Industries and Businesses (ARIB) (ARIB, 2009); and the Brazilian Ginga (ITU-T, 2009).

The execution environment used in MHP is based on the Java Virtual Machine. A DVB application developed in this environment is called DVB–J. Moreover, the MHP 1.1 allows the usage of a declarative language similar to HTML called DVB–HTML. These types of applications have the capabilities of downloading and storing iDTV applications (in storage devices like USB Flash Drive or Hard Disc), access smart cards readers, and control iDTV applications over the Internet.

Similar to MHP, ACAP enables the usage of declarative languages as XHTML-based or ECMAScript. However, applications developed to this middleware are not complatible to MHP. To overcome this problem, a stable subset of API was extracted from MHP and defined as a standard common API, assuming interoperability among applications built in any middleware. This interoperable platform is called *Globally Executable MHP (GEM)*. All the middleware specifications are supposed to have a GEM-compliance subset.

ARIB is composed by ARIB STD-B24 standard (Data Coding and Transmission Specification for Digital Broadcasting) which allows the development of declarative iDTV applications through the Broadcast Markup Language (BML).

Ginga is the middleware of the International Standard for Digital Television (ISDTV), the Brazilian Digital TV System. The specification is compliant with ITU J.200, J.201 and J.202 recommendations by providing an environment that supports declarative and procedural content, using an execution machine for Java-based applications (xlets) and a presentation machine for the treatment of declarative content based mainly on NCL (Nested Context Language) (Soares et al., 2007). In the Ginga software stack, a core structure (Ginga Common Core) is responsible for providing services that integrate the two environments. This part of the stack contains common content decoders that serve both the Ginga-NCL and the Ginga-J as well as implements a bridge mechanism to enable interaction between Java applications and NCL documents.

The first specifications released for Ginga-J defined the middleware as a set of 3 API's (named Green, Yellow and Blue), each one of them grouped some common functionalities for iDTV APIs (media management, life cicle control through JavaTV, return channel, and so on). This specification had a special feature of a device support API integrated to the middleware, which allowed sharing content among the iDTV and other devices. Currently, the Ginga-J specification has changed, and some of these APIs were replaced by the JavaDTV standard (ABNT NBR 15606-4, 2010), especially those related to GEM compliance. In spite of these modifications in Ginga-J, the basic functionalities of a Java-based iDTV programming environment were maintained, such as the xlet lifecycle model, media management, and the inter-xlet communication mechanism.

The Ginga-NCL provides a presentation engine for multimedia content based on scripts. The logical subsystem of Ginga-NCL handles documents in the pattern of the NCL language. NCL was designed for presentation and synchronization of multimedia content, based on NCM (Nested Context Model). Other types of content supported by Ginga-NCL are the ECMA Script, CSS and XHTML. Ginga-NCL also offers support for treatment of procedural content, through the implementation of the Lua API (Soares et al., 2007), allowing developers to construct audiovisual programs and to insert some sort of dynamic programming. The support for content (such as scripts, Lua, JPEG, PNG, and MPEG) is guaranteed by the Adapter, a component located on Ginga Common Core. Ginga-NCL also provides a device support mechanism, mainly related to sharing multimedia content among iDTV and mobile devices (Soares et al., 2009).

A summary of the procedural/declarative technologies available for the middleware specifications presented before is depicted in Table 1.

2.2 Home networks

The emergence and growth of the communication technologies enabled the interconnection of multiple devices located in a residence creating a smart home environment (Dixit & Prasad, 2008). This kind of home environment is characterized by allowing users to control, access and share information through these devices. Some applications can be cited, as for example, scheduling an air conditioner to turn on automatically when the environment temperature is above 25 celsius degrees.

Middleware	iDTV System	Declarative Environment	Procedural Environment
ACAP	ATSC (American)	ACAP-X [ATSC A-101 2005] Languages: XHTML like and ECMAScript	ACAP-J [ATSC A-101 2005] Language: Java
MHP	DVB (European)	DVB-HTML [ETSI TS 102 812 v 1.2.2 2006] Languages: XHTML like and ECMAScript	MHP [ETSI TS 102 812 v 1.2.2 2006] Language: Java
ARIB	ISDB (Japonese)	ARIB-BML [ARIB B-24 2004] Languages: BML(XHTML like) and ECMAScript	Optional (GEM [ETSI TS 102 819 v 1.3.1 2005]) Language: not implemented
Ginga	ISDTV (Brazilian)	Ginga-NCL [ABNT NBR 15606-2 2009] Languages: NCL and Lua	Ginga-J [ABNT NBR 15606-4 2010] Language: Java

Table 1. Declarative and procedural environments of iDTV middlewares

Furthermore, advanced types of systems may be constructed, in a near future such as those who have the ability to learn from user's everyday activities at home and, using artificial intelligence techniques, create an adaptable environment based on the user profiles. For example, when someone arrives at home, the environment recognizes his/her profile and sends a message to the stereo system which selects his/her favorite music track. Another point that have contributed to the creation of these kind of environment was the popularization of wireless communication which enabled the interconnection of several devices located in a home.

2.2.1 Open standards used in a home network

The Universal Plug-and-Play (UPnP) technology provides communication between electronic devices as well as the sharing of services, without the need of human intervention and configuration (Miller et al., 2001). The architecture has zero configuration support and the services discovery is automatic. A Device Control Protocol (DCP) was created for interconnection of electronic devices. Another important feature is that each manufacturer can create its own API and describe their services by an Extensible Markup Language (XML) file.

Jini, for example, is a middleware that offers APIs for the development of services, as well as network protocols allowing the data sharing among electronic devices with different types of communication technologies (Gupta et al., 2002). Each device supplies an interface to access available methods. Thus it ensures standardization and the sharing of services among them. This interface is represented by a Java object that implements its methods. The Remote Method Invocation (RMI) is used to access its methods through *invoke* and *lookup* commands.

The Home Audio Video Interoperability (HAVi) specification is used for sharing multimedia content between audio and video devices through FireWire (IEEE 1394) and their managment is centered on TV. To do so, a set of APIs and a middleware were created to implement functions, such as detect the devices in a Home Network, install the interfaces, and guarantee the interoperability between the devices (HAVi, 2001). The HAVi main features are that any device can control other device, each device has a Java interface which is available to other devices, the updates are done via download, and it gives support for legacy systems and Plug-and-Play (Marshall, 2001).

One of the most known specifications for Home Networking is the Open Services Gateway initiative (OSGi). The framework supports applications from modular units known as bundles. In fact it controls the bundles life-cycle (adding, removing and replacing bundles at run-time) and verifies the dependencies between them (Tavares & Valente, 2008). Each bundle is represented as a service in the OSGi architecture. The services are registered in the OSGi Service Registry, which allows the discovery and access of services in an OSGi environment (Marples & Kriens, 2001).

2.2.2 Communications technologies used in a home network

In a home, there are different types of CE (TV, mobile phone, digital camera, and so on) that have a communication technology which allows to exchange information among them. This trend is followed by the growth in the usage of some communication technologies (Bluetooth, Universal Serial Bus (USB), Firewire etc). Among the most promising communication technologies commonly used in a Home Network, the two types above deserve a special attention: Wireless Networks and No New Wires Networks.

Wireless networks, such as IEEE 802.15 (Bluetooth), IEEE 802.15.4 (ZigBee) and IEEE 802.11x (WiFi), have grown significantly in recent years because of their convenience in easily connecting with new placed devices, the integration with several types of devices, and the gradually low cost of these solutions. They provide a transmission rate from 115Kbps (ZigBee) to 54Mbps (802.11g), measurable Quality of Service (Bluetooth and Zigbee), and a transmission range from 1m (Bluetooth) to 1.6 km (ZigBee). This kind of network is very useful in a home environment because of the typical distance between the CE devices, which is, in general, between 1m and 50m, its ability to communicate with more than one device at the same time, and, most importantly, because of the lack of cables that facilitates the replacement of devices.

The No New Wires Networks reuses the existent wired infrastructure of the house, such as the electrical wiring (HomePlug) and phone line (HomePNA) to establish a communication mechanism. As a matter of fact, the electrical wiring used is not considered an apropriate network media for data transmission because of its noise, the presence of interference, and fading. However, the emergence of new techniques in digital signal processing and code error control has allowed the increase of data rate transmission through the power lines and the reduction of noise (Lin et al., 2002). The main features of these networks are data rate transmission between 10 Mbps (HomePNA) and 14 Mbps (HomePlug), transmission of multimedia contents and connection of up to 50 devices in the same network. Nevertheless, there are some technical difficulties in building these networks, such as scalability of the number of connected devices in the network and security issues in data traffic (Zahariadis et al., 2002).

3. State of the art

The design of solutions incorporating electronic devices with some communication technology that promotes the exchange of information among them has been the topic of research in several recent works. These works diverge on their respective adopted approaches. Three different aspects of these approaches were analyzed: the way a device communicates with others, the specification used to manage electronic devices, and the collaborative ways between iDTV and Home Gateway.

When talking about the diversity communication mechanisms, we may cite Kanma et al. (2003), which describes a scenario where a cellular phone communicates with electronic devices, such as an air conditioner and a washing machine, over Bluetooth. To do so, adapters with integrated Bluetooth technology through device's serial ports (RS 232) were developed. Some services were deployed, including the monitoring and remote controlling, updating of the adapter software, diagnosing of the failures, and getting technical information on the electronic devices. The need to create new adapters to each new device that joins to the network is a significant disadvantage.

The work described in Al Mehairi et al. (2007) used Short Message Service (SMS) to request different kinds of services from a Home Server that controls/monitors electronic devices through Bluetooth. To do so, in the SMS, the device and command names (turn on/off lamp, for example) were informed. In this approach, the Home Server receives the command and sends the information to the appropriate device. As a disadvantage of this work we may cite the fact that SMS is a payed service.

Considering the specification used for managing electronic devices, the work in Kim et al. (2007) used OSGi in a Residential Gateway to create a common ground for electronic devices from a wide range of communication technologies. In this work the electronic devices are managed remotely through a Web page available by the Residential Gateway. This proposal was focused on the use of limited resources, such as low data rate transmission and low energy consumption.

Another possibility may be illustrated by a scenario where UPnP and Jini specifications communicate with OSGi by offering a large scope to manage electronic devices (Dobrev et al., 2002). In this context, two components were created, a Jini Driver and an UPnP Base Driver. These components offer an access interface to registered services in OSGi environment. Thus, it is possible to create several applications, such as accessing a printer from Jini or a digital camera from UPnP. This way, when a device (a PC or cellular phone, for example) requests some service, such as printing a text or getting photos from a digital camera, the OSGi communicates with Jini requesting the printing of a text, or with UPnP requesting the content from a digital camera.

Some works related to the possible colaborative mechanims suggest the use of the TV-Sets as Residential Gateways mainly due to the emergence of the DTV and its potential for integrating other electronic devices in the Home Network. One of the first ideas was to create a protocol layer to control multimedia devices (audio and video) through HAVi specification (Marshall, 2001).

In Tkachenko et al. (2005) a framework named DTV-HNF (Digital TV - Home Network Framework) is described. This framework enables managing access requests from iDTV applications to available services from electronic devices on the Home Network. However, only iDTV applications access electronic devices services and there is a possibility of communication failure between iDTV and the Residential Gateway because of the technical nature of the communication used (TCP/IP).

To overcome these difficulties, the approaches in Cabrer et al. (2006), Bae et al. (2006), Yang et al. (2007), Redondo et al. (2007) and Lin et al. (2008; 2009) describe a collaboration mechanism between iDTV and Residential Gateway in the same environment, i.e., in the same device are included features from the iDTV and from the Residential Gateway. Other characteristic of these works is the bidirectional communication, i.e. an iDTV appl ication can access a service from an electronic device and vice-versa.

In Cabrer et al. (2006) and Redondo et al. (2007) a new kind of application named XBundLET was created, which has features of MHP applications (xlet) and OSGi services (bundle). XBundLET is in compliance with xlets and bundles specifications: it is managed by an Application Manager and communicates with other xlets through Inter-Xlet Communication (IXC). At the same time provides services to other bundles and/or invokes services from other bundles through OSGi Service Registry.

A convergent architecture between data broadcasting and home networking services is proposed in Bae et al. (2006), based on the ACAP middleware and the UMB (Universal Middleware Bridge) protocol stack. This model has two sets of software components; a Service Proxy under the ACAP architecture and a Service Broker on the UMB stack. These components establish connections through the Simple Service Discovery Protocol (SSDP) enabling the discovery and use of network services for ACAP-J applications.

The proposal in Yang et al. (2007) implements a collaborative model that modifies as little as possible the characteristics of the MHP and OSGi native components. The work defines bridge structures between the two platforms that allow the passing of context parameters from MHP xlets to OSGi bundles and vice-versa. These structures exploit the Java Class Loader features, as well as implement a security mechanism to ensure that unauthorized access will not occur. Although, this model is simpler than the previous ones, its main disadvantages are that the developers of both xlets and bundles need to know the new components, besides the need to export bridge-components as Java Virtual Machine (JVM) static libraries outside the MHP and OSGi environments.

The approach of Lin et al. (2008) used components under the Wrapper and Broker design patterns, to isolate iDTV and Home Network software components. MHP xlets and OSGi bundles communicate with specific proxies for each platform, implemented within a Broker bridge component. This model has the MHP Application Manager as an OSGi service, through *MHPAPPmanager* bundle. Inside this bundle are the Broker component and the proxies. A significant disadvantage is the need to modify the MHP and OSGi components to support this new model, which just increases its complexity. The work of Lin et al. (2009) is an extension of the previous one. It presents a general classification of MHP-OSGi architectures, designing some of them in order to make a qualitative/quantitative comparison, considering issues of resources consumption, time for loading components, startup time, etc.

4. Integrating digital TV in an ubiquitous environment

The iDTV usage as a part of the ubiquitous environment is a topic of recent research. The collaboration strategies presented in Section 3 offer software platforms to build new application scenarios to the home user. One possible trend, analysed by Maia et al. (2009), is to extend a software platform for iDTV in order to increase the scope of these new applications. This way, it is possible to create from monitoring/controlling to more ubiquitous related scenarios, such as personalizing the home configuration to the user preferences.

To deliver ubiquitous services to the Brazilian iDTV, it is desired to create an integration mechanism between the Ginga middleware and some Residential Gateway specification (OSGi, Jini or UPnP) that can live together in only one CE device. In the literature, there is the work of Viana et al. (2009) which shows an introductory idea of such integration. Moreover, some features from the DTV middleware can be used, such as spatial-temporal synchronization between media (video, audio, text) and electronic devices.

In this section will be described one constructed component-based model for the Brazilian DTV middleware Ginga and the OSGi framework. The proposed model explores the features of the two Ginga environments (Ginga-J and Ginga-NCL) offering software components that interact with applications (xlets) or declarative content (NCL), exporting its features to the OSGi domain. The components and the two Ginga-OSGi approaches (GingaJ-OSGi and GingaNCL-OSGi) will be shown in details. Similarly, it should be possible for Ginga-J and Ginga-NCL applications accessing OSGi services to have interactive control over devices in Home Networks.

The general architecture of the model is shown in Figure 3. In this figure are Ginga-J, Ginga-NCL and OSGi components and the software bridge between them. Some features for the new Ginga-OSGi platform have been identified to meet the needs of integration between Home Networks and the Brazilian Digital TV. They are:

- ***Allowing the registry and the discovery of OSGi services in a Home Network*** – Services are the basis of the OSGi model. A service is the interface to operations provided by the networked devices. The service discovery in a Home Network is a key step for integrating it with iDTV applications.
- ***Interoperation between OSGi services and Ginga functionalities*** – The environment must allow Ginga to access OSGi services. That is a difficult task because it requires an effort to integrate these different software platforms. Similarly, this model should enable the access of Ginga functions by OSGi.
- ***Providing a useful description of the services to the user*** – Service description is the key to success in attracting a user. In addition to the information provided by OSGi services, such as name, version, and provider, other information should be released, such as device name and methods description.

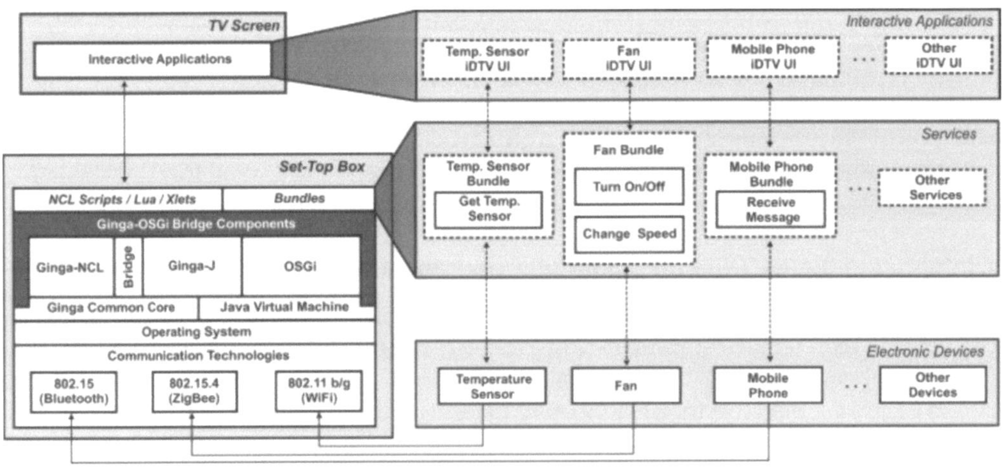

Fig. 3. General Ginga-OSGi Architecture.

The developed strategy considers mechanisms for collaboration between Ginga and OSGi. The two Ginga-OSGi approaches (GingaJ-OSGi and GingaNCL-OSGi) will be described in the next sections.

4.1 GingaJ-OSGi model

The procedural approach is in line with the desired requirements previously mentioned, and follows a model supported by components of the basic modules of Ginga-J and OSGi APIs. Therefore the model can be extended to other middleware like MHP. Indeed, it is based on the approaches of Cabrer et al. (2006), Yang et al. (2007), Lin et al. (2008) and Redondo et al. (2007), providing components that act as interfaces between the two frameworks. However, for this model, it was tried to change as little as possible both environments so that the xlets/services programmers do not need to know complex mechanisms of the platform.

The software layer of GingaJ-OSGi presents seven components that enable the flow of service objects between the two areas following one common pattern. The whole interaction process is focused in the registering of entities for Ginga-J features (IXCRegistry) and OSGi services (Service Registry). Once some Ginga-J functionality has been registered in the IXCRegistry, a component notifies the OSGi side through the registration of a corresponding service. Similarly, every time a bundle registers its service in OSGi, another entity will pass the service reference for the Ginga-J side. These entities act as listeners in both environments and the objects are registered through a generic interface following the Proxy and Decorator design patterns as described in Gamma et al. (1995). They protect the direct access to methods of the object, providing new methods for accessing the object with security, using features of the Java Reflection API. The seven developed components are:

- *GingaJ-OSGiRegister* – This component exports Ginga-J features as services in the OSGi domain. It implements a listener to registry events in the *IXCRegistry* (bind, unbind, rebind). *GingaJ-OSGiRegister* gets the Ginga-J and OSGi contexts through *ContextBridge*. Thus, it registers the Ginga-J functionality as an OSGi service using a *WrappedProxyObject*. This is done by accessing a service provided by the GingaJ-OSGiBundle component.
- *GingaJ-OSGiBundle* – This component provides a service in the Service Registry through which it is possible the registering of *WrappedProxyObject* objects relating to interfaces of the Ginga-J. This is necessary because since the *GingaJ-OSGiRegister* component is not a bundle, it is not authorized to directly register OSGi services.
- *OSGi-GingaJRegister* – Supports the reverse process, it implements a listener to registry events in the OSGi Service Registry and accesses the *ContextBridge* to export the OSGi service as a *WrappedProxyObject* related to the functionality to be registered on the Ginga-J IXCRegistry.
- *XletContextExporter* – This is an xlet that exports a singleton *XletContext* object (in textitjavax.tv.xlet package) to the *ContextBridge*.
- *BundleContextExporter* – It is a bundle that exports a singleton *BundleContext* object (in textitorg.osgi.framework package) to the *ContextBridge*.
- *ContextBridge* – This is a bridge component that allows accessing xlet/bundle contexts. This component receives context objects from *XletContextExporter* and *BundleContextExporter*, making these context objects available in the environment.
- *WrappedProxyObject* – That is a generic object that implements an interface (*WrappedProxyInterface*) which has methods for protecting the services that are being registered (into Service Registry or IXCRegistry).

These components, which are the basis of GingaJ-OSGi platform, operate with the aim of ensuring two interaction mechanisms between the platforms: OSGi services should be accessed by Ginga-J applications, and OSGi applications should access functionalities exported by Ginga-J. The two mechanisms are described in the following subsections.

4.1.1 Accessing OSGi services through Ginga-J applications

As ilustrated in Figure 4, this mechanism is supported by four components: *XletContextExporter*, *BundleContextExporter*, *ContextBridge* and *OSGi-GingaJRegister*.

Once the system is launched, the Application Manager defines a mechanism based on Java class loaders for activating *XletContextExporter* and *BundleContextExporter*. When these two objects are initialized, their contexts are passed to the Singleton object *ContextBridge* which remains active until the shutdown of the framework. At this point, the *OSGi-GingaJRegister* is waiting for notification of any OSGi service registration, through a ServiceListener object (in org.osgi.framework package). When a bundle registers its service in the OSGi (step 1), a reference is retrieved by the *OSGi-GingaJRegister* (step 2). The reference object (ServiceReference) provides methods for accessing some properties of the service through a query language expressed in Lightweight Directory Access Protocol (LDAP) (Howes, 1997). The *OSGi-GingaJRegister* has a key method that passes the service object to a *WrappedProxyObject* instance (step 3), which in turn is passed to IXCRegistry (step 4). This way, all access to the service object from Ginga-J applications is protected by the *WrappedProxyObject*, as outlined before. Thus the xlet, after retrieving the service object from IXCRegistry (step 5), needs only to know the name, the parameters and the types of the desired method in the service.

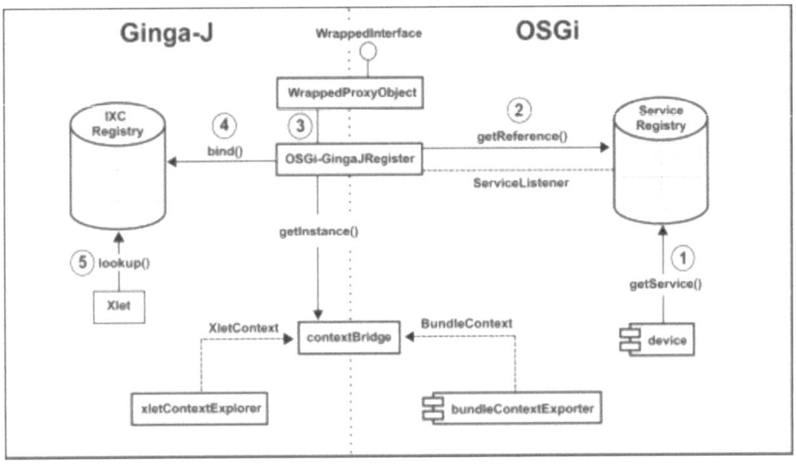

Fig. 4. Exporting OSGi services to Ginga-J domain

4.1.2 Accessing Ginga-J functionalities through OSGi bundles

To register xlet functionalities on the OSGi Service Registry, there are five components: *XletContextExporter*, *BundleContextExporter* and *ContextBridge*, *GingaJ-OSGiRegister*, and *GingaJ-OSGiBundle*(see Figure 5).

Once *XletContextExporter*, *BundleContextExporter* and *ContextBridge* are initialized, the xlet must register an interface in IXCRegistry (step 1). At this point a Singleton object, *GingaJ-OSGiRegister* is listening to events on the IXCRegistry (BIND, REBIND and UNBIND, which means that an interface has been registered, updated or removed, respectively) (step 2). From this point the process is similar to the previous one: the *GingaJ-OSGiRegister* activates a *WrappedProxyObject* to protect the methods of the object registered in IXCRegistry (step 3). After that, the *GingaJOSGiRegister* accesses a service from *GingaJ-OSGiBundle* to register the *WrappedProxyObject* as an OSGi service (step 4). A client bundle for this service needs to know how to get a ServiceReference for the *WrappedProxyObject* (step 5). A bundle that needs to access a method of the interface registered in IXCRegistry must pass the name, types and parameters to *WrappedProxyObject* which will automatically invoke the method. In this way, the bundle is enabled for using a Ginga-J functionality without directly interacting with the middleware.

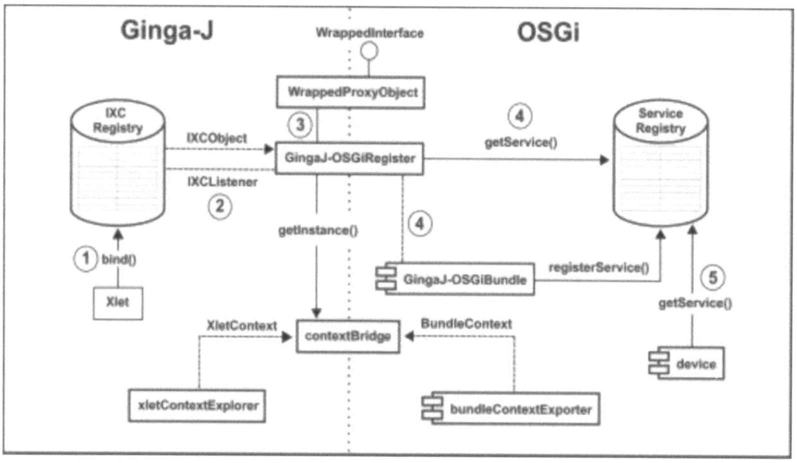

Fig. 5. Exporting Ginga-J funcionalities as OSGi services

4.2 GingaNCL-OSGi Model

The software layer created on the GingaNCL-OSGi platform has components that enable the passing of objects related to services between the OSGi and Ginga-NCL environments. Two Ginga-NCL Adapters are working as bridge components. An *Adapter* is a Java-based component that acts as a container for presenting the media in the interactive audiovisual NCL document. For each *Adapter* a specific region on the iDTV screen can be declared, having its properties defined by the *Descriptor*, that is associated with a *Player* component for playing the media. The six types of components presented in the GingaNCL-OSGi software layer are:

- *DeviceBundle* – This component represents a device located on the Home Network. The information contained in its Manifest file is used to describe it, such as the vendor, the interface name, and the service description. Moreover, a Property file is created to offer a useful description of its services, such as device name, and a description of the available methods.
- *ListenerServerBundle* – That is a component that listens to the registration of *DeviceBundle* services in the Service Registry and stores the information contained in the Manifest and Property files in the XML format.
- *Communication Bridge* – It is composed of two Java static classes (*BundleContextBridge* and *GingaNCLContextBridge*). These Java classes store a bundle context and a Ginga-NCL object, respectively, and enable the communication between Ginga-NCL applications and OSGi bundles.
- *ExporterBundle* – For a Ginga-NCL application to access some *DeviceBundle* services, it is necessary to get its reference on the Service Registry. To do so, this component exports its bundle context to *BundleContextBridge*. In this way, the Ginga-NCL application can use the *OSGiAdapter* for accessing the OSGi services.

- *GingaNCLBundle* – This bundle component registers a Ginga-NCL application as a service after getting the Ginga-NCL object stored in the *GingaNCLContextBridge*. After that, any *DeviceBundle* can access the Ginga-NCL services by retrieving its references on the Service Registry.
- *Extended Adapters and Players* – Two new Adapters were created, the *OSGiAdapter* and the *GingaNCLAdapter*. The first one is responsible for getting a bundle context stored in the *BundleContextBridge* and accessing the registered services by requesting to the *ListenerServerBundle*. After that, the *OSGiAdapter* accesses a *DeviceBundle* and uses its services. The last one exports a Ginga-NCL object to the *GingaNCLContextBridge* enabling the *GingaNCLBundle* to register it as a service on the Service Registry. Thus, a *DeviceBundle* can access this service to communicate with a Ginga-NCL application.

By using these components, the Ginga-NCL and OSGi characteristics were not modified, i.e. Ginga-NCL applications are accessed by OSGi bundles through a service that represents it in the OSGi environment and OSGi services are accessed by Ginga-NCL applications through their discovery in the Service Registry. The following subsections describe the proposed communication mechanism between Ginga-NCL applications and OSGi.

4.2.1 Accessing OSGi services by Ginga-NCL applications

In Figure 6 is shown how Ginga-NCL applications access OSGi services. The following components are presented: *ListenerServerBundle, DeviceBundle, ExporterBundle, BundleContextBridge*, and *OSGiAdapter*.

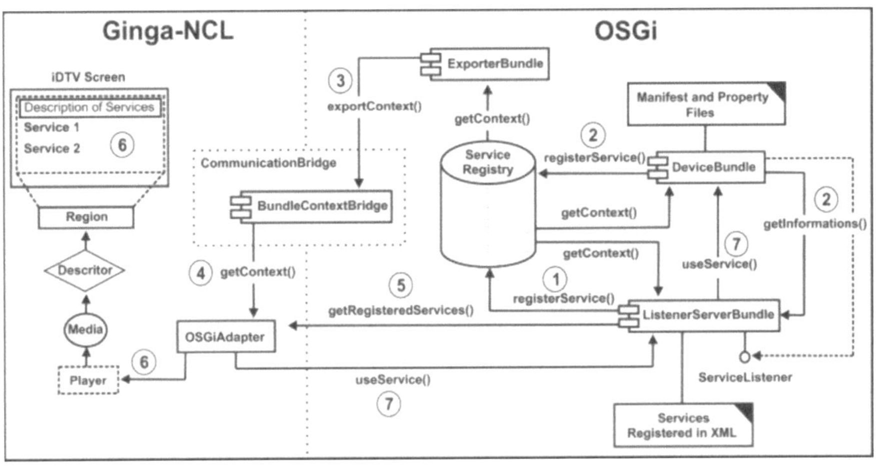

Fig. 6. Mechanism of exporting OSGi services to the Ginga-NCL domain.

When the system is launched, *ListenerServerBundle* registers its services in Service Registry (step 1). One of its functions is to provide a list of available services in the Service Registry in an XML format. To do this, it awaits the registration of new services on the Service Registry through a Listener. When a *DeviceBundle* registers its service, *ListenerServerBundle* gets some information contained on its Manifest and Properties files (step 2). Thus, this more detailed information helps the choosing of services by the users. To ensure that the services described in XML format by *ListenerServerBundle* are viewed by Ginga-NCL applications, another bundle named *ExporterBundle* is used, which exports its context to a bridge-structure named *BundleContextBridge* (step 3). With this, the *OSGiAdapter* gets a bundle context stored on the *BundleContextBridge* (step 4). After that, *OSGiAdapter* uses this context to get the desired service from *ListenerServerBundle* by searching In the Service Registry (step 5) and displaying on the TV screen the available services (step 6). Finally, the *OSGiAdapter* informs to the ListenerServerBundle to invoke the service chosen by the viewer (step 7).

4.2.2 Accessing Ginga-NCL applications by OSGi bundles

Figure 7 shows how the OSGi bundles access Ginga-NCL applications. The following components are involved: *GingaNCLAdapter, GingaNCLBundle, DeviceBundle* and *GingaNCLContextBridge.*

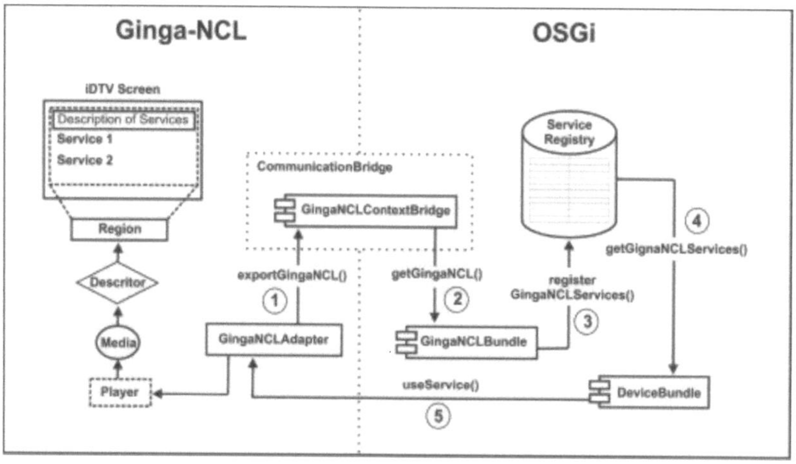

Fig. 7. Mechanism of exporting OSGi services to the Ginga-NCL domain.

When a *GingaNCLAdapter Player* executes a media object, *GingaNCLAdapter* exports a GingaNCL object to *GingaNCLContextBridge* (step 1). In this bridge-structure another Java static class named *GingaNCLContextBridge* is created, which stores the GingaNCL object. After that, *GingaNCLBundle* gets this object (step 2) and registers it in the Service Registry as a service (step 3). Finally, when a *DeviceBundle* needs to use this service, it is invoked after being searched in the Service Registry (step 4). In this way, the *DeviceBundle* sends an information to a specific region described on the NCL document through a correspondent GingaNCL object (step 5).

5. Implementation and experiments

The prototype was implemented in a PC platform with Intel Pentium 1.3GHz, 512MB RAM, 80GB HD, with WiFi, Serial RS-232 and USB interfaces. The operating systems was Windows XP SP2, with the Java 2 Platform Standard Edition 1.4.2_17 and 1.6.0_07. The PC simulates a single STB-HG (Set-Top Box Home Gateway) platform. The procedural part of the model used components of the XleTView 0.3.6 platform (XleTView, 2011), in which two main features were created: support for Inter-Xlet Communication through Java CDC Personal Profile RI (Personal Profile, 2006), and a model for IXC event listeners. The Ginga-NCL Emulator 1.1.1 (Ginga-NCL, 2011), a Java-based environment for creating interactive audiovisual documents based on NCL scripts, was chosen as a declarative middleware. The Knopflerfish 1.3.4 OSGi framework (Knopflerfish, 2011) was adopted for managing OSGi services. In order to test the proposed platform, some case studies were built under the new Ginga-OSGi platform for procedural and declarative environments.

5.1 Building the procedural environment

Once registered in the OSGi, the services must be exported to the Ginga-J as xlet remote objects, (using the platform components in the *br.ufam.tvdihn.* package*). In the Ginga-J environment, the Application Manager uses system API's (*havi, javatv, cdc personal profile, nanoxml*) to control the xlet execution (using *xjavax.microedition.xlet.** components), which can register java.rmi.Remote objects in the IXCRegistry (using *com.sun.xlet.ixc.IXCRegistry* package). A listening mechanism ensures the exporting of ICXRegistry objects to the OSGi. It is important to say that the API's for graphical interface such as HAVi and DAVIC (*Digital Audio Video Council*) are not present in the Ginga-J middleware but they were used on this project because of the MHP nature of the Java iDTV emulated environment (XleTView). In spite of that, as they are graphical components, they do not interfere in the GingaJ-OSGi components.

Inside the *br.ufam.tvdihn.** package there is the bridge entity *ContextBridge*. This is a Singleton object, which means there is only one instance of *ContextBridge* in the entire system. Once the system is started, *ContextBridge*, *XletContextExporter* and *BundleContextExporter* are activated. *XletContextExporter* is an xlet which exists in the Ginga-J only while performing its function of exporting an xlet context and *BundleContextExporter* is a bundle installed in the OSGi. The *ContextBridge* initialization is done in the startXlet of *XletContextExporter* and start of *BundleContextExporter*.

The central components of the model, *WrappedProxyObject* and *WrappedInterface* are in the *br.edu.ufam.tvdihn.wrapped* package. The former stores information about a service object (an object to be exported between the domains), and the later is an interface that contais the operations that can be done on the service object. *WrappedProxyObject* protects direct access to the service objects it represents (an OSGi service or a Ginga-J remote object). Thus, *WrappedProxyObject* is an implementation of the Wrapped and Proxy design patterns, described in Gamma et al. (1995).

The *WrappedProxyObject* uses three additional components to store service object information: *java.lang.Object object* (related to the service object), *java.reflect.Method method* (an object that represents a method to be invoked in the service object) and *java.lang.object.Object methodObject* (the result of the invocation of *method*). These components work together in order to guarantee the protection of the service object.

The last group of common components is in the *br.ufam.tvdihn.listeners* package, which presents classes for creating a listening mechanism for events in the IXC. This is an important mechanism because it allows registering Ginga-J remote objects from the IXCRegistry to the OSGi Service Registry. The main classes of this group are: *IXCEvent*, which represents three types of events: BIND (when an xlet registers a remote object), UNBIND (when an xlet unregisters a remote object) and REBIND (when the remote object is updated); *IXCListener*, which in fact is a listener to IXC events; and *IXCListeners*, responsible for storing all existing *IXCListener* objects.

In the proccess of exporting OSGi services to the Ginga-J domain, there is the *OSGiGingaJ-Register* component which is represented by the entity *OSGiGingaJRegister* in the *br.edu.ufam.tvdihn* package.

To implement its function, the *OSGiGingaJRegister* has a listening mechanism for service events on Service Registry, using the *org.osgi.framework.ServiceListener* component. Once is

detected a service registration, the related object is passed to Ginga-J through *ContextBridge* and *WrappedProxyObject*, following the *WrappedProxyObject* mechanism, described earlier.
The *OSGiGingaJRegister* has three main functions: catch OSGi service objects, register these objects in the Ginga-J IXC and remove the objects from the IXC. The first function is carried out using a standard OSGi element, the *ServiceEvent*, which represent three types of service events in the Service Registry: *ServiceEvent*.REGISTERED (a service has been registered), *ServiceEvent*.UNREGISTERING (a service has been removed) and *ServiceEvent*.MODIFIED (the service properties were changed).
When the service object is retrieved, the OSGiGingaJRegister checks the following service properties through a LDAP query: SERVICE_ALIAS = "HOME_NETWORK_ALIAS" and SERVICE_TYPE = "HOME_NETWORK_SERVICE". If it do not match, the service is invalid and it will not be exported to the IXC Registry; otherwise, the *OSGiGingaJRegister* will execute the second function: to register the object in the IXC. To do so, the service object is initialized (using a bundle context from *ContextBridge*), passed to *WrappedProxyObject*, and then the IXCRegistry is invocated (using an xlet context from *ContextBridge*) through the *IXCRegistry.bind* operation. An alias for identifying the object is retrieved from the OSGi service, using the SERVICE_IXC_ALIAS property. This process is illustrated in Figure 8.

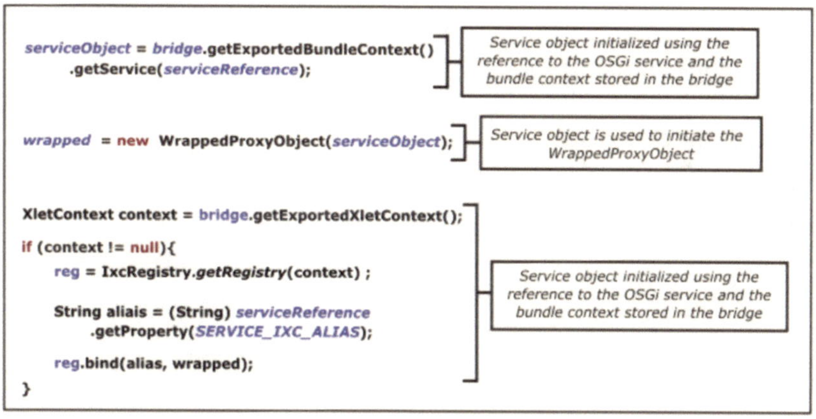

Fig. 8. *OSGiGingaJRegister*: code for registering an OSGi service as a Ginga-J remote object.

The last function of *OSGiGingaJRegister* is the reverse proccess: removing the IXC remote object from IXC Registry, when a service is uninstalled from the Service Registry. This is done by verifying the *ServiceEvent.UNREGISTERING* event, using the service properties to search for the corresponding object in IXC and then performing an *IXCRegistry.unbind* operation.
Regarding the process of registering remote objects from the IXCRegistry (in the *WrappedProxyObject* format) to the OSGi Service Registry, there are two components; *GingaJ-OSGiRegister* and *GingaJ-OSGiBundle*, both configured in a single bundle, *BundleGingaJOSGiRegister*, in the *br.edu.ufam.tvdihn* package.
The component *GingaJOSGiRegisterActivator* activates the *BundleGingaJOSGiRegister*. It implements a listener for events on the IXC Registry (through the *IXCListener* object in *br.ufam.tvdihn.listeners*). The main functions of *GingaJOSGiRegisterActivator* are: capturing the IXC remote object, registering and removing this object from the Service Registry. The registering/unregistering of service objects is preformed by the *GingaJOSGiRegisterActivator* in a different way of the *OSGiGingaJRegister*: in the OSGi domain there is only one service, *GingaJOSGiService*, which maintains an object repository, related to all IXC remote objects from

Ginga-J. The *GingaJOSGiService* can be accessed by bundles that need to use some functions of an IXC remote object. For each IXC remote object there is a corresponding *WrappedProxyObject* stored in the *GingaJOSGiService* repository.

5.2 Building the declarative environment

Similar to the procedural environment, the instances of Ginga-NCL and OSGi reference implementations were configured in a single JVM. The Ginga-NCL emulator source code was modified to define a specific ClassLoader for loading Ginga-NCL and Knopflerfish classes. In this way, the Ginga NCL Adapters can use OSGi code to access OSGi services. The same way, OSGi bundles can use functionalities of Ginga-NCL Adapters.

The two Ginga-OSGi adapters are Java classes built on Ginga-NCL middleware. As mentioned before, an Adapter is associated with media type and a Player object for this media. For each *Adapter* defined at *br.ginga.core.adapters.bridge* package, a corresponding Player which extends a *DefaultPlayerImplementation* object that represents *IPlayer* interface was created. The new *Adapter* must also extend a standard abstract class (*DefaultFormatterPlayerAdapter*) that has methods for managing the media presentation. The relationship between *Adapter* and *Player* objects is managed by *PlayerAdapterManager* object that works with two property-based standard files in the emulator: *controldefs.ini* and *mimedefs.ini*, both in *gingaNclConfigs.players* package. In the first file an alias for each *Adapter* class and its full name is defined. The second file defines the type of media for the *Adapter*, which can be played in Ginga-NCL Emulator. To show the media in the emulator, the node of the region and the corresponding media are configured in NCL file.

Figure 9 shows the description of the *GingaNCLAdapter* and the *OSGiAdapter* in the files mentioned above. In order to run an application the developer needs to create one region for each Adapter and define their presentation moment in the NCL file.

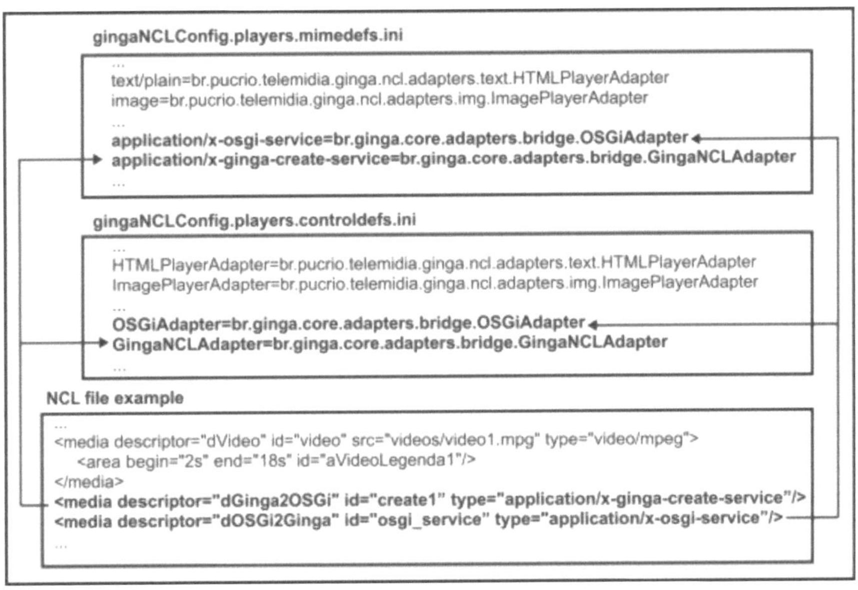

Fig. 9. Defining new Adapters in Ginga configuration files

5.3 Experiments

In order to clarify how the system works, two categories of examples are going to be explainded. The first contains one experiment based on procedural model (GingaJ-OSGi) and the second contains other experiment based on declarative model (GingaNCL-OSGi).

The first experiment allows bundles to use xlets functionalities, as described in Section 4. In this scenario we used an embedded microcontroller device (with WiFi interface) and a Webcam. When a user interacts with the device's keypad, it sends a request to a bundle server through the WiFi connection. The server bundle uses a Webcam service and takes a snapshot of the user attending to the request. The snapshot is passed to an iDTV area controlled by the xlet that exported its functionalities for the OSGi side as a service. At this moment, the iDTV user can use the remote control to send a reply message to the device. This situation simulates a home access control managed by the Digital TV. Figure 10 illustrates the final interface of the procedural application for the access control scenario.

Fig. 10. The Procedural Access Control Scenario

In the declarative experiment, a *BluetoothServerBundle* application was developed which provides a Bluetooth service in the OSGi network. It provides a Bluetooth connection server for mobile phones by means of Java Bluetooth API. It registers an interface in OSGi Service Registry that provides methods to send a simple text message from a mobile phone to an iDTV with Bluetooth interface. When a region on the TV screen is created to allow the *GingaNCLAdapter* to receive messages, the *GingaNCLAdapter* exports a GingaNCL object to the *GingaNCLContextBridge*. After that, the *GingaNCLBundle* gets a GingaNCL object and registers it as a service in the Service Registry. From now on, when a cellular phone sends a message to the iDTV screen, the *BluetoothServerBundle* will get the Ginga-NCL service and communicate with the *GingaNCLAdapter* sending the message information. After that, the message is shown on the TV screen. This scenario is illustrated in Figure 11.

For the last one the *TempSensorBundle* was created. It manages an interface with a temperature device (MSP430-based platform) through a RS-232 interface by means of a Java-based API, through which the master device can monitor some others installed in a WiFi sensors network. In this bundle, there are the Manifest and Property files that have some information about its services, such as description of methods, device name, version and so on. The *TempSensorBundle* is started and registers its services on the Service Registry.

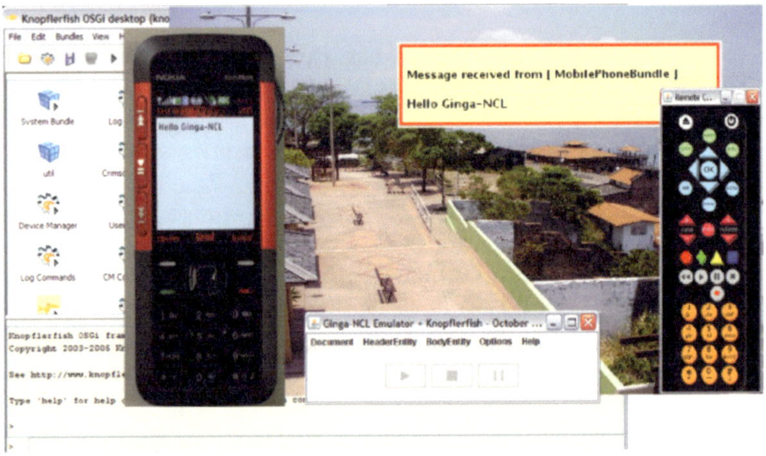

Fig. 11. The Declarative Mobile Scenario

After its registration, the *ListenerServerBundle* gets the information contained in Manifest and Property files of this bundle and saves into an XML format. After that, the *ExporterBundle* is activated. It exports its bundle context into the *BundleContextBridge*. In the user TV screen, the possible devices located in the house are shown. One of them is the Temperature Sensor. When the user selects this device, the *OSGiAdapter* is started and gets the bundle context located in *BundleContextBridge* to access the *ListenerServerBundle*. After that, the *OSGiAdapter* requests the service to *ListenerServerBundle* by searching the service on an XML document. After the desired service is found, *ListenerServerBundle* sends the method name to get the temperature sensor from *TempSensorBundle*. After a few seconds, is shown on the user TV screen the description and the methods available by *TempSensorBundle*. Finally, the user selects the desired service (Get Temp. Sensor Value, for example) and a few seconds later it is shown on the TV screen (see Figure 12).

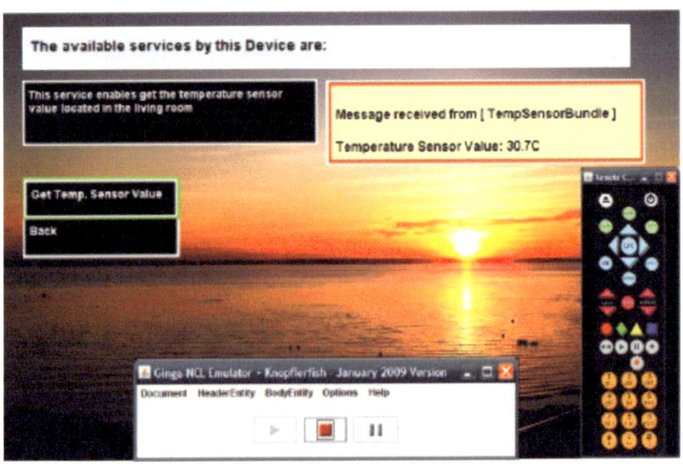

Fig. 12. The Declarative Temperature Monitoring Scenario

6. Conclusion and future scenarios

The expansion of the iDTV features and its recent use as a Home Gateway, makes the iDTV a key element for providing several kinds of services in the home networked environment buildind useful ubiquitous systems. Thus, this chapter aims to contribute to consolidate an iDTV-HN collaboration model, allowing the emergence of useful Home Automation applications and improving the user's experience and quality of life. The existing iDTV-HN convergence models were analyzed and a model that explores new features of the Brazilian iDTV middleware was proposed. This model can be easily exported to other iDTV standards. The main features obtained from this research are summarized in the key points described in the following:

- The fact of using two software platforms in a single environment allows the direct communication between the iDTV Ginga middleware and OSGi framework components. This is a useful advantage over some related proposals that use TCP/IP network.
- The xlet/bundle programmer does not need to know the new components: he/she can work with standard Ginga/OSGi components. In the case of the NCL programmer, he/she only needs to know the name of Adapters created for each service.
- The bridge-mechanism does not modify the Ginga/OSGi core components.
- In both models there is a difficulty in exporting iDTV functionalities (both for Ginga-J xlets and Ginga-NCL Adapters). It was necessary to use additional bundles to make this work (*GingaJ-OSGiBundle*, for example).
- In the case of the Ginga-NCL based model, the fact of managing the presentation of OSGi services just configuring some properties in a XML-based file, without any procedural code, is a useful advantage.
- In the case of Ginga-J-based model the components are less complex than the XBundLET of Cabrer et al. (2006); Redondo et al. (2007) and it is not necessary to allocate bridge components outside the GingaJ-OSGi environment, as Yang et al. (2007). In addition the Ginga-J Application Manager remains in its domain: it is not exported to OSGi, as in Lin et al. (2008).

In addition to the model based on the procedural specification (using Ginga-J middleware), the novelty of the work is in using declarative middleware features (through Ginga-NCL) to provide integration between script-based content and OSGi services. It considerably extends the scope of home automation applications that can be constructed using this new model. In the future the platform will be extended to support more kinds of ubiquitous scenarios, inserting components that have some intelligence to provide a dynamic adaptation of the application to the user's context. This model will allow to build user centered scenarios, such as those related to context aware systems and ambient intelligence.

7. Acknowledgements

The authors would like to thank the following funding institutions: CAPES (Coordenação de Aperfeiçoamento de Pessoal de Nível Superior) and CNPq (Conselho Nacional de Desenvolvimento Científico e Tecnológico) which provided support for the implementation of the work described in this chapter.

8. References

ABNT NBR 15606-4 (2010). Digital terrestrial television – Data coding and transmission specification for digital broadcasting Part 4: Ginga-J – The environment for the execution of procedural applications, Document ABNT NBR 15606-4, 2010.

ACAP (2009). ATSC Standard: Advanced Common Application Platform (ACAP), Document A/101A, 12 February 2009.

Al Mehairi, S., Barada, H. & Al Qutayri, M. (2007). Integration of Technologies for Smart Home Application, *Computer Systems and Applications, 2007. AICCSA '07. IEEE/ACS International Conference on*, pp. 241 –246.

ANATEL (2010). Brazilian National Agency of Telecommunications. Mobile users exceed 185 million subscribers in June 2010. Report on Personal Mobile Services, *Available at http://www.anatel.gov.br/Portal/exibirPortalNoticias.do?acao = carregaNoticia&codigo=20824. Accessed on January 10, 2011.*

ARIB B-24 (2009). ARIB Standard B-24 Data Coding and Transmission Specification for Digital Broadcasting, version 5.2-E1, 2009.

ATSC (2009). Digital Television Standard: Part 1 - Digital Television System, Document A/53 Part 1:2009, 2009.

Bae, Y.-S., Oh, B.-J., Moon, K.-D. & Kim, S.-W. (2006). Architecture for Interoperability of Services between an ACAP Receiver and Home Networked Devices, *Consumer Electronics, IEEE Transactions on* 52(1): 123–128.

Cabrer, M., Diaz Redondo, R., Vilas, A. & Pazos Arias, J. (2006). Controlling the smart home from TV, *Consumer Electronics, 2006. ICCE '06. 2006 Digest of Technical Papers. International Conference on*, pp. 255–256.

Dixit, S. & Prasad, R. (2008). *Technologies For Home Networking*, Wiley-Interscience, New Jersey.

Dobrev, P., Famolari, D., Kurzke, C. & Miller, B. (2002). Device and service discovery in home networks with OSGi, *Communications Magazine, IEEE* 40(8): 86–92.

DVB (2010). Multimedia Home Platform (MHP) Specification 1.2.2, ETSI Doc. No. TS 102 727 V1.1.1, 2010.

ELETROBRAS (2011). PROCEL. Brazilian Center for Information on Energy Efficiency. Research on Appliances Own and Energy Consuption Habbits. Summary from 2005-2007, *Available at http://www.eletrobras.com/pci/main.asp?View=05070313-120A-45FD-964D-5641D6083F80. Accessed on January 10, 2011.*

Gamma, E., Helm, R., Johnson, R. & Vlissides, J. (1995). *Design patterns: elements of reusable object-oriented software*, Addison-Wesley Longman Publishing Co., Inc., Boston, MA, USA.

ITU-T (2009). Consented Recommendation H.761. Nested Context Language (NCL) and Ginga-NCL for IPTV Services, 2009.

Ginga-NCL (2011). Ginga-NCL tools. Ginga-NCL Emulator, *in* Ginga-NCL (ed.), *Available at http://www.gingancl.org.br/ferramentas.html. Accessed on January 10, 2011.*

Gupta, R., Talwar, S. & Agrawal, D. (2002). Jini home networking: a step toward pervasive computing, *Computer* 35(8): 34 – 40.

HAVi (2001). The HAVi Specification: Specification of the Home Audio/Video Interoperability (HAVi) Architecture, version 1.1, 2001.

Howes, T. (1997). The String Representation of LDAP Search Filters, Document RFC 2254, December 1997.

ISDB (2011). Integrated Services Digital Broadcasting, *Available at http://www.dibeg.org. Accessed on January 10, 2011.*

ISDTV (2011). International Standard for Digital Television. Brazilian Digital TV System Forum (SBTVD), *Available at http://www.forumsbtvd.org.br. Accessed on January 10, 2011.*

ISO (2000). ISO/IEC 13818-1:2000. Information Technology - Generic Coding of Moving Pictures and Associated Audio Information.

ISO (2002). ISO/IEC 13818-6:1998/Cor2:2002. Information Technology - Generic Coding of Moving Pictures and Associated Audio Information: Part VI: Extensions for DSMCC.

Kanma, H., Wakabayashi, N., Kanazawa, R. & Ito, H. (2003). Home appliance control system over Bluetooth with a cellular phone, *Consumer Electronics, IEEE Transactions on* 49(4): 1049 – 1053.

Kim, K.-S., Park, C., Seo, K.-S., Chung, I.-Y. & Lee, J. (2007). ZigBee and The UPnP Expansion for Home Network Electrical Appliance Control on the Internet, *Advanced Communication Technology, The 9th International Conference on*, Vol. 3, pp. 1857 –1860.

Knopflerfish (2011). Open Source OSGi Service Platform, *in* Knopflerfish (ed.), *Available at http://www.knopflerfish.org. Accessed on January 10, 2011.*

Lin, C.-L., Wang, P.-C. & Hou, T.-W. (2008). A wrapper and broker model for collaboration between a set-top box and home service gateway, *Consumer Electronics, IEEE Transactions on* 54(3): 1123–1129.

Lin, C.-L., Wang, P.-C. & Hou, T.-W. (2009). Classification and Evaluation of Middleware Collaboration Architectures for Converging MHP and OSGi in a Smart Home, *Information Science and Engineering, Journal on* 25(1): 1337–1356.

Lin, Y.-J., Latchman, H., Lee, M. & Katar, S. (2002). A power line communication network infrastructure for the smart home, *Wireless Communications, IEEE* 9(6): 104 – 111.

Maia, O., Viana, N. & de Lucena, V. (2009). Using the iDTV for Managing Services in the Ubiquitous Computing Environment, *Ubiquitous, Autonomic and Trusted Computing, 2009. UIC-ATC '09. Symposia and Workshops on*, pp. 143 –148.

Marples, D. & Kriens, P. (2001). The Open Services Gateway Initiative: an introductory overview, *Communications Magazine, IEEE* 39(12): 110 –114.

Marshall, P. (2001). Home networking: a TV perspective, *Electronics Communication Engineering Journal* 13(5): 209 –212.

MHP (2010). Digital Video Broadcasting (DVB); Multimedia Home Platform (MHP) Specification 1.2.2, ETSI Doc. No. TS 102 727 V1.1.1, 2010.

Miller, B., Nixon, T., Tai, C. & Wood, M. (2001). Home networking with Universal Plug and Play, *Communications Magazine, IEEE* 39(12): 104 –109.

Morris, S. & Smith-Chaigneau, A. (2005). *Interactive TV Standards: A Guide to MHP, OCAP and JavaTV*, Focal Press, Burlington.

Personal Profile, R. I. (2006). JSR-000216 Personal Profile 1.1 (Final Release). Java Community Process, 2006.

Redondo, R. P. D., Vilas, A. F., Cabrer, M. R. & Arias, J. J. P. (2007). Exploiting OSGi capabilities from MHP applications, *Journal of Virtual Reality and Broadcasting* 4(16).

Schwalb, E. M. (2004). *iTV Handbook: Technologies and Standards*, Pearson Education, New Jersey.

Soares, L. F. G., Costa, R. M., Moreno, M. F. & Moreno, M. F. (2009). Multiple exhibition devices in DTV systems, *MM '09: Proceedings of the seventeen ACM international conference on Multimedia*, ACM, New York, NY, USA, pp. 281–290.

Soares, L. F. G., Rodrigues, E. F. & Moreno, M. F. (2007). Ginga-NCL: The Declarative Environment of the Brazilian Digital TV System, *in* B. C. Society (ed.), *Journal of the Brazilian Computer Society*, Vol. 13, Brazilian Computer Society, pp. 37–46.

Tavares, A. L. & Valente, M. T. (2008). A gentle introduction to OSGi, *SIGSOFT Softw. Eng. Notes* 33(5): 1–5.

Tkachenko, D., Kornet, N., Dodson, A., Li, L. & Khandelwal, R. (2005). A framework supporting interaction of iDTV applications and CE devices in home network, *Consumer Communications and Networking Conference, 2005. CCNC. 2005 Second IEEE*, pp. 605 – 607.

Viana, N., Maia, O., de Lucena, V. & Pinto, L. (2009). A Convergence Proposal between the Brazilian Middleware for iDTV and Home Network Platforms, *Consumer Communications and Networking Conference, 2009. CCNC 2009. 6th IEEE*, pp. 1 –5.

XleTView (2011). MHP Emulator for viewing xlets on PC, *in* M. Svenden (ed.), *Available at http://www.xletview.org/. Accessed on January 10, 2011.*

Yang, M.-C., Sheng, N., Huang, B. & Tu, J. (2007). Collaboration of Set-Top Box and Residential Gateway Platforms, *Consumer Electronics, IEEE Transactions on* 53(3): 905–910.

Zahariadis, T., Pramataris, K. & Zervos, N. (2002). A comparison of competing broadband in-home technologies, *Electronics Communication Engineering Journal* 14(4): 133 – 142.